THE WORLD
JOKE
BOOK

Other collections by Phillip Adams and
Patrice Newell

The Penguin Book of Australian Jokes
The Penguin Book of More Australian Jokes
The Penguin Bumper Book of Australian Jokes
The Penguin Book of Jokes from the Net
The Penguin Book of Schoolyard Jokes
The Penguin Book of All-New Australian Jokes
The A-Z of Knock-Knock Jokes
The Great Australian Joke Book
Pocket Jokes
More Pocket Jokes
What a Joke!
What a Giggle!
What a Laugh!
What a Hoot!

THE WORLD
JOKE
BOOK

PHILLIP ADAMS
& PATRICE NEWELL

Penguin Books

PENGUIN BOOKS

Published by the Penguin Group
Penguin Group (Australia)
250 Camberwell Road, Camberwell, Victoria 3124, Australia
(a division of Pearson Australia Group Pty Ltd)
Penguin Group (USA) Inc.
375 Hudson Street, New York, New York 10014, USA
Penguin Group (Canada)
10 Alcorn Avenue, Toronto, Ontario, Canada M4V 3B2
(a division of Pearson Penguin Canada Inc.)
Penguin Books Ltd
80 Strand, London WC2R 0RL, England
Penguin Ireland
25 St Stephen's Green, Dublin 2, Ireland
(a division of Penguin Books Ltd)
Penguin Books India Pvt Ltd
11 Community Centre, Panchsheel Park, New Delhi – 110 017, India
Penguin Group (NZ)
Cnr Airborne and Rosedale Roads, Albany, Auckland, New Zealand
(a division of Pearson New Zealand Ltd)
Penguin Books (South Africa) (Pty) Ltd
24 Sturdee Avenue, Rosebank, Johannesburg 2196, South Africa

Penguin Books Ltd, Registered Offices: 80 Strand, London, WC2R 0RL, England

First published by Penguin Group (Australia),
a division of Pearson Australia Group Pty Ltd, 2004

1 3 5 7 9 10 8 6 4 2

Design by George Dale © Penguin Group (Australia)
Typeset in 12/16pt Sabon by Midland Typesetters, Maryborough, Victoria
Printed and bound in Australia by McPherson's Printing Group, Maryborough, Victoria

National Library of Australia
Cataloguing-in-Publication data:

Adams, Philip, 1939– .
The world joke book.
ISBN 014 300209 0.
1. Wit and humor. I. Newell, Patrice 1956– . II. Title.
808.882

www.penguin.com.au

Introduction

On the face of it, you'd hardly expect our troubled times to be propitious for humour. Australia has had to deal with Howard's prime ministership – and while Gough's tenure was at least mildly amusing and Billy McMahon's verged on the hilarious, John's has been far less funny than Fraser's. We've had the bad jokes of Tampa, detention centres, the worst drought in a hundred years, the bombing in Bali and the war in Iraq. Not to mention the unalloyed joys of the Bush presidency, the War Against Terror, the massacre in Madrid, the worsening symptoms of global warming, an endless and expensive succession of corporate scandals and collapses on both sides of the Pacific and the implosion of dot-communism. All in all, one might have expected every smile to have evaporated, all laughter to have drowned in tears.

Yet the opposite seems true. Never before have so many people told so many jokes. No matter how great the catastrophe, within minutes there's a humorous response. Not so long ago we wondered – even winced – at how fast a shuttle tragedy turned NASA into 'Needs Another Seven Astronauts'. Now the speed of the Internet, that global provider of pornography, spam, conspiracy theories, bigotries and sundry social comment, has produced a fusillade of jokes for every tragedy, every crisis, before the dust has settled or the blood dried.

Humour has, of course, always been therapeutic. As we said in the introduction to the first Penguin book of jokes, humour's purpose is to deal with our demons, to exorcise our anxieties about everything from sexuality to mortality. Should something cause concern or provoke hostility, be it politician, lawyer, employer or mother-in-law, we transform it into a joke – in much the same way but far more quickly than an oyster transforms an irritant into a pearl. Thus jokes are replete with racism, sexism, religious intolerance and every imaginable form of bad taste.

In a fascinating essay in the *New Yorker* (19 April, 2004), Jim Holt provided an archaeological study of jokes and joke books. He'd learnt that in the Athens of Demosthenes there was a comedians' club called the Group of Sixty 'which met in the temple of Heracles to trade wisecracks, and it's said that Philip of Macedon paid handsomely to have their jokes written down.' Unfortunately, all copies of the volume have long since disappeared. However, Rome's Plautus refers to jest books in a couple of his plays, 'while Seuetonius tells us that Melissus, a favourite professor of the Emperor Augustus, compiled no fewer than 150 joke anthologies.'

Sadly, only a single joke book survives from ancient times: the *Philogelos* or *Laughter-Lover* dating from the fourth or fifth century AD. Holt describes a book of 264 items, several of which appear twice in slightly different form. Examples include: ' "How shall I cut your hair?" a talkative barber asked a wag. "In silence!" '

The jokes concerned drunks, misers, blackguards, sex-starved women, a bloke with bad breath and the 'scholastikos', which Holt translates as 'pedant, absent-minded professor or egghead'. Here's a sample of the genre: 'An egghead was on a sea voyage when a big storm blew up, causing his slaves to weep in terror. "Don't cry," he consoled them, "I have freed you all in my will." '

Thus begins a long history of compilations and it's clear that quite a few of the examples in this tome, though harvested from the Internet, began their lives a few millennia back. For example, joke number 263, deriving from Plutarch, sounds very familiar: ' "I had your wife for nothing," someone sneered at a wag. "More fool you. I'm her husband. I have to have the ugly bitch. You don't." '

Versions of that, equally misogynist and unfunny, continue to circulate.

History records joke books throughout history. Poggio Bracciolini (1380–1459), a distinguished Italian humanist and secretary to eight popes over half a century, was an inveterate collector of just about everything. He fathered fourteen children with a mistress, and late in life took for himself an eighteen-year-old bride, who bore him another six. He collected precious manuscripts, rotting in medieval monasteries, concerning everything from the orations of Cicero to the architectural writings of Vitruvius and Apicius's works on cooking. But he's best remembered, it seems, for a book of jokes: his *Facetiae*, published in his seventieth year. This venerable volume contains jokes about drunks, fatties, erections and farts. Quite a few are translated by William Caxton, England's first printer of books. In 1484 he used them to pad his own translation of *Aesop*, thus giving us the first joke book in English. And by Shakespeare's time they were very popular. As, praise the Lord, they remain today. Now, as then, jokes blow raspberries in the face of fate and display the full range of bigotries. But it would seem to your editors that these days there is an increasing emphasis on jokes that attack the mighty. While such jokes certainly existed in the past, it was probably unwise to print them. Now, political jokes demonstrate that the new technologies are destroying old-style censorships and eroding the authorities of dogmatisms.

Consider the inundation of jokes about George Bush, bin Laden and Saddam Hussein. They might conceal a subtext of desperation, even despair, but they come thick and fast. In the era of Shock and

Awe, humour seems a psychological version of Son of Star Wars, deflecting not missiles but miseries.

Your editors receive many hundreds of jokes a week from people across the country and the planet. They come by word of mouth, in letters, in emails, scrawled on the backs of postcards. While most are familiar – having appeared in one form or another in the dozen collections preceding this book – we're constantly astonished by the ingenuity and originality of the anonymous authors. True, many of the latest jokes are simply old jokes in new costumes, with changes of name and location. Others, however, seem to be truly original, particularly in the area of social satire or comment, as opposed to the formal structure of the traditional joke. These writings, these offerings, are thrown into the electronic air like paper aeroplanes, fluttering around to be enjoyed, modified and relaunched by others.

Jokes and humorous comment are one of the redeeming features of the Internet, compensating for the tsunamis of pornography, spam and hate pages. Fewer and fewer global corporations dominate the realms of information and entertainment, and governments have been using September 11 to gather more power unto themselves at the cost of hard-won rights and the notion of privacy. Jokes represent a marvellously democratic response to a troubled and troubling world and a subversive use of the technologies that seem to be curtailing freedom while they pretend to extend it.

Here is a random selection of some of the funnier – and nastier – jokes told by human beings around the world. As with most forms of popular culture, the US seems to dominate and in many countries, certainly Australia, we witness a process of hybridising American originals – in jokes as much as in music, film or television. However, as long as people exercise the democratic right to derision, all is not lost.

At last! The Second Coming! The Messiah returns! His Holiness the Pope calls an urgent meeting of all his cardinals. One by one the Boeings land at Rome airport and the highest in the church hierarchy assemble, fully robed, in the Sistine Chapel. Despite his frailty, the Pope speaks with passionate urgency. 'I've some great news and some terrible news.' The cardinals mumble and mutter, their faces showing both apprehension and excitement. Understandably, they want to hear the great news first, so the Pope tells them, 'Jesus Christ has returned. The time of judgment is at hand, and our faith has been justified.'

There is joyous genuflection and faces wreathed in smiles.

After the euphoria dies down, one of the cardinals asks, 'And, Holy Father, what is the terrible news?'

'The Saviour was calling from Salt Lake City.'

***

The young blonde, the secret mistress of an Australian tycoon, has all the windows in her Centennial Park mansion replaced with the latest in double-insulated, energy-efficient windows. And every month, for a year, she gets a call from the contractor asking for a cheque.

After twelve months, the bills are piled high on her desk, but she hasn't responded. Nor has the contractor received a cheque from the tycoon.

Finally, the contractor becomes threatening. 'Do you want me to put this into the hands of a debt collector? Think about the publicity!'

The blonde calmly replies, 'Now, don't try to pull a fast one on me. Your salesman told me that in a year the windows would pay for themselves.'

***

A drunk staggers into St Mary's, enters a confessional box and sits there grunting but saying nothing. After a few moments the priest coughs once, then twice, to get his attention. But the drunk just sits there grunting. Finally, the priest pounds three times on the wall. The drunk mumbles, 'Ain't no use knocking. There's no dunny paper on this side either.'

***

Spell Checker Poem

Eye halve a spelling chequer.
It came with my pea sea.
It plainly marques four my revue
Miss steaks eye kin knot sea.

Eye strike a key and type a word
And weight four it two say
Weather eye am wrong oar write
It shows me strait a weigh

As soon as a mist ache is maid
It nose bee fore two long
And eye can put the error rite
Its rare lea ever wrong.

Eye have run this poem threw it
I am shore your pleased two no
Its letter perfect awl the weigh
My chequer tolled me sew.

Sauce unknown

✳✳✳

The blonde from Centennial Park calls the tycoon
and says, 'Darling, you've got to call in and help me. I
haven't seen you for weeks and I got really, really bored.
So I bought this huge jigsaw puzzle but I can't work out
how to get started.'

The tycoon says, 'What's it supposed to be when
it's finished?'

The blonde says, 'Well, according to the picture on the box, it's a tiger.'

The tycoon detours in the middle of a busy day and goes over to help with the jigsaw. The blonde lets him in and shows him the puzzle spread all over the dining table.

'You're a twit,' says the tycoon. 'This isn't a jigsaw. It's a packet of cornflakes.'

***

If most people said what's on their minds, they'd be speechless.

An argument is two people trying to get the last word in first.

When most people put in their two cents' worth, they're not overcharging.

The man who has everything is envious of the man who has two of everything.

A masochist is someone who paints himself into a corner and then applies a second coat.

Every notice how people who say, 'that's the way the ball bounces' are usually the ones who dropepd it?

***

A brunette goes to the doctor and says to him, 'Doctor, I'm hurting all over my body.'

'That's odd,' replies the doctor, 'show me what you mean.'

So the girl takes her finger and pokes her elbow, and screams in pain. She touches her knee and cries in agony, and so on.

The doctor says to her, 'You're not a natural brunette, are you?'

'No, I'm a blonde,' she replies.

'I thought so,' replies the doctor. 'Your finger is broken.'

***

Office Mathematics
Smart boss + smart employee = profit.
Smart boss + dumb employee = production.
Dumb boss + smart employee = promotion.
Dumb boss + dumb employee = overtime.

✱✱✱

My aunts used to come up to me at weddings, poke me in the ribs and, with a big smile, tell me, 'You're next.' They stopped that after I started doing the same thing to them at funerals.

✱✱✱

Three senior military men are discussing what to do if and when bin Laden is caught by America's war against terror. One, a Pentagon general, says, 'If we catch him, and shoot him, he'll be made into a martyr.'

A British field marshal says, 'By Jove, yes, what! If we put him in jail, there'll be people endlessly trying to get him out, what!'

The Australian brigadier, from North Queensland, says, 'If we catches 'im, wot we'll do is take 'im orff ter 'ospital an' give 'im a sex-change operation. Then we send 'im home. That'll fix the bastard!'

✱✱✱

There was a competition to swim across Sydney Harbour doing only breaststroke, and the three women who entered the race were a brunette, a redhead and a blonde.

After many hours, the brunette staggered up the shore and was declared the fastest breaststroker. About half an hour later, the redhead crawled up the sand to the finishing line to win second place.

Nearly four hours afterwards, the blonde finally arrived, more dead than alive, and passed out on the sand.

When she regained consciousness, a reporter from *The Daily Telegraph* asked her why it had taken her so long to cover the distance. She said, 'I don't want to sound like a sore loser, but I think those other two girls were using their arms.'

***

A highway cop observed a car puttering along a highway at 22km/h. He turned on his blue lights and pulled the car over. Approaching the vehicle, he saw that it contained five old ladies – two in the front seat and three in the back. They were wide-eyed and white as ghosts.

The driver said, 'Officer, I don't understand. I was doing exactly the speed limit. What's the problem?'

'Ma'am,' the officer replied, 'you weren't speeding. But you should know that driving far, far slower than the speed limit can also be dangerous. To other drivers.'

'Slower than the speed limit? But I'm following the posted speed exactly.'

The officer couldn't help but grin. He explained that '22' was the route number, not the speed limit.

The embarrassed woman smiled and thanked him for pointing out her error.

Before waving her on, the officer asked, 'Is everyone in this car okay? Your passengers seem somewhat distressed and they haven't said a word since I stopped you.'

'Oh, they'll be all right in a minute. You see, we just got off route 220.'

***

APHORISMS

When all fails, read the instructions.

The other queue moves faster.

Proofreading is more effective after publication.

Paper is always strongest at the perforations.

Life is a whole series of circumstances beyond your control.

If at first you don't succeed, you're doing about average.

If you do a job too well, you'll get stuck with it.

He who hesitates is not only lost, but several kilometres from the next freeway exit.

***

WISE WORDS

You can't tell which way the train went by looking at the track.

Indecision is the key to flexibility.

There is absolutely no substitute for a genuine lack of preparation.

Nostalgia isn't what it used to be.

The facts, although interesting, are irrelevant.

If you can smile when things go wrong, you have someone in mind to blame.

If you think there is good in everybody, you haven't met everybody.

Years and skill is no match for experience and treachery.

By the time you make ends meet, they move the ends.

Money can't buy happiness but it can rent it.

If you can smile when everything goes wrong, you probably don't understand the problem.

Experience is what you get when you were expecting something else.

✶✶✶

THE AXIS PANDEMIC

International reaction to Bush's Axis of Evil declaration was swift, as within minutes France surrendered.

Elsewhere, peer-conscious nations rushed to gain triumvirate status in what became a game of geopolitical chairs. Cuba, Sudan and Serbia said they had formed the Axis of Somewhat Evil, forcing Somalia to join with Uganda and Myanmar in the Axis of Occasionally Evil, while Bulgaria, Indonesia and Russia established the Axis of Not So Much Evil Really as Just Generally Disagreeable.

With the criteria suddenly expanding and all the desirable clubs filling up, Sierra Leone, El Salvador and Rwanda applied to be called the Axis of Countries that Ain't the Worst but Certainly Won't Be Asked to Host the Olympics; Canada, Mexico and Australia formed the Axis of Nations that Are Actually Quite Nice but Secretly Have Nasty Thoughts About America; while Spain, Scotland and New Zealand established the Axis of Countries That Be Allowed to Ask Sheep to Wear Lipstick.

While wondering if the other nations of the world weren't perhaps making fun of him, a cautious Bush granted approval for most axes, although he rejected the establishment of the Axis of Countries Whose Names End in 'Guay', accusing one of its members of filing a false application. Officials from Paraguay, Uruguay and Chadguay denied the charges. Israel, meanwhile, insisted it didn't want to join any Axis, but privately world leaders said that's only because no one asked them.

***

Two aerials met on a roof. They fell in love and got married. The ceremony didn't go very well but the reception was brilliant.

***

Two fat blokes were sitting in a pub. One turned to the other and said, 'Your round.'

And the other one replied. 'So are you, you big fat bastard.'

***

A distressed business executive lay on the couch in his psychiatrist's office singing, 'The Green, Green Grass of Home'.

'Why are you singing that?' asked the psychiatrist.

'I can't stop singing it. I sing it all the time.'

'I haven't seen a case like this in all my years of practice – but I've read about it in textbooks. What you have is the Tom Jones Syndrome.'

'Is it common?' asked the patient.

'Well, it's not unusual.'

***

Having been cured of the Tom Jones Syndrome, the patient returned to his psychiatrist wearing the top half of his Armani suit but with only cling wrap to protect his nether regions. 'I can clearly see,' said the psychiatrist, 'you're nuts.'

***

A young bloke was hitchhiking on the Hume Highway, waving his thumb in the air and holding a piece of cardboard on which he'd written MELBOURNE. A bloke in a four-wheel drive pulled up beside him. The hitchhiker said, 'Could you give me a lift?'

The driver said, 'Yes, of course I can. You look really, really great. The world is your oyster. Go for it!' And he drove off.

***

The tycoon visits his mistress and discovers a huge pile of documents that she'd collected from under her windscreen wiper. 'Good God, look at all these! You owe the council a bloody fortune.'

'No, I don't,' she says. 'They all say "Parking Fine". Isn't that nice?'

***

You know you've been in the corporate world far too long when:

You ask the waiter what the restaurant's core competencies are.

You decide to reorganise your family into a 'team-based organisation'.

You refer to going out on a date as 'test marketing'.

You understand your airline's frequent flyer points system.

You write executive summaries in your love letters.

You celebrate your wedding anniversary by conducting a performance review.

Your Valentine's Day cards have bullet points.

You believe you never have any problems in your life, just 'issues' and 'improvement opportunities'.

You can explain to someone the difference between 're-engineering', 'downsizing', 'right-sizing' and 'firing people'.

You talk to the waiter about 'process flow' when dinner arrives late.

You refer to your significant other as 'my co-CEO'.

You insist that you do some more market research before you and your spouse produce another child.

You use the term 'value added' without falling down laughing.

You give constructive feedback to your dog.

***

The Skoda car was one of the proudest products of the former Czechoslovakia. But they did have some quality-control problems. Hence the proliferation of Skoda jokes. For example:

What do you call a Skoda with a sunroof?
A skip.

What's the correct name for a Skoda with the windows open?
A bottle bank.

Why do Skodas have heated rear windows?
To keep your hands warm when you're pushing them.

What's the difference between a Jehovah's Witness and a Skoda?

You can always shut the door on a Jehovah's Witness.

***

Why did the chicken cross the road?

Philip Ruddock: It didn't. I sent it back to where it came from. Who knows what might happen if we keep letting any old chicken cross the road? We could be inundated with them. Send them to the farmer up the road a bit and we can pay him to deal with the problem.

Jeff Kennett: If the chicken did cross the road it should have been fitted with an E-tag and should pay the same toll as all other road users.

Steve Bracks: Regional chickens should have the same opportunities to cross the road as chickens living in Melbourne.

John Howard: The chicken never crossed the road. And it was not forcibly removed from its mother! Anyway, that's a matter for the State and is of no interest to us. The United Nations should butt out.

Kim Beazley: There was a chicken. And it did cross the road. This is a deliberate act by the government to hide the fact that chickens continue to cross Australian roads.

Natasha Stott Despoja: What if it was not a chicken but a bantam? Minority sectors of our community shouldn't be discriminated against purely on the size of their legs and eggs.

Evelyn Scott: To demonstrate a commitment to reconciliation with indigenous chickens.

Peter Costello: According to documentation submitted to the Live Food Processing Authority, the chicken in question was uncooked at the time of its journey and therefore will not incur a GST charge. However if that chicken actually crossed the road for profit, regardless of its raw/cooked status, the road crossing would be considered by the ATO to be a service for which GST will be imposed.

Pauline Hanson: Please explain.

Robert de Niro: Are you tellin' me the chicken crossed that road? Is that what you're tellin' me?

Martin Luther King Jr: I envisage a world where all chickens, be they black, white or brown or red or speckled, will be free to cross the road without having their motive called into question.

Grandpa: In my day we didn't ask why the chicken crossed the road. Someone told us that the chicken crossed and that was good enough for us.

The Rev. Fred Nile: Because the chicken is gay! Isn't it obvious? Can't you people see the plain truth in front of your face? The chicken was going to the 'other side'. That's what they call it. The 'other side'. Yes, my friends!

Captain James T. Kirk: To go boldly where no chicken has gone before.

Hansie Cronje: What if I could guarantee that it won't get to the other side?

Freud: The fact that you are at all concerned that the chicken crossed the road reveals your underlying sexual insecurity. How do you feel about your mother?

The CIA: Who told you about the chicken? Did you see the chicken? There was no chicken. Please step into the car.

Einstein: Did the chicken really cross the road or did the road move beneath the chicken?

Bill Clinton: I did not cross the road with *that* chicken. What do you mean by chicken? Could you define the word chicken?

Homer Simpson: Mmmmmm. Chicken!

★★★

A Native American, an Al Qaeda spokesman and a Texan get involved in a discussion. The Indian says, 'I come from an ancient and noble people, with a profound sense of history. Unfortunately, my tribe is in decline and daily becomes less numerous and less politically influential.'
    The Al Qaeda man says, 'I too belong to people of ancient and noble origin. And we, too, have a profound sense of history. However, we are becoming more numerous and more significant in world affairs.'
    And the Texan says, 'That's because we ain't played Cowboys and Arabs yet.'

★★★

An elderly bloke invites a lady with a similar amount of mileage on her clock to go rowing with him. When they reach a fork in the river he asks her, 'Up or down?' To his astonishment, she drops her knickers and pulls him to the bottom of the boat.

Next day, he takes her rowing again. They get to the fork in the river and he asks, 'Up or down?' And again she responds in the same energetically amorous way.

Third time lucky? This time he breaks all geriatric records in reaching the fork in the river. 'Up or down?' he cries enthusiastically. She, however, tells him to turn the boat around and row for home.

'But I don't understand,' he says, 'the last two days we've made mad, passionate love. What's the difference today?'

'Today? Today, I've got my hearing aid turned on,' she says. 'Yesterday I thought my choices were fuck or drown.'

✱✱✱

MAXIMS

Logic is a system of coming to the wrong conclusion with confidence.

If it weren't for the last minute nothing would get done.

Only someone who understands something absolutely can explain it so no one else can understand it.

If you don't understand it, it must be intuitively obvious.

How long a minute is depends on which side of the bathroom door you're on.

Complex problems have simple, easy-to-understand, wrong answers.

There's no time like the present for postponing what you ought to be doing.

After your hands become coated with grease, your nose will begin to itch.

Any tool, when dropped, will roll into the least accessible corner.

The first rule of intelligent tinkering is to save all the parts.

If it jams, force it. If it breaks, it needed replacing anyway.

***

Marc Antony has had a bugger of a day campaigning. Fighting the Gauls, the Goths, the Franks, whoever. Thoroughly exhausted, he can't wait to hit the cot in his tent. He drops his shield, unbuckles his sword, denudes himself of helmet, breastplate and tunic, and kicks off his Roman sandals.

With a sigh of relief he lies down and is starting to doze off when, all of a sudden, he's awakened by an urgent cry of 'Marc! Marc!' Leaping from the cot he struggles into his Roman sandals, his tunic, his breastplate and his helmet. He snatches up his sword and his shield and races out into the night, fearing the worst but prepared to fight.

Nothing. Silence. Stillness.

He returns to his tent, lays aside sword and shield, helmet, breastplate and tunic and sheds his Roman sandals. This time, no sooner does his head hit the pillow than there's the unmistakable call of 'Marc! Marc!'

On goes the tunic, the breastplate, the helmet and the Roman sandals. On goes the sword. Up goes the shield. And once more he sallies forth and peers into the surrounding shrubbery.

And there he spots a dog with a harelip.

***

Ballet impresarios always audition Trees in the morning and Water Sprites in the arvo. They don't believe in casting swirls before pine.

***

A teenager with spiky, multicoloured hair was sitting on a park bench. After a time, he noticed that an old bloke, sitting at the other end of the bench, was staring at him. 'What's the matter, you silly old bugger?' he said defiantly. 'Didn't you ever do anything unusual?' 'I got drunk once and had sex with a parrot,' the old bloke said. 'So I just thought we might be related.'

***

Reality is that which, when you stop believing in it, refuses to go away.

***

Three violin manufacturers have done business for years on the same block in the small town of Cremona, Italy. After years of peaceful coexistence the Amati shop decided to put a sign in the window saying, 'We make the best violins in Italy'. The Guarneri shop soon followed suit with a sign in their window proclaiming, 'We make the best violins in the world'. Finally, the Stradivarius family put up a sign outside their shop stating, 'We make the best violins on the block'.

***

Why is it considered necessary to nail down the lid of a coffin?

Why does the sun lighten our hair, but darken our skin?

Why can't women apply mascara with their mouths closed?

Why doesn't glue stick to the inside of the bottle?

Why don't you ever see the headline 'Psychic Wins Lottery'?

Why is 'abbreviated' such a long word?

Why is a boxing ring square?

Why is it called lipstick if you can still move your lips?

Why is it that doctors call what they do 'practice'?

Why is it that rain drops but snow falls?

Why is it that when you're driving and looking for an address, you turn down the volume of the radio?

Why is lemon juice made from artificial flavour and dishwashing liquid made from real lemons?

Why is the man who invests all his money called a broker?

Why isn't there mouse-flavoured cat food?

Why can't they make the whole plane out of the material used to make that little indestructible black box?

***

Mum and Dad took their six-year-old son to a nude beach. As the kid walked along the sand, he noticed that some of the ladies had bigger titties than his mum. So he asked her why. She said, 'The bigger they are the less intelligent the person.'

Pleased with the answer, the kid went to splash

THE WORLD JOKE BOOK

in the shallows. But he returned to tell his mum that some of the men had bigger dickies than his dad. And his mother replied, 'The bigger they are, the dumber the person.'

Once more, the child was satisfied with the answer and returned to the water to play.

But he came back almost immediately telling his mum, 'Daddy is talking to the dumbest girl on the beach and the longer he talks, the dumber he gets.'

***

A bloke is camping in a national park and is just eating the last scraps of a tiger snake he's baked in an open fire when the park ranger nabs him. He's dragged in front of the magistrate on a charge of eating a protected species and in view of the incontrovertible evidence – namely, a half-masticated snake – he's pronounced guilty. Before passing sentence, the magistrate invites the bloke to speak in litigation.

What follows is the most heart-rending and inspiring tale of hardship and survival, of a bloke's battle with tough times and bad luck culminating with the dilemma of an environmentally aware but starving man agonising over whether he should preserve his rapidly ebbing life by eating the (already dead) tiger snake that providence had left in his path.

Moved to tears, the magistrate pardons the bloke and wishes him well.

Just as the bloke is exiting the courtroom, the magistrate calls him back. 'Just out of curiosity,' he asks, 'what does tiger snake taste like?'

'Well, it's sort of like a cross between a dolphin and lyrebird.'

***

George W. Bush was walking through an airport when he saw an old man with white hair and a long beard wearing a long white robe and holding a wooden staff. He walked up to the man who was staring at the ceiling and said, 'Excuse me, sir, but are you by any chance Moses?' (Bush could make that identification because he'd seen Charlton Heston in Cecil B. DeMille's *The Ten Commandments*.)

The man stood perfectly still and continued to stare at the ceiling, saying nothing. He entirely ignored the most powerful man in the world.

Again Bush asked, a little louder this time, 'Excuse me, sir, but aren't you Moses?'

The old man continued to be unresponsive. He just stared at the ceiling.

Bush wasn't used to being ignored so he tried a third time, louder yet. 'Excuse me, sir, but aren't you Moses?'

Again no movement or words from the old man.

One of Bush's aides asked him if there was a problem and the President said, 'Either this man is deaf or extremely rude. I've asked him three times if he was Moses and he hasn't answered me.' To which the man, still staring at the ceiling, finally responded, 'Verily, I can hear you. And yes, I am Moses. But the last time I spoke to a bush, I ended up spending forty years wandering in the wilderness.'

***

How you can tell it's going to be a lousy day:

You wake up face-down in the gutter.

You put your bra on backwards and it fits better.

You call Suicide Prevention and they put you on hold.

You see the *A Current Affair* news crew waiting on your doorstep.

You turn on the news and they're showing emergency routes out of the city.

You wake up and discover your waterbed broke. Then you remember you don't have a waterbed.

Your car horn goes off accidentally and remains stuck as you follow a group of Hell's Angels up the freeway.

Your boss tells you not to bother taking off your coat.

The bird singing outside your window is a vulture.

***

Maria is a devout Catholic. She gets married and, in the next few years, has seventeen kids. Soon after her last child is born her husband dies. A few weeks later she remarries and, over the following years, has another twenty-two children. After the last child is born her second husband dies.

Refusing to be discouraged, Maria finds another suitable husband and, within a month, is married for a third time. Unfortunately she becomes very ill and dies.

At her wake the priest looks tenderly at Maria lying in her coffin. And he looks up to the heavens and says,

'At last they're finally together!'

A bloke standing next to the priest asks, 'Excuse me, father, but do you mean Maria and her first husband? Or Maria and her second husband? Or Maria and –'

The priest interrupts. 'I mean her legs.'

***

Lachlan and Jamie were driving back from lunch at Machiavelli restaurant in Sydney when they passed the Ferrari dealership in William Street and dropped in for a quick perve. Particularly taken with a twelve-cylinder model, about a metre high and half a block long, Lachlan writes out a cheque for two of them. Jamie says, 'No, let me buy these. You bought lunch.'

***

I nearly had a psychic girlfriend. But she dumped me before we met.

***

What the doctor says versus what the doctor means

'Well, well, well. What have we here?'
(I haven't the faintest idea what's wrong with this poor old bugger!)

'We should take care of this straightaway.'
(I need some extra cash to pay for my golf clubs.)

'Let's first check your medical history.'
(I wonder if this little creep paid his last bill.)

'Can we make an appointment for later in the week?'
(I wish you'd nick off. My golf game starts at three.)

'No, I wouldn't really recommend a second opinion.'
(Why should I let those mongrels rake in more money?)

'We've got some good news and some bad news.'
(We've amputated the wrong leg, but we got a good price for your carpet slippers.)

'Let's see how it develops.'
(Maybe it'll grow into something we can cure.)

'I'd like to prescribe a new drug.'
(I get paid by the drug company for each guinea pig I can book.)

'This might hurt a little.'
(The last two patients bit their tongues off before they fainted.)

***

Why can't life's big problems come when we are twenty and know everything?

Why do kamikaze pilots wear crash helmets?

Why is a wrong number never engaged?

***

GOOD ADVICE

Beware! The toes you tread on today may belong to the feet that are attached to the legs that hold up the backside you may have to kiss tomorrow.

Only an average person is always at his best.

People who matter don't mind. People who mind don't matter.

'I must do something' will always solve more problems

than 'something must be done'.

It's easier to get forgiveness than permission.

Inside every small problem there is a major disaster trying to get out.

When faced with two evils, always pick the one you haven't tried before.

✱✱✱

A bloke in a country town in New South Wales bought an emu from an emu farmer for $100. He wanted it as a pet for his kids. The farmer agreed to deliver the emu the next day but, come morning, he phoned to say that he had some bad news. 'I'm sorry, but the emu died.'

'Oh, bugger it. Well, you'd better give me my money back.'

'Can't do that. I've spent it already.'

'Okay, then just drop off the emu.'

'What are you going to do with a dead emu?'

'I'm going to raffle it.'

'You can't raffle a dead emu!'

'Sure I can. I used to raffle ducks in country pubs – so an emu ought to be easy. I just won't tell anyone it's dead.'

A month later the farmer met up with the bloke and asked, 'What happened with the dead emu?'

'I raffled it, like I said I would. I sold 500 tickets at $2 a piece and made a profit of $898.'

'Didn't anyone complain?'

'Just the bloke who won. So I gave him his $2 back.'

***

James Bond walks into a posh bar in Knightsbridge and takes a seat next to a very, very elegant woman. He gives her a quick glance, then looks at his watch for a few moments.

The woman notices this and says, 'Excuse me, Mr Bond, but is your date running late?'

'No,' he replies. 'Q has just given me a high-tech, state-of-the-art watch and I was just testing it.

Intrigued, the woman says, 'A state-of-the-art watch? What's so special about it?'

Bond explains. 'It uses alpha waves to talk to me telepathically.'

The lady says, 'What's it telling you now?'

'Well, it says that you're not wearing any knickers.'

The woman giggles and replies, 'Well, it must be broken. Because I am wearing knickers.'

Bond tut-tuts, taps the watch and says, 'The damn thing's an hour fast.'

★★★

A bloke was walking along St Kilda beach when he found a bottle half buried in the sand. It appeared to be a bottle of very good champagne, the cork intact. He looked around and didn't see anyone so he opened it. Instantly, a genie appeared and thanked the bloke for letting him out. 'It really wasn't very good champagne. Non-vintage. So for your kindness I'll grant you one wish.'

The bloke thought about it for a minute and said, 'I've always wanted to go to Hawaii but have never been able to because I'm afraid of flying and I get claustrophobic on ships. So I wish for a road to be built from St Kilda to Hawaii.'

The genie thought about it for a minute and said, 'No, I don't think I can do that. Just think of all the work involved. The pilings needed to hold up the highway. How deep they'd have to be to reach the bottom of the ocean. Think of all the pavement that would be needed. And think of all the environmental problems that might be caused. We could finish up disturbing the breeding places of whales or stopping the migratory paths of shrimp. No, that's just too much to ask.' And the genie prepared to return to the bottle, because a deal's a deal.

But the bloke told the genie to hold on. 'Let me think about it again. There is something else I've always wanted. I would like to be able to understand women. What makes them laugh? Or cry? Why are they temperamental? Why are they so difficult to get along with? What do they want? Basically, what makes a woman tick?'

The genie considered this wish for a few moments, then said, 'So, do you want two lanes or four?'

***

A street walker in Kings Cross visited her doctor for a regular check-up. 'Any specific problems you should tell me about?' asked the GP.

'Well, I've noticed if I get a cut – even the tiniest cut – it seems to bleed for hours. Do you think I might be a haemophiliac?'

'Well,' the doctor answered, 'haemophilia is a genetic disorder and it's more often found in men. But it's possible for a woman to be a haemophilic. Tell me, how much do you lose when you have your period?'

After calculating for a moment, the prostitute replied, 'Oh, about $700 or $800, I guess.'

***

A good pun is its own reword.

Dijon vu – the same mustard as before.

Practise safe eating – always use condiments.

Shotgun wedding: a case of wife or death.

A man needs a mistress just to break the monogamy.

A hangover is the wrath of grapes.

Sea captains don't like crew cuts.

Does the name Pavlov ring a bell?

Condoms should be used on every conceivable occasion.

Reading while sunbaking makes you well-red.

When two egotists meet, it's an I for an I.

***

Twenty-one reasons why the English language is so hard to learn:

The bandage was wound around the wound.

The farm was used to produce produce.

The dump was so full that it had to refuse more refuse.

We must polish the Polish furniture.

He could lead if he would get the lead out.

The soldier decided to desert his dessert in the desert.

Since there is no time like the present, he thought it was time to present the present.

A bass was painted on the head of the bass drum.

When shot at, the dove dove into the bushes.

I did not object to the object.

The insurance was invalid for the invalid.

There was a row among the oarsmen about how to row.

They were too close to the door to close it.

The buck does funny things when the does are present.

A seamstress and a sewer fell down into a sewer line.

To help with planting, the farmer taught his sow to sow.

The wind was too strong to wind the sail.

After a number of injections, my jaw got number.

Upon seeing the tear in the painting I shed a tear.

I had to subject the subject to a series of tests.

How can I intimate this to my most intimate friend?

***

Women already know everything. Nonetheless, training courses are now available for women on the following subjects:

1. Silence, the Final Frontier: Where No Woman Has Gone Before

2. The Undiscovered Side of Banking: Making Deposits

3. Parties: Going Without New Outfits

4. Man Management: Minor Household Chores Can Wait until After the Game

5. Bathroom Etiquette I: Men Need Space in the Bathroom Cabinet too

6. Bathroom Etiquette II: His Razor is His

7. Communication Skills I: Tears – The Last Resort, not the First

8. Communication Skills II: Thinking Before Speaking

9. Communications Skills III: Getting What you Want Without Nagging

10. Driving a Car Safely: A Skill You *Can* Acquire

11. Telephone Skills: How to Hang Up

12. Introduction to Parking

13. Advanced Parking: Backing Into a Space

14. Water Retention: Fact or Fat

15. Cooking I: Bringing Back Bacon, Eggs and Butter

16. Cooking II: Bran and Tofu are Not for Human Consumption

17. Cooking III: How Not to Inflict Your Diets on Other People

18. Compliments: Accepting Them Gracefully

19. PMS: Your Problem – Not His

20. Dancing: Why Men Don't Like It

21. Classic Clothing: Wearing Outfits You Already Have

22. Household Dust: A Harmless Natural Occurrence Only Women Notice

23. Integrating Your Laundry: Washing It All Together

24. Oil and Petrol: Your Car Needs Both

25. TV Remotes: For Men Only

26. Getting Ready to Go Out: Start the Day Before

***

He: Baby, I can play you just like my violin.
She: I'd rather have you play me like a harmonica.

***

'Haven't I seen your face before?' the judge demanded, looking down at the defendant.

'You have, Your Honour,' the man answered hopefully, 'I gave your son violin lessons last winter.'

'Ah yes,' recalled the judge. 'Twenty years.'

***

What do you get when you drop a piano down a mineshaft?
A flat minor.

What do you get when you drop a piano on an army base?
A flat major.

Why was the piano invented?
So the musician would have a place to put his beer.

***

A letter from an Irish mother to her son in Australia:

Dear Son,

Just a few lines to let you know I'm still alive. I'm writing this letter slowly as I remember you can't read fast. You won't know the house when you come home. We've moved.

Your father has a lovely new job with 500 men under him. He cuts the grass at the cemetery.

There's a washing machine in our new house but it isn't working too well. I put fourteen shirts into it, pulled the chain, and I haven't seen the shirts since.

Your sister Colleen had a baby last week. I haven't found out if it's a boy or a girl yet so I don't know if you're an uncle or auntie.

Your Uncle Dick drowned in a vat of whisky in Dublin a few days ago. Some of his mates dived in to save him but he fought them off bravely. We cremated his body and it took three days for the fire to go out.

I went to the doctor on Thursday and your father came with me. The doctor put a tube in my mouth and told me not to open it for ten minutes, then your father offered to buy it from him.

It rained twice last week, the first time for three days, and the second time for four days. On Monday it was so windy the hen laid the same egg four times.

We had a letter from the undertaker. He said if we don't pay the final instalment on your granny, up she comes.

Your loving Mum.

PS: I was going to send you some money, but I already sealed the envelope.

★★★

Sixty things not to say to a naked bloke:

1. I've smoked fatter joints than that.
2. Oh, it's cute.
3. Why don't we just cuddle?
4. Make it dance.

5. You know there's a tower like that in Italy.
6. Wow! And your feet are so big!
7. It's okay, we'll work around it.
8. Yuk, there's an inch worm on your thigh.
9. Can I be honest with you?
10. Let me go get my tweezers.
11. This explains your car.
12. Maybe if we water it, it'll grow.
13. Thanks, I needed a toothpick.
14. Ever heard of Clearasil?
15. Why is God punishing you?
16. But it still works, right?
17. Maybe it looks better in natural light.
18. Why don't we skip straight to the cigarettes?
19. Aw, it's hiding.
20. It's a good thing you have other talents.
21. Where's the rest of it?

***

Two musicians are walking down the street and one says to the other: 'Who was that piccolo I saw you with last night?'

The other replies, 'That was no piccolo, that was my wife.'

***

Bush and Gore go fishing. Gore fishes one side of the lake and Bush the other. Later that day, Bush returns with 129 fish and Gore comes back with none.

Gore screams for a revote.

The next day Bush comes back with 173 fish and Gore once again screams for a revote.

On the third day Gore sends a Secret Service man to spy on Bush who comes back with 293 fish this time while Gore has none. Gore goes to the Secret Service man and asks whether Bush is cheating.

'Yes,' says his spy, 'he's putting holes in the ice.'

***

Why do bagpipe players walk while they play?
To get away from the noise.

How many country-and-western singers does it take to change a light bulb?
Three. One to change the bulb and two to sing about the old one.

What happens if you play blues music backwards?
Your wife returns to you, your dog comes back to life and you get out of prison.

What do you get when you play New Age music backwards?
New Age music.

What does it say on a blues' singer's tombstone?
'I didn't wake up this morning'.

What's the difference between a puppy and a singer-songwriter?
Eventually the puppy stops whining.

How many punk rockers does it take to change a light bulb?
Two. One to screw in the bulb and the other to smash the old one on his forehead.

Know how to make a million dollars singing jazz?
Start with two million.

Michael Caine goes up to Milton Berle during a party and asks, 'What kind of cigar are you smoking there?'

'It's a Lawrence Welk,' says Berle.

'What's a Lawrence Welk?' asks Caine.

Milton says, 'It's a piece of crap with a band wrapped around it.'

***

How do you tell the difference between a violist and a dog?
The dog knows when to stop scratching.

***

Son: Mum, when I grow up I want to be a rock 'n' musician.
Mum: Now, son, you'll have to pick one or the other. You can't do both.

What's the first thing a musician says at work?
Would you like fries with that?

What do you call a musician without a significant other?
Homeless.

There were two people walking down the street. One was a musician, the other didn't have money either.

***

St Peter is checking IDs at the Pearly Gates. First up is a Texan. 'Tell me what you've done in your life?' asks

St Peter. The Texan says, 'Well, I struck oil so I became rich but I didn't sit on my laurels. I divided all my money among my family in my will, so my descendants are all set for about three generations.'

St Peter says, 'That's very good. Come in. Next?'

The second bloke in line has been listening. He says, 'I struck it big on the stock market. But I didn't selfishly provide for my own like that Texan guy. I donated $5 million to Save the Children.'

'Wonderful,' says St Peter. 'Come in. Who's next?'

The third bloke has been listening and says timidly, with a downcast look, 'Well, I only made $5000 in my entire lifetime.'

'Heavens!' says St Peter. 'What instrument did you play?'

***

A bloke walks into his doctor's office and says, 'Doc, I haven't had a bowel movement in a week.'

The doctor gives him a prescription for a mild laxative and tells him, 'If it doesn't work, let me know.'

A week later the bloke comes back. 'Doc, still no movement.'

The doctor says, 'Hmm, you need something stronger,' and prescribes a powerful laxative.

Another week passes. 'Doc, still nothing.'

The doctor, worried, says, 'We'd better get some information to try and figure out what's going on. What do you do for a living?'

'I'm a musician.'

The doctor looks up and says, 'Well, that's it. Here's $5. Go get something to eat.'

***

It was the night of the big symphony concert and all the town notables arrived for the performance. However, close to eight o'clock, there was no sign of the conductor. The orchestra's manager was desperate, knowing they'd have to refund everyone's money. So he went backstage and asked the musicians if any of them could conduct.

None of them could. So he went around and asked the staff if any of them could conduct. No luck there either.

So he started asking people in the lobby in the hope that maybe one of them could conduct the night's concert.

When he didn't find anyone he went into the streets and asked passersby. By now the concert was fifteen minutes late in starting, and the assistant manager said the crowd was getting restless and were about to demand their money back.

Whereupon the desperate manager spied a cat, a dog and a horse. 'Oh, what the hell,' he said, 'let's ask them. We've got nothing to lose.' So the manager and assistant manager went up to the cat. 'Mr Cat, do you know how to conduct?'

The cat miaowed, 'I don't know but I'll try.' But although it tried really hard it just couldn't stand upright on its hind legs.

So the manager moved onto the dog. 'Mr Dog, do you think you can conduct?'

The dog woofed, 'Let me see.' But although it was able to stand up on its hind legs and wave its front paws around, it just couldn't stay upright long enough for an entire movement.

'Nice try,' the manager told the dog and turned to the horse. 'Mr Horse, how about you? Can you conduct?'

The horse looked at him for a second and without a word turned around, presented its hind end, and started swishing its tail in perfect four-four time. 'That's it!' the manager exclaimed. 'The concert can go on.' However, right then the horse dropped a load of plop onto the street. The assistant manager was horrified and told the manager, 'We can't have this horse conduct. What would the orchestra think?'

The manager looked at the horse's arse and then

at the plop lying in the street and replied, 'Trust me – from this angle the orchestra won't even know they have a new conductor.'

***

A bloke walks into a pet store wanting a parrot. The clerk shows him two beautiful ones in posh cages. 'This one's $5000 and the other is $10 000.'

'Wow! What does the $5000 one do?'

'This parrot can sing every aria Mozart ever wrote.'

'And the other?' asked the customer.

'This one can sing Wagner's entire *Ring Cycle*. And there's another one in the back room for $30 000.'

'Holey moley, what does that one do?'

'Nothing that I can tell. But the other two parrots call him "maestro".'

***

CONFUCIUS SAY:

Virginity like bubble. One prick, all gone.

Man who run in front of car get tyred.

Man who run behind car get exhausted.

Man with hand in pocket feel cocky all day.

Foolish man give wife grand piano.

Wise man give wife upright organ.

Man who walks through airport turnstile sideways going to Bangkok.

Man with one chopstick go hungry.

Man who scratch arse should not bite fingernail.

Man who eat many prunes get good run for money.

Panties not best thing on earth but next to best thing on earth.

War does not determine who is right. War determine who is left.

Wife who put husband in dog house soon find him in cat house.

Man who fight with wife all day get no piece at night.

It take many nails to build cot, but one screw to fill it.

Man who drive like hell bound to get there.

Man who stand on toilet is high on pot.

Man who live in glass house should change clothes in basement.

Man who fish in other man's well often catch crabs.

Man who fart in church sit in own pew.

***

Why did the tycoon's blonde mistress always have an empty milk carton in the fridge?
In case someone came around and wanted black coffee.

***

Why do violinists put a cloth between their chin and their instrument?
Violins don't have spit valves.

***

A lawyer and a blonde are sitting beside each other, in the first class cabin, on a Qantas flight from Sydney to LA. The lawyer leans over and asks if she'd like to play a game.

The blonde is tired and just wants to sleep. So she politely declines and turns to the window. But the lawyer persists, insisting that the game is really easy and lots and lots of fun. He explains how it works. I ask you a question and if you don't know the answer you pay me and vice versa. Again she declines and tries to get some sleep.

The lawyer reckons that because she's a blonde he'll easily win the match, so he makes another offer. 'Okay, how about this. If you don't know the answer you pay me just $5. But if I don't know the answer I have to pay you $500.'

This catches the blonde's attention and realising there'll be no end to her torment unless she plays, she agrees. The lawyer asks the first question. 'What's the distance from the earth to the moon?' The blonde doesn't say a word. Instead she reaches into her purse, pulls out a $5 bill and hands it to the lawyer.

Now it's the blonde's turn. She asks the lawyer, 'What goes up a hill with three legs and comes down with four?' The lawyer looks at her with a puzzled expression. He hasn't got the foggiest idea. So he pulls out his Toshiba Satellite and searches all his references. He taps into the earphone with his modem and searches the Net and every nook and cranny of the Library of Congress. Frustrated, he sends emails to all his co-workers and friends. All to no avail.

After an hour of searching, searching, searching, he finally concedes defeat. He wakes up the blonde who's enjoyed an hour of peace and hands her $500. She politely takes the money and snuggles back into her pillow.

More than a little frustrated, he taps her on the shoulder and says, 'Okay. Okay. So what is the answer?'

Without a word, the blonde reaches into her purse, hands the lawyer $5, and goes back to sleep.

✳✳✳

What's the difference between fat and cholesterol?
You don't wake up in the morning with a cholesterol.

Why aren't there any Puerto Ricans on *Star Trek*?
Because they're not going to work in the future either.

How do you get a sweet little eighty-year-old grand-mother to say 'fuck'?

You get another sweet little eighty-year-old grand-mother to yell 'Bingo!'

What's the Cuban national anthem?
Row, row, row your boat.

What's the difference between a zoo in New York State and a zoo in Arkansas?
The Arkansan zoo has a description of the animal on the front of the cage, along with a recipe.

What's the difference between a New York fairytale and an Arkansan fairytale?
The New York fairytale begins 'Once upon a time'. And the Arkansan fairytale begins 'Y'all ain't gonna believe this shit!'

★★★

A lawyer, a priest and a kid were sitting side-by-side in a Boeing when one by one its engines filled with ash from a volcano they'd flown over and the pilot announced that, sadly, they were going to crash. 'There's not a damned thing I can do about it. All the engines are out and we're plummeting towards the earth. Thanks for choosing to fly United.'

The lawyer, the priest and the kid searched the plane

high and low and found a total of two parachutes. The lawyer said that he deserved to survive because he was the best-educated bloke on the plane. He took a chute and jumped.

The priest looked at the young boy and, reflecting back on his life, told him to take the last parachute since he'd already lived a wonderful and full life. In any case, very soon he'd join his Saviour, Jesus Christ, in paradise.

The kid said, 'You can have the other chute because the best-educated bloke on the plane just jumped out with my schoolbag.'

***

The lovers were passionately embracing on her bed, their bodies fused together as they gyrated.

The woman cocked her ear. 'Christ! That's my husband's car! He'll be coming through the front door in a couple of seconds! Hide in the bathroom!'

The lover ran into the bathroom while she hid his clothes under the bed. She just had time to sprawl on top of it as her husband came through the door.

'Why are you lying on the bed naked?' he asked a little suspiciously.

'Darling, I heard you coming up the drive and got ready to welcome you,' she replied with a fond smile.

'Great,' he said, 'I'll just nip into the bathroom and be with you in two shakes.'

Before she could stop him, he opened the bathroom door and found a man standing there, clapping his hands together in mid-air.

'Who the fuck are you?' the husband demanded.

'I'm from the exterminator company. You wife called me in to get rid of these pesky moths,' the lover replied.

'But you've got no clothes on,' stammered the husband.

The lover looked down, jumped backwards in surprise and said, 'The little bastards!'

***

Two blokes were sitting at a bar telling each other about last night's dreams.

'I dreamt I was on holidays,' one bloke said fondly. 'It was just me and my fishing rod and this big, beautiful lake. What a dream.'

'I had a great dream too,' said the other. 'I dreamt I was in bed with two beautiful women having the time of my life.'

His mate looked a bit sulky. 'You dreamed you had two women and you didn't call me?'

'Oh, I did,' said the other, 'but when I called your wife said you'd gone fishing.'

***

A mother and son were walking through a cemetery and passed by a headstone inscribed with 'Here lies a good lawyer and an honest man'.

The little boy read the inscription, looked up and asked, 'Mummy, why did they bury two men there?'

***

The trouble with life is there's no background music.

Suicidal twin kills sister by mistake.

Quoting one is plagiarism; quoting many is research.

My husband and I divorced over religious differences. He thought he was God and I didn't.

My wild oats have turned to shredded wheat.

***

Three rednecks, Bubba, Earl and Jeb, are stumbling home late one night and find themselves on the road that leads past the old graveyard.

'Come and have a look over here,' says Bubba. 'It's

Zeb Jones's grave. God bless his soul, he lived to the ripe old age of eighty-seven.'

'That's nothing,' says Earl, 'here's one named Butch Smith. It says here that he was ninety-five when he died.'

Just then Jeb yells out, 'But here's a fellow who died when he was 145 years old.'

'What was his name?' asks Bubba. Jeb lights a match to see what else is written on the stone marker and says, 'Miles, from Georgia.'

***

How do you know when you're really ugly?
Dogs hump your leg with their eyes closed.

What is the quickest way to clear out a men's rest room?
Say, 'Nice dick'.

How do you know when you're leading a sad life?
When a nymphomaniac tells you, 'Let's just be friends.'

Why don't bunnies make a noise when they have sex?
Because they have cotton balls.

Why is being in the military like a blow job?
The closer you get to discharge, the better you feel.

What has a whole bunch of little balls and screws old ladies?
A bingo machine.

What did the blonde say when she found out she was pregnant?
Are you sure it's mine?

What three two-letter words mean small?
Is it in?

Why does Mike Tyson cry during sex?
Mace will do that to you.

A beggar walked up to a well-dressed woman on Rodeo Drive and said, 'I haven't eaten anything in four days.'

She looked at him and said, 'God, I wish I had your willpower.'

***

A bloke came home from work one day to find his wife sitting on the front porch with her bags packed. He asked where she was going and she said, 'I'm going to Sydney. I'm going to hang out at the Darling Harbour casino.'

'Why are you doing that?' said the bloke. 'You've never shown any interest in gambling.'

She said, 'I've just found out that I can make $400 a night doing what I give you for free.'

He thought about this, went into the house and packed his bags.

Returning to the porch he sat beside his wife waiting for the taxi. She said, 'Where do you think you're going?'

'Same place,' he replied.

'Why?' she asked.

'I want to see how you can live on $800 a year.'

***

IMPORTANT MEASUREMENTS

Radius of an igloo's circumference to its diameter: Eskimo pi

2000 pounds of Chinese soup: Won ton

1 millionth of a mouthwash: 1 microScope

Time between slipping on a banana skin and smacking the pavement: a bananosecond

Weight an evangelist carries with God: 1 billigram

Time it takes to sail 220 yards at 1 nautical mile per hour: Knot-furlong

365.25 days of drinking low-calorie beer: 1 lite year

Half of a large intestine: 1 semicolon

1000 aches: 1 kilohurtz

Basic unit of laryngitis: 1 hoarsepower

Shortest distance between two jokes: a straight line

453.6 graham crackers: 1 pound cake

1 million bicycles: 2 megacycles

1 million microphones: 1 megaphone

2000 mockingbirds: two kilo mockingbirds

10 cards: 1 decacard

1000 kilograms of falling figs: 1 Fig Newton

100 cubic centimetres of wet socks: 1 literhosen

1 millionth of a fish: 1 microfiche

1 trillion pins: 1 terrapin

10 rations: 1 decoration

100 rations: 1 C-ration

2 monograms: 1 diagram

Statute miles of intravenous surgical tubing at Yale University Hospital: One I.V. League

100 politicians: not 1 decision

★★★

Shortly before his marriage to Jodie, James Packer is at his favourite table in Machiavelli restaurant, when he notices a very beautiful woman sitting at a table nearby. All alone. He calls the waiter over and asks for their most expensive bottle of Bollinger to be sent to her, knowing that if she accepts, he's in like Flynn.

The waiter gets the bottle and presents it to the woman saying, 'This is from the gentleman.'

She looks at James, who she clearly doesn't recognise. She looks at the champagne, and she decides to send a note. It reads, 'For me to accept this bottle, you'd need to have a Mercedes in your garage, a million dollars in the bank and seven inches in your pants.'

After reading the note, James sends one of his own back to her. It reads, 'Just so you know, I happen to have a Ferrari Testarossa, a BMW 850 iL, and a Mercedes 560 SEL in my garage, plus over a billion dollars in the bank. But not even for a woman as beautiful as you would I cut off three inches. Just send the bottle back.'

***

A woman gives birth to a baby at St Vincent's and, afterwards, her doctor comes in looking very, very solemn. 'I'm afraid I have to tell you something about your baby.'

She sits up in her bed and says, panic-stricken, 'What's wrong with it? What's wrong?'

The doctor says, 'Well, now, nothing's wrong exactly. But your baby is a little bit different.'

'A little bit different? What do you mean?'

'Well, your baby is a hermaphrodite.'

'An hermaphra what?'

'An hermaphrodite. It means your baby has the . . . er . . . features . . . of a male and a female.'

The young mother is aghast. She says, 'Oh my God. You mean it has a penis *and* a brain?'

***

Ever stop to think and forget to start again?

Beer – the reason I get up each afternoon.

I must be a proctologist because I work with arseholes.

Frankly, Scallop, I don't give a clam.

Wrinkled was not one of the things I wanted to be when I grew up.

Procrastinate now.

Rehab is for quitters.

Finally eighteen and legally able to do what I've been doing since I was fifteen.

Failure is not an option. It comes bundled with the software.

I'm out of oestrogen and I've got a gun.

Stupidity is not a handicap. Park elsewhere.

A journey of a thousand miles starts with a cash advance.

Time's fun when you've having flies – Kermit the Frog.

Police station toilet stolen – cops have nothing to go on.

The meek shall inherit the earth, after we're through with it.

Time flies like an arrow. Fruit flies like a banana.

***

It was a Friday morning in the primary school and the teacher came up with a clever way to motivate her inattentive class. She told them that she would read a quote and the first student to correctly identify who'd said it would get the rest of the day off.

She started with, 'This was England's finest hour,' and a little girl jumped up and said, 'Winston Churchill!'

'Congratulations,' said the teacher, 'you may go home.'

Then the teacher said, 'Ask not what your country can do for you,' and before she could finish the quote, another little girl yelled out, 'John F. Kennedy!'

'Very good,' said the teacher, 'you may go.'

Irritated that he'd missed two golden opportunities, and seeing his teacher writing a third quote on the blackboard, and with her back to the class, a little boy said, 'I wish those fucking girls would just shut up.'

Outraged, the teacher turned to the class and demanded to know who'd said it. The little boy rose to his feet and said, 'Bill Clinton. I'll see you Monday.'

✳✳✳

I asked Mum if I was a gifted child. She said they certainly wouldn't have paid for me.

We childproofed our home three years ago. And they're still getting in.

Children are natural mimics who act like their parents despite every effort to teach them good manners.

The main purpose of having kids' birthday parties is to remind yourself that there are children more awful than your own.

Children seldom misquote you. Instead they repeat, word-for-word, what you shouldn't have said.

***

It used to be that only death and taxes were inevitable. Now, of course, there's postage and handling too.

***

What do a council worker and a shotgun with a broken firing pin have in common?
They won't work and you can't fire them.

***

A drunk who stank of beer and cheap wine sat on a subway seat next to a priest. His clothes were filthy, his face covered in stubble, yet there was red lipstick on his forehead. The drunk picked up a discarded newspaper from the floor and began reading it. After a while he turned to the priest and said, 'Father, what causes arthritis?'

'My son, it's caused by loose living, being with cheap, wicked women, by too much alcohol, a contempt for your fellow man and poor personal hygiene.'

'Well, I'll be fucked,' the drunk muttered, returning to his paper.

The priest regretted being so aggressive and said, 'Look, I'm sorry. I didn't mean to be so critical. How long have you had arthritis?'

'I don't have it, Father. I was just reading here that the Pope does.'

***

A kid is doing very badly in maths at the local state school. So his mother sends him to the local Catholic school. Instantly, the boy's grades improve.

Delighted, his mother asks him how he likes the Catholic school. 'Oh, it's fine, I suppose,' he says.

'They must be teaching you a lot better.'

'No, not really.'

'Then why the big difference in your grades – particularly your mathematics?'

'Well,' he said, 'as soon as I saw that bloke nailed to the plus sign, I knew they meant business!'

***

After a long illness a woman died and arrived at the gates of heaven. While she was waiting for St Peter to greet her she peeked through the gates and saw a beautiful banquet table. Sitting all around, in golden chairs, eating golden fruit, were her parents and all the other people she had loved and who had died before her. They saw her and began calling out greetings. 'Hello. How are you? We've been waiting for you. Welcome. Good to see you.'

When St Peter appeared the woman said to him, 'This is such a wonderful place. How do I get in?'

'You have to spell a word,' St Peter told her.

'Which word?' the woman asked.

'Love.'

The woman was delighted. 'L-O-V-E,' she recited and St Peter opened the Pearly Gates.

Six months later St Peter came to the woman and asked her to watch the gates for him that day. While she was guarding the gates of heaven, her husband arrived. 'I'm surprised to see you,' the woman said. 'How have you been?'

'Oh, I've been doing pretty well since you died,' her husband told her. 'I married the beautiful young nurse who took care of you when you were ill. Then I won the lottery. I sold our little house and I bought a big mansion and my new wife and I travelled all around the world, flying first class and staying in five-star hotels.'

'And what happened?'

'Well, I was water-skiing today, in Hawaii, when I fell and the ski hit my head. So here I am. How do I get in?'

'You have to spell a word,' the woman told him.

'Which word?' her husband asked.

'Czechoslovakia.'

***

And God created woman and she was good. And she had two arms, two legs and three breasts. God asked woman what she would like to have changed about herself. And she asked for her middle breast to be removed. God removed her middle breast and it was good. She stood there with her third breast in her hand and asked God what should be done with this useless boob. And God created man.

***

A man walked into the ladies' department of David Jones and approached the woman behind the counter. 'I'd like to buy a bra for my wife,' he whispered.

'What type of bra,' said the woman, so loudly that the customer was embarrassed.

'Type?' he whispered. 'There's more than one type?'

'Look around,' said the saleswoman, as she indicated a sea of bras in every shape, size, colour and material. 'But don't worry, even with all this variety there's really only three types,' she said.

Confused, the man asked what they were.

She explained. 'There's the Catholic type, the Salvation Army type and the Baptist type. Which one do you need?'

Still confused, the man asked, 'What's the difference between them?'

The lady explained. 'It's all really quite simple. The Catholic type supports the masses, the Salvation Army type lifts up the fallen and the Baptist type makes mountains out of molehills.'

***

Three blokes die and on arriving at the Pearly Gates, St Peter says, 'Before I let you into heaven I have to ask you a couple of questions. Make sure you tell the truth because if you don't you'll forfeit your privilege of being here and we'll have to ask you to visit our friend below. Your answers will also determine what kind of car you get. You have to have a car here because heaven is so big.'

St Peter asks the first bloke, 'How long were you married?'

He says, 'Twenty-four years.'

'Did you ever cheat on your wife?'

'Yes, about ten times, but I thought sins were forgiven.'

St Peter said, 'Yes, they are, but your record's not too good. Here's a Barina for you to drive.'

Then Peter put the same questions to the second bloke. 'I was married for forty-one years and cheated on my wife once. But that was during our first year. And we worked it out and I was faithful thereafter.'

Peter said, 'I'm pleased to hear that. Here's a BMW 3 series for you to drive.'

Whereupon the third bloke said, 'Peter, I know what you're going to ask. I was married for sixty-three years and didn't even look at another woman. I treated my wife like a queen.'

And Peter said, 'That's what we like to hear. Here's an S series Mercedes for you.'

A little while later the blokes with the smaller cars saw the bloke with the Mercedes crying on a golden sidewalk. So they went to see what was the matter. He tearily explained, 'I just saw my wife and she was on a skateboard.'

✷✷✷

The following key business terms have been updated to fit today's turbulent financial news.

CEO: Chief Embezzlement Officer.

CFO: Corporate Fraud Officer.

Bull Market: A random market movement causing an investor to mistake himself for a financial genius.

Bear Market: A six to eighteen-month period when the kids get no allowance, the wife gets no jewellery, and the husband gets no sex.

Value Investing: The art of buying low and selling lower.

P/E Ratio: The percentage of investors wetting their pants as the market keeps crashing.

Broker: What my broker has made me.

Standard & Poors: Your life in a nutshell.

Stock Analyst: Idiot who just downgraded your stock.

Stock Split: When your ex-wife/husband and her/his lawyer split your assets equally between themselves.

Financial Planner: Someone whose phone has been disconnected.

Market Correction: The day after you buy stocks.

Cashflow: The movement your money makes as it disappears down the toilet.

Yahoo: What you yell after selling it to some poor sucker for $240 per share.

Windows 2000: What you jump out of when you're the sucker who bought Yahoo at $240 per share.

Institutional Investor: Past-year investor who's now locked up in a nuthouse.

Profit: An archaic word no longer in use.

★★★

A patient awakened after a serious operation to find herself in a room with all the blinds drawn. 'Why are the blinds closed?' she asked a doctor.

'Well,' the surgeon explained, 'there's a big fire across the street. Flames 30 metres high. And we didn't want you to wake up and think that you'd died in the operating theatre.'

★★★

A married couple was holidaying in Pakistan, just before the war against terror. They were exploring the marketplace, looking at the exotic merchandise, when they passed a small sandal shop. From inside they heard a gentleman with a Pakistani accent say, 'You foreigners, come in! Come into my humble shop.' So they walked in and the shopkeeper said, 'I have some special sandals I think you would be interested in. They have special power. They make you wild at sex like a great desert camel.'

Needless to say the wife was interested in buying the sandals – but her husband insisted he didn't really need them.

'Yes you do, darling,' whispered the wife, 'go on, buy them.'

The husband asked the shopkeeper how sandals could improve his abilities.

'Just try them on, sahib. The sandals will prove it to you.'

After some gentle urging from his wife, he finally

conceded. And as soon as he slipped them onto his feet, he got a wild look in his eyes – something his wife hadn't seen in years – and a feeling of raw sexual power! In the blink of an eye, he grabbed the Pakistani shopkeeper, bent him violently over a table, yanked down his pants and grabbed firm hold of the Pakistani's buttocks. The shopkeeper began screaming, 'You have them on the wrong feet!'

***

Captain Cook stood on the bridge of the *Endeavour*, heading for Tahiti. When, suddenly, over the horizon, a pirate ship was seen. Cook yelled, 'Everyone prepare for battle and hand me my red jacket.'

The battle ended victoriously for the ship and Cook and the *Endeavour* continued on their voyage.

Later again they spotted two French ships. 'Men, we must go to battle again. Someone get me my red jacket.'

After fierce engagement the French retreated, defeated.

At this point the first officer asked Captain Cook to explain the significance of the red jacket. 'Well, if for some reason I should be injured and bleed, the red jacket will not show my wounds and thus the crew will not be alarmed.'

Later that day, over the horizon came a massive fleet of French ships. The nervous crew looked up at the bridge as Captain Cook yelled, 'Everyone prepare for battle. And hand me my brown pants!'

***

The tour bus was travelling through northern Nevada and approached the mustang ranch Sparks. The guide said to the tourists, 'We are now passing the largest house of prostitution in America' and a male passenger shouted, 'Why?!'

***

A young doctor was establishing a new practice on Oxford Street. He had a sign painted and hung it in front of the surgery, proclaiming his specialities: Homosexuals and Haemorrhoids. The locals were upset by the sign and asked him to change it. Eager to please, the doctor put up a new sign saying, 'Queers and Rears'. This caused even more offence – and people from the gay community insisted that the sign come down. Finally the doctor came up with a sign that was acceptable: 'Odds and Ends'.

***

According to the fossil records, for millions of years Neanderthal men were not fully erect, which is pretty easy to understand if you've looked at a Neanderthal woman.

***

A study in Scotland showed that the kind of 'male face' a woman finds attractive differs depending on where she is in her menstrual cycle. For example, if she's post-menstrual she may be attracted to plain facial features. When pre-menstrual she can be attracted to more feminine features in a man. If she is ovulating she is attracted to men with rugged masculine features, and if she's menstruating she's more prone to be attracted to a man with a pair of scissors shoved in his temple.

***

Although born to a Catholic family, Chester had always wanted to be Jewish. At college he decided to take the plunge and go through the formal conversion process. He studied Judaism all semester. Finally, he felt he was ready to take the test and complete the conversion.

On the appointed day, he arrived at the rabbi's office, ready to be tested.

The rabbi said, 'I'm sorry, but before I give you the test, I must discuss my fee. It's $5000.'

'$5000!' exclaimed Chester. 'That's a lot of money. How about $500?'

'Congratulations, you pass,' said the rabbi.

***

Grandma and Grandpa were watching a televangelist. He called on all who wanted to be healed to go to their television set, place one hand on the screen and the other on the afflicted body part. Grandma got up, slowly hobbled to the television set, placed her right hand on the screen and her left on her arthritic shoulder. Then Grandpa got up, went to the TV, placed his right hand on the screen and his left hand on his crotch. Grandma wasn't impressed. 'You just don't get it. The purpose of doing this is to heal the sick, not raise the dead.'

***

Husband: Oh, you're wonderfully tight tonight, darling.
Wife: Get that big hairy thing out of my navel.

***

A distraught husband gets a call from the hospital – his wife's been in a terrible car accident. He rushes into the emergency room and is directed to the doctor handling the case. They page him. He comes out to the waiting room to see the husband.

'Mr Smith?' the doctor asks.

'Yes, sir. What happened? How's my wife?'

The doctor sits next to him and says, 'Not good news. Your wife's accident resulted in two fractures of her spine.'

'Oh my God. What will her prognosis be?'

'Well, her vital signs are stable. However, her spine is inoperable. She'll have no motor skills or capability. This means you'll have to feed her; and you'll have to move her in her bed every two hours to prevent bed sores and pneumonia.'

The husband began to wail loudly.

'Then, of course,' the doctor continued cheerfully, 'you'll have to diaper her as she'll have no control over her bladder and these diapers must be changed at least five times a day.'

The husband's howls grew louder.

'And you'll have to clean up her faeces on a regular basis, as she'll have no control over her sphincter. Her bowel will engorge whenever and quite often, I'm afraid, and you must immediately clean her to avoid accumulation of the putrid effluent she'll be emitting regularly.'

Now the husband was convulsed with uncontrollable sobbing and began to slide off the bench onto the floor. Whereupon the doctor reached out his hand, patted him on the shoulder and said, 'Hey, I'm just kidding. There's good news. She's dead.'

***

A bloke and his wife returned to their honeymoon hotel to celebrate their twenty-fifth anniversary. As the couple reflected on that magical evening a quarter of a century ago, the wife asked the husband, 'When you first saw my naked body in front of you, what went through your mind?'

He replied, 'All I wanted to do was fuck your brains out and suck your tits dry.'

Then as the wife undressed, she asked, 'What are you thinking now?'

He replied, 'It looks as if I did a pretty good job.'

***

On September 11, as the Boeing approached the World Trade Centre, a female passenger jumped up and announced, 'If I'm going to die, I want to die feeling like a woman.' She removed all her clothing and said, 'Is there someone on this plane who's man enough to make me feel like a woman?'

And a bloke stood up, removed his shirt and said, 'Here, iron this.'

***

The Japanese eat very little fat and suffer fewer heart attacks than the British or Americans.

On the other hand, the French eat a lot of fat and also suffer fewer heart attacks than the British or Americans.

The Japanese drink very little red wine and suffer fewer heart attacks than the British or Americans.

The Italians drink excessive amounts of red wine and also suffer fewer heart attacks than the British or Americans.

Conclusion: Eat and drink what you like. It's speaking English that kills you.

***

Editor: How many authors does it take to change a light globe?

Author: I'm not going to change a bloody thing.

***

In a bar in Washington, the barman is astonished to see George W. Bush and Colin Powell come in and grab a couple of stools. The President orders a beer and Powell orders a Jack Daniels.

'Sir,' says the breathless barman, 'it's such a great honour to have you both here. Can I ask you why you've chosen this place? We don't usually get important folk here.'

'Well,' said the President, 'we wanted somewhere quiet to discuss World War III.'

'World War III?'

'Yep, we're going to wipe out 140 million Iraqis and one blonde with big tits.'

The barman is astonished, and curious. 'Why a blonde with big tits?'

And the President turned to Colin Powell and said, 'Told you no one would give a stuff about the 140 million Iraqis.'

***

A little white bloke walks into an office building and presses the Up button for the lift. The doors open and he finds himself standing beside a huge African-American, who looks down at him and says, 'Seven foot tall, 350 pounds, 20-inch dick, three-pound left ball, three-pound right ball, Turner Brown.'

The little white bloke drops to the floor of the lift in a faint. The big black bloke brings him round and says, 'What's wrong?'

And the little white bloke says, 'Excuse me, but what did you say?'

The African-American repeats his formal introduction. 'Seven foot tall, 350 pounds, 20-inch dick, three-pound left ball, three-pound right ball. My name is Turner Brown.'

'Thank God,' says the little white bloke. 'I thought you said "turn around".'

***

These days, the only time politicians are telling the truth is when they call each other liars.

It's no wonder politicians don't listen to their consciences. They don't want to take advice from a total stranger.

The reason politicians are so busy is that they spend half their time passing laws and the other half helping their friends get around them.

Elections are when people find out what politicians stand for and politicians find out what people will fall for.

Political-campaign speeches are like horns: a point here, a point there, and a lot of bull in between.

***

The reason most people are lost in thought is because it's unfamiliar territory.

***

How is it that people looking for a helping hand tend to overlook the one at the end of their arm?

***

Most of us don't know exactly what we want, but we're pretty sure we don't have it.

***

Good hospitality is making your guests feel at home, even when you wish they were!

***

When you give back all your ill-gotten gains, you're a reformed crook. When you keep most of the loot and only give back a small part of it, you're a philanthropist.

***

Living on a budget is the same as living beyond your means, except that you have a record of it.

***

The best scheme for doubling your money is to fold it in half and stuff it back in your wallet.

***

You know the world's in trouble when it takes 2000 laws just to enforce the Ten Commandments.

***

The suburbs are where they cut down all the trees and then name the streets after them.

***

Nuclear energy may prove that all men are cremated equal.

***

The great advantage of small cars is that you can get twice as many of them into traffic jams.

***

The trouble with most neighbourhoods is that there are too many hoods and not enough neighbours.

***

A kiss is proof that two heads are better than one.

***

Some people are like blisters: they show up after the work is done.

***

The big guns in business are those who escape being fired!

***

A born manager is someone whose father owns the business.

***

A boss is someone who's late when you're early and early when you're late.

***

A lawyer is someone who writes an eighty-page document and calls it a brief.

***

It's amazing how unimportant your job is when you ask for a raise, and how important it is when you want a day off!

***

A family vacation is when you go away with people you need to get away from.

***

Marriage is like a bath: once you're in it and you're used to it, it's not so hot.

***

Things you will never hear a woman say:

You know, I've been complaining a lot lately. I don't blame you for ignoring me.

The new girl in my office is beautiful and a part-time stripper. So I've invited her over for dinner on Friday.

I liked that wedding even more than ours. Your ex-girlfriend has class.

That girl is wearing the same outfit as I am. Cool, I'm going over to talk to her.

Let's just leave the toilet set up at all times, then you won't have to mess with it any more.

It's only the third quarter, you should order a couple more pints.

My mother is going to take care of the tab, so order another round for you and your friends.

I'm so happy with my new hairstyle, I don't think I'll ever change it again.

I love it when my pillow smells like your cigars and

beer. You passed out before brushing your teeth again, you big silly!

You're so much smarter than my father.

If we're not going to have sex, then you have to let me watch football.

Are you sure you've had enough to drink?

I've decided to stop wearing clothes around the house.

You're so sexy when you're hungover.

I'd rather watch football and drink beer with you than go shopping.

Let's subscribe to *Hustler*.

I'll be out painting the house.

I love it when you ride your Harley. I just wish you had more time to ride.

Our new neighbour's daughter is sunbaking again, come and see.

No, no, I'll take the car to have the oil changed.

Your mother is way better than mine.

Do me a favour, forget the stupid Valentine's thing and buy yourself something.

Listen, I make enough money for the both of us. Why don't you retire?

Look, my arse is fatter than yours!

***

Useful expressions for high-stress days:

Well, aren't we just a ray of fucking sunshine?

Not the brightest crayon in the box now, are we?

Do I look like a fucking people person?

This isn't an office. It's hell with fluorescent lighting.

I pretend to work. They pretend to pay me.

You! Off my planet!

Practise random acts of intelligence and senseless acts of self-control.

I like cats too. Let's exchange recipes.

Did the aliens forget to remove your anal probe?

And your crybaby, whiny-arsed opinion would be?

How many times do I have to flush before you go away?

Aw, did I step on your poor itty-bitty ego?

How do I set a laser printer to stun?

I'm not tense, just terribly, terribly alert.

When I want your opinion, I'll give it to you.

Earth is full. Go home.

***

My first job was working in an orange-juice factory, but I got canned. Couldn't concentrate.

After that I tried to be a tailor, but I just wasn't suited for it, mainly because it was a so-so job.

Then I tried to be a chef – figured it would add a little spice to my life – but I just didn't have the thyme.

Next I tried working in a muffler factory but that was too exhausting.

I managed to get a good job working for a pool-maintenance company, but the work was just too draining.

I attempted to be a deli worker, but any way I sliced it, I couldn't cut the mustard.

Then I worked in the woods as a lumberjack, but I just couldn't hack it, so they gave me the axe.

Next was a job in a shoe factory, but I just didn't fit in.

So then I got a job in a workout centre, but they said I wasn't fit for the job.

After many years of trying to find steady work, I finally got a job as a historian until I realised there was no future in it.

I studied a long time to become a doctor, but I didn't have any patience.

My best job was being a musician, but eventually I found I wasn't noteworthy.

I became a professional fisherman, but discovered that I couldn't live on my net income.

My last job was working at Starbucks, but I had to quit because it was always the same old grind.

So I retired and found I'm perfect for the job!

***

A little old lady answered a knock on the door one day, only to be confronted by a well-dressed young man carrying a vacuum cleaner.

'Good morning,' said the young man. 'If I could take a couple of minutes of your time, I would like to demonstrate the very latest in high-powered vacuum cleaners.'

'Go away!' said the old lady. 'I haven't got any money!' And she proceeded to close the door.

Quick as a flash, the young man wedged his foot in the door and pushed it wide open. 'Don't be too hasty!' he said. 'Not until you have at least seen my demonstration.'

And with that, he emptied a bucket of horse manure onto her hallway carpet.

'If this vacuum cleaner does not remove all traces of this horse manure from your carpet, madam, I will personally eat the remainder.'

'Well,' she said, 'I hope you've got a darned good appetite, because the electricity was cut off this morning.'

***

Married men live longer than single men, but married men are more willing to die.

***

WHAT THE DOCTOR REALLY MEANS

Says: We have some good news and some bad news.
Means: The good news is I'm going to buy that new BMW; the bad news is you're going to pay for it.

Says: I'd like to have my associate look at you.
Means: He's going through a messy divorce and owes me a small fortune.

Says: How are we today?
Means: I feel great. You, on the other hand, look like crap.

Says: I'd like to run some more tests.
Means: I can't figure out what's wrong. Maybe the kid in the lab can solve this one.

Says: Do you suppose all of this stress could be affecting your nerves?
Means: I think you're crazy and I'm hoping to find a psychiatrist who will split fees.

Says: Why don't you slip out of your things.
Means: I haven't had a good laugh all day.

Says: If these symptoms persist, call for an appointment.
Means: I've never heard of anything so disgusting. Thank God I'm off next week.

✳✳✳

How to keep a healthy level of sanity at work while driving your colleagues insane:

Page yourself over the intercom.

Send emails to the rest of the company to tell them what you're doing. For example: 'If anyone needs me, I'll be in the toilet.'

Put mosquito netting around your cubicle.

Every time someone asks you to do something, ask if they want fries with that.

Put your waste-paper bin on your desk and label it 'IN'.

Develop an unnatural fear of staplers.

Put decaf in the coffee-maker for three weeks. Once everyone is over their caffeine addictions, switch to espresso.

Reply to everything someone says with, 'That's what you think.'

Practise making fax and modem noises.

Finish all your sentences with 'in accordance with the prophecy'.

Ask people what sex they are.

While making presentations, occasionally bob your head like a parakeet.

At lunchtime, sit in your parked car and point a hair dryer at passing cars to see if they slow down.

***

Four worms were placed into four separate jars. The first worm was put into a jar of alcohol. The second worm was put into a jar of cigarette smoke. The third worm was put into a jar of sperm. The fourth worm was put into a jar of soil.

After one day, these were the results: The first worm in alcohol – dead. Second worm in cigarette smoke – dead. Third worm in sperm – dead. Fourth worm in soil – alive.

Lesson: As long as you drink, smoke and have sex, you won't get worms.

***

German scientists dug 50 metres below ground and discovered small pieces of copper. After studying these pieces for a long time, Germany announced that the Germans 25 000 years ago had a nationwide telephone network.

Naturally, the British Government was not that easily impressed. They ordered their own scientists to dig even deeper. A hundred metres down they found small pieces of glass and they soon announced that the Brits 35 000 years ago already had a nationwide fibre network.

Israeli scientists were outraged. They dug 50, 100 and 200 metres underground but found absolutely nothing. They concluded that the Hebrews 55 000 years ago had mobile phones.

★★★

The year is 2222 and Mike and Maureen land on Mars after accumulating enough frequent-flyer points. They meet a Martian couple and are talking about all sorts of things. Mike asks if Mars has a stock market, if they have laptop computers, how they make money etc. Finally Maureen brings up the subject of sex.

'Just how do you guys do it?' asks Maureen.

'Pretty much the way you do,' responds the Martian.

Discussion ensues and finally the couples decide to swap partners for the night and experience one another.

Maureen and the male Martian go off to a bedroom where the Martian strips. He's got only a teeny, weeny member – about half an inch long and just a quarter of an inch thick. 'I don't think this is going to work,' says Maureen.

'Why?' he asks. 'What's the matter?'

'Well,' she replies, 'it's just not long enough to reach me.'

'No problem,' he says, and proceeds to slap his forehead with his palm. With each slap of his forehead, his member grows until it's quite impressively long.

'Well,' she says, 'that's quite impressive, but it looks like a long pencil, it's still pretty narrow.'

'No problem,' he says, and starts pulling his ears. With each pull his member grows wider and wider until the entire measurement is extremely exciting to the woman.

'Wow!' she exclaims, as they fall into bed and make mad, passionate love.

The next day the couple rejoin their normal partners and go their separate ways. As they walk along, Mike asks, 'Well, was it any good?'

'I hate to say it,' says Maureen, 'but it was damn good. How about you?'

'It was horrible,' he replies. 'All I got was a headache. She kept slapping my forehead and pulling my ears.'

***

HOW TO SPEAK NEW ZEALAND

Milburn – capital of Victoria
Peck – to fill a suitcase
Pissed aside – chemical that kills insects
Pigs – for hanging out washing
Pump – to act as agent for prostitute
Pug – large animal with a curly tail
Nin tin dough – computer game
Munner stroney – soup
Min – male of the species
Mess Kara – eye make-up
McKennock – person who fixes cars
Mere – Mayor
Leather – foam produced from spa
Lift – departed
Kiri Pecker – famous Australian businessman
Kittle crusps – potato chips
Ken's – Cairns
Jumbo – pet name for someone called Jim
Jungle Bills – Christmas carol
Inner me – enemy

Guess – vapour
Fush – marine creatures
Fitter cheney – type of pasta
Ever cardeau – avocado
Fear hear – blonde
Ear – mix of nitrogen and oxygen
Ear roebucks – exercise at the gym
Duffy cult – not easy
Amejen – visualise
Day old chuck – very young poultry
Bug hut – popular recording
Bun button – been bitten by insect
Beard – a place to sleep
Chully bun – Esky
Sucks peck – half a dozen beers
Ear New Zulland – an extinct airline
Beers – large savage animals found in US forests
Veerjun – mythical New Zealand maiden
One doze – well-known computer program
Sex – one less than sivven
Iggs ecktly – precisely
Beggage chucken – place to leave your suitcase at the earport

***

A body builder picks up a woman at a bar and takes her home with him. He takes off his shirt and the woman says, 'What a great chest you have.'

The body builder tells her, 'That's 50kg of dynamite.'

He takes off his pants and the woman says, 'What massive calves you have.'

The body builder tells her, 'That's another 50kg of dynamite.'

He then takes off his underwear and the woman goes running and screaming out of the apartment.

The body builder puts his clothes back on and chases after her.

He finally catches up to her and asks why she ran out of the apartment.

The woman replies, 'I was afraid to be around all that dynamite after I saw how short the fuse was.'

✱✱✱

Many, many years ago, when I was thirty-three, I got married to a widow who was pretty as could be. The widow had a grown-up daughter who had hair of red. My father fell in love with her and soon the two were wed. This made my dad my son-in-law and changed my very life. My daughter was my mother, for she was my father's wife. To complicate matters more, although it brought me joy, I soon became the father of a bouncing baby boy. My little baby then became a brother-in-law to dad. And so became my uncle, though it made me very sad. For if he was my uncle, then that also made him brother to the widow's grown-up daughter who, of course, was my stepmother. Father's wife then had a son, who kept them on the run. And he became my grandson, for he was my daughter's son. My wife is now my mother's mother and it makes me blue. Because although she is my wife, she's my grandma too. If my wife is my grandmother, then I am her grandchild. And every time I think of it, it simply drives me wild. For now I have become the strangest case you ever saw. As the husband of my grandma, I am my own grandpa!

***

A couple drove several miles down a country road, not saying a word. An earlier discussion had led to an argument and neither wanted to concede their position.

As they passed a barnyard of mules and pigs, the wife sarcastically asked, 'Relatives of yours?'

'Yep,' the husband replied, 'in-laws'.

***

A priest was called away for an emergency. Not wanting to leave the confessional unattended, he called his rabbi friend from across the street and asked him to cover for him. The rabbi told him he wouldn't know what to say, but the priest told him to come on over and he'd stay with him for a little while and show him what to do. The rabbi came and he and the priest were in the confessional.

A few minutes later, a woman came in and said, 'Father, forgive me, for I have sinned.' The priest asked, 'What did you do?' The woman said, 'I committed adultery.'

Priest: 'How many times?'

Woman: 'Three times.'

Priest: 'Say two Hail Marys, put $5 in the poor box and go and sin no more.'

A few minutes later a man entered the confessional. He said, 'Father, forgive me, for I have sinned.'

Priest: 'What did you do?'

Man: 'I committed adultery.'

Priest: 'How many times?'

Man' 'Three times.'

Priest: 'Say two Hail Marys, put $5 in the poor box and go and sin no more.'

The rabbi told the priest that he'd got the hang of it so the priest left. A few minutes later another woman entered and said, 'Father, forgive me, for I have sinned.'

Rabbi: 'What did you do?'

Woman: 'I committed adultery.'

Rabbi: 'How many times?'

Woman: 'Once.'

Rabbi: 'Go do it two more times. We have a special this week, three for $5.'

***

A married woman is having an affair. Whenever her lover comes over, she puts her nine-year-old son in the closet. One day while her lover is visting the woman hears a car in the driveway and puts her lover in the closet as well.

Inside the closet, the little boy says, 'It's dark in here, isn't it?'

'Yes, it is,' the man replies.

'You wanna buy a baseball?' the little boy asks.

'No, thanks,' the man replies.

'I think you do want to buy a baseball,' the little extortionist continues.

'Okay. How much?' the man asks, after considering the position he is in.

'Twenty-five dollars,' the little boy says.

'*Twenty-five dollars!*' the man repeats incredulously, but complies to protect his hidden position.

The following week, the lover is visiting the woman again when she hears a car in the driveway and, again, places her lover in the closet with her little boy.

'It's dark in here, isn't it?' the boy starts off.

'Yes, it is,' replies the man.

'Wanna buy a baseball glove?' the little boy asks.

'Okay. How much?' the hiding lover responds, acknowledging his disadvantage.

'Fifty dollars,' the boy replies and the transaction is completed.

The next weekend, the boy's father says, 'Hey son. Go get your ball and glove and we'll play some catch.'

'I can't. I sold them,' replies the little boy.

'How much did you get?' asks the father, expecting to hear the profit in terms of lizards and lollies.

'Seventy-five dollars,' the little boy says.

'*Seventy-five dollars!* That's thievery! I'm taking you to the church right now. You must confess your sin and ask for forgiveness,' the father explains, as he hauls the child away.

At the church, the little boy goes into the confessional, draws the curtain, sits down and says, 'It's dark in here, isn't it?'

'Don't you start that shit in here,' says the priest.

***

A man in a hot-air balloon realised he was lost. He reduced altitude and spotted a woman below.

He descended a bit more and shouted, 'Excuse me, can you help me? I promised a friend I would meet him an hour ago, but I don't know where I am?'

The woman below replied, 'You are in a hot-air balloon hovering approximately 30 feet above the ground. You are between 40 and 41 degrees north latitude and between 59 and 60 degrees west longitude.'

'You must be an engineer,' said the balloonist.

'I am,' replied the woman. 'How did you know?'

'Well,' answered the balloonist, 'everything you told me is technically correct, but I have no idea what to make of your information and the fact is I'm still lost. Frankly, you've not been much help so far.'

The woman below responded, 'You must be in management.'

'I am,' replied the balloonist. 'But how did you know?'

'Well,' said the woman, 'you don't know where you are or where you are going. You have risen to where you are due to a large quantity of hot air. You made a promise, which you have no idea how to keep, and you expect people beneath you to solve your problems. The fact is you are in exactly the same position you were in before we met, but now, somehow, it's my fault.'

***

A man is in a hotel lobby. He wants to ask the clerk a question. As he turns to go to the front desk, he accidentally bumps into a woman beside him and as he does, his elbow goes into her breast. They are both startled and he says, 'Madam, if your heart is as soft as your breast, I know you'll forgive me.'

She replies, 'If you penis is as hard as your elbow, I'm in room 1221.'

***

One night, as a couple lay down in bed, the husband gently taps his wife on the shoulder and starts rubbing her arm. The wife turns over and says, 'I'm sorry, honey. I've got a gynaecologist appointment tomorrow and want to stay fresh.'

The husband, rejected, turns over and tries to sleep.

A few minutes later, he rolls back over and taps his wife again. This time he whispers in her ear, 'Do you have a dentist appointment tomorrow too?'

***

On a plane bound for New York, the flight attendant approached a blonde sitting in the first-class section and requested that she move to the coach section since she did not have a first-class ticket.

The blonde replied, 'I'm blonde, I'm beautiful, I'm going to New York, and I'm not moving.'

Not wanting to argue with a customer, the flight attendant asked the co-pilot to speak with her. He went to talk to the woman, asking her to please move out of the first-class section. Again, the blonde replied, 'I'm blonde, I'm beautiful, I'm going to New York, and I'm not moving.'

The co-pilot returned to the cockpit and asked the captain what he should do. The captain said, 'I'm married to a blonde, and I know how to handle this.'

He went to the first-class section and whispered in the blonde's ear. She immediately jumped up and ran to the coach section, mumbling to herself, 'Why didn't someone just say so.'

Surprised, the flight attendant and the co-pilot asked what he said to her that finally convinced her to move from her seat.

The pilot replied, 'I told her the first-class section wasn't going to New York.'

✱✱✱

Recently a worldwide survey was conducted by the United Nations. The question was: 'What is your opinion on the food shortage in the rest of the world?'

The survey was a huge failure. In Africa, they did not know what 'food' meant. In western Europe, they did not know what 'shortage' meant. In eastern Europe, they did not know what 'opinion' meant. In South America, they did not know what 'please' meant. And in the USA, they did not know what 'the rest of the world' meant.

***

Morris returns from the doctor and tells his wife that the doctor has told him he has only twenty-four hours to live. Given the prognosis, Morris asks his wife for sex. Naturally, she agrees, so they make love.

About six hours later, the husband goes to his wife and says, 'Honey, you know I now have only eighteen hours to live. Could we do it one more time?' Of course the wife agrees and they do it again.

Later, as the man gets into bed, he looks at his watch and realises that he now has only eight hours left. He touches his wife's shoulder and asks, 'Honey, please, just one more time before I die.'

'Of course, dear,' the wife says, and they make love for the third time.

After this session, the wife rolls over and falls asleep. Morris, however, worried about his impending demise, tosses and turns until he's down to four more hours. He taps his wife, who rouses. 'Honey, I have only four more hours. Do you think we could . . . ?'

At this point, the wife sits up and says, 'Listen Morris, I have to get up in the morning, you don't.'

***

A man walks into a dentist's and asks how much it will cost to extract wisdom teeth.

'It will be $160,' says the dentist.

'That's a ridiculous amount,' the man says. 'Isn't there a cheaper way?'

'Well,' the dentist says, 'if you don't use anaesthetic, I can knock it down to $120.'

'That's still too expensive,' says the man.

'Okay,' says the dentist, 'if I save on anaesthesia and simply rip the teeth out with a pair of pliers, I could get away with charging $40.'

'Nope,' moans the man, 'it's still too much.'

'Hmmm,' says the dentist, scratching his head. 'If I let one of my students do it for the experience, I suppose I could charge you just $20.'

'Marvellous,' says the man. 'Book my wife in for next Tuesday.'

***

AUSTIN POWERS' CHAT-UP LINES

I wish you were a door so I could bang you all day long.

(Lick finger and wipe on her shirt.) Let's get you out of those wet clothes.

Nice legs. What time do they open?

Do you work for the post office? I thought I saw you checking out my package.

You've got 206 bones in your body, want one more?

Can I buy you a drink or do you just want the money?

I may not be the best-looking guy in here, but I'm the only one talking to you.

I'm a bird watcher and I'm looking for a Big Breasted Bed Thrasher, have you seen one?

I'm fighting the urge to make you the happiest woman on earth tonight.

Wanna play army? I'll lie down and you can blow the hell outta me.

I'd really like to see how you look when I'm naked.

You might not be the best-looking girl here, but beauty is only a light switch away.

You must be the limp doctor, because I've got a stiffy.

If it's true that we are what we eat, then I could be you by morning.

***

A comely redhead was thrilled to have obtained a divorce and dazzled by the skill and virtuosity of her lawyer, not to mention his healthy income and good looks. In fact, she realised she had fallen head over heels in love with him, even though he was a married man.

'Oh, Sam,' she sobbed at the conclusion of the trial. 'Isn't there some way we can be together, the way we were meant to be?'

Taking her by the shoulders, Sam proceeded to scold her. 'Snatched drinks in grimy bars on the edge of town, lying on the phone, hurried meetings in sordid

117

motel rooms – is that really what you want for us?'

'No, no . . .' she sobbed, heartsick.

'Oh,' said the lawyer, 'well it was just a suggestion.'

***

He was too old to have a birth certificate, so when asked to prove his age he opened his shirt and showed the grey hairs on his chest. This was accepted as proof and he got his first pension cheque.

He went home to his wife, showed her the cheque and explained to her what had happened.

She replies, 'Well, get back down there, drop your pants, and see if you can also get disability!'

***

Three men were discussing ageing on the steps of the nursing home. 'Sixty is the worst age to be,' announced the sixty-year-old. 'You always feel like you have to pee. And most of the time you stand at the toilet and nothing comes out!'

'Ah, that's nothing,' said the seventy-year-old. 'When you're seventy, you can't take a crap any more. You take laxatives, eat bran – you sit on the toilet all day and nothing comes out!'

'Actually,' said the eighty-year-old, 'eighty is the worst age of all.'

'Do you have trouble peeing too?' asked the sixty-year-old.

'No, not really. I pee every morning at six o'clock. I pee like a racehorse – no problem at all.'

'Do you have trouble taking a crap?' asked the seventy-year-old.

'No, not really. I have a great bowel movement every morning at six-thirty.'

With great exasperation, the sixty-year-old said, 'Let me get this straight. You pee every morning at six o'clock and take a crap every morning at six-thirty. What's so tough about being eighty?'

To which the eighty-year-old replied, 'I don't wake up until ten!'

★★★

A LETTER TO A BANK

Dear Sir,

I am writing to thank you for bouncing my cheque with which I endeavoured to pay my plumber last month. By my calculations, some three nanoseconds must have elapsed between his presenting the cheque and the arrival in my account of the funds needed to honour it. I refer, of course, to the automatic monthly deposit of my entire salary, an arrangement that, I admit, has only been in place for eight years. You are to be commended for seizing that brief window of opportunity, and also for debiting my account $50 by way of penalty for the inconvenience I caused to your bank. My thankfulness springs from the manner in which this incident has caused me to rethink my errant financial ways. You have set me on the path of fiscal righteousness. No more will our relationship be blighted by these unpleasant incidents, for I am restructuring my affairs in 2005, taking as my model the procedures, attitudes and conduct of your very bank. I can think of no greater compliment and I know you will be excited and proud to hear it. To this end, please be advised of the following changes.

I have noticed that whereas I personally attend to your telephone calls and letters, when I try to contact you I am confronted by the impersonal, ever-changing, pre-recorded, faceless entity that your bank has become.

From now on I, like you, choose only to deal with a flesh-and-blood person. My mortgage and loan repayments will, therefore and hereafter, no longer be automatic, but will arrive at your bank by cheque, addressed personally and confidentially to an employee at your branch whom you must nominate. You will be aware that it is an offence under the Postal Act for any other person to open such an envelope. Please find attached an Application Contact Status, which I require your chosen employee to complete. I am sorry it runs to eight pages, but in order that I know as much about him or her as your bank knows about me, there is no alternative.

Please note that all copies of his or her medical history must be countersigned by a notary public, and the mandatory details of his/her financial institution (income, debts, assets and liabilities) must be accompanied by documented proof. In due course, I will issue your employee with a PIN number that he/she must quote in dealings with me. I regret that it cannot be shorter than twenty-eight digits but, again, I have modelled it on the number of button presses required to access my account balance on your phone-banking service.

As they say, imitation is the sincerest form of flattery. Let me level the playing field even further by introducing you to my new telephone system, which you will notice is very much like yours.

My authorised contact at your bank, the only person with whom I will have any dealings, may call me at any time and will be answered by an automated voice service. He/she may press buttons as follows:

1. To make an appointment to see me.
2. To query a missing payment.
3. To transfer the call to my living room in case I am there.
4. To transfer the call to my bedroom in case I am sleeping.
5. To transfer the call to my toilet in case I am attending to nature.
6. To transfer the call to my mobile phone if I am not at home.
7. To leave a message on my computer. A password to access my computer is required. The password will be communicated at a later date to the authorised contact.
8. To return to the main menu and to listen to options 1 through 7.
9. To make a general complaint or inquiry. The contact will then be put on hold, pending the attention of my automated answering service. While this may on occasion involve a lengthy wait, uplifting music will play for the duration of the call. This month I've chosen a refrain from *The Best of Woody Guthrie*.

'Oh, the banks are made of marble,
With a guard at every door,
And the vaults are filled with silver,

That the miners sweated for.'

On a more serious note, we come to the matter of cost. As your bank has often pointed out, the ongoing drive for greater efficiency comes at a cost that you have always been quick to pass on to me. Let me repay your kindness by passing some costs back. First, there is a matter of advertising material you send me. This I will read for a fee of $20 per page. Inquiries from the authorised contact will be billed at $5 per minute of my time spent in response. Any debits to my account as, for example, in the matter of the penalty for the dishonoured cheque, will be passed back to you. New phone service runs at 75 cents a minute. You will be well advised to keep your inquiries brief and to the point. Regrettably, but again following your example, I must also levy an establishment fee to cover the setting up of this new arrangement.

May I wish you a happy, if ever-so-slightly less prosperous, New Year?

Your humble client

***

These are the only ten times in history that the 'F' word has been acceptable and appropriate in open conversation:

'What the @#$% was that?'

Mayor Hiroshima, 1945

'Where did all those @#$%ing Indians come from?'

Custer, 1877

'Any @#$%ing idiot could understand that.'

Einstein, 1938

'It does so @#$%ing look like her!'

Picasso, 1926

'How the @#$% did you work that out?'

Pythagoras, 126 BC

'You want *what* on the @#$%ing ceiling?'

Michelangelo, 1566

'Where the @#$% are we?'

Amelia Earhart, 1937

'Scattered @#$%ing showers, my arse!'

Noah, 4314 BC

'Aw, c'mon. Who the @#$% is going to find out?'

Bill Clinton, 1999

'Geez, I didn't think they'd get this @#$%ing mad!'
                    Osama bin Laden, November 2001

***

There is no egg in eggplant, nor is there ham in hamburger, or apple or pine in pineapple. English muffins weren't invented in England or French fries in France. Sweetmeats are candies while sweetbreads, which aren't sweet, are meat.

We take English for granted. But if we explore its paradoxes, we find that quicksand can work slowly, boxing rings are square and a guinea pig is neither from Guinea nor is it a pig. And why is it that writers write but fingers don't fing, grocers don't groce and hammers don't ham? If the plural of tooth is teeth, why isn't the plural of booth beeth? One goose, two geese. So one moose, two meese? One index, two indices.

Doesn't it seem crazy that you can make amends but not one amend. If you have a bunch of odds and ends and get rid of all but one of them, what do you call it? If teachers taught, why didn't preachers praught? If a vegetarian eats vegetables, what does a humanitarian eat?'

In what language do people recite at a play and play at a recital? Ship by truck and send cargo by ship? Have noses that run and feet that smell? How can a slim chance and a fat chance be the same, while a wise man and a wise guy are opposites?

You have to marvel at the unique lunacy of a language in which your house can burn up as it burns down, in which you fill in a form by filling it out and in which an alarm goes off by going on.

English was invented by people, not computers, and it reflects the creativity of the human race, which, of course, is not a race at all.

That is why, when the stars are out, they are visible, but when the lights are out, they are invisible.

✱✱✱

A herd of buffalo can only move as fast as the slowest buffalo. And when the herd is hunted, it is the slowest and weakest ones at the back that are killed first. This natural selection is good for the herd as a whole, because the general speed and health of the whole group keeps improving by the regular killing of the weakest members. In much the same way, the human brain can only operate as fast as the slowest brain cells. Excessive intake of alcohol, as we all know, kills brain cells, but naturally it attacks the slowest and weakest brain cells first. In this way, regular consumption of beer eliminates the weaker brain cells, making the brain a faster and more efficient machine.

That's why you always feel smarter after a few beers.

***

A small-town prosecuting attorney called his first witness to the stand in a trial – a grandmotherly, elderly woman. He approached her and asked, 'Mrs Jones, do you know me?'

She responded, 'Why yes, I do know you, Mr Burns. I've known you since you were a young boy, and frankly you've been a big disappointment to me. You lie, cheat on your wife, you manipulate people and talk about them behind their backs. You think you're a rising big shot when you haven't the brains to realise you will never amount to anything more than a two-bit pusher. You, I know you.'

The lawyer was stunned. Not knowing what else to do, he pointed across the room and asked, 'Mrs Jones, do you know the defence attorney?'

She again replies, 'Why yes, I do. I've known Mr Trevino since he was a youngster, too. I used to babysit him for his parents. And he, too, has been a real disappointment to me. He's lazy, bigoted, and he has a drinking problem. The man can't build a normal relationship with anyone and his law practice is one of the shoddiest in the entire state. Yes, I know him.'

At this point, the judge rapped the courtroom to silence and called both counsellors to the bench. In a very quiet voice, he said with menace, 'If either of you asks her if she knows me, you'll be jailed for contempt.'

***

A blonde is driving home and she gets caught in a really bad hailstorm. The hail is as big as tennis balls, and she ends up with her car covered with large dents. The next day she takes her car to the panel beater.

The shop owner, seeing she's a blonde, decides to send her up. He tells her just to go home and blow into the exhaust pipe really hard, and all the dents will just pop out.

The blonde drives home, gets out of the car, gets down on her hands and knees and starts blowing into the exhaust. Nothing happens. So she blows a little harder, and still nothing happens.

Meanwhile, her flatmate, also a blonde, comes home and asks, 'What in the world are you doing?'

She tells her how the repairman had instructed her to blow into the exhaust in order to get all the hail dents to pop out.

Her blonde friend rolls her eyes and says, 'Helloooo! Don't you think you should roll up the windows first?'

***

A woman walks into the chemist and asks the pharmacist if he sells size extra-large condoms. He replies, 'Yes, we do. Would you like to buy some?'

She responds, 'No, but do you mind if I wait around here until someone does?'

***

Dear Abby,

I have always wanted to have my family history traced, but I can't afford to spend a lot of money to do it. Any suggestions?

Sam.

Dear Sam,

Yes. Run for public office.

***

A man staggers into an emergency room with two black eyes and a golf club wrapped tightly around his throat. Naturally, the doctor asks him what happened. 'Well, it was like this,' said the man. 'I was having a quiet round of golf with my wife when she sliced her ball into a pasture of cows. We went to look for it and while I was rooting around, I noticed one of the cows had something white at its rear end.

'I walked over and lifted up the tail and sure enough, there was my wife's golf ball – stuck right in the middle of the cow's butt. That's when I made my mistake.'

'What did you do?' asks the doctor.

'Well, I lifted the tail and yelled to my wife, "Hey, this looks like yours!" '

***

A kindergarten class had a homework assignment to find out about something exciting to relate to the class the next day.

The first little boy called upon walked up to the front of the class and, with a piece of chalk, made a small white dot on the blackboard, then sat back down. Puzzled, the teacher asked him just what it was. 'It's a period,' said the little boy.

'Well, I can see that,' she said, 'but what is so exciting about a period?'

'Darned if I know,' said the little boy, 'but this morning my sister was missing one, Dad had a heart attack, Mum fainted, and the man next door shot himself.'

***

Two buddies, Tony and Steve, are getting very drunk at a bar when suddenly Steve throws up all over himself.

'Oh, no. Now Jane will kill me!'

Tony says, 'Don't worry, pal. Just tuck a twenty in your breast pocket, tell Jane that someone threw up on you and gave you $20 for the dry-cleaning bill.' So they stay for another couple of hours and get even drunker.

Eventually Steve comes home and Jane starts to give him a bad time. 'You reek of alcohol and you've puked all over yourself! My God, you're disgusting!'

Speaking very carefully so as not to slur, Steve says, 'Hangonaminit, I can e-splain everythin! Itsh snot wha jew think. I only had a cupla drrrinks. But this other guy got sick on me . . . He had one too many and he juss couldin hold hiz liquor. He said he was verrry sorry an gave me twennie bucks for the cleaning bill!'

Jane looks in the breast pocket and says, 'But this is forty bucks.'

'Oh yeah . . . I almos fergot, he shhhit in my pants, too.'

***

My mum taught me to appreciate a job well done.
'If you're going to kill each other, do it outside.
I just finished cleaning!'

My mum taught me religion.
'You better pray that will come out of the carpet.'

My mum taught me about time travel.
'If you don't clean up this room, I'm going to knock
you into the middle of next week!'

My mum taught me logic.
'Because I said so, that's why.'

My mum taught me foresight.
'Make sure you wear clean underwear in case you're
involved in an accident.'

My mum taught me irony.
'Keep crying and I'll give you something to cry
about.'

My mum taught me the science of osmosis.
'Shut your mouth and eat your supper!'

My mum taught me contortionism.
'Will you look at the dirt on the back of your neck!'

My mum taught me stamina.
'You'll sit there 'til all the vegetables are finished.'

My mum taught me weather.
'It looks as if a cyclone came through here.'

My mum taught me how to solve physics problems.
'If I yelled because I saw a meteor coming toward you, would you listen then?'

My mum taught me hypocrisy.
'If I've told you once, I've told you a thousand times. Don't exaggerate!'

My mum taught me the circle of life.
'I brought you into this world and I can take you out.'

My mum taught me envy.
'There are millions of less-fortunate children in this world who don't have wonderful parents like you do!'

***

SIGNS

Illiterate! Write today for free help.

Auto Repair Service. Free pick-up and delivery. Try us once, you'll never go anywhere again.

Our experienced mum will care for your children. Fenced yard, meals and smacks included.

Dog for sale: eats anything and is fond of children.

Man wanted to work in dynamite factory. Must be willing to travel.

Stock up and save. Limit: one.

Three-year-old teacher needed for pre-school. Experience preferred.

Mixing-bowl set designed to please a cook with round bottom for efficient beating.

Dinner special – turkey $2.35; chicken or beef $2.25; children $2.00.

For sale: antique desk suitable for lady with thick legs and large drawers.

Now is your chance to have your ears pierced and get an extra pair to take home, too.

We do not tear your clothing with machinery. We do it carefully by hand.

Tired of cleaning yourself? Let me do it.

Vacation special: have your home exterminated.

Get rid of aunts. Zap does the job in 24 hours.

Toaster: a gift that every member of the family appreciates. Automatically burns toast.

For rent: six-room hated apartment.

Man, honest. Will take anything.

Used Cars: Why go elsewhere to be cheated? Come here first.

Christmas tag-sale. Handmade gifts for the hard-to-find person.

Wanted: hair cutter. Excellent growth potential.

Wanted: man to take care of cow that does not smoke or drink.

Our bikinis are exciting. They are simply the tops.

Wanted: widower with school-age children requires person to assume general housekeeping duties. Must be capable of contributing to growth of family.

And now, the superstore unequalled in size, unmatched in variety, unrivalled inconvenience.

***

The sex was so good that even the neighbours had a cigarette.

I work hard because millions on welfare depend on me.

Some people are alive only because it's illegal to kill them.

You're jealous because the voices only talk to me.

Beauty is in the eye of the beer holder.

I don't have to be dead to donate my organ.

I want to die in my sleep like my grandfather. Not screaming and yelling, like the passengers in his car.

It *is* as bad as you think and they *are* out to get you.

***

How to tell if your cat is overweight:

Your cat door is retro-fitted with a garage-door opener.

Visitors to your house constantly mistake her for a beanbag chair.

She waits for the third bowl of food before getting finicky.

There are fewer calls to the fire department, but there is a sudden upsurge in broken branches.

After a fifteen-month gestation period, there are still no kittens!

He only catches mice that get trapped in his gravitational pull.

His enormous tummy keeps your hardwood floors freshly buffed.

She has more chins than lives.

***

It is well documented that for every minute you exercise, you add one minute to your life. This enables you at eighty-five years to spend an additional five months in a nursing home at $5000 per month.

The only reason I would take up exercising is so that I could hear heavy breathing again.

I have to exercise early in the morning before my brain figures out what I'm doing.

I like long walks, especially when they are taken by people who annoy me.

I have flabby thighs, but fortunately my stomach covers them.

The advantage of exercise every day is that you die healthier.

If you are going to try cross-country skiing, start with a small country.

***

An old farmer went to a pub and ordered a drink. As he sat there sipping his beer a young lady sat down next to him. She turned to him and said, 'Are you a real farmer?'

He replied, 'Well, I've spent my whole life on the place, herding sheep, mending fences and branding cattle. So I reckon I am.'

She replied, 'I'm a lesbian. I spend my whole day thinking about women. As soon as I get up in the morning, I think about women. When I shower, watch TV, everything seems to make me think of women.'

A little while later, a couple sat down next to the old bloke and asked him, 'Are you a real farmer?'

His answer, 'I always thought I was. But I just found out I'm a lesbian.'

***

The most unfair thing about life is the way it ends. I mean, life is tough. It takes up a lot of your time. What do you get at the end of it? A death. What's that, a bonus? I think the life cycle is all backwards.

You should die first, get it out of the way. Then you go and live in an old age home. You get kicked out when you're too young, go collect all your super, then, when you start work, you get a gold watch on your first day.

You work forty years until you're young enough to enjoy your retirement. You drink alcohol, you party, and you get ready for high school. You go to primary school, you become a kid, you play, you have no responsibilities. You become a little baby, you go back into the womb. You spend your last nine months floating with luxuries like central heating, spa, room service on tap, then you finish off as an orgasm!

***

We have all been to those meetings where someone wants 'more than 100 per cent'. Well here's how to do that. Here's how to achieve 103 per cent.

IF:

A = 1	B = 2	C = 3
D = 4	E = 5	F = 6
G = 7	H = 8	I = 9
J = 10	K = 11	L = 12
M = 13	N = 14	O = 15
P = 16	Q = 17	R = 18

S = 19   T = 20   U = 21
V = 22   W = 23   X = 24
Y = 25   Z = 26

THEN:

H A R D W O R K =
8 + 1 + 18 + 4 + 23 + 15 + 18 + 11 = only 98%

Similarly,

K N O W L E D G E =
11 + 14 + 15 + 23 + 12 + 5 + 4 + 7 + 5 = only 96%

But interestingly,

A T T I T U D E =
1 + 20 + 20 + 9 + 20 + 21 + 4 + 5 = 100%. This is how
to achieve 100% in life.

But even more importantly,

B U L L S H I T =
2 + 21 + 12 + 12 + 19 + 8 + 9 + 20 = 103%

So now you know what all those high-priced
consultants, upper management and motivational

speakers really mean when they want you to exceed 100 per cent!

***

What's the connection between a space shuttle and a horse's arse? Read on to find out.

The US standard railroad gauge (distance between the rails) is an odd 4 feet 8.5 inches. That gauge was used because that's the way they built them in England, and the US railroads were built by English expatriates.

Why did the English build them that way? Because the first rail lines were built by the same people who built the pre-railroad tramways, and that's the gauge they used.

Why did *they* use that gauge then? Because the people who built the tramways used the same jigs and tools that they used for building wagons, which used that wheel spacing.

So why did the wagons have that particular odd spacing? Well, if they tried to use any other spacing, the wagon wheels would break on some of the old, long-distance roads in England, because that's the spacing of the wheel ruts.

Why built those old rutted roads? The first long-distance roads in Europe (and England) were built by

Imperial Rome for their legions. The roads have been used ever since.

And the ruts in the roads? The ruts in the roads, which everyone had to match for fear of destroying their wagon wheels, were first formed by Roman war chariots. Since the chariots were made for (or by) Imperial Rome, they were all alike in the matter of wheel spacing.

The US standard railway gauge of 4 feet 8.5 inches derives from the original specification for an Imperial Roman war chariot. Specifications and bureaucracies live forever. So, the next time you are handed a specification and wonder what horse's arse came up with it, you may be exactly right, because the Imperial Roman war chariots were made just wide enough to accommodate the back end of two war horses. Thus we have the answer to the original question.

Now the twist to the story. When we see a space shuttle sitting on its launch pad, there are two booster rockets attached to the side of the main fuel tank. These are Solid Rocket Boosters or SRBs. The SRBs are made by Thiokol at their factory in Utah. The engineers who designed the SRBs might have preferred to make them a bit fatter, but the SRBs had to be shipped by train from the factory to the launch site. The railroad line from the factory had to run through a tunnel in the mountains. The tunnel is slightly wider than the railroad track, and the railroad track is about as wide as two horses' behinds. So, the major design feature of what is arguably the world's most advanced transportation system was determined more than 2000 years ago by the width of a horse's arse!

★★★

The local bar was so sure its bartender was the strongest man around, they offered a standing $1000 bet. The bartender would squeeze a lemon until all the juice ran into a glass, and hand the lemon to a patron. Anyone who could squeeze one more drop of juice out would win the money. Many people had tried over time – weightlifters, longshoremen, etc. – but nobody could do it.

One day a scrawny little man wearing thick glasses and a polyester suit came into the bar and said in a tiny, squeaky voice, 'I'd like to try the bet.' After the laughter had died down, the bartender said okay, grabbed a lemon and squeezed away. Then he handed the wrinkled remains of the rind to the little man.

But the crowd's laughter turned to total silence as the man clenched his fist around the lemon and six drops fell into the glass. As the crowd cheered, the bartender paid the $1000 and asked the little man, 'What do you do for a living? Are you a lumberjack, a weightlifter, what?'

The man replied, 'I work for the tax department.'

***

A young woman, down on her luck, decided to end it all one night by casting herself into the cold, dark waters of Sydney Harbour. As she stood on the edge of the dock, pondering the infinite, a young sailor noticed her as he strolled by. 'You're not thinking of jumping, are you?' he asked.

'Yes, yes I am,' replied the sobbing girl.

Putting his arm around her, the kind sailor coaxed her back from the edge. 'Look, nothing's worth that. I'll tell you what. I'm sailing off for Europe tomorrow. Why don't you stow away on board and start a new life over there? I'll set you up in one of the lifeboats on the deck, bring you food and water every night, and I'll look after you if you look after me.'

The girl, having no better prospects, agreed and the sailor snuck her on board that night. For the next three weeks the sailor would come to her lifeboat every night, bringing food and water, and make love to her until dawn.

Then, during the fourth week, the captain was performing a routine inspection of the ship and its lifeboats. He peeled back the cover to find the startled young woman and demanded an explanation. The young woman came clean, 'I've stowed away to get to Europe. One of the sailors is helping me out, he set me up in here and brings me food and water every night and . . . he's screwing me.'

The puzzled captain stared at her for a moment before a small grin cracked his face and he replied, 'He sure is. This is the Manly ferry.'

***

Monica went to the dry cleaners and said, 'Excuse me, I would like to get my dressed cleaned.'

The little old man was barely able to hear her and said, 'What did you say?'

She replied, 'I would like to get my dress cleaned.'

And the old man still could not hear her and said, 'Come again?'

She replied, 'No, mustard.'

***

Dusty goes to the patents office with some designs.
Dusty: I'd like to register my new invention, a folding bottle.
Clerk: Oh yes, what do you call it?
Dusty: A fottle.
Clerk: That's a silly name. Can you think of something else?
Dusty: I'll think about it. I've got something else here,

THE WORLD JOKE BOOK

a folding carton.
Clerk: And what do you call that?
Dusty: A farton.
Clerk: That's rude, you can't possibly use that name.
Dusty: Gee, something tells me you're not going to be impressed with my folding bucket.

***

Job application for McDonald's, from a seventeen-year-old boy:

NAME: Greg Bulmash.
SEX: Not yet. Still waiting for the right person.
DESIRED POSITION: Company's president or vice president. But seriously, whatever's available. If I were in a position to be picky, I wouldn't be applying here in the first place.
DESIRED SALARY: $185 000 a year, plus stock options and a Jodee Rich-style bonus. If that's not possible, make an offer and we can haggle.
EDUCATION: Yes.
LAST SALARY: Less than I'm worth.
MOST NOTABLE ACHIEVEMENT: My incredible collection of stolen pens.
MAY WE CONTACT YOUR CURRENT EMPLOYER: If I had one, would I be here?

DO YOU HAVE ANY PHYSICAL CONDITIONS THAT WOULD PROHIBIT YOU FROM LIFTING UP TO 20KG? Of what?

DO YOU HAVE A CAR? I think the more appropriate question here would be, 'Do you have a car that runs?'

WHAT WOULD YOU LIKE TO BE DOING IN FIVE YEARS? Living at Port Douglas with a fabulously wealthy, dumb, sexy blonde supermodel who thinks I'm the greatest thing since sliced bread. Actually, I'd like to be doing that now.

DO YOU CERTIFY THAT THE ABOVE IS TRUE AND COMPLETE TO THE BEST OF YOUR KNOWLEDGE? Yes. Absolutely.

★★★

WORLD'S THINNEST BOOKS

Things I Can't Afford by Bill Gates
Beauty Secrets by Bronwyn Bishop
Things I Love About Bill by Hillary Clinton
My Life's Memories by Alan Bond
Things I Would Not Do For Money by Alan Jones
The Wild Years by Fred Nile
Amelia Earhart's Guide to the Pacific Ocean
Rushdie's Most Popular Lawyers
Philip Nitschke's Collection of Motivational Speeches

148

Everything Men Know About Women
Everything Women Know About Men
All the Men I've Loved Before by Kerryn Phelps
Mike Tyson's Guide To Dating Etiquette
My Plan to Find the Real Killers by O.J. Simpson
My Book of Morals by Bill Clinton

***

It's good to be a bloke:

Your last name stays put.

The garage is all yours.

Chocolate is just another snack.

You can be Prime Minister.

Car mechanics tell you the truth.

You don't give a rat's arse if someone notices your new haircut.

The world is your urinal.

You never have to drive to another petrol station

because this one's just too 'yucky'.

Same work . . . more pay.

Wrinkles add character.

Wedding dress $5000; suit rental $100.

People never stare at your chest when you're talking to them.

The occasional well-rendered belch is practically expected.

New shoes don't cut, blister or mangle your feet.

Your pals can be trusted never to trap you with, 'So, notice anything different?'

A five-day holiday requires only one suitcase.

You can open all your own jars.

Dry cleaners and hair stylists don't rob you blind.

You can leave the motel bed unmade.

You can kill your own food.

You get extra credit for the slightest act of thoughtfulness.

If someone forgets to invite you to something, he or she can still be your friend.

Your underwear is $8.95 for a three-pack.

If you are 34 and single, nobody notices.

Three pairs of shoes are more than enough.

You can quietly watch a game with a mate for hours without thinking, 'He must be angry with me.'

You can drop by to see a friend without having to bring a little gift.

You are not expected to know the names of more than five colours.

You are unable to see wrinkles in your clothes.

The same hairstyle lasts for decades.

You don't have to shave below your neck.

One wallet and one pair of shoes, one colour, all seasons.

You have freedom of choice concerning growing a moustache.

You can do Christmas shopping for twenty-five relatives, on 24 December, in forty-five minutes.

***

Why is a conductor like a condom?
It's softer with one, but more fun without.

***

During a recent staff meeting in heaven, God, Moses and Saint Peter concluded that the behaviour of ex-President Clinton had brought about the need for an eleventh commandment.

They worked long and hard in a brainstorming session to try to settle on the wording of the new commandment because they realised that it should have the same majesty and dignity as the other ten.

After many revisions they finally agreed that the

eleventh commandment should be: 'Thou shalt not comfort thy rod with thy staff.'

***

One evening a young woman came home from a date rather sad. She told her mother, 'Anthony proposed to me an hour ago.'

'Then why are you so sad?' asked her mother.

'Because he also told me he is an atheist. Mum, he doesn't even believe there's a hell.'

Her mother replied, 'Marry him anyway. Between the two of us, we'll show him just how wrong he is.'

***

David received a parrot for his birthday. The parrot was fully grown with a bad attitude and worse vocabulary. Every other word was an expletive. F this and F that. Those that weren't expletives were, to say the least, rude.

David tried hard to change the bird's attitude and was constantly saying polite words, playing soft music, anything he could think of to try and set a good example. Nothing worked.

He yelled at the bird and the bird got worse. He shook the bird and the bird got more angry and more rude. Finally, in a moment of desperation, David put the parrot in the freezer. For a few moments he heard the bird squawking, kicking and screaming. Then, suddenly, there was quiet.

David was concerned that he might have hurt the bird and quickly opened the freezer door. The parrot calmly stepped out onto David's extended arm and said, 'I'm sorry that I might have offended you with my language and action and I ask your forgiveness. I will endeavour to correct my behaviour.'

David was astonished at the bird's change in attitude and was about to ask what had made such a dramatic change, when the parrot continued, 'May I ask what the chicken did?'

***

THE FOUR STAGES OF LIFE

1. You believe in Santa Claus.
2. You don't believe in Santa Claus.
3. You are Santa Claus.
4. You look like Santa Claus.

***

Yasser Arafat, not feeling well and concerned about his mortality, goes to consult a psychic about the date of his death.

Closing her eyes and silently reaching into the realm of the future, she finds the answer, 'You will die on a Jewish holiday.'

'Which one?' Arafat asks nervously.

'It doesn't matter,' replies the psychic, 'whenever you die, it will be a Jewish holiday.'

***

A man is driving down a road. A woman is driving down the same road from the opposite direction.

As they pass each other, the woman leans out the window and yells, '*Pig!*'

The man immediately leans out his window and yells, '*Slut!*'

They each continue on their way, and as the man rounds the next bend, he crashes into a huge pig in the middle of the road and dies.

If only men would listen.

***

A lady walks into a Lexus dealership. She browses around, spots the perfect car and goes to inspect it.

As she bends to feel the fine leather upholstery, a loud fart escapes her.

Very embarrassed, she looks around nervously to see if anyone has noticed her little accident and hopes a salesperson doesn't pop up right now.

As she turns back, there standing next to her is a salesman.

'Good day, madam. How may we help you today?'

Very uncomfortably she asks, 'What is the price of this lovely vehicle?'

He answers, 'Madam, if you farted just touching it, you are going to shit yourself when you hear the price.'

***

A little girl asked her mother, 'Mum, may I take the dog for a walk around the block?'

Mum said, 'No, because the dog is in heat.'

'What does that mean?' asked the child.

Mum replied, 'Go ask your father. I think he's in the garage.'

The little girl went out to the garage and said, 'Dad, may I take Belle for a walk around the block? I asked Mum, but she said the dog was in heat and to come and talk to you.'

Dad said, 'Bring Belle over here.'

He took a rag, soaked it with petrol and scrubbed the dog's backside with it saying, 'Okay, you can take a walk, but keep Belle on the leash and only go around the block one time.'

The little girl left with the dog, but returned a few minutes later with no dog.

Dad asked, 'Where's Belle?'

The little girl answered, 'She ran out of petrol about halfway around the block, so another dog's pushing her home.'

***

A woman was walking along the beach when she stumbled upon a genie's lamp. She picked it up and rubbed it and, lo and behold, a genie appeared. The amazed woman asked if she got three wishes. The genie said, 'Nope. Due to inflation, constant downsizing, low wages in third world countries and fierce global competition, I can only grant you one wish. So what'll it be?'

The woman didn't hesitate. She said, 'I want peace in the Middle East. See this map? I want these countries to stop fighting with each other.'

The genie looked at the map and exclaimed, 'Gadzooks, lady! These countries have been at war for thousands of years. I'm good but not *that* good!

I don't think it can be done. Make another wish.'

The woman thought for a minute and said, 'Well, I've never been able to find the right man. You know, one that's considerate and fun, likes to cook and helps with the house cleaning, is good in bed and gets along with my family, doesn't watch sport all the time and is faithful. That's what I wish for – a good mate.'

The genie let out a long sigh and said, 'Let me see that fuckin' map.'

***

An old preacher was dying. He sent a message for his accountant and his lawyer (both church members) to come to his home. When they arrived, they were ushered up to his bedroom. As they entered the room, the preacher held out his hands and motioned for them to sit on each side of the bed.

The preacher grasped their hands, sighed contentedly, smiled and stared at the ceiling. For a time, no one said anything. Both the accountant and the lawyer were touched and flattered that the old preacher would ask them to be with him during his final moment. They were also puzzled because the preacher had never given any indication that he particularly liked either one of them.

Finally, the lawyer asked, 'Preacher, why did you

ask the two of us to come?'

The old preacher mustered up some strength, then said weakly, 'Jesus died between two thieves, and that's how I want to go, too.'

***

A bloke died and found himself in hell. As he was wallowing in despair, he had his first meeting with a demon. The demon asked, 'Why so glum?'

The bloke responded, 'What do you think? I'm in hell!'

'Hell's not so bad,' the demon said. 'We actually have a lot of fun down here. You a drinking man?'

'Sure,' the man said, 'I love to drink.'

'Well, you're gonna love Mondays then. On Mondays all we do is drink. Whisky, tequila, Guinness, wine coolers, diet cola and Fresca. We drink till we throw up and then we drink some more!'

The bloke is astounded. 'Damn, that sounds great.'

'You a smoker?' the demon asked.

'You better believe it!'

'You're gonna love Tuesday. We get the finest cigars from all over the world and smoke our lungs out. If you get cancer, no big deal. You're already dead, remember?'

'Wow,' the man said, 'that's awesome!'

The demon continued, 'I bet you like to gamble.'

'Why yes, as a matter of fact I do.'

'Wednesdays you can gamble all you want. Craps, blackjack, roulette, poker, whatever. If you go bankrupt, well, you're dead anyway. You into drugs?'

The bloke said, 'Are you kidding! I love drugs! You don't mean . . .'

'That's right! Thursday is drug day. Help yourself to a great big bowl of crack, or smack. Smoke a doobie the size of a submarine. You can do all the drugs you want, you're dead, who cares!'

'Wow!' the bloke said, starting to feel better about his situation. 'I never realised hell was such a cool place!'

The demon said, 'You gay?'

'No.'

'Ooooh, you're gonna hate Fridays!'

***

If you're a bear, you get to hibernate. You do nothing but sleep for six months. I could deal with that.

Before you hibernate, you're supposed to eat yourself stupid. I could deal with that, too.

If you're a bear, you birth your offspring (who are

the size of walnuts) while you're sleeping and wake to partially grown, cute cuddly cubs. I could definitely deal with that.

If you're a mama bear, everyone knows you mean business. You swat anyone who bothers your cubs. If your cubs get out of line, you swat them too. I could deal with that.

If you're a bear, your mate *expects* you to wake up growling. He *expects* that you will have hairy legs and excess body fat.

Yep, I wanna be a bear.

***

Two Palestinian women are walking through Tel Aviv. One turns to the other and says, 'Be honest, Habeebera, does my bomb look big in this?'

***

A prominent young barrister was on his way to court to begin arguments on a complex lawsuit when he suddenly found himself at the gates of heaven. St Peter started to escort him inside when he began to protest that his untimely death had to be some sort of mistake.

'I'm much too young to die! I'm only thirty-five!' St

Peter agreed that thirty-five did seem to be a bit young to be entering the pearly gates and agreed to check on his case.

When St Peter returned he told the barrister, 'I'm afraid that the mistake must be yours, my son. We verified your age on the basis of the number of hours you've billed to your clients, and you're at least 108.'

***

GEOGRAPHY OF A WOMAN

Between eighteen and twenty a woman is like Africa, half discovered, half wild, naturally beautiful with fertile deltas.

Between twenty-one and thirty a woman is like America, well developed and open to trade, especially for someone with cash.

Between thirty-one and thirty-five she is like India, very hot, relaxed and convinced of her own beauty.

Between thirty-six and forty a woman is like France, gently aging but still a warm and desirable place to visit.

Between forty-one and fifty she is like Yugoslavia, lost the war, haunted by past mistakes. Massive reconstruction is now necessary.

Between fifty-one and sixty she is like Russia, very

wide and borders are unpatrolled. The frigid climate keeps people away.

Between sixty-one and seventy a woman is like Mongolia, with a glorious and all conquering past but, alas, no future.

After seventy, she becomes Afghanistan. Almost everyone knows where she is, but no one wants to go there.

GEOGRAPHY OF A MAN

Between fifteen and seventy a man is like Iraq – ruled by a dick.

***

A husband took his wife to play her first game of golf. Of course, the wife promptly hacked her first shot right through the window of the biggest house adjacent to the course.

The husband cringed. 'I warned you to be careful! Now we'll have to go up there, find the owner, apologise and see how much your lousy drive is going to cost us.'

So the couple walked up to the house and knocked on the door. A warm voice said, 'Come on in.'

When they opened the door they saw the damage

that was done: glass was all over the place, and a broken antique bottle was lying on its side near the broken window. A man, reclining on the couch, asked, 'Are you the people that broke my window?'

'Yes, sir. We're very sorry about that,' the husband replied.

'Oh, no apology is necessary. Actually I wanted to thank you. You see, I'm a genie and I've been trapped in that bottle for a thousand years. Now that you've released me, I'm allowed to grant three wishes. I'll give you each one wish, but if you don't mind, I'll keep the last one for myself.'

'Wow, that's great!' the husband said. He pondered a moment and blurted out. 'I'd like a million dollars a year for the rest of my life.'

'No problem,' said the genie. 'You've got it, it's the least I can do. And I'll guarantee you a long, healthy life! And now you, young lady, what do you want?' the genie asked.

'I'd like to own a gorgeous home complete with servants in every country in the world,' she said.

'Consider it done,' the genie said. 'And your homes will always be safe from fire, burglary and natural disasters!'

'And now,' the couple asked in unison, 'what's your wish, genie?'

'Well, since I've been trapped in that bottle and

haven't been with a woman in more than a thousand years, my wish is to have sex with your wife.'

The husband looked at his wife and said, 'Gee honey, you know we both now have a fortune and all those houses. What do you think?'

She mulled it over for a few moments and said, 'You know, you're right. Considering our good fortune, I guess I wouldn't mind, but what about you, honey?'

'You know I love you sweetheart,' said the husband. 'I'd do the same for you.'

So the genie and the woman went upstairs where they spent the rest of the afternoon enjoying each other. The genie was insatiable. After about three hours of non-stop sex, the genie rolled over and looked directly into her eyes and asked, 'How old are you and your husband?'

'Why, we're both thirty-five,' she responded breathlessly.

'Good God! Thirty-five years old and both of you still believe in genies!'

✱✱✱

Two bored Crown Casino dealers were waiting at a craps table. A very attractive blonde woman arrived and bet $20 000 on a single roll of the dice.

She said, 'I hope you don't mind, but I feel much luckier when I'm completely nude.'

With that she stripped from her neck down, rolled the dice and yelled, 'Mama needs new clothes!'

Then she yelled, '*Yes! Yes! I won! I won!*' She jumped up and down and hugged each of the dealers. She then picked up all the money and clothes and quickly departed.

The dealers just stared at each other dumbfounded. Finally, one of them asked, 'What did she roll?'

The other answered, 'I don't know. I thought *you* were watching!'

***

At a spiritual awareness retreat, Sam and Annie were told to individually write a sentence using the words 'sex' and 'love'.

Annie wrote: 'When two mature people are passionately and deeply in love with one another to a high degree that they respect each other very much, just like Sam and I, it is spiritually and morally acceptable for them to engage in the act of physical sex with one another.'

Sam wrote: 'I love sex.'

***

An attractive blonde woman from New York was driving through a remote part of Arizona when her car broke down. An Indian on horseback came along and offered her a ride to a nearby town. She climbed up behind him on the horse and they rode off. The ride was uneventful except that every few minutes the Indian would let out a whoop so loud that it would echo from the surrounding hills. When they arrived in town, he let her off at the local service station, yelled one final 'Yahoo!' and rode off.

'What did you do to get that Indian so excited?' asked the service-station attendant.

'Nothing,' shrugged the woman. 'I merely sat behind him on the horse, put my arms around his waist and held onto his saddle horn so I wouldn't fall off.'

'Lady,' the attendant said, 'Indians ride bareback.'

***

Two accountancy students were walking across campus when one said, 'Where did you get such a great bike?'

The second student replied, 'Well, I was walking along yesterday minding my own business when a beautiful woman rode up on this bike. She threw the bike to the ground, took off all her clothes and said, 'Take what you want.'

The first accountant nodded approvingly. 'Good choice; the clothes probably wouldn't have fit.'

***

An architect, an artist and an accountant were discussing whether it was better to spend time with the wife or a mistress.

The architect said he enjoyed time with his wife, building a solid foundation for an enduring relationship.

The artist said he enjoyed time with his mistress, because of the passion and mystery he found there.

The accountant said, 'I like both.'

'Both?'

The accountant explained, 'Yes. If you have a wife and a mistress, they will each assume you are spending time with the other woman, and you can go to the office and get some work done.'

***

Henry Ford dies and goes to heaven. At the gates, St Peter greets Ford and tells him, 'Well, you've been such a good guy, and your invention, the T-Model, changed the world. As a result you can hang out with anyone in heaven you want.'

Ford thinks about it and says, 'I want to hang out with God himself.'

So the befuddled St Peter takes Ford to the throne

room and introduces him to God. Ford then asks God, 'When you invented woman, what were you thinking?'

God asks, 'What do you mean?'

'Well,' says Ford, 'you have some major design flaws in your invention:

1.   There's too much front-end protrusion.
2.   It chatters way too much at high speeds.
3.   Maintenance is extremely high.
4.   It constantly needs repainting and refinishing.
5.   It is out of commission at least five or six of every twenty-eight days.
6.   The rear end wobbles too much.
7.   The intake is placed too close to the exhaust.
8.   The headlights are usually too small.
9.   Fuel consumption is outrageous.
     Just to name a few.'

'Hmmm,' replies God. 'Hold on a minute.'

God goes over to the Celestial Super Computer, types in a few keystrokes and waits for the results. In no time the computer prints out a report and God reads it.

God then turns to Ford and says, 'It may be that my invention is flawed, but according to these statistics, more men are riding my invention than yours.'

***

A new young monk arrives at the monastery. He is assigned to help the other monks in copying the old canons and laws of the church by hand. He notices, however, that all of the monks are copying from copies, not from the original manuscript. So the new monk goes to the head abbot to question this, pointing out that if someone made even a small error in the first copy it would never be picked up. In fact, that error would be continued in all of the subsequent copies.

The head monk says, 'We have been copying from the copies for centuries, but you make a good point, my son.'

So he goes down into the dark caves underneath the monastery where the original manuscript is held in a locked vault that hasn't been opened for hundreds of years. Hours go by and nobody sees the old abbot. So the young monk gets worried and goes downstairs to look for him.

He sees him banging his head against the wall. His forehead is all bloody and bruised and he is crying uncontrollably. The young monk asks the old abbot, 'What's wrong, father?'

With a choking voice, the old abbot replies, 'The word is celebrate.'

***

A blonde dials 000 to report that her car has been broken into. She is hysterical as she explains her situation to the operator. 'They've stolen the dashboard, the steering wheel, the brake pedal and even the accelerator,' she cries.

The 000 operator says, 'Stay calm. An officer is on the way. He will be there in two minutes.'

Before the police get to the crime scene, however, the 000 operator's telephone rings a second time and the same blonde is on the line. 'Never mind,' giggles the blonde, 'I was in the back seat by mistake.'

★★★

SIGNS

On a gynaecologist's office door: 'Dr Jones, at your cervix'

On a plumber's truck: 'We repair what your husband fixed'

Outside a muffler shop: 'No appointment necessary. We hear you coming'

In a veterinarian's waiting room: 'Be back in five minutes. Sit! Stay!'

On the door of a plastic surgeon's office: 'We can help you pick your nose!'

On an electrician's truck: 'Let us remove your shorts'

On a maternity room door: 'Push. Push. Push'

At an optometrist's office: 'If you don't see what you're looking for, you've come to the right place'

In the front yard of a funeral home: 'Drive carefully. We'll wait'

***

A minister, a priest and a rabbi went for a hike one very hot day. They were sweating profusely by the time they came upon a small lake with a sandy beach. Since it was a secluded spot, they left all their clothes on a big log, ran down the beach to the lake and jumped in the water for a long, refreshing swim.

Refreshed, they were halfway back up the beach to the spot they'd left their clothes when a group of ladies from town came along. Unable to get to their clothes in time, the minister and the priest covered their privates and the rabbi covered his face while they ran for cover in the bushes.

After the ladies wandered on and the men got dressed again, the minister and the priest asked the rabbi why he covered his face rather than his privates.

The rabbi replied, 'I don't know about you, but in *my* congregation it's my face they would recognise.'

***

A good Irish man, John O'Reilly, met regularly with his toastmasters club. One evening they were hitting the Guinness Stout and having a contest to see who could make the best toast.

John O'Reilly hoisted his beer and said, 'Here's to spending the rest of me life between the legs of me wife!'

That won him the top prize for the best toast of the night! He went home and told his wife, Mary, 'I won the prize for the best toast of the night.'

She said, 'Aye, what was your toast?'

John said, 'Here's to spending the rest of me life sitting in church beside me wife.'

'Oh, that's very nice indeed, John!' said Mary.

The next day, Mary ran into one of John's toasting buddies on the street corner. The man chuckled leeringly and said, 'John won the prize the other night, with a toast to you, Mary.'

She said, 'Aye, and I was a bit surprised meself! You know, he's only been there twice! Once he fell asleep and the other time I had to pull him by the ears to make him come!'

***

An Arab diplomat, visiting the US for the first time, was being wined and dined by the State Department.

The Great Emir was not accustomed to the salt in American foods (French fries, cheese, salami, anchovies etc.) and was constantly sending his manservant, Abdul, to fetch him a glass of water. Time and again Abdul would scamper off and return with a glass of water. But then came the time when he returned empty handed.

'Abdul, you son of an ugly camel, where is my water?' demanded the Great Emir.

'A thousand pardons, O Illustrious One,' stammered the wretched Abdul, 'a man is sitting on the well.'

***

Howard is ninety-five and lives in a senior citizen's home. Every night after dinner, Howard goes to a secluded garden behind the centre to sit and ponder his accomplishments and long life.

One evening, Mildred, aged eighty-seven, wanders into the garden. They begin to chat and before they know it, several hours have passed. After a short lull in their conversation, Howard turns to Mildred and asks, 'Do you know what I miss most of all?' She asks, 'What?' And he replies, '*Sex!!!*'

Mildred exclaims, 'Why, you old fart, you couldn't get it up if I held a gun to your head!'

'I know,' Howard says, 'but it would be nice if a woman just held it for a while.'

'Well, I can oblige,' says Mildred, who gently unzips his trousers, removes his penis and proceeds to hold it.

Afterwards they agreed to meet secretly each night in the garden where they would sit and talk and Mildred would hold Howard's penis.

Then, one night, Howard didn't show up at their usual meeting place. Alarmed, Mildred decided to find Howard and make sure he was okay.

She walked around the senior citizens' home where she found him sitting by the pool with another female resident, Ethel, who was holding his penis.

Furious, Mildred yelled, 'You two-timing creep! What does Ethel have that I don't have?'

Howard smiled happily and replied, 'Parkinson's.'

✳✳✳

175

A young driver, still on P plates, was driving through the country when, suddenly, a bull wandered onto the road. Unable to stop in time, the boy drove into it, killing it outright.

Feeling the need to confess, he knocked at the homestead door. 'I'm sorry, but I've killed your bull. I'd very much like to replace him.'

'Okay,' said the farmer. 'You'll find the cows in the next paddock.'

***

Once upon a time there were two marble statues. One depicted a Grecian athlete and the other a Roman goddess. They'd been standing side-by-side in a park for so many years they were covered in pigeon shit.

Needless to say they'd been in love with each other for ages. But they were too far away to touch. And although they faced each other, it was quite impossible for them to kiss.

Then, once day, God said, 'You've been good statues so I'm going to reward you with half an hour of human life. Do with it what you wish.'

So the statues jumped off their pedestals and disappeared into some nearby bushes where passersby heard a lot of rustling noises.

After a time the statues emerged from the bushes

looking hot and happy.

And God said, 'Look, I think you deserve a little longer. So I'll grant you another ten minutes of flesh-and-blood life.'

'Will we do it again?' giggled the marble goddess.

'Yes!' agreed the marble athlete. 'Let's do it again. Only this time I'll hold down the fucking pigeon and you can shit on it.'

***

A bloke working for the local council is having his fifth tea break for the day. He's talking with his mates, a meat pie in one hand and a mug of tea in the other, with a fag hanging from his lips. All of a sudden he moves fast – to crush a snail beneath his wellies.

'Why did you do that?' asks one of the blokes. 'He wasn't hurting you.'

'No, but he's been following me around all day.'

***

An Englishman, a Frenchman and an Irishman were condemned to the guillotine. And being brave, they all decided to look death in the face. They would lie down facing up.

The first to face the blade was the Englishman,

and three times it was dropped to behead him. But, amazingly, each time it stopped at the last second. So, in accordance with French tradition, he was granted an unconditional pardon.

Next they tried the Frenchman and, once again, the blade was dropped three times and three times failed to decapitate him. So he, too, was pardoned.

Then came the Irishman. Twice the blade plummeted towards his bare throat and twice it stopped at the last nanosecond. And as he lay looking up and waiting for the third attempt, the Irishman said, 'Ah, begorrah! I can see the problem! There's a wire sticking in the pulley at the cross arm.'

***

The cops are about to smash through a door and arrest three drug dealers when God intervenes. He stops time and tells the dealers, in his great, booming voice, that he'll give them a second chance. 'If you can educate the population about the dangers of drugs, I'll turn back the clock. But you've only got twenty-four hours.'

Twenty-four hours later, God asks the first dealer, 'How did you go?'

'Very well,' he says, 'I convinced twenty people not to take drugs.'

'And how did you do that?' asks God.

'Easy. I held up a fifty-cent coin and a five-cent coin and I pointed to the fifty-cent coin and said, "This is your mind before you smoke dope." And then, pointing to the five cent coin I said, "And this is your mind after you smoke dope."'

'Were they convinced?' asks God.

'Yep.'

'Very good,' says God. 'Go forth and sin no more.'

Then God talked to the second bloke. 'How did you go?'

'Bonzer,' said the second bloke. 'I did the same thing with the two coins. "This is your mind before you smoke dope and this is your mind after you smoke dope." And I persuaded fifty people to give up drugs.'

'Excellent,' says God. 'Go forth and sin no more.'

Whereupon God spoke to the third bloke who said, 'I did better than them. I convinced 10 000 people not to smoke dope.'

'Did you do it the same way?'

'More or less,' says the bloke. 'I held up the two coins . . .'

'Don't tell me,' says God. 'You held up the fifty-cent coin and said, "This is your mind before you smoke dope."'

'No,' said the bloke, 'I held up the five-cent coin and said, "This is your arsehole before you go to jail."'

***

The Pope met with his cardinals to discuss a proposal from Ariel Sharon, the leader of Israel.

'Your Holiness,' said one of his cardinals, 'Mr Sharon wants to challenge you to a game of golf to show the friendship and ecumenical spirit shared by the Jewish and Catholic faiths.'

The Pope thought this was a good idea, but he had never held a golf club in his hand. 'Don't we have a cardinal to represent me?' he asked.

'None that plays very well,' a cardinal replied. 'But,' he added, 'there is a man named Jack Nicklaus, an American golfer who is a devout Catholic. We can offer to make him a cardinal, then ask him to play Mr Sharon as your personal representative. In addition to showing our spirit of cooperation, we'll also win the match.'

Everyone agreed it was a good idea. The call was made. Of course Nicklaus was honoured and agreed to play.

The day after the match Nicklaus reported to the Vatican to inform the Pope of the result.

'I have some good news and some bad news, Your

Holiness,' said the golfer.

'Tell me the good news first, Cardinal Nicklaus,' said the Pope.

'Well, Your Holiness, I don't like to brag but even though I've played some pretty terrific rounds of golf in my life, this was the best I have ever played, by far. I must have been inspired from above. My drives were long and true, my irons were accurate and purposeful, and my putting was perfect. With all due respect, my play was truly miraculous.'

'There's bad news?' the Pope asked.

'Yes,' Nicklaus sighed. 'I lost to Rabbi Tiger Woods by three strokes.'

***

Paddy had been drinking at his local Dublin pub all day and most of the night celebrating Ireland's draw with Germany.

Mick, the bartender, said, 'You'll not be drinking any more tonight, Paddy.'

Paddy replied, 'Okay, Mick, I'll be on my way then.'

Paddy spins around on his stool and steps off. He falls flat on his face. 'Shite,' he says and pulls himself up on the stool and dusts himself off. He takes a step towards the door and falls flat on his face. He looks to the doorway and thinks to himself that if he can just get to the door and some fresh air he'll be fine. He belly crawls to the door and shimmies up the door frame. He sticks his head outside and takes a deep breath of fresh air, feels much better and takes a step out onto the sidewalk. He falls flat on his face. 'I'm fockin' focked,' he says.

He can see his house just a few doors down and crawls to the door and shimmies up the door frame, opens the door and shimmies inside. He takes a look up the stairs and says, 'No fockin' way.' He crawls up the stairs to his bedroom door and says, 'I can make it to the bed.' He takes a step into the room and falls flat on his face. He says, 'Fock it,' and falls into bed.

The next morning, his wife, Jess, comes to the room carrying a cup of coffee and says, 'Get up, Paddy. Did you have a bit to drink last night?'

Paddy says, 'I did, Jess. I was fockin' pissed. But how'd you know?'

'Mick called. You left your wheelchair at the pub.'

***

Amazingly, due to pressure from feminists, Guinness have been forced to publish a female version of the *Guinness Book of Records*. Here are a few excerpts from the British Edition.

CAR PARKING

The smallest curbside space successfully reversed into by a woman was one of 19.36m (63ft 2ins), equivalent to three standard parking spaces, by Mrs Elizabeth Simpkins, driving an unmodified Vauxhall Nova 'Swing' on 12 November 1993. She started the manoeuvre at 11.15 a.m. in Ropergate, Pontefract, and successfully parked within three feet of the pavement eight hours fourteen minutes later. There was slight damage to the bumpers and wings of her own and two adjoining cars, as well as a shop frontage and two lampposts.

FILM CONFUSION

The greatest length of time a woman has watched a film with her husband without asking a stupid plot-related question was achieved on 28 October 1990, when Mrs Ethel Brunswick sat down with her husband to watch *The Ipcress File*. She watched in silence for a breathtaking two minutes forty seconds before asking, 'Is he a goodie or a baddie, him in the glasses?' This broke her own record set in 1962 when she sat through two minutes thirty-eight seconds of *633 Squadron* before asking, 'This a war film, is it?'

INCORRECT DRIVING

The longest journey completed with the handbrake

on was one of 504km (313 miles) from Stranraer to Holyhead by Dr Julie Thorn (GB) at the wheel of a Saab 900 on 2 April 1987. Thorn smelled burning two miles into her journey at Aird, but pressed on to Holyhead with smoke billowing from the rear wheels. This journey also holds the record for the longest completed journey with the choke fully out and the right indicator flashing.

JUMBLE SALE MASSACRE

The greatest number of old ladies to perish while fighting at a jumble sale is ninety-eight, at a Methodist church hall in Castleford, West Yorkshire, on 12 February 1991. When the doors opened at 10 a.m., the initial scramble to get in cost sixteen lives, a further twenty-five being killed in a crush at the first table. A seven-way skirmish then broke out over a pinafore dress costing 10 pence, which escalated into a full-scale melee, resulting in another eighteen lives being lost. A pitched battle over a headscarf then ensued and quickly spread throughout the hall, claiming thirty-nine old women. The jumble sale raised £5.28 for the local boy scouts.

GOSSIPING

On 18 February 1992, Joyce Blatherwick, a close friend of Agnes Banbury, popped around for a cup of tea and a chat, during the course of which she told Mrs Banbury, in the strictest confidence that she was having an affair with the butcher. After Mrs Blatherwick left at 2.10 p.m. Mrs Banbury immediately began to tell everyone, swearing them to secrecy. By 2.30 p.m. she had told 128 people of the news. By 2.50 p.m. it had risen to 372 and by 4 p.m. that afternoon 2774 knew of the affair, including the local Amateur Dramatic Society, several knitting circles, a coach-load of American tourists that she flagged down, and the butcher's wife. When a tired Mrs Banbury went to bed at 11.55 p.m. that night, Mrs Blatherwick's affair was common knowledge to a staggering 75 338 people, enough to fill Wembley Stadium.

GROUP TOILET VISIT

The record for the largest group of women to visit a toilet simultaneously is held by 147 workers at the Department of Social Security, Longbenton. At their annual Christmas celebration at a nightclub in Newcastle-upon-Tyne on 12 October 1994, Mrs Beryl Crabtree got up to go to the toilet and was immediately followed by 146 other members of the party. Moving as a mass, the group entered the toilet at 9.52 p.m. and, after waiting for everyone to finish, emerged two hours thirty-seven minutes later.

SINGLE-BREATH SENTENCE

An Oxfordshire woman today became the first ever to break the thirty-minute barrier for talking without drawing breath. Mrs Mavis Sommers, forty-eight, of Cowley, smashed the previous record of twenty-three minutes when she excitedly reported an argument she'd had in the butcher's to her neighbour. She ranted on for a staggering thirty-two minutes and twelve seconds without pausing for air, before going blue and collapsing in a heap on the ground. She was taken to Radcliffe Infirmary in a wheelbarrow but was released later after check-ups. At the peak of her mammoth motor-mouth marathon, she achieved an unbelievable 680 words per minute, repeating the main points of the story an amazing 114 times, while her neighbour, Mrs Dolly Knowles, nodded and tutted. The last third of the sentence was delivered in a barely audible croak, the last two minutes being mouthed only, accompanied by vigorous gesticulations and indignant spasms.

★★★

A husband is at home watching the football when his wife interrupts: 'Honey, could you fix the light in the hallway? It's been flickering for weeks now.'

He looks at her and says angrily, 'Fix the light? Now? Does it look like I have an electrical logo printed on my forehead? I don't think so!'

'Well, could you fix the fridge door? It won't close properly.'

'Fix the fridge door? Does it look like I have Westinghouse written on my forehead? I don't think so.'

'Fine!' she says. 'Then could you at least fix the steps at the front door? They're about to break.'

'Does it look like I have Mitre 10 written on my forehead? I don't think so. I've had enough of this, I'm going to the pub!'

So he goes to the pub and drinks for a couple of hours. When he arrives home he notices the steps are fixed and the light is no longer flickering. He goes to the fridge to get a beer and notices that the fridge door is also fixed.

'Honey, how'd this all get fixed?'

'Well,' she says, 'when you left I sat outside and cried. Just then a nice young man asked me what was wrong, so I told him. He offered to do all the repairs and all I had to do was bake him a cake or have sex with him.'

'So, what kind of a cake did you bake him?' asks her husband.

She replied, '*Hello!* Do you see Sara Lee written on my forehead? I don't think so!'

***

A woman was sitting at a bar, enjoying an after-work cocktail with her girlfriends, when an exceptionally tall, handsome, extremely sexy young man entered. He was so striking that the woman could not take her eyes off him. The young man noticed her overly attentive stare and walked directly towards her.

Before she could offer her apologies for staring so rudely, he leaned over and whispered to her, 'I'll do anything, absolutely anything, that you want me to do, no matter how kinky, for $20 – on one condition.'

Flabbergasted, the woman asked what the condition was. The young man replied, 'You have to tell me what you want me to do in just three words.'

The woman considered his proposition for a moment, then slowly removed from her purse a $20 bill, which she pressed into the young man's hand, along with her address. She looked deeply into his eyes and slowly, meaningfully whispered, 'Clean my house.'

***

International academics were asked to write a book about elephants. The English version was titled *The Elephants and Empire: A Thousand Years of Glory*.

The French was *Les Elephants: Les Implications Sensuelles et Existentielles*, the German was *Achtung! The Training and Discipline of Elephants*. The American version came out in two editions. On the east coast it was titled *Raising Elephants for Fun and Profit* and on the west coast *The Joy of Elephants*. As for the Australian edition, the title was *Elephants – Federal or State Responsibility?*

∗∗∗

Ted and his wife are working in their garden one day when Ted looks over at his wife and says, 'Your butt is getting really big! I mean *really* big! I bet your butt is bigger than the barbecue.'

With that, he proceeds to get a measuring tape to measure the grill and then goes over to where his wife is working and measures his wife's bottom. 'Yes, I was right. Your butt is two inches wider than the barbecue!!'

The wife chooses to ignore her husband.

Later that night in bed, Ted is feeling a little frisky. He makes some advances towards his wife who completely brushes him off. 'What's wrong?' he asks.

She answered, 'Do you really think I'm going to fire up this big-arse grill for one little sausage?'

***

Recently, a Husband Shopping Centre opened in Dallas, where women could go to choose a husband from among many men. It was laid out in five floors, with the men increasing in positive attitudes as you ascended the floors. The only rule was, once you opened the door to any floor, you must choose a man from that floor. And if you went up a floor, you couldn't go back down except to leave the place, never to return.

A couple of girlfriends go to the place to find men.

First floor, the door had a sign saying, 'These men have jobs and love kids.' The women read the sign and said, 'Well, that's better than not having jobs, or not loving kids. But I wonder what's up further?' So up they go.

Second floor said, 'These men have high-paying jobs, love kids and are extremely good-looking. 'Hmmm,' said the girls. 'But I wonder what's up further?'

The third-floor sign read, 'These men have high-paying jobs, are extremely good-looking, love kids and help with the housework.'

'Wow!' said the women. 'Very tempting. But there's more up further!' And up they go.

On the fourth floor they read: 'These men have high-paying jobs, love kids, are extremely good-looking, help with the housework, and have a strong romantic streak.'

'Oh, mercy me. But just think! What must be waiting further up!'

So up to the fifth floor they go. The sign on that door read, 'This floor is empty and exists only to prove that women are impossible to please. Goodbye.'

***

Two elderly women were eating breakfast in a restaurant one morning. Ethel noticed something funny about Mabel's ear and said, 'Mabel, did you know you've got a suppository in your left ear?'

Mabel answered, 'I have? A suppository?' She pulled it out and stared at it. Then she said, 'Ethel, I'm glad you saw this thing. Now I think I know where my hearing aid is.'

***

When the husband finally died, his wife put the usual death notice in the paper, but added that he died of gonorrhoea. No sooner were the papers delivered than a good friend of the family phoned and complained bitterly. 'You know very well that he died of diarrhoea, not gonorrhoea.'

The widow replied, 'I nursed him night and day, so of course I know he died of diarrhoea. But I thought it would be better for posterity to remember him as a great lover rather than the big shit he always was.'

***

An elderly couple was on a cruise and it was really stormy. They were standing on the back of the boat watching the moon when a wave came up and washed the old woman overboard. They searched for days and couldn't find her, so the captain sent the old man back to shore with the promise that he would notify him as soon as they found something.

Three weeks went by and finally the old man got a fax from the boat. It read: 'Sir, sorry to inform you, we found your wife dead at the bottom of the ocean. We hauled her up to the deck and attached to her butt was an oyster that had a pearl worth $50 000. Please advise.'

The old man faxed back: 'Send me the pearl and rebait the trap.'

***

A funeral service is being held for a woman who has just passed away. At the end of the service, the pallbearers are carrying the casket out when they accidentally bump into a wall, jarring the casket. They hear a faint moan! They open the casket and find that the woman is actually alive! She lives for ten more years, and then dies.

Once again, a ceremony is held, and at the end of it the pallbearers are again carrying out the casket. As they carry the casket towards the door, the husband cries out, 'Watch that wall!'

***

When I went to lunch today I noticed an old lady sitting on a park bench sobbing her eyes out. I stopped and asked her what was wrong. She said, 'I have a 22-year-old husband at home. He makes love to me every morning and then gets up and makes me pancakes, sausages, fresh fruit and freshly ground coffee.'

I said, 'Well then, why are you crying?'

She said, 'He makes me homemade soup for lunch and my favourite brownies and then makes love to me for half the afternoon.'

I said, 'Well, why are you crying?'

She said, 'For dinner he makes me a gourmet meal with wine and my favourite dessert and then makes love to me until two a.m.'

I said, 'Well, why in the world would you be crying?'

She said, 'I can't remember where I live!'

THE WORLD JOKE BOOK

***

Two elderly ladies had been friends for many decades. Over the years they had shared all kinds of activities and adventures. Lately, their activities had been limited to meeting a few times a week to play cards. One day they were playing cards when one looked at the other and said, 'Now, don't get mad at me. I know we've been friends for a long time. But I just can't think of your name! I thought and thought but I can't remember it. Please tell me what your name is.'

Her friend glared at her. For at least three minutes she just glared. Finally, she said, 'How soon do you need to know?'

***

EXCERPTS FROM A CAT'S DIARY

DAY 752 – My captors continue to taunt me with bizarre little dangling objects. They dine lavishly on fresh meat, while I am forced to eat dry cereal. The only thing that keeps me going is the hope of escape and the mild satisfaction I get from ruining the occasional piece of furniture. Tomorrow I may eat another house plant.

DAY 761 – Today my attempt to kill my captors

by weaving around their feet while they were walking almost succeeded. Must try this at the top of the stairs. In an attempt to disgust and repulse these vile oppressors, I once again induced myself to vomit on their favourite chair. Must try this on their bed.

DAY 765 – Decapitated a mouse and brought them the headless body in an attempt to make them aware of what I am capable of, and to try to strike fear into their hearts. They only cooed and condescended about what a good little cat I was. Hmmm. Not working according to plan.

DAY 768 – I am finally aware of how sadistic they are. For no good reason I was chosen for the water torture. This time, however, it included a burning foamy chemical called 'shampoo'. What sick minds could invent such a liquid? My only consolation is the piece of thumb still stuck between my teeth.

DAY 771 – There was some sort of gathering of their accomplices. I was placed in solitary confinement throughout the event. However, I could hear the noise and smell the foul odour of the glass tubes they call 'beer'. More importantly I overheard that my confinement was due to my power of 'allergies'. Must learn what this is and how to use it to my advantage.

DAY 774 – I am convinced the other captives are flunkies and maybe snitches. The dog is routinely released and seems more than happy to return. He is obviously a half-wit. The bird on the other hand has got to be an informant and speaks with them regularly. I am certain he reports my every move. Due to his current placement in the metal room his safety is assured. But I can wait; it is only a matter of time.

***

Rodney Adler dies and goes to hell. He notices a sign that says CAPITALIST HELL and one a few metres away saying SOCIALIST HELL. There's a long, long queue of souls waiting for the Socialist Hell, including many famous identifies from the Australian business community. Whereas no one is queuing to get into the Capitalist Hell.

Rodney asked the guard, 'What do they do to you in the Socialist Hell?'

'They boil you in oil. They whip you. They put you on the rack,' said the guard with a grin.

'And what do they do in the Capitalist Hell?' asked Rodney.

'Exactly the same thing.'

'Then why is everyone lining up for the Socialist Hell – particularly all the people who were prominent in the Australian business community?'

'Because in Socialist Hell,' the guard explained, 'they're always out of oil, whips and racks.'

***

A bloke comes home, flakes out in front of the telly and says to his wife, 'Quick! Give me a beer before it starts.'

She scowls but brings him the beer. A few minutes later he says, 'Give me another beer. It's gonna start any time now.'

She's furious. 'So that's all you're gonna do tonight? Sit in front of the TV drinking beer? You're an absolute slob.'

He interrupts her with a heavy sigh and says, 'It's started.'

***

A working mother returned from a business trip and asked her little boy what he'd been up to while she'd been away.

'Mummy, there was a really terrible storm on Monday night,' he said. 'Lots of thunder and lightning. I was so scared that me and Daddy snuggled up together in your bed.'

'You mean "Daddy and I",' corrected the boy's attractive young nanny.

'No, that was on Tuesday, Wednesday and Thursday,' said the boy.

***

THE WISDOM OF GEORGE W. BUSH

The vast majority of our imports come from outside the country.

I have made good judgements in the past. I have made good judgements in the future.

A low voter turnout is an indication of fewer people going to the polls.

We are ready for any following unforeseen event that may or may not occur.

It isn't pollution that's harming the environment. It's the impurities in our air that are doing it.

***

Letter from the White House regarding captives taken during the Afghanistan war:

Dear Concerned Citizen,
    Thank you for your recent letter roundly criticising our treatment of the Taliban and Al Qaeda detainees

currently being held at Guantanamo Bay, Cuba. My administration takes these matters seriously, and your opinion was heard loud and clear here in Washington.

You'll be pleased to learn that, thanks to the concerns of citizens like you, we are creating a new division of the Terrorist Retraining Program to be called the 'Liberals Accept Responsibility for Killers' program, or LARK for short. In accordance with the guidelines of this new program, we have decided to place one terrorist under your personal care. Your personal detainee has been selected and scheduled for transportation under heavily armed guard to your residence next Monday.

Ali Mohammed Ahmed bin Mahmud (you can just call him Ahmed) is to be cared for pursuant to the standards you personally demanded in your letter of admonishment. It will likely be necessary for you to hire some assistant caretakers. We will conduct weekly inspections to ensure that your standards of care for Ahmed are commensurate with those you so strongly recommended in your letter.

He generally bathes quarterly with the change of seasons, assuming that it rains, and he washes his clothes simultaneously. This should help with your water bill. Also, your new friend has a really bad case of body lice that hasn't been completely remedied. Please heed the large orange notice attached to your detainee's cage: 'Does not play well with others'. Although Ahmed is sociopathic and extremely violent, we hope that your sensitivity to what you described as his 'attitudinal problem' will help him overcome these character flaws. Perhaps you are correct in describing these problems as mere cultural differences.

He will bite you, given the chance, but his rabies test came back negative, so not to worry.

We understand that you plan to offer counselling and home schooling. Your adopted terrorist is extremely proficient in hand-to-hand combat and can extinguish human life with such simple items as a pencil or nail clippers. We do not suggest that you ask him to demonstrate these skills at your next yoga group.

He is also expert at making a wide variety of explosive devices from common household products, so you may wish to keep those items locked up, unless (in your opinion) this might offend him.

Ahmed will not wish to interact with your wife or daughters (except sexually), since he views females as a subhuman form of property. However, he will be eager to assist with the education of your sons; have available for their use several copies of the Koran.

Oh, and rest assured he absolutely loves animals, especially cats and dogs. He prefers them roasted, but raw is fine, too, if they aren't more than two or three days dead.

Thanks again for your letter. We truly appreciate it when folks like you, who know so much, keep us informed of the proper way to do our job. We think this watching over each other's shoulder is such a good way for people to interact that we will be sending a team of federal officials with expertise in your line of work to your place of business soon, just to help you do your job better.

Don't be concerned that they have the power to close your business, seize your property, and arrest you for any violation of the 4 850 206 laws, codes, regulations and rules that apply to your profession. They're really there just to make sure you're doing everything the proper way. That is what you wanted, right?

Well, thank you for this opportunity to interact with such a valued member of the citizenry.

You take good care of Ahmed – and remember, we'll be watching!

Cordially,

GWB President

Toodle Pip Banksie

***

A Melbourne company, feeling it is time for a shake-up, hire a new CEO. He's a follower of Al 'Chainsaw' Dunlap, the bloke who put the cleaners through Consolidated Press – and he's determined to improve the bottom line by ridding the company of all slackers.

On a tour of the facilities, the new CEO notices a bloke leaning against a wall. The room is full of employees and he thinks this is his chance to show everyone that he means business.

So the CEO walks up to the bloke and says, 'How much money do you make a week?'

The young bloke looks at him and says, '$200. Why?'

The CEO peels four $50 notes off his thick bankroll and screams, 'Here's a week's pay. Now piss off! And don't come back!'

Feeling pretty good about his demo, the CEO looks around the room and says, 'Does anyone want to tell me what that slacker was doing here?'

With a grin, one of the employees mutters, 'Delivering pizza.'

***

A skinhead and his girlfriend are walking through a shopping mall late at night. They're holding hands and looking in the windows. As they pass a jeweller's, the girlfriend sees a diamond ring. 'Look, Arthur. I'd love to have that.'

So he throws a brick through the window, reaches in and grabs the ring. 'Here you go,' he says.

She's impressed. The next shop is a posh boutique and, again, she sees something she likes. 'Look at that, Arthur. That coat is really beautiful.'

The skinhead shrugs, tosses another brick through the window and, brushing the broken glass from the coat, hands it to her.

In the next shop she spots a pair of boots and is just about to ask for them when the skinhead says, 'For Christ sake, do you think I'm made of bricks?'

***

Two blokes from the bush are walking through Kings Cross and, outside a shop, see a sign that reads 'Suits $10, shirts $2, trousers $5'.

'Look at that,' says one of the bushies. 'That's really, really cheap. We should go in and buy some of this gear – and sell them to the shearers when we get back home. We could make a lot of dough.'

So they go into the shop and ask for ten suits, thirty shirts and a dozen pairs of trousers.

'You're not locals, are you?' says the woman behind the counter.

'No,' says one of the bushies, adjusting his soiled Akubra and hitching his trousers. 'How can you tell?'

She says, 'Because this is a dry cleaners.'

***

If you take an Oriental person and spin him around several times, does he become disoriented?

If people from Poland are called Poles, why aren't people from Holland called Holes?

Why do we say something is out of whack? What's a whack?

Do infants enjoy infancy as much as adults enjoy adultery?

If a pig loses its voice, is it disgruntled?

If love is blind, why is lingerie so popular?

When someone asks you, 'A penny for your thoughts' and you put your two cents in, what happens to the other penny?

Why is a person who plays the piano called a pianist but a person who drives a racecar not called a racist?

Why are a wise man and a wise guy opposites?

Why do overlook and oversee mean opposite things?

Why isn't 11 pronounced onety-one?

'I am' is reportedly the shortest sentence in the English language. Could it be that 'I do' is the longest sentence?

If lawyers are disbarred and clergymen defrocked, doesn't it follow that electricians can be delighted, musicians denoted, cowboys deranged, models deposed, tree surgeons debarked, and dry cleaners depressed?

I was thinking about how people seem to read the Bible a whole lot more as they get older. Then it dawned on me. They're cramming for their final exam.

I thought about how mothers feed their babies with tiny spoons and forks so I wondered what do Chinese mothers use? Toothpicks?

Why do they put pictures of criminals up in the post office? What are we supposed to do, write to them? Why don't they just put their pictures on the postage stamps so the mailmen can look at them while they deliver the mail?

If it's true that we are here to help others, then what exactly are the others here for?

You never really learn to swear until you learn to drive.

No one ever says, 'Its only a game' when their team is winning.

Ever wonder what the speed of lightning would be if it didn't zigzag?

Ever wonder about those people who spend $2 apiece on those little bottles of Evian water? Try spelling Evian backwards: *naive*.

Isn't making a smoking section in a restaurant like making a peeing section in a swimming pool?

If four out of five people *suffer* from diarrhoea, does that mean that one enjoys it?

***

After their first blue, which occurred in the middle of their honeymoon at Surfer's, a young husband complained to his new bride, 'When we were married just last week you promised to love, honour and obey.'

And she said, 'Yes, that's because I didn't want us to have a row in front of all those people.'

***

Two corrupt mayors were comparing notes on the dirty doings in their respective shires. One boasted of his new big house and his late-model BMW – saying that he'd got the money by skimming six per cent off the budget of a newly built bridge.

The other produced a photograph of a river in the middle of his shire. 'See that bridge?' he said, pointing at the photograph.

'What bridge?' asked the other mayor.

'One hundred per cent,' said the mayor.

***

What do bungee jumping and hookers have in common? They both cost a hundred bucks and if the rubber breaks, you're screwed.

***

Q: What is the definition of an engineer?
A: Someone who solves a problem you didn't know you had in a way you don't understand.

Q: How can you tell an extroverted engineer?
A: When he talks to you, he looks at your shoes instead of his own.

Q: Why did the engineer cross the road?
A: Because they looked in the file and that's what they did last year.

Q: How do you drive an engineer completely insane?
A: Tie him to a chair, stand in front of him and fold up a road map the wrong way.

***

YOU'RE A BORN ENGINEER IF:

Choosing to buy flowers for your girlfriend or upgrading your RAM is a moral dilemma.

You take a cruise so you can go on a personal tour of the engineer room.

In college you thought spring break was a metal fatigue failure.

The salesperson at the local computer store can't answer any of your questions.

At an air show you know how far the skydivers are falling.

You bought your wife a new CD-ROM drive for her birthday.

You can quote scenes from any Monty Python movie.

You can type seventy words per minute but can't read your own handwriting.

You comment to your wife that her straight hair is nice and parallel.

You sit backwards on the Disneyland rides to see how they do the special effects.

You have saved every power cord from all your broken appliances.

You have more friends on the Internet than in real life.

You look forward to Christmas so you can put the kids' toys together.

You see a good design and still have to change it.

You spent more on your calculator than you did on your wedding ring.

You still own a slide rule and know how to use it.

You think that people yawning around you are sleep deprived.

You window shop at radio stores.

Your laptop computer costs more than your car.

Your wife hasn't the foggiest idea of what you do at work.

You've already calculated how much you make per second.

You've tried to repair a two-way radio.

***

What's the difference between mechanical engineers and civil engineers?
Mechanical engineers build weapons, civil engineers build targets.

***

To the optimist, the glass is half full. To the pessimist, the glass is half empty.

To the engineer, the glass is twice as big as it needs to be.

***

A group of QA inspectors were given the assignment to measure the height of a flagpole. So they go out to the flagpole with ladders and tape measures, and they're falling off the ladders, dropping the tape measures – the whole thing is just a mess. An engineer comes along and sees what they're trying to do, walks over, pulls the flagpole out of the ground, lays it flat, measures it from end to end, puts the pole back and gives the measurement to one of the inspectors and walks away. After the engineer has gone, one inspector turns to another and laughs, 'Isn't that just like an engineer. We've been looking for the height and he gives us the length.'

***

Last week we took some friends to a new restaurant and noticed that the waiter who took our order carried a spoon in his shirt pocket. It seemed a little strange, but I ignored it. However, when the busboy brought out water and utensils, I noticed he also had a spoon in his shirt pocket, then looked around the room and saw that all the staff had spoons in their pockets.

When the waiter came back to serve our soup I asked, 'Why the spoon?'

'Well,' he explained, 'the restaurant's owners hired Anderson Consulting, experts in efficiency, in order to revamp all our processes. After several months of statistical analysis, they concluded that customers drop their spoons 73.84 per cent more than any other utensil. This represents a drop frequency of approximately three spoons per table per hour. If our personnel are prepared to deal with that contingency, we can reduce the number of trips back to the kitchen and save fifteen man hours per shift.'

As luck would have it, I dropped my spoon and he was able to replace it with his spare spoon.

'I'll get another spoon next time I go to the kitchen instead of making an extra trip to get it right now.' I was rather impressed.

The waiter served our main course and I continued to look around. I then noticed that there was a very thin string hanging out of the waiter's fly. Looking around, I noticed that all the waiters had the same string hanging from their flies. My curiosity got the better of me and before he walked off, I asked the waiter, 'Excuse me, but can you tell me why you have that string right there?'

'Oh certainly!' he answered, lowering his voice. 'Not everyone is as observant as you. That consulting firm I mentioned also found out that we can save time in the restroom.'

'How so?'

'See,' he continued, 'by tying this string to the tip of you-know-what, we can pull it out over the urinal without touching it and that way eliminate the need to wash the hands, shortening the time spent in the restroom by 76.39 per cent.'

'Okay, that makes sense, but if the string helps you get it out, how do you put it back in?'

'Well,' he whispered, lowering his voice even further, 'I don't know about the others, but I use the spoon.'

***

US homeland security director asked another critical question, 'What if Bill Clinton had run after a car? Could we have saved him?'

Buddy was adopted by the Clintons as a three-month-old puppy in December 1997 and quickly asserted himself as the nation's top dog. He accompanied Bill Clinton on many of his travels, met foreign leaders who visited the White House, and spent more time under the President's desk than an intern.

When tension mounted between Clinton and Al Gore, political observers wondered if Buddy had become 'the real vice president'. Said political analyst George Stephanopoulos, 'Buddy once chased a pesticide company's van, barking louder than ever. That made us realise that Buddy, like Al Gore, cared deeply about the environment.'

When Hillary Clinton left the White House to campaign in New York, Buddy moved into the presidential bedroom and had his way with the presidential pillows. 'I tried to get him to stop,' Clinton said. 'I said, "Buddy, if you don't cut it out, the Republicans will try to impeach you."'

Aside from chasing cars, his favourite hobbies included chewing socks, eating anything that looked like food, and barking at Sam Donaldson. 'He loved to fetch things,' Clinton said. 'I'd be sitting in the Oval Office and I'd say, "Buddy, go fetch the ball," and he'd run outside and get a ball. I'd say "Buddy, go fetch Monica," and he'd run outside and get a ball. He really knew what was good for me.'

Despite his friendly nature, Buddy did not get along with the Clintons' other pet, Socks the cat, which often hissed at the dog. 'Buddy likes socks,' Clinton said, 'just not that kind of socks.'

Socks and Buddy were featured in a 1998 book *Dear Socks, Dear Buddy: Kids' Letters to the First Pets*. Socks later authored several other books, including *Buddy is Not My Buddy*, *Buddy is Cruddy*, and *Buddy, You Fuddy-Duddy*.

Buddy is survived by his mother, Bunny, an unknown deadbeat dad, four brothers, five sisters, twenty-four half-brothers, thirty-two half-sisters, four pillows and a tattered sock.

On the night of his death, Buddy was honoured at sporting events throughout the country. Fans and players rose to their feet and observed a moment of barking.

Buddy was laid to rest with full honours, his funeral attended by dignitaries from around the world, both human and canine. Socks the cat did not attend and did not send a representative. Socks released a statement through his spokesman, saying, 'The death of Buddy proves what I have been saying for a long time: dogs are dumb! You'll never see a cat chasing a van. We don't have nine lives – we have brains!'

***

RAC MOTORING SERVICES

Caller: Does your European Breakdown Policy cover me when I am travelling in Australia?'
Operator: Does the product name give you a clue?'

Caller: If I register my car in France, do I have to change the steering wheel to the other side of the car?

***

DIRECTORY INQUIRIES

Caller: I'd like the number of the Argoed Fish Bar in Cardiff, please.
Operator: Sorry, there's no listing. Is the spelling correct?
Caller: Well, it used to be called the Bargoed Fish Bar but the 'B' fell off.

Then there was the caller who asked for a knitwear company in Woven.

Operator: Woven? Are you sure?
Caller: Yes. That's what it says on the label – Woven in Scotland.

Caller: I'd like the RSPCA please.
Operator: Where are you calling from?
Caller: The living room.

On another occasion, a man making heavy breathing sounds from a phone box told a worried operator, 'I haven't got a pen, so I'm steaming up the window to write the number on.'

***

COMPUTER CAPERS

Tech support: I need you to right-click on the Open Desktop.
Customer: Okay.
Tech support: Did you get a pop-up menu?
Customer: No.
Tech support: Okay. Right-click again. Do you see a pop-up menu?
Customer: No.
Tech support: Okay, sir. Can you tell me what you have done up until this point?

Customer: Sure. You told me to write 'click' and I wrote 'click'.

Tech support: Okay. In the bottom left-hand side of the screen, can you see the 'OK' button displayed?
Customer: Wow. How can you see my screen from there?

Caller: I deleted a file from my PC last week and I have just realised that I need it. If I turn my system clock back two weeks, will I have my file back again?

***

BRITISH RAIL

Customer: How much does it cost to Bath on the train?
Operator: If you can get your feet in the sink, then it's free.

Customer: I've been ringing 0700 2300 for two days and can't get though to inquiries. Can you help?
Operator: Where did you get that number from, sir?
Customer: It was on the door to the Travel Centre.
Operator: Sir, they are our opening hours.

***

It is important to find a woman who cooks and cleans. It is important to find a woman who makes good money. It is important to find a woman who likes to have sex. It is important that these three women never meet.

***

Jim decided to propose to Sandy, but prior to her acceptance Sandy had to confess to her man about her childhood illness. She informed Jim that she suffered a disease that left her breasts at the maturity of a twelve-year-old. He stated that it was okay because he loved her so much. However, Jim felt that this was also the time for him to open up and admit that he also had a deformity. Jim looked Sandy in the eyes and said, 'I too have a problem. My penis is the same size as an infant and I hope you could deal with that once we are married'.

She said, 'Yes, I will marry you and learn to live with your infant-sized penis.'

Sandy and Jim got married and they could not wait for the honeymoon. Jim whisked Sandy off to their hotel suite and they started touching, teasing, holding one another. As Sandy put her hands in Jim's pants, she began to scream and ran out of the room! Jim ran after her to find out what was wrong.

She said, 'You told me your penis was the size of an infant!'

'Yes it is – 8lbs, 7oz, 19 inches long.'

***

He isn't quiet. He's a Conversational Minimalist.

He isn't stupid. He suffers from Minimal Cranial Development.

He isn't balding. He's in Follicle Repression.

He doesn't fart or belch. He is Gastronomically Expressive.

He isn't a cradle snatcher. He prefers Generationally Different Relationships.

He's not an arsehole. He's developed a case of Rectal-Cranial Inversion.

He isn't short. He's Anatomically Compact.

He didn't have a rich dad. He's a recipient of Parental Asset Infusion.

He doesn't eat like a pig. He suffers from Reverse Bulimia.

He isn't afraid of commitment. He's Monogamously Challenged.

***

I went to the butcher the other day and bet him $50 that he couldn't reach the meat on the top shelf. He said, 'No, the steaks are too high.'

***

My friend drowned in a bowl of muesli. He was pulled in by a strong currant.

***

A man regained consciousness in his hospital bed. He shouted, 'Doctor, doctor. I can't feel my legs.'
    And the doctor said, 'Of course you can't. I've cut your arms off.'

***

I went to a seafood disco last week – and pulled a mussel.

***

A bloke walks into his doctor's surgery. 'What seems to be the problem?' asks the doctor.

'Well, it's a bit embarrassing.'

'Don't be embarrassed. I'm a doctor. I've seen everything. I've heard everything.'

'You haven't heard this. I've got five penises.'

Good heavens!' says the doctor. 'How do your trousers fit?'

'Like a glove!'

***

An ice-cream man was found lying on the floor of his van covered with hundreds and thousands of hundreds and thousands. The police said that he'd topped himself.

***

Two cannibals were eating a clown. One says to the other, 'Does that taste funny to you?'

***

Two cows are standing next to each other in a paddock. Daisy says to Dolly, 'I was artificially inseminated this morning.'

'I don't believe you,' says Dolly.

Daisy says, 'It's true, straight up, no bull.'

***

Two hydrogen atoms walk into a bar. One says, 'I think I've lost an electron.'

The other says, 'Are you sure?'

The first says, 'Yes, I'm positive.'

***

Answerphone message: If you want to buy marijuana, press the hash key.

Deja moo: The feeling that you've heard this bullshit before.

***

Two peanuts walk into a bar. One is a salted.

A jumper lead walks into a bar. The barman says, 'I'll serve you, but don't start anything.'

A sandwich walks into a bar. The barman says, 'Sorry, we don't serve food in here.'

A dyslexic man walks into a bra.

A man walks into a bar with a roll of asphalt under his arm and says, 'Pint please, and one for the road.'

***

Three sheilas are sitting in a sauna. Their names are Beryl, Cheryl and Kylie. Suddenly there's a beeping sound. Cheryl presses her forearm and the beeping immediately stops. Beryl and Kylie look at her curiously. 'That's my pager,' says Cheryl, 'I've got a microphone under the skin of my arm.'

A few moments later a phone rings. Beryl lifts her empty hand to her ear and talks into her palm. When she's finished she says, 'That's my mobile phone. I've got a microchip in my hand.'

Kylie, feeling decidedly low-tech, steps out of the sauna and returns a few minutes later with a piece of toilet paper dangling from her bum.

Cheryl and Beryl raise their eyebrows. 'Sorry, girls,'

she says cheerfully, 'but I'm getting a fax.'

***

DATING VS MARRIAGE

When you are dating, farting is never an issue.
When you are married, you make sure there's nothing flammable near your husband at all times.

When you are dating, he takes you out to have a good time.
When you are married, he brings home a six-pack and says, 'What are you going to drink?'

When you are dating, he holds your hand in public.
When you are married, he flicks your ear in public.

When you are dating, a single bed for two isn't *that* bad.
When you are married, a king-size bed feels like an army cot.

When you are dating, you are turned on at the sight of him naked.
When you are married, you think to yourself, 'Was he always this hairy?'

When you are dating, you enjoy foreplay.
When you are married, you tell him, 'If we have sex, will you leave me alone?'

When you are dating, he hugs you when he walks by you for no reason.
When you are married, he grabs your boob any chance he gets.

When you are dating, you picture the two of you growing old together.
When you are married, you wonder who will die first.

When you are dating, he knows what the hamper is.
When you are married, the floor will suffice as a dirty clothes-storage area.

When you are dating, he understands if you aren't in the mood.
When you are married, he says, 'It's your job.'

When you are dating, he understands that you have male friends.
When you are married, he thinks they are all out to steal you away.

When you are dating, he likes to discuss things.
When you are married, he develops a blank stare.

When you are dating, he calls you by name.
When you are married, he calls you 'Hey' and when speaking to others refers to you as 'She'.

***

If you yelled for eight years, seven months and six days you would produce enough sound energy to heat one cup of coffee. So it hardly seems worth it.

If you farted consistently for six years and nine months, enough gas is produced to create the energy of an atomic bomb. Now that's more like it!

The human heart creates enough pressure to squirt blood 9m. Which I'd rather not think about.

A pig's orgasm lasts thirty minutes. So three cheers for reincarnation. I'm coming back as a pig.

A cockroach will live nine days without its head before it starves to death.

Banging your head against a wall uses 150 calories an hour.

The male praying mantis cannot copulate while its head is attached to its body. The female initiates sex by ripping the male's head off. So I'm going to stick with being a pig.

A flea can jump 350 times its body length. It's like a human jumping the length of a football field. Trouble is, I can't get my mind off that thirty-minute orgasm.

The catfish has over 27 000 tastebuds. Most of which are wasted in the mud.

Some lions mate more than fifty times a day.

Pig first, lion second.

Butterflies taste with their feet. Fancy that.

The strongest muscle in the body is the tongue. So who needs Viagra?

Right-handed people live on average nine years longer than left-handed people. If you're ambidextrous, do you split the difference?

The elephant is the only animal that can't jump. Thank God for that.

A cat's piss glows under a black light. And the scientist who discovered that was probably on a grant.

An ostrich's eye is bigger than its brain. A bit like John Howard.

Starfish have no brains. A bit like Wilson Tuckey.

Polar bears are left-handed. If they switched, they'd live longer.

Humans and dolphins are reckoned to be the only species to have sex for pleasure. I bet the pig disagrees.

***

Phil Ruddock is standing on the Sydney Harbour Bridge, singing 'Twenty-one today, twenty-one today.' He looks very, very happy.

A man of Middle Eastern appearance approaches the Minister for Immigration and says, 'Twenty-one today? I'm surprised. You look much older.'

'Oh, it's not my birthday,' says Ruddock.

'Then what is it?'

At this point Ruddock tosses the Middle Eastern gentleman off the harbour bridge and bursts into song again, 'Twenty-two today, twenty-two today.'

***

On the outskirts of a small town in Queensland there was an old macadamia tree just inside the cemetery fence. One day, a couple of kids who'd filled a bucket with nuts were sitting beneath the tree, out of sight, dividing them. Several nuts dropped and rolled towards the fence.

Another kid came along the road on his bike. As he passed he thought he heard voices from inside the cemetery and slowed down to investigate.

'One for you, one for me, one for you, one for me.'

Being the son of a Pentecostal minister the boy shuddered. 'It's Satan and the Lord dividing the souls.' Then he jumped back on his bike and belted off.

At the corner he met an old bloke hobbling along. 'Come here quick,' he said, 'you won't believe what I've heard! Satan and the Lord are down at the cemetery divvying up the souls.'

The old bloke pooh-poohed him. 'Don't talk nonsense.' But the boy insisted, and the old bloke hobbled to the cemetery. Standing side by side, they heard, 'One for you, one for me, one for you, one for me.'

The old bloke shivered with fear. Then he heard the voice saying, 'Now let's go and get those nuts by the fence and we'll be done.'

The old bloke made it back to town fully five minutes ahead of the boy on the bike.

***

A little girl goes to the barber shop with her dad. She stands next to the barber's chair eating her cake while her dad gets his hair cut.

The barber smiles at her and says, 'Sweetheart, you're going to get hair on your muffin.'

'I know,' she says, 'I'm going to get tits, too.'

***

A bloke gets on a Virgin flight from Sydney to Adelaide. He's plonked in the aisle seat with another bloke at the window. And in between them is a dog.

He's not very happy about being stuck next to a dog for the two-hour flight, so he decides to complain to the owner. 'Is this your dog?'

'Yes, but he's no ordinary dog.'

'What do you mean?'

'Well, I'm a customs officer. And he's a sniffer dog. Actually, he's on duty right now.'

Pleased with the explanation, the bloke relaxes, whereupon the dog unbuckles its seatbelt, jumps over his lap and walks up and down the aisles. It then puts its right paw on the custom officer's left knee.

'What's all that about?' inquires the bloke.

'The dog told me that the man in seat 22B has some heroin.'

A few minutes later the dog unbuckles its seatbelt, leaps over the bloke's lap and does another trot up and down the aisle. On his return, he taps the customs officer's knee again.

'What is it this time?' asks the bloke.

'The man in seat 46C has some cocaine.'

'That's bloody marvellous,' says the bloke, 'I'm very, very impressed.'

A few minutes later the dog repeats the routine and, on its return, spins around three times and does a great crap on the seat. 'Well, that's a bit rich,' says the bloke, thoroughly disgusted. 'What's that all about?'

'He just told me the bloke in 11F has a bomb!'

***

Our fervour which art in footy
Followed by thy game
All kids can come
All will be shown on 9 and 10 as it was on 7
Give us this week our weekly round
Forgive us our excessive barracking
As we forgive those who excessively barrack again us
Lead us not into the tribunal
But deliver us from the bottom of the ladder
For the bouts down
To the final siren
We will be roaring
Forever and ever.
He-men!!

***

If you take the inside out of a hot dog, what have you got?
A hollow-weeny.

***

Men are invited to sign up for one or more of the
following classes to be held at our local learning centre
for adults. (Note: Due to the complexity and difficulty
of their content, each course will accept a maximum
of eight participants.)

Topic One: How to fill ice-cube trays, step-by-step, with slide presentation.

Topic Two: Toilet-paper rolls. Do they grow on the holders? Round-table discussion.

Topic Three: Is it possible to relieve oneself using the technique of lifting the seat up and avoiding the floor/walls? Group practice.

Topic Four: Fundamental differences between the laundry hamper and the floor. Pictures and explanatory graphics.

Topic Five: After-dinner dishes and cutlery. Can they levitate and fly into the kitchen sink? Examples on video.

Topic Six: Loss of identity – losing the remote to your significant other. Helpline and support groups.

Topic Seven: Learning how to find things starting with looking in the right place instead of turning the house upside down while screaming. Open forum.

Topic Eight: Health watch. Bringing her flowers is not harmful to her health. Graphics and audiotape.

Topic Nine: Real men ask for directions when lost. Real-life testimonials.

Topic Ten: Is it genetically impossible to sit quietly as she parallel parks? Driving simulation.

Topic Eleven: Learning to live – basic differences between mother and wife. Online class and role playing.

Topic Twelve: How to be the ideal shopping companion. Relaxation exercises, meditation and breathing exercises.

Topic Thirteen: How to fight cerebral atrophy – remembering birthdays, anniversaries and other important dates, and calling when you're going to be late. Cerebral shock-therapy sessions and full lobotomies offered.

***

Leaving Newcastle and heading for Sydney, a bloke makes a stop at the Caltex service station just before the Gosford turnoff and heads straight for the toilet. The first cubicle is taken so he goes into the second. No sooner has he sat down than he hears a voice from next door. 'Hi there, how ya goin'?'

'Fine, thank you.'

Not the type to strike up conversations with strangers in loos, he's somewhat embarrassed. For all he knows, the bloke next door is a homosexual.

'So what are you doing?' the stranger asks.

'Well, obviously I'm in the loo at the moment, then I'm driving straight to Sydney.'

Whereupon the disembodied voice sounds somewhat flustered. 'Look, I'll call you back – every time I ask you a question an idiot in the next toilet keeps answering me.'

✳✳✳

Three blokes are waiting at the Pearly Gates when St Peter tells them of a slight delay. A bit of a backlog with the bookkeeping. But not to worry – Albert Einstein wants to have a chat while they wait.

Albert appears, introduces himself to the first bloke and asks, 'What's your IQ?'

He replies, 'It's 241.'

'That's wonderful,' says Albert, 'we'll talk about the Grand Unification Theory and the mysteries of the Universe. We'll have much to discuss.'

He turns to the second man, 'And what's your IQ?'

His reply, 'It's 144.'

'That's great,' responds Albert. 'We can discuss politics

and current affairs. We will have much to discuss.

The he turns to the third man and asks, 'What is your IQ?'

To which the man answers, 'It's 51.'

'How about Alec Waugh!' says Albert.

***

A blonde drove into a petrol station. She went to the counter for parts and accessories and asked for a 710 cap.

The young man at the counter asked, 'Excuse me, miss, but what's a 710 cap and what's it for?'

The blonde replied, 'You know, it's the one that's always on the engine. Mine got lost somehow and I need a new one.'

'But I don't get it. A seven-ten cap?' he asked.

She replied, 'It's always been there on the engine, except this time it's gone missing.'

The clerk gave her a pen and notepad and asked her to draw a picture of what the cap looked like.

The blonde drew a circle about 8cm in diameter and in the middle of it wrote '710'.

After looking at the drawing, the counter clerk sold her the cap and she walked away. Someone from inside the office then asked him what a 710 cap was.

He said, 'It's just oil, upside down.'

***

An eighty-year-old couple were having problems remembering things, so they decided to go to their doctor to get checked out just in case they were getting Alzheimer's. When they arrived at the surgery they spoke to the GP about their memory problems but, after checking them out, he told them they were physically okay. 'And your mental processes seem to be quite good.' But he suggested they start writing things down and making notes to help them remember things.

Thanking him, they left. Later that night, while watching *Blue Heelers*, the old bloke got up from his chair and his wife asked, 'Where are you going?'

He said, 'To the kitchen.'

She said, 'Then get me a bowl of ice-cream, will you?' She then added, 'Don't you think you should write it down so you can remember it?'

He said, 'No, I can remember that.'

Then she said, 'Well, I'd also like some strawberries on top. You'd better write that down, because I know you'll forget.'

He said, 'I can remember that. You want a bowl of ice-cream with strawberries.'

'Yes,' she said, 'but I'd also like some whipped cream on top. I know you'll forget that, so you'd better write it down.'

He became quite crabby. 'I don't need to write it down. I can remember that.' And he then stomped off to the kitchen.

About twenty minutes later, he returned and handed her a plate of bacon and eggs. She stared at the plate for a moment and said, 'You forgot my toast!'

***

A bloke had worked his whole life in a chutney and mustard pickles factory in East Brunswick. One day he came home in some distress and told his wife that he'd been sacked from his job. She was very upset.

'You've given those bastards twenty years of devoted service. Why did they fire you?'

'Well, for twenty years I've wanted to stick my penis in the pickle slicer,' he explained. 'And today I finally did it.'

The wife ran over, pulled down his pants to see what damage had been done.

'It looks okay,' she said with a sigh of relief. 'So what happened to the pickle slicer?'

'They sacked her too.'

***

THE WEAKEST LINK

Here is a simple little test comprising four questions. They will determine the level of your intellect. Your replies must be spontaneous and immediate. No deliberation or wasting time allowed. And no cheating!

On your marks, get set . . . *go!*

Q: You are competing in a race and overtake the runner in second place. In which position are you now?
A: If you answered that you're now coming first, you're wrong. You overtook the second runner and took their place. Therefore you're coming second. You'll have to try harder for the next question.

Q: If you overtake the last runner, what position are you in now?
A: If you answered second last you are, once again, completely wrong. Think about it. How can you overtake the person coming last? If you're behind them, they can't be last. The answer is impossible! It would appear that thinking is not one of your strong points. You would make a good weak link!

Anyway, here's another one to try, but don't take any

notes, and don't use a calculator. And remember that your reply must be instantaneous!

Q: Take 1000
Add 40
Add another 1000
Add 30
Add 1000
Add 20
Add 1000
Add 10
What is the total?
A: 5000? Wrong again. The correct answer is 4100.

But even you should manage to get the last question right.

Q: Marie's father had five daughters:
1: Cha Cha
2: Che Che
3: Chi Chi
4: Cho Cho
5: ?????
What is the fifth daughter's name? Think quickly – Answer *now*.
A: Chu Chu? *Wrong*! It's obviously Marie. Read the question properly. You are the weakest link. Goodbye.

***

I always wanted to see my name up in lights. So I changed it to Hoyts.

***

I've got this thing in the car that tells you when you're going too fast and you've taken the wrong turn. It's called . . . the wife!

***

QUOTES FROM LITTLE CHILDREN

When your mum is mad at your dad, don't let her brush your hair.

If your sister hits you, don't hit her back. They always catch the second person.

Don't sneeze when someone is cutting your hair.

Never hold a dust-buster and a cat at the same time.

If you throw a ball at someone, they'll probably throw it back.

School lunches stick to the wall.

You can't hide a piece of broccoli in a glass of milk.

Don't wear polka-dot underwear under white shorts.

A pencil without an eraser may as well be just a pen.

Don't say 'last one is a rotten egg' unless you're absolutely sure there's a slow kid behind you.

If you don't like the birthday girl, don't go to the party.

If you want a kitten, start out by asking for a horse.

Silence can be an answer.

***

DR SEUSS EXPLAINS WHY COMPUTERS CRASH

If a packet hits a pocket on a socket on a port, and the bus is interrupted as a very last resort, and the access of the memory makes your floppy disk abort, then the socket packet pocket has an error to report.

If your cursor finds a menu item followed by a dash, and the double-clicking icon puts your window in the trash, and your data is corrupted 'cos the index doesn't hash, then your situation's hopeless and your system's gonna crash!

If the label on the able on the table at your house says the network is connected to the button on your mouse, but your packets want to tunnel to another protocol, that's repeatedly rejected by the printer down the hall, and your screen is all distorted by the side effects of gauss, so your icons in the window are as wavy as a souse; then you may as well reboot and go out with a bank, 'cos sure as I'm a poet, the sucker's gonna hang!

When the copy of your floppy's getting sloppy in the disk, and the macro code instructions cause unnecessary risk, then you'll have to flash the memory and you'll want to RAM your ROM. Quickly turn off the computer and be sure to tell your mum!

***

WHAT I'VE LEARNED AS I'VE MATURED

I've learned that you cannot make someone love you.

All you can do is stalk them and hope they panic and give in.

I've learned that no matter how much I care, some people are just arseholes.

I've learned that it takes years to build up trust, and it only takes suspicion, not proof, to destroy it.

I've learned that you can get by on charm for about fifteen minutes. After that, you'd better have a big willy.

I've learned that you shouldn't compare yourself to others – they are more screwed up than you think.

I've learned that you can keep vomiting long after you think you've finished.

I've learned that we are responsible for what we do, unless we are celebrities.

I've learned that regardless of how hot and steamy a relationship is at first, the passion fades, and there had better be a lot of money to take its place.

I've learned that the people you care most about in life

are taken from you too soon and all the less important ones just never go away.

I've learned to say 'F☠-© 'em if they can't take a joke' in six languages.

***

Ever wonder why ABCDEF are used to define bra sizes?
A – Almost Boobs
B – Barely There
C – Can Do
D – Damn Good
E – Enormous
F – Fake

***

An Asian man walked into the currency exchange in New York with 2000 Japanese yen and walked out with $72.

The following week, he walked in with 2000 yen and was handed $66. He asked the teller why he got less than the previous week.

The teller said, 'Fluctuations.'

The Asian man stormed out and, just before

slamming the door, turned around and shouted, 'Fluck you Amelicans, too!'

***

An amateur is someone who supports himself with outside jobs that enable him to paint.

A professional is someone whose wife works to enable him to paint.

***

After being nearly snowbound for two weeks last winter, a Seattle man departed for his vacation in Miami Beach, where he was to meet his wife the next day at the conclusion of her business trip to Minneapolis. They were looking forward to pleasant weather and a nice time together.

Unfortunately, there was some sort of a mix-up at the boarding gate, and the man was told he would have to wait for a later flight. He tried to appeal to a supervisor but was told the airline was not responsible for the problem and it would do no good to complain.

Upon arrival at the hotel the next day, he discovered that Miami Beach was having a heatwave, and its weather was almost as uncomfortably hot as Seattle's was cold. The desk clerk gave him a message that his wife would arrive as planned. He could hardly wait to get to the pool area to cool off, and quickly sent his wife an email, but due to his haste, he made an error in the email address. His message therefore arrived at the home of an elderly preacher's wife whose even older husband had died only the day before. When the grieving widow opened her email, she took one look at the monitor, let out an anguished scream, and fell to the floor dead. Her family rushed to her room where they saw this message on the screen:

Dearest wife, departed yesterday as you know. Just now got checked in. Some confusion at the gate. Appeal was denied. Received confirmation of your arrival tomorrow. Your loving husband. PS: Things are not as we thought. You're going to be surprised at how hot it is down here.

✳✳✳

Everyone should believe in something – I believe I'll have another drink.

Build a system that even a fool can use, and only a fool can use it.

In any hierarchy, each individual rises to his own level of incompetence, and then remains there.

You'll remember that you forgot to take out the trash when the garbage truck is two doors away.

The race is not always to the swift, or the battle to the strong, but that's the way to bet.

There's never time to do it right, but there's always time to do it over.

When it doubt, mumble. When in trouble, delegate.

Anything good in life is either illegal, immoral or fattening.

It is morally wrong to allow suckers to keep their money.

A bird in hand is safer than one overhead.

Murphy's Golden Rule: Whoever has the gold makes the rules.

Everything east of the San Andreas Fault will eventually plunge into the ocean.

Nature always sides with the hidden flaw.

The light at the end of the tunnel is the headlamp of an oncoming train.

Celibacy is not hereditary.

Beauty is only skin deep, ugly goes to the bone.

To know yourself is the ultimate form of aggression. (Freudian psychology)

Never play leapfrog with a unicorn.

If everything seems to be going well, you obviously don't know what the heck is going on.

If more than one person is responsible for a miscalculation, no one will be at fault.

In case of doubt, make it sound convincing.

Never argue with a fool; people might not know the difference.

***

A man boards an aeroplane and takes his seat. As he settles in, he glances up and sees a most beautiful woman boarding the plane. He soon realises she is heading straight towards his seat. A wave of nervous anticipation washes over him. Lo and behold, she takes the seat right beside his. Eager to strike up a conversation, he blurts out, 'Business trip or holiday?'

'Nymphomaniac convention in Chicago,' she states.

Wow! He swallows hard and is instantly crazed with excitement. Here's the most gorgeous woman he has ever seen, sitting right next to him and she's going to a meeting of nymphomaniacs! Struggling to maintain his outward cool, he calmly asks, 'What's your role at this convention?'

'Lecturer,' she says, 'I use my experiences to debunk some of the popular myths about sexuality.'

'Really,' he says, swallowing hard. 'What myths are those?'

'Well,' she explains, 'one popular myth is that African-American men are the most well endowed when, in fact, it is the Native American Indian who is most likely to possess that trait. Another popular myth is that French men are the best lovers, when actually it is men of Greek descent.'

Suddenly the woman becomes very embarrassed and blushes. 'I'm sorry,' she says, 'I shouldn't be discussing this with you. I don't even know your name!'

'Tonto,' the man says, as he extends his hand. 'Tonto Papadopoulos.'

***

The year is 1902. What a difference a century makes:

The average life expectancy in the US was forty-seven.

Only 14 per cent of homes had a bathtub.

Only 8 per cent of homes had a telephone. A three-minute call from Denver to New York City cost $11.

There were only 8000 cars in the US and only 230km of paved roads.

The maximum speed limit in most cities was 16km/h.

Alabama, Mississippi, Iowa and Tennessee were each more heavily populated than California.

The tallest structure in the world was the Eiffel Tower.

The average worker made between $200 and $400 per year.

A competent accountant could expect to earn $2000 a year, a dentist $2500, a veterinarian between $1500 and $4000 and a mechanical engineer about $5000 a year.

More than 95 per cent of all births took place at home. 90 per cent of US physicians had no college education. Instead they attended medical schools, many of which were condemned in the press and by the government as substandard.

Sugar cost 4 cents a pound. Eggs were 14 cents a dozen. Coffee cost 15 cents a pound.

Most women only washed their hair once a month and used borax or egg yolk for shampoo.

The six leading causes of death were pneumonia, influenza, tuberculosis, diarrhoea, heart disease and stroke.

The American flag had forty-five stars. Arizona, Oklahoma, New Mexico, Hawaii and Alaska hadn't been admitted to the Union.

The population of Las Vegas was thirty.

Crossword puzzles, canned beer and iced tea hadn't been invented.

There was no Mother's Day or Father's Day.

One in ten US adults couldn't read or write.

Only 6 per cent of all Americans had graduated from high school.

Marijuana, heroin and morphine were all available over the counter at corner drug stores. According to one pharmacist, heroin clears the complexion, gives buoyancy to the mind, regulates the stomach and bowels and is, in fact, a perfect guardian of health.

Eighteen per cent of households had at least one full-time servant or domestic.

There were only about 230 reported murders in the entire USA.

★★★

Knock, knock.
Who's there?
Howard.

Howard who?
Howard you like to be an Afghan refugee?

***

As Paddy lay dying, at the great age of ninety, the priest asked him to renounce the devil and all his works. Paddy shook his head. 'This is no time to antagonise anybody.'

***

A Canadian man was having coffee and croissants with butter and jam in a diner when an American man, chewing gum, sat down next to him. The Canadian politely ignored the American who, nevertheless, started up a conversation.

The American snapped his gum and said, 'You Canadian folk eat the whole bread?'

The Canadian frowned, annoyed at being bothered during his breakfast, and replied, 'Of course.'

The American blew a huge bubble. 'We don't. In the States, we only eat what's inside. The crusts we collect in a container, recycle them, transform them into croissants and sell them to Canada.' The American had a smirk on his face.

The Canadian listened in silence. The American

persisted. 'D'ya eat jelly with the bread?'

Sighing, the Canadian replied, 'Of course.'

Cracking his gum between his teeth, the American said, 'We don't. In the States, we eat fresh fruit for breakfast, then we put all the peels, seeds and leftovers in containers, recycle them, transform them into jam and sell it to Canada.'

The Canadian then asked, 'Do you have sex in the States?'

The American smiled and said, 'Why of course we do.'

The Canadian leaned closer to him and asked, 'And what do you do with the condoms once you've used them?'

'We throw them away, of course.'

Now it was the Canadian's turn to smile. 'We don't. In Canada, we put them in a container, recycle them, melt them down into chewing gum and sell them to the United States.'

***

A rich Texan walked into the offices of the president of a small Texan college and said, 'I'd like to donate a million dollars tax-free to this institution. But there's a condition. I would like to have an honorary degree.'

The president nodded agreeably. 'That's not a

problem. We can certainly arrange that!'

The rich man said, 'An honorary degree for my horse.'

'For your horse?'

'Yep, you betcha. She carried me for many years and I owe her a lot. I'd like her to receive a TrD, a Doctor of Transportation.'

'But, we can't give a degree to a horse!'

'Then I'm afraid I'll have to take my million dollars to another educational institution.'

'Well, wait a minute,' said the president, seeing the million slip through his fingers. 'Let me consult with the school's trustees.'

A hurried trustee meeting was brought to order and the president related the deal and the condition. All of the board reacted with shock and disbelief – except the oldest trustee. He appeared almost asleep.

One trustee snorted, 'We can't give a horse an honorary degree – no matter *how* much money is involved. The oldest trustee opened his eyes and said, 'Take the money and give the horse the degree.'

The president asked, 'Don't you think that would be a disgrace to us?'

'Of course not,' the wise old trustee said. 'It would be an honour. It'd be the first time we ever gave a degree to an *entire* horse.'

***

A man takes his wife to the cattle show. They start heading down the alley that houses all the bulls. The sign on the first bull's stall states, 'This bull mated fifty times last year.'

The wife turns to her husband and says, 'He mated fifty times in a year, isn't that nice!'

They proceed to the next bull and his sign states, 'This bull mated sixty-five times last year.'

The wife turns to her husband and says, 'This one mated sixty-five times last year. That's over five times a month. You could learn from this one!'

They proceed to the last bull and his sign says 'This bull mated 365 times last year.'

The wife's mouth drops open and she says, 'Wow! He mated 365 times last year. That is *once a day!* You could really learn from this one.'

The annoyed man turns to his wife and says, 'Go up and inquire if it was 365 times with the same cow.'

***

A reporter was doing a story on gender roles in Kuwait several years before the Gulf War. She noted then that women customarily walked about ten feet behind their husbands.

She returned to Kuwait recently and observed that the men now walked several yards behind their wives.

The reporter approached one of the women and said, 'This is marvellous. Can you tell the free world just what enabled women here to achieve this reversal of roles.'

'Land mines,' said the Kuwaiti woman.

***

It was the first day of school and a new student named Huong, the son of a Vietnamese businessman, entered the fourth grade in Australia.

The teacher said, 'Let's begin by reviewing some Australian history. Who said, "Vinegar Hill!"?'

She saw a sea of blank faces, except for Huong. 'Captain Henry Ross, Eureka Stockade, Ballarat, 1854,' he said.

'Very good! Who said, "We shall form a Commonwealth and govern from Canberra"?'

Again, no response except from Huong. 'General Sir John Monash, 1915,' said Huong.

The teacher snapped at the class. 'Class, you should be ashamed. Huong, who is new to our country, knows more about its history than you do.'

She heard a loud whisper: 'Screw the Vietnamese.'

'Who said that?' she demanded. Huong put up his hand. 'Bruce Ruxton, 1975.'

At that point, a student in the back said, 'I'm gonna puke.'

The teacher glared and asked, 'All right! Now, who said that?'

Again, Huong said, 'Paul Keating, meeting Malaysian Prime Minister Dr Mahathir, 1991.'

Now furious, another student yelled, 'Oh yeah? Suck this!'

Huong jumped out of his chair waving his hand and shouted to the teacher, 'Gareth Evans to Cheryl Kernot, 1999!'

With almost mob hysteria, someone said, 'You little shit. If you say anything else, I'll kill you.'

Huong frantically yelled at the top of his voice, 'Peter Reith to Rear Admiral Chris Ritchie at the "children overboard" inquiries, 2001.'

The teacher fainted. And as the class gathered around the teacher on the floor, someone said, 'Oh shit, we're in *big* trouble!'

And Huong said, 'Ansett Australia, 2002!'

***

Mother Teresa dies and goes to heaven. God greets her at the Pearly Gates. 'Be thou hungry, Mother Teresa?'

asks God.

'I could eat,' replies Mother Teresa.

So God opens a can of tuna and reaches for a chunk of rye bread and they share it.

While eating this humble meal, Mother Teresa looks down into hell and sees the inhabitants devouring huge steaks, lobsters, pheasants, pastries and wines. Curious, but deeply trusting, she remains quiet.

The next day God again invites her to join him for a meal. Again, it's tuna and rye bread.

Once again, Mother Teresa can see the denizens of hell enjoying caviar, champagne, lamb, truffles and chocolates. Still she says nothing.

The following day, mealtime arrives and another can of tuna is opened.

She can't contain herself any longer. Meekly, she says, 'God, I am grateful to be in heaven with you as a reward for the pious, obedient life I led. But here in heaven all I get to eat is tuna and a piece of rye bread and in the other place they eat like emperors and kings! I just don't understand.'

God sighs, 'Let's be honest,' he says, 'For just two people, does it pay to cook?'

***

The Pope was finishing his sermon. He ended it with the Latin phrase, *Tuti homini* – blessed be mankind.

A women's rights group approached the Pope. They noticed that the Pope blessed all mankind, but not womankind. The next day, after his sermon, the Pope concluded by saying, *Tuti homini et tuti femini* – blessed be mankind and womankind.

The next day, a gay-rights group approached the Pope. They said that they noticed that he blessed mankind and womankind, and asked if he could also bless gay people. The Pope said, 'Sure.'

So the next day, the Pope concluded his sermon with *Tuti homini et tuti femini et tuti fruiti*.

***

Why does your gynaecologist leave the room when you get undressed?

If a person owns a piece of land do they own it all the way down to the core of the earth?

Why is it called Alcoholics Anonymous when the first thing you do is stand up and say, 'My name is Bob, and I am an alcoholic'?

Why are they called stairs inside but steps outside?

Why is there a light in the fridge and not in the freezer?

Why does mineral water that 'has trickled through mountains for centuries' have a use-by date?

Is French kissing in France just called kissing?

Who was the first person to look at a cow and say, 'I think I'll squeeze these dangly things here and drink whatever comes out'?

If the professor on *Gilligan's Island* can make a radio out of a coconut, why can't he fix a hole in a boat?

***

General Norman Schwarzkopf was asked if he didn't think there was room for forgiveness toward the people who have harboured and abetted the terrorists who perpetrated the 9/11 attacks on America. His answer: 'I believe that forgiving them is God's function. Our job is simply to arrange the meeting.'

***

An Aboriginal walked into the local unemployment office, marched straight up to the counter and said,

'G'day mate, I'm lookin' for a job.'

The man behind the counter replied, 'Your timing is amazing. We've just got a listing from a very wealthy man who wants a chauffeur for his daughter. You'll have to drive around in a big black Mercedes, uniform provided. Because of the long hours of this job, meals will be provided and once a year you will also be required to escort the young lady on her overseas holiday. The salary package is $200 000 a year.'

The Aboriginal said, 'Nah, you're tellin' me bullshit!'

The man behind the counter said, 'Well you fucking started it.'

***

ANAGRAMS

DORMITORY. When you rearrange the letters:
DIRTY ROOM

DESPERATION
A ROPE ENDS IT

THE MORSE CODE
HERE COME DOTS

SLOT MACHINES
CASH LOTS IN 'EM

ANIMOSITY
IS NO AMITY

MOTHER-IN-LAW
WOMAN HITLER

SNOOZE ALARMS
ALAS! NO MORE Z'S

A DECIMAL POINT
I'M A DOT IN PLACE

THE EARTHQUAKES
THAT QUEER SHAKE

ELEVEN PLUS TWO
TWELVE PLUS ONE

ALEC GUINNESS
GENUINE CLASS

SEMOLINA
IS NO MEAL

CONTRADICTION
ACCORD NOT IN IT

ASTRONOMER
MOON STARER

PRINCESS DIANA
END IS A CAR SPIN

THE PUBLIC ART GALLERIES
LARGE PICTURE HALLS I BET

YEAR TWO THOUSAND
A YEAR TO SHUT DOWN

PRESIDENT CLINTON OF THE USA
TO COPULATE HE FINDS INTERNS

***

Sue and Bob, a pair of tight wads, lived in the Midwest and had been married for years. Bob had always wanted to go flying. The desire deepened each time a barnstormer flew into town, offering rides. Bob would ask, and Sue would say, 'No way. Ten dollars is ten dollars.'

As the years went by Bob figured he didn't have

much longer. He finally convinced Sue to go to the show by explaining it's free to watch.

Once they got there the feeling became so strong he and Sue started arguing.

The pilot, between flights, overheard and listened to their problem. He said, 'I'll tell you what. I'll take you both up flying and if you don't say a word the ride is on me. But if you make one sound, you pay ten dollars.' So off they flew.

The pilot did as many rolls and dives as he could. He headed the plane to the ground as fast it would go and pulled out of the dive at the very last second. Not a word. Finally he admitted defeat and went back to the airport. 'I'm surprised, why didn't you say anything?'

'Well, I almost said something when Sue fell out, but ten dollars is ten dollars.'

***

A woman tells her friend that when lions mate they remain joined for thirty hours. To which the friend replies, 'Thank God I'm married to a Rotarian.'

***

How do you know when you're staying in a Kentucky hotel?

When you call the front desk and say, 'I've got a leak in my sink,' and the person at the front desk says, 'Go ahead.'

***

An Arkansas State trooper pulls over a pickup truck and says to the driver, 'Got any ID?' The driver says, ''Bout what?'

***

Two Mississippians are walking towards each other and one is carrying a sack. When they meet, one says, 'Hey, Tommy Ray, whatcha got in th' bag?'

'Jes some chickens.'

'If I guesses how many they is, kin I have one?'

'Shoot, if ya guesses right, I'll give you both of 'em!'

'Okay. Ummm. Five?'

***

Why do folks in Kentucky go to R-rated movies in groups of eighteen or more? Because they heard seventeen and under aren't admitted.

***

Billy Bob and Lester were talking one afternoon when Billy Bob tells Lester, 'Ya know, I reckon I'm about ready for a vacation. Only this year I'm gonna do it a little different. The last few years I took your suggestions as to where to go. Three years ago you said to go to Hawaii. I went to Hawaii and Betty Sue got pregnant. Then two years ago, you told me to go to the Bahamas, and Betty Sue got pregnant again. Last year you suggested Tahiti and darned if Betty Sue didn't get pregnant again.'

Lester asks Billy Bob, 'So, what you gonna do this year that's different?'

Billy Bob says, 'This year I'm taking Betty Sue *with* me.'

***

Know why they raised the minimum drinking age in Tennessee to thirty-two?
They wanted to keep alcohol out of high schools.

***

What do they call reruns of 'Hee Haw' in Mississippi?
Documentaries.

***

Where was the toothbrush invented?
Arkansas. If it were invented anywhere else, it would have been called a teethbrush.

***

Did you hear about the $3 million Tennessee State Lottery?
The winner gets $3 a year for a million years.

***

A new law was recently passed in North Carolina so that when a couple gets divorced, they're still brother and sister.

***

SHE WAS SOOOO BLONDE:
She took a ruler to bed to see how long she slept.
She sent me a fax with a stamp on it.
She thought a quarterback was a refund.
She tried to put M&Ms in alphabetical order.
She thought Boyz II Men was a day-care centre.

HE WAS SOOOO BLONDE:
He thought General Motors was in the Army.
He thought Meow Mix was a CD for cats.
He thought TuPac Shakur was a Jewish holiday.
Under 'education' on his job application, he put 'Hooked on Phonics'.

SHE WAS SOOO BLONDE:
She tripped over a cordless phone.
She spent twenty minutes looking at the orange juice because it said 'concentrate'.
She told me to meet her at the corner of 'WALK' and 'DON'T WALK'.
At the bottom of the application where it says 'sign here', she put 'Sagittarius'.
She asked for a price check at the two-dollar shop.

HE WAS SOOOO BLONDE:
He studied for a blood test.
He sold the car for petrol money.
When he missed the 44 bus, he took the 22 bus twice instead.
When he went to the airport and saw a sign that read 'Airport Left', he turned around and went home.

SHE WAS SOOOO BLONDE:
When she heard that 90 per cent of all crimes occur around the home, she moved.
She thinks Taco Bell is the Mexican phone company.
If she spoke her mind, she'd be speechless.
She thought she could not use her AM radio in the evening.

***

My seven-year-old son asked me why I didn't have a boyfriend. I was recovering from surgery and spent most of the week in bed. I told him the TV was my boyfriend, he entertained me all the time.

The TV set was old and would just shut itself off for no reason. I'd give it a few hard whacks on the side and it would come back on.

The pastor stopped by to check on my recovery and my son answered the door. At that time I was trying to get the TV to come back on. The pastor asked my son if I was busy.

My little one said, 'No, sir, she is just in the bedroom banging her boyfriend.'

***

A GIRL'S PRAYER

Lord,
Before I lay me down to sleep
I pray for a man, who's not a creep.
One who's handsome, smart and strong,
One whose willy is thick and long.
One who thinks before he speaks,
When he promises to call, he won't wait weeks.
I pray that he is gainfully employed,
And when I spend his cash, won't be annoyed.
Pulls out my chair and opens my door,
Massages my back and begs to do more.
Oh! Send me a man who'll make love to my mind,
Knows just what to say, when I ask, 'How big's my behind?'
One who'll make love till my body's a twitchin',
In the hall, the loo, the garden and the kitchen!
I pray that this man will love me to no end,
And never attempt to shag my best friend.
And as I kneel and pray by my bed,
I look at the creep you sent me instead.
Amen.

***

A BOY'S PRAYER

Lord, I pray for a nympho with huge boobs who owns a beer store.

***

A blonde is walking down the street with her blouse open and her right breast hanging out. A policeman approaches her and says, 'Ma'am, are you aware that I could cite you for indecent exposure?'

She says, 'Why officer?'

'Because your breast is hanging out.'

She looks down and says, '*Oh my God!* I left the baby on the bus again!'

***

A blonde is out for a walk when she comes to a river and sees another blonde on the opposite bank. 'Yoohoo,' she shouts, 'how can I get to the other side?'

The second blonde looks up the river, then down the river, then shouts back, 'You *are* on the other side.'

***

A man walks up to the same woman in the office each

day, stands very close to her, draws in a large breath of air and tells her that her hair smells nice.

After a week of this, she can't stand it any longer, and goes to personnel. Without identifying the guy, she tells them what the co-worker does, and that she wants to file a sexual harassment suit against him.

The personnel manager is puzzled by this approach, and asks, 'What's sexually threatening about a co-worker telling you your hair smells nice?'

The woman replies, 'It's Keith, the midget.'

***

On a tour of New Zealand, the Pope took a couple of days off his itinerary to visit the wild east coast near Gisborne on an impromptu sightseeing trip.

His 4×4 Popemobile was driving along the golden sands when there was an enormous commotion heard just off the headland. They rushed to see what it was and upon approaching the scene the Pope noticed just outside the surf, a hapless man wearing a green and gold football jersey, struggling frantically to free himself from the jaws of a six metre shark.

At that moment a speedboat containing three men wearing All Black football tops roared into view from around the point. Spontaneously, one of the men took aim and fired a harpoon into the shark's ribs, immobilising it instantly. The other two reached out and pulled the Aussie from the water and then, using long clubs, beat the shark to death.

They bundled the bleeding, semi-conscious man into the speedboat along with the dead shark and then prepared for a hasty retreat, when they heard frantic shouting from the shore. It was, of course, the Pope, and he summoned them to the beach.

When they reached the shore, the Pope went into raptures about the rescue and said, 'I give you my blessing for your brave actions. I had heard that there were some racist xenophobic people trying to divide Australia and New Zealand, but now I have seen with my own eyes this is not true. I can see that your society is a truly enlightened example of racial harmony and could serve as a model on which other nations could follow.' He blessed them all and drove off in a cloud of dust.

As he departed, the harpoonist asked the others, 'Who was that?'

'That,' one answered, 'was His Holiness the Pope. He is in direct contact with God and has access to all God's wisdom.'

'Well,' the harpoonist replied, 'he knows fuck-all about shark hunting. How's that bait holding up or do we need to get another one?'

***

While trying to escape through Pakistan, Osama bin Laden found a bottle on a beach and picked it up. Suddenly, a female genie rose from the bottle and, with a smile, said, 'Master, may I grant you one wish?'

'You ignorant, unworthy daughter of a dog! Don't you know who I am? I don't need any common woman giving me anything,' barked bin Laden.

The shocked genie said, 'Please, I must grant you a wish or I will be returned to that bottle forever.'

Bin Laden thought a moment. Then grumbled about the impertinence of the woman and said, 'Very well. I want to awaken with three white women in my bed in the morning, so just do it and be off with you!'

The annoyed genie said, 'So be it!' and disappeared. The next morning bin Laden woke up in bed with Lorena Bobbitt, Tonya Harding and Hillary Clinton. His penis was gone, his knee was broken and he had no health insurance.

***

WHICH CONDOM WOULD YOU USE?

Nike condoms: Just Do It!

Toyota condoms: Oh, what a feeling!

Diet Pepsi condoms: You got the right one, baby!

Avis condoms: Trying harder than ever!

KFC condoms: Finger-lickin' good!

Coca-Cola condoms: Always the real thing!

Campbell's Soup condoms: Mm mmm good!

Energizer condoms: It keeps going and going . . .!

M&M condoms: It melts in your mouth, not in your hands!

Doublemint condoms: Double your pleasure, double your fun!

★★★

An elderly couple had been dating for some time and decided it was finally time to marry. Before the wedding, they had a long conversation regarding how their marriage might work. They discussed finances, living arrangements and so on.

Finally, the old man decided it was time to broach the subject of their physical relationship.

'How do you feel about sex?' he asked, rather hopefully.

'Well, I'd have to say I like it infrequently,' she responded.

He paused, then asked, 'Was that one word, or two?'

***

A blonde reports for her university final examination that consists of yes/no-type questions. She takes her seat in the examination hall, stresses at the question paper for five minutes and then, in a fit of inspiration, takes her purse out, removes a coin and starts tossing it and marking the answer sheet 'yes' for heads and 'no' for tails.

Within half an hour she is all done, whereas the rest of the class is sweating it out. During the last few minutes, she is seen desperately throwing the coin, muttering and sweating. The moderator, alarmed, approaches her and asks what is going on.

'I finished the exam in half an hour,' she says, 'but I'm rechecking my answers.'

***

There was a blonde woman who was having financial troubles, so she decided to kidnap a child and demand a ransom. She went to a local park, grabbed a little boy, took him behind a tree and wrote this note: 'I have kidnapped your child. Leave $10 000 in a plain brown bag behind the big oak tree in the park tomorrow at 7 a.m. Signed, "The Blonde".'

She pinned the note inside the little boy's jacket and told him to go straight home.

The next morning, she returned to the park to find the $10 000 in a brown bag, behind the big oak tree, just as she had instructed.

Inside the bag was the following note: 'Here is your money. I cannot believe that one blonde would do this to another!'

***

Three blokes were on a desert island and wanted desperately to get home. Then a bottle was washed up on the shore and, when they opened it, out popped a genie.

'Gentlemen,' said the genie, 'thank you for releasing me from the bottle. I've been stuck in there for hundreds of years. In return, I shall grant you three wishes. That's one each.'

The first bloke wished he was back with his wife

and family – and suddenly he was!

The second bloke wanted to be home with his family and friends. And suddenly he was!

Whereupon the third bloke said, 'I'm really lonely now. I wish I were back with my mates.' And, lo and behold, they were all back on the island.

✱✱✱

I was travelling home on the train from Newcastle to Glasgow and I was sitting with a group of people who, through no fault of their own, had recently been travelling in the first-class carriage. They told me of this incident that occurred while they were living the high life with their complimentary coffee and biscuits.

Apparently there had been a woman on the train with a small dog. When the ticket inspector came round he told her she'd have to buy a ticket for her dog. Understandably galled, she replied that if she was paying for a ticket for the dog, the dog would be entitled to a seat of its own. The ticket inspector graciously agreed but on one condition: he pointed to the sign by the window and said, 'Just as long as he keeps his feet off the seat.'

✱✱✱

When Peters learned that he was being fired, he went to see the head of human resources. 'Since I've been with the firm for so long,' he said, 'I think I deserve at least a letter of recommendation.'

The human resources director agreed and said he'd have the letter the next day.

The following morning, Peters found the letter on his desk. It read: 'Jonathan Peters worked for our company for eleven years. When he left, we were very satisfied.'

***

An old man lived alone. He wanted to dig his potato garden, but it was very hard work. His only son, who would have helped him, was in prison. The old man wrote a letter to his son and mentioned his predicament.

A few days later, at 4 a.m., a dozen people showed up and, without explanation, dug up the entire garden and left.

Shortly after, the old man received a letter that had obviously been read by the prison censor that had a PS from his son saying, 'For heaven's sake, Dad, don't dig up the garden, that's where I buried the guns!'

Confused, the old man wrote another note to his son telling him what had happened and asked him what to do next. His son's reply was, 'Go ahead and plant your potatoes, Dad. I'm glad I could help.'

✸✸✸

My therapist told me the way to achieve true inner peace is to finish what I start. So far today I have finished two bags of chips and a chocolate cake.

I feel better already.

✸✸✸

Did you hear about the new restaurant on the moon? Great food, but no atmosphere.

✸✸✸

A man had not been feeling well and went to the doctor for a check-up. After the physical examination and a battery of blood tests and X-rays, he asked the doctor about his situation.

The doctor replied, 'You are very sick. You might not live longer than perhaps three or four months.'

The man, in despair, yet with a glimmer of hope, said, 'If you don't mind doctor, I would like to have a second opinion.'

'Okay,' the doctor answered, 'you're ugly, too!'

***

A perfect summer day is when the sun is shining, the breeze is blowing, the birds are singing, and the lawn mower is broken.

***

A blonde appeared at the Pearly Gates seeking admission. The gatekeeper said there was a test that had to be passed before continuing to paradise, and that the test consisted of three questions.

The blonde said, 'Go ahead, ask the questions.'

'Okay,' said the angel. 'For the first question, tell me which two days of the week begin with the letter T.'

'That's easy,' said the candidate for admission, 'Today and Tomorrow.'

'Hmmmm,' said the angel. 'Well I can't argue with that. Now for the second question. Tell me how many seconds there are in a year.'

'There are twelve,' said the blonde.

'Twelve?!' exclaimed the angel. 'How do you figure that?'

'Well, there's January second, February second, March second, etc.'

'Okay,' said the angel. 'For the third question, tell

me God's first name.'

'God's first name is Andy.'

'Oh? What makes you say that?' asked the angel.

And the blonde replied, 'It's right there in the song.' The blonde begins singing an excerpt from the hymn 'In the Garden': 'And He walks with me. And he talks with me. And he tells me I am his own.'

***

Little Johnny returns from school and tells his father he got an 'F' in arithmetic today.

'Why?' asks his father.

'The teacher asked, "How much is two times three?" I said six.'

'But that's right,' said his father.

'Then she asked me, "How much is three times two?"'

'What's the fucking difference?' asks his father.

'That's what I said!'

***

Two Arabs are chatting. One of them has his wallet out and is flipping through pictures. 'Yeah, this is my oldest. He's a martyr. And here's my second son. He's a martyr, too.'

There's a pause.

The second Arab says wistfully, 'Ah, they blow up fast, don't they?'

***

Shirley and Abe, a retired couple from New York City, living in Miami, are getting ready to go out to dinner. Shirley says, 'Abe, darling, do you want me to wear this Chanel suit or the Gucci?'

Abe says, 'Do I care?'

A few minutes later Shirley says, 'Abe, should I wear my Cartier watch or my Rolex?'

Abe says, 'Who cares?'

A few more minutes pass and Shirley says, 'Abe, love, shall I wear my five-carat pear-diamond ring or my six-carat round-diamond ring with the baguettes?'

Abe says, 'Shirley, I really don't care what you wear, but if you don't move your butt, we're going to miss the Early Bird Special at McDonald's.'

***

SIGN AT THE LOCAL GOLF CLUB:

1. Back straight, knees bent, feet shoulder-width apart.

2.   Form a loose grip.
3.   Keep your head down.
4.   Avoid a quick back swing.
5.   Stay out of the water.
6.   Try not to hit anyone.
7.   If you are taking too long, please let others go ahead of you.
8.   Don't stand directly in front of others.
9.   Quiet please, while others are preparing.
10. Don't take extra strokes.

Well done! Now flush the urinal. Go outside and tee off!

***

FOOT-IN-MOUTH SPORTS COMMENTARIES

Weightlifting commentator at the Olympic Snatch and Jerk event: 'This is Gregoriava from Bulgaria. I saw her snatch this morning during her warm-up and it was amazing.'

Ted Walsh, horseracing commentator: 'This is really a lovely horse and I speak from personal experience since I once mounted her mother.'

Grand Prix race announcer: 'The lead car is absolutely,

truly unique, except for the one behind it, which is exactly identical to the one in front of the similar one in back.'

Greg Norman, pro golfer: 'I owe a lot to my parents, especially my mother and father.'

Ringside boxing analyst: 'Sure there have been injuries and even some deaths in boxing, but none of them really that serious.'

Baseball announcer: 'If history repeats itself, I should think we can expect the same thing again.'

Basketball analyst: 'He dribbles a lot and the opposition doesn't like it. In fact, you can see it all over their faces.'

At a trophy ceremony BBC TV boat race, 1988: 'Ah, isn't that nice, the wife of the Cambridge president is hugging the cox of the Oxford crew.'

Metro Radio, college football: 'Julian Dicks is everywhere. It's like they've got eleven Dicks on the field.'

US Open TV commentator: 'One of the reasons Arnie

Palmer is playing so well is that, before each final round, his wife takes out his balls and kisses them. Oh my God, what have I just said?!'

***

LOUD SEX

A wife went to see a therapist and said, 'I've got a big problem, doctor. Every time we're in bed and my husband climaxes, he lets out this ear-splitting yell.'

'My dear,' the shrink said, 'that's completely natural. I don't see what the problem is.'

'The problem is,' she complained, 'it wakes me up!'

***

QUIET SEX

Tired of a listless sex life, the man came right out and asked his wife during a recent lovemaking session, 'How come you never tell me when you have an orgasm?'

She glanced at him casually and replied, 'You're never home!'

***

DECEPTIVE SEX

A married man and his secretary were having a torrid affair. One afternoon they couldn't contain their passion, so they rushed over to her place where they spent the afternoon making passionate love. When they were finished, they fell asleep, not waking until eight o'clock. They got dressed quickly. Then the man told his secretary to take his shoes outside and rub them on the lawn. Bewildered, she did as he asked, thinking him pretty weird.

The man finally got home and his wife met him at the door. Upset, she asked where he'd been. The man replied, 'I cannot tell a lie. My secretary and I are having an affair. Today we left work early, went to her place, spent the afternoon making love, and then fell asleep. That's why I'm late.'

The wife looked at him, noticed his shoes and yelled, 'I can see those are grass stains on your shoes. *You damn liar!* You've been playing golf again, haven't you?'

***

WEDDING ANNIVERSARY SEX

A husband and his wife had a bitter quarrel on the day of their fortieth wedding anniversary. The husband yelled, 'When you die, I'm getting you a headstone that reads: "Here Lies My Wife – Cold As Ever".'

'Yeah,' she replied, 'when you die, I'm getting you a headstone that reads "Here Lies My Husband – Stiff At Last".'

***

My husband came home with a tube of KY jelly and said, 'This will make you happy tonight.'

He was right. When he went out of the bedroom, I squirted it all over the doorknobs so he couldn't get back in.

***

Jacob, ninety-two, and Rebecca, eighty-five, are very excited about their decision to get married. They go for a stroll to discuss the wedding and on the way go past a pharmacy. Jacob suggests they go in. Jacob addresses the man behind the counter:

Jacob: Are you the owner?

Pharmacist: Yes.

Jacob: Do you sell heart medication?

Pharmacist: Of course we do.

Jacob: How about medicine for circulation?

Pharmacist: All kinds.

Jacob: Medicine for rheumatism?

Pharmacist: Definitely.

Jacob: How about Viagra?

Pharmacist: Of course.

Jacob: Medicine for memory?

Pharmacist: Yes, a large variety.

Jacob: What about vitamins and sleeping pills?

Pharmacist: Absolutely.

Jacob turns to Rebecca: Sweetheart, we might as well register our wedding-gift list with them.

★★★

A woman and a man are involved in a bad car accident. Both cars are totally demolished, but amazingly neither of them is hurt.

After they crawl out of their cars, the woman says, 'So you're a man. That's interesting. I'm a woman. Wow, just look at our cars! There's nothing left, but fortunately we are unhurt. This must be a sign from God that we should meet and be friends and live in peace for the rest of our days.

The man replied, 'I agree with you completely. This must be a sign from God!'

The woman continued, 'And look at this. Here's another miracle. My car is completely demolished but this bottle of wine didn't break! Surely God wants us to drink this wine and celebrate our good fortune.'

She hands the bottle to the man, as he nods his head in agreement. He opens the bottle and drinks half the contents, then hands it back to the woman. The woman takes the bottle immediately, replaces the cork and hands it back to the man.

He asked, 'Aren't you having any?'

The woman replied, 'No, I think I'll just wait for the police to arrive.'

***

TOP 20 WAYS TO SAY 'YOUR FLY IS OPEN'

20. The cucumber has left the salad.

19. I can see the gun of Navarone.

18. Someone tore down the wall and your Pink Floyd is hanging out.

17. You've got Windows in your laptop.

16. Sailor Ned's trying to take a little shore leave.

15. Your soldier isn't so unknown now.

14. Quasimodo needs to go back in the tower and tend to his bell.

13. Paging Mr Johnson. Paging Mr Johnson.

12. You need to bring your tray table to the upright and locked position.

11. Your pod bay door is open, Hal.

10. Elvis Junior has *left* the building!

9. Mini Me is making a break for the escape pod.

8. Ensign Haynes is reporting a hull breach on the lower desk, sir!

7. The Buick is not all the way in the garage.

6. Dr Kimble has escaped!

5. You've got your fly set for 'Monica' instead of 'Hillary'.

4. Our next guest is someone who needs no introduction.

3. You've got a security breach at Los Pantalones.

2. I'm talking about Shaft, can you dig it?

And the number one way to tell someone his fly is unzipped:
1. I thought you were crazy, now I see your nuts.

***

In 1993, the American government funded a study to see why the head of a man's penis was larger than the shaft. After one year and $180 000, they concluded that the reason the head was larger than the shaft was to give the man more pleasure during sex.

After the US published the study, France decided to do their own study. After $250 000 and three years of research, they concluded that the reason was to give the woman more pleasure during sex.

Canada, unsatisfied with these findings, undertook its own study. After two weeks and a cost of around $75.45 and two cases of beer, they concluded that it was to keep a man's hand from flying off and hitting him in the forehead.

***

A sick pig rarely curls its tail.
A woodpecker's tongue is long enough to wrap around its head two times.
Ants prefer not to walk through baby powder.

Snakes can't blink.

A rat can tread water for three days.

A snail takes twenty hours to crawl 1km.

The bigger the navel, the sweeter the orange.

The dot over the lower case i is called a tittle.

In an average lifetime the human heart circulates 250 million litres of blood.

Nutmeg is extremely poisonous if injected intravenously.

It is illegal in the state of Kentucky to marry your wife's grandmother.

If a frog's mouth is held open too long the frog will suffocate.

Peanuts are used in the manufacture of dynamite.

No word in the English language rhymes with month.

Worcestershire sauce is basically anchovy ketchup.

A duck's quack does not echo.

The ashes of an average cremated person weigh 4kg.

Roosters cannot crow if they cannot extend their necks.

Oak trees do not grow acorns until they are fifty years old.

Shirley Temple always had fifty-six curls in her hair.

An office chair with wheels travels 13km a year.

Bubblegum contains rubber.

Every time you sneeze, some of your brain cells die.

An animal epidemic is called an epizootic.

Camel's milk does not curdle.

A cat has four rows of whiskers.

Maine, USA, is the toothpick capital of the world.

The space between the two front teeth is called a diastema.

Alexander the Great was an epileptic.

A group of owls is called a parliament.

The ball on top of a flagpole is called the truck.

Giraffes have no vocal chords.

The dragonfly has a life span of twenty-four hours.

Professional ballerinas use about twelve pairs of point shoes per week.

Mel Blanc (the voice of Bugs Bunny) was allergic to carrots.

The glue on Israeli postage stamps is certified kosher.

In *Casablanca*, Humphrey Bogart never said. 'Play it again, Sam.'

The average person falls asleep in seven minutes.

Money isn't made out of paper, it's made out of cotton.

Every time you lick a stamp, you're consuming 0.1 calories.

All dogs, no matter what size, scratch at the same speed.

There are no turkeys in Turkey.

The term 'checkmate' comes from the Arabic meaning 'the king is dead'.

There are 293 ways to make change for a dollar.

A giraffe's tongue is blue.

The average person blinks 313 million times in a lifetime.

Robert E. Lee wore size 4½ shoes.

If a spider dismantles his web, a bad storm is near.

Tug of War was an Olympic event between 1900 and 1920.

The right lung takes in more air than the left.

There is no rice in rice paper.

More than 25 per cent of the world's forests are in Siberia.

***

My wife uses fabric softener. I never knew what that stuff was for. Then I noticed women coming up to me, sniffing, then saying under their breath, 'Married!' and walking away. Fabric softeners are how our wives mark their territory.

***

My grandmother has a bumper sticker on her car that says, 'Sexy Senior Citizen'. You don't want to think of your grandmother that way, do you? Out entering wet shawl contests. Makes you wonder where she got that dollar she gave you for your birthday.

***

Over the past few years, more money has been spent on breast implants and Viagra than on Alzheimer's disease research. So it is believed that by the year 2030 there will be a large number of people wandering around with huge breasts and erections who can't remember what to do with them.

***

A couple of rednecks are out in the woods hunting, when one of them falls to the ground. He doesn't seem to be breathing; his eyes are rolled back in his head.

The other guy whips out his mobile and dials 000. He gasps to the operator, 'My friend is dead! What can I do?'

The operator, in a calm soothing voice, says, 'Just take it easy. I can help. First, let's make sure he's dead.'

There is a silence, then a shot is heard. The guy's voice comes back on the line. He says, 'Okay, now what?'

***

First-year students at Med School were receiving their first anatomy class with a real dead human body. They all gathered around the surgery table with the body covered with a white sheet.

The professor started the class by telling them, 'In medicine, it is necessary to have two important qualities as a doctor. The first is that you should not be disgusted by anything involving the human body.'

As an example, the professor pulled back the sheet, stuck his finger in the butt of the corpse, withdrew it and stuck it into his mouth. 'Go ahead and do the same thing,' he told his students.

The students freaked out, hesitated for several minutes, but eventually took turns sticking a finger in the butt of the dead body, pulling it out and sucking it.

When everyone had finished, the professor looked at them and told them, 'The second most important quality is observation. I stuck in my middle finger and sucked on my index finger. Now learn to pay attention!'

***

OFFICE TERMINOLOGY:

BLAMESTORMING: Sitting around in a group, discussing why a deadline was missed or a project failed, and who was responsible.

SEAGULL MANAGER: A manager who flies in, makes a lot of noise, craps on everything, then leaves.

ASSMOSIS: The process by which some people seem to absorb success and advancement by kissing up to the boss rather than working hard.

SALMON DAY: The experience of spending an entire day swimming upstream only to get screwed and die in the end.

CUBE FARM: An office filled with cubicles.

PRAIRIE DOGGING: When someone yells or drops something loudly in a cube farm, and people's heads pop up over the walls to see what's going on.

MOUSE POTATO: The online, wired generation's answer to the couch potato.

STRESS PUPPY: A person who seems to thrive on being stressed out and whiny.

XEROX SUBSIDY: Euphemism for swiping free photocopies from one's workplace.

PERCUSSIVE MAINTENANCE: The fine art of whacking the crap out of an electronic device to get it to work again.

ADMINISPHERE: The rarefied organisation layers beginning just above the rank and file. Decisions that fall from the adminisphere are often profoundly inappropriate or irrelevant to the problems they were designed to solve.

CROP DUSTING: Surreptitiously farting while passing through a cube farm, then enjoying the sounds of dismay and disgust. Leads to PRAIRIE DOGGING.

★★★

WILL THE REAL DUMMY PLEASE STAND UP!
AT&T fired president John Walter after nine months, saying he lacked intellectual leadership. He received a $26 million severance package.

WITH A LITTLE HELP FROM OUR FRIENDS

Police in Oakland, California, spent two hours attempting to subdue a gunman who had barricaded himself in his home. After firing ten tear gas canisters, officers discovered the man standing beside them in the police line, shouting, 'Please come out and give yourself up!'

WHAT WAS PLAN B?

An Illinois man, pretending to have a gun, kidnapped a motorist and forced him to drive to two different ATMs, wherein the kidnapper proceeded to withdraw money from his own bank accounts.

THE GETAWAY

A man walked into a Kansas Kwik Stop and asked for all the money in the cash drawer. Apparently, the take was too small, so he tied up the store clerk and worked the counter himself for three hours until police showed up and grabbed him.

DID I SAY THAT?

Police in Los Angeles had good luck with a robbery suspect who just couldn't control himself during a line-up. The detectives asked each man in the line-up to repeat the words 'Give me all your money or I'll shoot'. The man shouted, 'That's not what I said!'

ARE WE COMMUNICATING?

A man spoke frantically into the phone: 'My wife is pregnant and her contractions are only two minutes apart!'

'Is this her first child?' the doctor asked.

'No,' the husband shouted, 'this is her husband!'

NOT THE SHARPEST TOOL IN THE SHED

In Modesto, California, Steven Richard King was arrested for trying to hold up a Bank of America branch without a weapon. King used a thumb and a finger to simulate a gun, but unfortunately he failed to keep his hand in his pocket!

THE GRAND FINALE

One summer down on Lake Isabella, located in the high desert an hour east of Bakersfield, California, some folks, new to boating, were having a problem. No matter how hard they tried, they couldn't get their brand new 22ft boat going. It was very sluggish in almost every manoeuvre, no matter how much power was applied.

After about an hour of trying to make it go, they putted to a nearby marina, thinking someone there could tell them what was wrong. A thorough topside check revealed everything in perfect working condition. The engine ran fine, the out-drive went up and down, and the prop was the correct size and pitch.

So, one of the marina guys jumped in the water to check underneath. He came up choking on water, he was laughing so much. Under the boat, still strapped securely in place was the trailer!

***

GREAT PEARLS OF WISDOM

The journey of a thousand miles starts with a broken fan belt and a leaky tyre.

It's always darkest just before dawn, so if you're going to steal your neighbour's newspaper, that's the time to do it.

Don't be irreplaceable. If you can't be replaced, you can't be promoted.

Always remember: you're unique. Just like everyone else.

Never test the depth of the water with both feet.

It may be that your sole purpose in life is simply to serve as a bad example.

Don't squat with your spurs on.

It is far more impressive when others discover your good qualities without your help.

If you think nobody cares if you're alive, try missing a couple of car payments.

Before you criticise someone, you should walk a mile in their shoes. That way, when you criticise them, you're a mile away and you have their shoes.

If at first you don't succeed, skydiving is not for you.

Give a man a fish and he'll eat for a day. Teach him how to fish and he'll sit in a boat and drink beer all day.

If you lend someone $20 and never see them again, it was probably worth it.

If you tell the truth, you don't have to remember anything.

Some days you are the bug, some days you are the windshield.

Good judgement comes from bad experience, and a lot of that comes from bad judgement.

Timing has an awful lot to do with the outcome of a rain dance.

A closed mouth gathers no foot.

Generally speaking, you aren't learning much when your mouth is moving.

Experience is something you don't get until just after you need it.

Never miss a good chance to shut up.

We are born naked, wet and hungry. Then things get worse.

***

An Amish woman and her daughter were riding in an old buggy one cold blustery day. The daughter said to her mother, 'My hands are freezing cold!'

The mother replied, 'Put them between your legs. Your body heat will warm them up.'

So the daughter did and her hands warmed up.

The next day the daughter was riding with her boyfriend and he said, 'My hands are freezing cold.'

The girl replied, 'Put them between my legs. The

warmth of my body will warm them up.'

So he did and warmed his hands.

The following day the boyfriend was again in the buggy with the daughter. He said, 'My nose is cold.'

The girl replied, 'Put it between my legs. The warmth of my body will warm it up.'

So he did and warmed his nose.

The next day the boyfriend was again driving with the daughter and he said, 'My penis is frozen solid.'

The following day the daughter was driving in the buggy with her mother and she said to her mother, 'Have you ever heard of a penis?'

Slightly concerned the mother said, 'Why yes! Why do you ask?'

The daughter replied, 'Well, they make one hell of a mess when they defrost, don't they!'

✳✳✳

Hung Chow calls in to work and says, 'Hey boss, I not come to work today. I really sick. I got headache, stomach ache and my legs hurt. I not come to work.'

The boss says, 'You know, Hung Chow, I really need you today. When I feel like this I go to my wife and tell her to give me sex. That makes everything better and I can go to work. You should try that.'

Two hours later Hung Chow calls again. 'Boss, I do

what you say and feel great. I be at work soon. You got nice house.'

***

EXCUSE NOTES FROM PARENTS

My son is under a doctor's care and should not take PE today. Please execute him.

Please excuse Lisa for being absent. She was sick and I had her shot.

Dear School, Please excuse John being Absent on Jan. 28, 29, 30, 31, 32 and also 33.

Please excuse Gloria from Jim today. She is administrating.

Please excuse Roland from PE for a few days. Yesterday he fell out of a tree and misplaced his hip.

John has been absent because he had two teeth taken out of his face.

Carlos was absent yesterday because he was playing football. He was hurt in the growing part.

Megan could not come to school today because she has been bothered by very close veins.

Chris will not be in school cus he has an acre in his side.

Please excuse Ray Friday from school. He has very loose vowels.

Please excuse Burma, she has been sick and under the doctor.

Irving was absent yesterday because he missed his bust.

Please excuse Jimmy for being sick. It was his father's fault.

I kept Billie home because she had to go Christmas shopping because I don't know what size she wears.

Please excuse Jennifer for missing school yesterday. We forgot to get the Sunday paper off the porch, and when we found it Monday, we thought it was Sunday.

Sally won't be in school for a week from Friday. We have to attend her funeral.

My daughter was absent yesterday because she was tired. She spent a weekend with the Marines.

Please excuse Jason for being absent yesterday. He had a cold and could not breed well.

Please excuse Mary for being absent yesterday. She was in bed with gramps.

Maryann was absent December 11–16 because she had a fever, sore throat, headache and upset stomach. Her sister was also sick, fever and sore throat, her brother had a low grade fever and ached all over. I wasn't the best either, sore throat and fever. There must be something going around, her father even got hot last night.

Please excuse little Jimmy for not being in school today. His father is gone and I could not get him ready because I was in bed with the doctor.

***

ONLY IN AMERICA

A Charlotte, North Carolina, lawyer purchased a box of very rare and expensive cigars, then insured them against fire among other things.

Within a month, having smoked his entire stockpile of these great cigars and without yet having made even his first premium payment on the policy, the lawyer filed a claim against the insurance company. In his claim, the lawyer stated the cigars were lost 'in a series of small fires'. The insurance company refused to pay, citing the obvious reason: that the man had consumed the cigars in the normal fashion. The lawyer sued – and won!

In delivering the ruling the judge agreed with the insurance company that the claim was frivolous. The judge stated, nevertheless, that the lawyer held a policy from the company in which it had warranted that the cigars were insurable and also guaranteed that it would insure them against fire, without defining what is considered to be unacceptable fire, and was obligated to pay the claim. Rather than endure a lengthy and costly appeal process, the insurance company accepted the ruling and paid $15 000 to the lawyer for his loss of the rare cigars, lost in the 'fires'.

After the lawyer cashed the cheque, the insurance company had him arrested on twenty-four counts of arson, with his own insurance claim and testimony from the previous case being used against him. The lawyer was convicted of intentionally burning his insured property and was sentenced to twenty-four months in jail and fined $24 000.

This is a true story and was the winner in a US Criminal Lawyers Award Contest.

***

QUOTES

'Oh, you hate your job? Why didn't you say so? There's a support group for that. It's called Everybody, and they meet at the bar.'   Drew Carey

'Instead of getting married again, I'm going to find a woman I don't like and just give her a house.'

Rod Stewart

'The problem with the designated driver program is it's not a desirable job. But if you ever get sucked into doing it, have fun with it. At the end of the night, drop them off at the wrong house.'   Jeff Foxworthy

'If a woman has to choose between catching a fly ball and saving an infant's life, she will choose to save the infant's life without even considering if there is a man on base.'   Dave Barry

'What do people mean when they say the computer went down on them?'   Marilyn Pittman

'Relationships are hard. It's like a full-time job, and we should treat it like one. If your boyfriend or girlfriend wants to leave you, they should give you two weeks' notice. There should be severance pay, and before they leave, they should have to find you a temp.'

Bob Ettinger

'My mum said she learned how to swim when someone took her out in the lake and threw her off the boat. I said, "Mum, they weren't trying to teach you how to swim."' Paula Poundstone

'Why does Sea World have a seafood restaurant? I'm halfway through my fish burger and I realise, "Oh my God! I could be eating a slow learner."'

Lynda Montgomery

'I think that's how Chicago got started. A bunch of people in New York said, "Gee, I'm enjoying the crime and poverty, but it just isn't cold enough. Let's go west."' Richard Jeni

'Sometimes I think war is God's way of teaching us geography.' Paul Rodriguez

'My parents didn't want to move to Florida, but they turned sixty, and that's the law.' Jerry Seinfeld

314

'Remember in elementary school you were told that in case of fire you have to line up quietly in a single file line from smallest to tallest. What is the logic in that? What, do tall people burn slower?'

Warren Hutcherson

'Bigamy is having one wife/husband too many. Monogamy is the same.'　　　　Oscar Wilde

'Suppose you were an idiot. And suppose you were a member of Congress – but I repeat myself.'

Mark Twain

Our bombs are smarter than the average high-school student. At least they can find Afghanistan.'

A. Whitney Brown

'Ah, yes, divorce – from the Latin word meaning to rip out a man's genitals through his wallet.'

Robin Williams

'Women complain about premenstrual syndrome, but I think of it as the only time of the month that I can be myself.'　　　　Roseanne

'Banning the bra was a big flop.'　　　Author unknown

'The length of a film should be directly related to the endurance of the human bladder.'   Alfred Hitchcock

'Always drink upstream from the herd.'   Will Rogers

***

Most people have heard of the Darwin Awards, given annually to individuals who do the most for mankind by removing themselves from the gene pool. Now we have the Stella Awards, given to the individuals who win the most frivolous lawsuits ever. The Stella Awards are named in honour of 81-year-old Stella Liebeck, the woman who won $2.9 million for spilling a cup of McDonald's coffee on herself. The following are candidates for the award:

1. January 2000: Kathleen Robertson of Austin, Texas, was awarded $780 000 after breaking her ankle tripping over a toddler who was running amok inside a furniture store. The owners of the store were understandably surprised at the verdict, considering that the misbehaving little fellow was Ms Robertson's son.

2. June 1998: Nineteen-year-old Carl Truman of Los Angeles won $74 000 and medical expenses when his

neighbour ran over his hand with a Honda Accord. Mr Truman apparently didn't notice there was someone at the wheel of the car when he was trying to steal his neighbour's hubcaps.

3. October 1998: Terrence Dickson of Bristol was leaving a house he had just finished robbing by way of the garage. He was not able to get the garage door to go up, because the automatic door opener was malfunctioning. He couldn't re-enter the house because the door connecting the house and garage locked when he pulled it shut. The family was on vacation. Mr Dickson found himself locked in the garage for eight days. He subsisted on a case of Pepsi he found in the garage and a large bag of dry dog food. Mr Dickson sued the homeowners, claiming the situation caused him undue mental anguish. The jury agreed to the tune of a half million dollars.

4. October 1999: Jerry Williams of Little Rock, Arkansas, was awarded $14 500 and medical expenses after being bitten on the buttocks by his next-door neighbour's beagle. The dog was on a chain in its owner's fenced-in yard at the time. Mr Williams was also in the fenced-in yard. The award was less than was sought because the jury felt the dog may have been provoked by Mr Williams who, at the time, was

repeatedly shooting it with a pellet gun.

5. December 1997: A Philadelphia restaurant was ordered to pay Amber Carson of Lancaster $113 500 after she slipped on soft drink and broke her coccyx. The beverage was on the floor because Ms Carson threw it at her boyfriend thirty seconds earlier during an argument.

6. December 1997: Kara Walton of Clamant successfully sued the owner of a nightclub when she fell from the bathroom window to the floor and knocked out her two front teeth. This occurred while Ms Walton was trying to sneak through the window in the ladies' room to avoid paying the $3.50 cover charge. She was awarded $12 000 and dental expenses.

***

On the first day God created the cow. God said, 'You must go to field with the farmer all day long and suffer under the sun, have calves and give milk to support the farmer. I will give you a lifespan of sixty years.'

The cow said, 'That's kind of a tough life you want me to live for sixty years. Let me have twenty years and I'll give back the other forty.' And God agreed.

On the second day, God created the dog. God said,

'Sit all day by the door of your house and bark at anyone who comes in or walks past. I will give you a lifespan of twenty years.'

The dog said, 'That's too long to be barking. Give me ten years and I'll give back the other ten.' So God agreed.

On the third day, God created the monkey. God said, 'Entertain people, do monkey tricks, make them laugh. I'll give you a twenty-year lifespan.'

The monkey said, 'How boring, monkey tricks for twenty years? I don't think so. The dog gave you back ten, so that's what I'll do, too, okay?' And God agreed again.

On the fourth day, God created man. God said, 'Eat, sleep, play, enjoy. Do nothing, just enjoy, enjoy. I'll give you twenty years.' Man said, 'What? Only twenty years? No way, man. Tell you what: I'll take my twenty, and the forty the cow gave back, and the ten the dog gave back, and the ten monkey gave back. That makes eighty, okay?'

'Okay,' said God. 'You've got a deal.'

So that is why for the first twenty years we eat, sleep, play, enjoy, and do nothing. For the next forty years we slave in the sun to support our family; for the next ten years we do monkey tricks to entertain our grandchildren; and for the last ten years we sit in front of the house and bark at everyone.

Life has now been explained.

***

A man picks up a young woman in a bar and convinces her to come back to his hotel. When they are relaxing afterwards, he asks, 'Am I the first man you ever made love to?'

She looks at him thoughtfully for a second before replying, 'You might be. Your face looks vaguely familiar.'

***

Two guys are working in a sawmill one day when one of the guys gets too close to the blade and his arm is severed. His buddy puts the arm in a plastic bag and rushes it down to the hospital to have it reattached.

The next day he goes to see his chum, and finds him playing tennis. 'Incredible!' says his friend. 'Medical science is amazing.'

Another month goes by and the two guys are again working at the sawmill when the same guy gets too close to the spinning blade and this time his leg gets cut off. Again his buddy takes the leg, puts it in a plastic bag and takes it to the hospital to have it reattached.

The next day, he goes down to see his chum and finds him outside playing football. 'Incredible!' says his friend. 'Medical science is amazing!'

Another month goes by and again the two friends are at the mill cutting wood when, suddenly, the same guy bends down too close to the blade and off comes his head. Well, his friend takes the head, puts it in a plastic bag and heads to the hospital to have it reattached.

The next day he goes to see his friend but can't find him. He sees the doctor walking down the hall and says, 'Doc, where is my friend? I brought him in yesterday.'

The doctor thinks for a minute, and says, 'Oh yeah. Some idiot put his head in a plastic bag and he suffocated.'

***

Michael the Dragon Master was an official in King Arthur's court. He had a longstanding desire to nuzzle the beautiful queen's voluptuous breasts. But he knew the penalty for this would be death.

One day, he revealed his secret desire to his colleague, Horatio, who was the king's chief physician. Horatio said, 'I can arrange it, but I will need 1000 gold coins to pay bribes.' Michael the Dragon Master readily agreed.

The next day Horatio made up a batch of itching powder and poured a little of it into the queen's brassiere while she was taking a bath. Soon after she dressed, the itching commenced and grew in intensity. Upon being called to the royal chambers, Horatio told the king that only a special saliva, if applied for four hours, would cure this type of itch, and that tests had shown such a saliva was only to be found in Michael the Dragon Master's mouth. King Arthur summoned Michael the Dragon Master.

Michael the Dragon Master slipped the antidote lotion into his mouth and for the next four hours worked passionately on the queen's magnificent breasts.

Satisfied, he returned to his chamber and found Horatio demanding payment. However, with his obsession now satisfied, he refused to pay Horatio anything and shooed him away, knowing that Horatio could never report this matter to the king.

The next day, Horatio slipped a massive dose of the same itching powder onto King Arthur's loincloth. King Arthur summoned Michael the Dragon Master . . .

✳✳✳

A rich white guy in Louisiana decided that he wanted to throw a party and invited all of his buddies and neighbours. He also invited Leroy, the token black guy in the neighbourhood. He held the party around the pool in the backyard of his mansion.

Everyone was having a good time drinking, dancing, eating shrimp. At the height of the party, the rich white dude said, 'I have a 10ft man-eating 'gator in my pool and I'll give a million dollars to anyone who has the balls to jump in.'

The words were barely out of his mouth when there was a loud splash and everyone turned around to see Leroy in the pool! Leroy was fighting the 'gator, jabbing its eyes with his thumbs, throwing punches, biting it on the tail and flipping it through the air like some kind of Japanese judo instructor. The water was churning and splashing everywhere. Both Leroy and the 'gator were screaming and raising hell.

Finally, Leroy strangled the 'gator and let it sink to the bottom. Leroy then slowly climbed out of the pool. Everyone was just staring at him in disbelief.

At last the rich white guy says, 'Well, Leroy, I reckon I owe you a million dollars.'

'No, that's okay, I don't want it,' said Leroy.

The rich white guy said, 'Man, I have to give you something. You won the bet. How about half a million bucks then?'

'No thanks. I don't want it,' answered Leroy.

The white dude said, 'Come on, I insist on giving you something. That was amazing. How about a new Porsche, a Rolex, some stock options?'

Leroy said no.

The confused rich guy said, 'Well, Leroy, then what do you want?'

Leroy said, 'I want the name of the son of a bitch who pushed me in the pool.'

***

There was a German, an Italian and an Irishman on death row. The warden gave them a choice of three ways to die: to be shot, hanged, or injected with the AIDS virus for a slow death.

The German said, 'Shoot me right in the head.'

Boom, he was dead instantly.

The Italian said, 'Just hang me.'

Snap, he was dead.

The Irishman said, 'Give me some of that AIDS stuff.' They gave him the shot and the Irishman fell down laughing. The guards looked at each other and wondered what was wrong with this guy. Then the Irishman said, 'Give me another one of those shots.' So the guards obliged. Now he was laughing so hard, tears rolled from his eyes and he doubled over.

Finally the warden said, 'What's wrong with you?'

The Irishman replied, 'You guys are so stupid – I'm wearing a condom!'

***

One day, in line at the company cafeteria, Jack says to Mike behind him, 'My elbow hurts like hell. I guess I'd better see a doctor.'

'Listen, you don't have to spend that kind of money,' Mike replies. There's a diagnostic computer at the pharmacy at the corner. Just give it a urine sample and the computer will tell you what's wrong and what to do about it. It takes ten seconds and costs $10, a hell of a lot cheaper than a doctor.'

So Jack deposits a urine sample in a small jar and takes it to the pharmacy. He deposits $10, and the computer lights up and asks for the urine sample. He pours the sample into the slot and waits. Ten seconds later, the computer ejects a printout reading, 'You have tennis elbow. Soak your arm in warm water and avoid heavy activity. It will improve in two weeks.'

That evening, while thinking how amazing this new technology was, Jack began wondering if the computer could be fooled. He mixed some tap water, a stool sample from his dog, urine samples from his wife and daughter, and masturbated into the mixture for good measure.

Jack hurried back to the pharmacy, eager to check the results. He deposited $10, poured in his concoction and waited for the results. The computer printed the following:

1. Your tap water is too hard. Get a water softener.

2. Your dog has ringworm. Bathe him with anti-fungal shampoo.
3. Your daughter has a cocaine habit. Get her into rehab.
4. Your wife is pregnant – twin girls. They aren't yours. Get a lawyer.
5. If you don't stop playing with yourself, your elbow will never get better.

***

A man and a woman were driving down the road and arguing about his deplorable infidelity when suddenly she reaches over and slices off the man's penis. Angrily, she tosses it out the car window.

Driving behind the couple is a man and his nine-year-old daughter. The little girl is just chatting away to her father when all of a sudden the penis smacks their windscreen, sticks for a moment, then flies off.

Surprised, the daughter asks her father, 'Daddy, what the heck was that?'

Not wanting to expose his little girl to anything sexual at such a young age, the father replies, 'It was only a bug, honey.'

The daughter sits with a confused look on her face, and after a few minutes, she says, 'Sure had a big dick, didn't it!'

★★★

A nurse was on duty in the emergency room, when in came a young woman with purple hair styled into a punk rocker mohawk, sporting a variety of tattoos and wearing strange clothing. It was quickly determined that the patient had acute appendicitis, so she was scheduled for immediate surgery. When she was completely disrobed on the operating table, the staff noticed that her pubic hair had been dyed green, and above it there was a tattoo that read, 'Keep off the grass'.

Once the surgery was completed, the surgeon wrote a short note on the patient's dressing, which said, 'Sorry, had to mow the lawn.'

★★★

A redneck, a sheep and a dog were survivors of a terrible shipwreck. They found themselves stranded on a desert island. After being there a while, they got into the habit of going to the beach every evening to watch the sun go down.

One particular evening, the sky was red with beautiful cirrus clouds, the breeze was warm and gentle, a perfect night for romance. As they sat there, the sheep started looking better and better to the redneck.

Soon, he leaned over to the sheep and put his arm around it. But the dog got jealous, growling fiercely until the redneck took his arm from around the sheep.

After that, the three of them continued to enjoy the sunsets together, but there were no more attempts to cuddle.

A few weeks passed by and, lo and behold, there was another shipwreck. The only survivor was a beautiful young woman, the most beautiful woman the redneck had ever seen. She was in a pretty bad way when they rescued her, so they slowly nursed her back to health.

When the young maiden was well enough, they introduced her to their evening beach ritual.

It was another beautiful evening with a red sky, cirrus clouds, a warm gentle breeze, and the redneck started to get 'those feelings' again. He fought them as long as he could, but finally gave in and leaned over to the young woman cautiously and whispered in her ear, 'Would you mind taking the dog for a walk?'

***

A blonde suspects her boyfriend of cheating on her, so she goes out and buys a gun.

She goes to his apartment unexpectedly and, when

she opens the door, finds him in the arms of a redhead. Well, the blonde is really angry! She opens her purse and takes out the gun, which she puts to her head.

The boyfriend yells, 'No honey, don't do it!'

The blonde replies, 'Shut up! You're next!'

***

An old hillbilly farmer had a wife who nagged him unmercifully. From morning 'til night she was always complaining about something. The only time he got any relief was when he was out ploughing with his old mule. He tried to plough a lot!

One day, when he was ploughing, his wife brought him lunch in the field. He drove the old mule into the shade, sat down on a stump and began to eat his lunch. Immediately his wife began haranguing him; on and on it went.

All of a sudden, the old mule lashed out with both hind feet, caught her smack in the back of the head and killed her on the spot.

At the funeral several days later, the minister noticed something rather odd. When a female mourner approached the old farmer, he would listen for a minute and then nod his head in agreement. But when a male mourner approached, he'd listen for a minute, then shake his head in disagreement. This was so consistent, the minister decided to ask the old farmer about it.

So after the funeral, the minister spoke to the old farmer and asked why he nodded his head and agreed with the women, but always shook his head and disagreed with the men.

The old farmer said, 'Well, the women would come up and say something about how nice my wife looked, or how pretty her dress was, so I'd nod my head in agreement.'

'And what about the men?' the minister asked.

'They wanted to know if the mule was for sale.'

***

An Amish boy and his father had come into the city from their isolated farming community and were visiting a city mall. They were amazed by almost everything they saw, but especially by two shiny, silver walls that could move apart and then slide back together again. The boy asked, 'What is this thing, Father?'

The father, having never seen an elevator before, responded, 'Son, I have never seen anything like this in my life. I don't know what it is.'

While the boy and his father were watching with amazement, a fat old lady in a wheelchair rolled up to the moving walls and pressed a button. The walls opened and the lady rolled between them into a small room. The walls closed and the boy and his father watched the small circular numbers above the wall light up sequentially. They continued to watch until it reached the last number and then the numbers began to light in the reverse order.

Finally, the walls opened again and a gorgeous, voluptuous young blonde stepped out. The father, not taking his eyes off the young woman, said quietly to his son, 'Go get your mother as quick as you can!'

***

Two gay men are walking through a zoo. They come across the gorillas and, after a while, they notice that the male gorilla has a massive erection.

The gay men are fascinated by this. One of the men just can't bear it any longer and he reaches into the cage to touch it. The gorilla grabs him, drags him into the cage and mates with him for six hours nonstop.

When he's done, the gorilla throws the man out of the cage. An ambulance is called and the man is taken away to hospital. A few days later his friend visits him in hospital and asks, 'Are you hurt?'

'Am I *hurt*?' he shouts. 'Wouldn't you be? He hasn't called, he hasn't written . . .'

***

On hearing that her elderly grandfather had just passed away, Katie went straight to her grandparents' house to visit her 95-year-old grandmother to comfort her. When she asked how her grandfather had died, her grandmother replied, 'He had a heart attack while we were making love on Sunday morning.'

Horrified, Katie told her grandmother that two people, nearly 100 years old and having sex would surely be asking for trouble.

'Oh no, my dear,' replied granny. 'Many years ago, realising our advanced age, we figured out the best time to do it was when the church bells would start to ring. It was just the right rhythm. Nice and slow and even. Nothing too strenuous, simply in on the ding and out on the dong.'

Granny paused, wiped away a tear and then continued, 'And if that damned ice-cream truck hadn't come along, he'd still be alive today!'

***

A middle-aged woman had a heart attack and was taken to the hospital. While on the operating table she had a near-death experience. Seeing God, she asked, 'Is my time up?' God said, 'No, you have another forty years, two months and eight days to live.'

Upon recovery, the woman decided to stay in the hospital and have a face-lift, liposuction and a tummy tuck. She even had someone come in and change her hair colour. Since she had so much more time to live, she figured she might as well make the most of it.

After her last operation, she was released from hospital. While crossing the street on her way home, she was killed by an ambulance.

Arriving in front of God, she angrily demanded, 'I thought you said I had another forty years? Why didn't you pull me from out of the path of the ambulance?'

God replied, 'I didn't recognise you.'

***

BILL GATES' ADVICE TO HIGH-SCHOOL STUDENTS:

1. Life is not fair – get used to it.
2. The world won't care about your self-esteem. The world will expect you to accomplish something *before* you feel good about yourself.
3. You will *not* make $40 000 a year right out of high school. You won't be vice-president with a car phone until you earn both.

4. If you think your teacher is tough, wait 'til you get a boss.

5. Flipping hamburgers is not beneath your dignity. Your grandparents had a different word for burger-flipping – they called it opportunity.

6. If you mess up, it's not your parents' fault, so don't whine about your mistakes, learn from them.

7. Before you were born, your parents weren't as boring as they are now. They got that way from paying your bills, cleaning your clothes and listening to you talk about how cool you are. So before you save the rainforest from the parasites of your parents' generation, try delousing the closet in your own room.

8. Your school may have done away with winners and losers, but life has not. In some schools they have abolished failing grades and they'll give you as many times as you want to get the right answer. This doesn't bear the slightest resemblance to *anything* in real life.

9. Life is not divided into semesters. You don't get summers off and very few employers are interested in helping you find yourself. Do that in your own time!

10. Television is *not* real life. In real life people actually have to leave the coffee shop and go to jobs.

11. Be nice to nerds. Chances are you'll end up working for one.

***

After hearing that one of the patients in a mental hospital had saved another from a suicide attempt by pulling him out of a bathtub, the director reviewed the rescuer's file and called him into his office.

'Mr James, your records and your heroic behaviour indicate that you're ready to go home. I'm only sorry that the man you saved later killed himself with a rope around his neck.'

'Oh, he didn't kill himself,' Mr James replied, 'I hung him up to dry.'

***

There was a zebra who had lived her entire life in a zoo and was getting on in age, so the zookeeper decided as a treat that she could spend her final years in bliss on a farm. The zebra was so excited, she got to see this huge space with green grass and hills and trees and all these strange animals. She saw a big, fat, weird-looking brown thing and ran up to it all excited. 'Hi, I'm a zebra! What are you?'

'I'm a cow.'

'Right, right. What do you do?'

'I make milk for the farmer.'

'Cool.'

The zebra then saw this funny-looking little white thing and ran over to it. 'Hi, I'm a zebra. What are you?'

'I'm a chicken.'

'Oh right. What do you do?'

'I make eggs for the farmer.'

'Right, great. See you around.'

The zebra then saw this very handsome beast that looked almost exactly like her without the stripes. She ran over to it and said, 'Hi, I'm a zebra. What are you?'

'I'm a stallion,' said the stallion.

'Wow!' said the zebra. 'What do you do?'

'Take off your pyjamas, darling, and I'll show you.'

***

Happiness is like peeing in your pants. Everyone can see it, but only you can feel the warmth.

***

THE SENILITY PRAYER

God, grant me the senility to forget the people I never liked anyway, the good fortune to run into the ones I do and the eyesight to tell the difference.

***

When the surgeon came to see his blonde patient on the day after her operation, she asked him somewhat hesitantly just how long it would be before she could resume her sex life.

'Uh, I haven't really thought about it,' replied the stunned surgeon. 'You're the first one ever to ask that after a tonsillectomy.'

***

Husband's note on the fridge to his wife: 'Someone from the Guyna Colleges called. They said the Pabst beer is normal. I didn't know you liked beer.'

***

A chicken and an egg are lying in bed. The chicken is leaning against the headboard smoking a cigarette with a satisfied smile on its face. The egg, looking a bit pissed off, grabs the sheet and rolls over and says, 'Well, I guess we finally answered *that* question!'

***

After years of frustration, the Smiths had no children and decided to use a proxy father to start their family. On the day the proxy father was to arrive, Mr Smith kissed his wife and said, 'I'm off. The man should be here soon.'

Half an hour later, just by chance, a door-to-door baby photographer rang the doorbell, hoping to make a sale. 'Good morning, madam. You don't know me, but I've come to –'

'Oh, no need to explain. I've been expecting you,' Mrs Smith cut in.

'Really?' the photographer asked. 'Well, good! I've made a specialty of babies.'

'That's what my husband and I had hoped. Please come in and have a seat. Just where do we start?' asked Mrs Smith, blushing.

'Leave everything to me. I usually try two in the bathtub, one on the couch and perhaps a couple on the bed. I also like to try some outdoors, like on the swing or just on the grass. Towards the end of the day it's nice to use some favourite toys – you understand what I'm saying, don't you?'

'Bathtub, living-room floor, *toys*! No wonder it didn't work for Harry and me.'

'Well, madam, none of us can guarantee a good one every time. But if we try several different positions and I shoot from six or seven angles, I'm sure you'll be pleased with the results.'

'I hope we can get this over with quickly,' gasped Mrs Smith.

'Madam, in my line of work, a man must take his time. I'd love to be in and out in five minutes, but you'd be disappointed with that, I'm sure.'

'Don't I know!' Mrs Smith exclaimed, tugging at her handkerchief.

'And these twins turned out exceptionally well when you consider their mother was so difficult to work with.' The photographer handed Mrs Smith the picture.

'She was difficult?' asked Mrs Smith.

'Yes, I'm afraid so. I finally had to take her to the park to get the job done right. People were crowding around four and five deep, trying to get a look.'

'Four and five deep?' asked Mrs Smith, eyes wide in amazement.

'Yes,' the photographer said, 'and for more than three hours, too. The mother was constantly squealing and yelling. I could hardly concentrate. The darkness approached and I began to rush my shots. Finally, when the squirrels began nibbling on my equipment, I just packed it all in.'

Mrs Smith leaned forward. 'You mean they actually chewed on your, eh, equipment?'

'That's right. Well, madam, if you're ready, I'll set

up my tripod so that we can get to work.'

'Tripod?' Mrs Smith looked extremely worried now.

'Oh yes. I have to use a tripod to rest my Canon on. It's much too big for me to hold steady while I'm shooting. Madam? Madam? Good Lord, she's fainted!'

***

A rookie police officer was out for his first ride in a cruiser with an experienced partner. A call came in telling them to disperse some people who were loitering.

The officers drove to the street and observed a small crowd standing on a corner. The rookie rolled down his window and said, 'Let's get off that corner, people.'

A few glances, but no one moved, so he barked again, 'Let's get off that corner – *now!*'

Intimidated, the group of people began to leave, casting puzzled stares in his direction.

Proud of his first official act, the young policeman turned to his partner and asked, 'Well, how did I do?'

'Pretty good,' laughed his partner, 'especially since this is a bus stop.'

***

A doctor of psychology was doing his normal morning rounds, and he entered a patient's room to find his patient sitting on the floor, sawing at a piece of wood with the side of his hand. Meanwhile, another patient was in the room, hanging from the ceiling by his feet. The doctor asked his patient what he was doing, sitting on the floor.

The patient replied in an irritated fashion, 'Can't you see I'm sawing this piece of wood in half?'

The doctor inquired, 'And what is the fellow hanging from the ceiling doing?'

'Oh, he's my friend, but he's a little crazy. He thinks he's a light bulb.'

The doctor asked, 'If he's your friend, don't you think you should get him down from there before he hurts himself?'

'What? And work in the dark?'

***

Two elderly ladies from the old country were sitting on a park bench. Ruschke asked Tschotchke, 'And how is your son?'

'Ah, 'e is a fine man. A doctor, a mansion in the best street, three cars . . . And how is your son doing?'

Ruschke lowered her eyes, 'Well, to tell you the truth, not so well. He is a homosexual.'

'Oh, darling! I am so sorry for you!'

Ruschke perked up. 'Oh, don't be. He lives with a doctor, in a mansion, with three cars!'

***

A magician worked on a cruise ship. The audience was different each week, so the magician did the same tricks over and over again.

There was one problem. The captain's parrot saw the shows each week and began to understand how the magician did every trick. Once he understood, he started shouting in the middle of the show. 'Look, it's not the same hat!' Or, 'Look, he's hiding the flowers under the table!' Or, 'Hey, why are all the cards the ace of spades?'

The magician was furious but couldn't do anything. It was, after all, the captain's parrot. Then, unfortunately, the ship sank.

The magician found himself on a piece of wood in the middle of the ocean with, as fate would have it, the parrot. They stared at each other with hatred, but did not utter a word. This went on for a day, and then another.

Finally, on the third day, the parrot could not hold

back and said, 'Okay, I give up. Where's the fucking ship?'

***

A mortician was working late one night. It was his job to examine the dead bodies before they were sent off to be buried or cremated. As he examined the body of Mr Schwartz, who was about to be cremated, he made an amazing discovery. Schwartz had the longest private part he had ever seen!

'I'm sorry, Mr Schwartz,' said the mortician, 'but I can't send you off to be cremated with a tremendously huge private part like this. It has to be saved for posterity.'

And with that the coroner used his tools to remove the dead man's schlong. The coroner stuffed his prize into a briefcase and took it home.

The first person he showed was his wife. 'I have something to show you that you won't believe,' he said, and opened his briefcase.

'Oh my God!' she screamed, 'Schwartz is dead!'

***

A woman was in bed with her lover when she heard her husband opening the front door.

'Hurry!' she said, 'Stand in the corner!' She quickly rubbed baby oil all over him and then dusted him with talcum powder. 'Don't move until I tell you to,' she whispered. 'Just pretend you're a statue.'

'What's this, honey?' the husband inquired as he entered the room.

'Oh, it's just a statue,' she replied. 'The Smiths bought one for their bedroom. I liked it so much, I got one for us, too.'

No more was said about the statue, not even later when that night when they went to sleep. Around two in the morning the husband got out of bed, went to the kitchen and returned a little while later with a sandwich and a glass of milk.

'Here,' he said to the statue. 'Eat something. I stood like an idiot at the Smiths' for three days, and nobody offered me so much as a glass of water.'

★★★

A man walks into a bar one night and asks for a beer. 'Certainly, sir,' the barman replies. 'That'll be one cent.'

'One cent!' exclaims the guy. The barman nods. So the guy glances over at the menu and he asks, 'Could I have a nice juicy T-bone steak, with chips, peas and a fried egg?'

'Certainly sir,' replies the bartender, 'but all that comes to real money.'

'How much money?' inquires the guy.

'Four cents,' he replies.

'Four cents!' exclaims the guy. 'Where's the guy who owns this place?'

'Upstairs with my wife.'

'What's he doing with your wife?'

The bartender replies, 'Same as what I'm doing to his business.'

***

Jake was dying. His wife Becky was maintaining a candlelight vigil by his side. She held his fragile hand, tears running down her face. Her praying roused him from his slumber. He looked up and his pale lips began to move slightly.

'My darling Beck,' he whispered.

'Hush, my love,' she said. 'Rest. Shhh, don't talk.'

He was insistent. 'Becky,' he said in his tired voice, 'I have something I must confess to you.'

'There's nothing to confess,' replied the weeping Becky. 'Everything's all right, go to sleep.'

'No, No, I must die in peace, Becky. I . . . I slept with your sister, your best friend, her best friend and your mother!'

'I know,' Becky whispered softly. 'That's why I poisoned you.'

***

A cabbie picks up a nun. She gets into the cab and the cab driver won't stop staring at her. She asks him why he is staring and he replies, 'I have a question to ask you but I don't want to offend you.'

She answers, 'My dear son, you cannot offend me. When you're a nun, you get a chance to see and hear just about everything. I'm sure that there's nothing you could say or ask that I would find offensive.'

The cabbie says, 'Well, I've always had a fantasy to have a nun kiss me.'

She replies, 'Well, let's see what we can do about that. First, you have to be single and second, you must be Catholic.'

The cab driver becomes very excited and says, 'Yes, I am single and I'm Catholic too!'

'Okay,' the nun says, 'pull into the next alley.'

He does and the nun fulfils his fantasy with a kiss that would make a hooker blush.

But when he gets back on the road, the cab driver starts crying.

'My dear child,' says the nun, 'why are you crying?'

He sobs, 'Forgive me sister, but I have sinned. I lied.

I must confess. I'm married and I'm Jewish.'

The nun says, 'That's okay. My name is Frank and I'm going to a Halloween party.'

***

When I stopped the bus to pick up Chris for preschool, I noticed an older woman hugging him as he left the house. 'Is that your grandmother,' I asked.

'Yes,' Chris said, 'she's come to visit us for Christmas.'

'How nice,' I said, 'where does she live?'

'At the airport,' Chris replied. 'Whenever we want her, we just go out there and get her.'

***

Jack and Betty are celebrating their fiftieth wedding anniversary when Jack asks his wife, 'Betty, have you ever cheated on me?'

Betty replies, 'Oh Jack, why would you ask such a question now? You don't want to know that.'

'Yes, Betty, I really want to know. Please.'

'Well then,' replies Betty, giving in, 'I'm afraid so. Three times.'

'Three! Well, when were they?' he asks.

'Well, Jack, remember when you were thirty-five

years old and you really, really wanted to start a business on your own, and no bank would give you a loan? But suddenly one day the bank president himself came over to the house and signed the loan papers, no questions asked?'

'Oh, Betty, you did that for me? I guess I can't be too upset about that. When was number two?'

'Well, Jack, remember when you had that last heart attack and you really, really needed that very risky operation that no surgeon was willing to perform? And remember how Dr Baker suddenly came all the way up here to perform the surgery himself?'

'Betty, that you should do such a thing for me, to save my life. To do such a thing, you must truly love me. How could any man be upset with that? And so, finally, when was number three?'

'Well Jack, remember a few years ago, when you really, really wanted to be the president of the golf club – and you were twenty-seven votes short?'

***

There are only two reasons to worry. Either you're successful or you're not successful. And if you're successful, there's nothing to worry about.

If you're not successful, there are only two things to worry about. Your health is either good or you're sick. And if your health is good, there's nothing to worry about.

And if you're sick, there are only two things to worry about. You're either going to get well, or you're going to die. If you're going to get well, there's nothing to worry about.

If you're not going to get well, there's only two things to worry about. You're either going to heaven or you're not going to heaven. If you're going to heaven, there's nothing to worry about.

And if you're going to the other place, you'll be so doggone busy shaking hands with old friends you won't have time to worry.

So why worry?

✶✶✶

John Howard has made the startling claim that incoming asylum seekers to Australia were responsible for the assassination of US President John F. Kennedy in 1963.

The claim comes as another group of about 160 Afghan refugees sails from Indonesia towards the Australian coast.

'Details are sketchy at the moment, but I have it on very good authority that a large proportion of this next wave of illegals were implicated in the murder of the American President. The question has to be asked: do we want these kinds of people in Australia?' the Prime Minister said.

Mr Howard said that he would not compromise security protocol by revealing the exact origin of the information, but he mentioned a video showing a shadowy figure on a grassy knoll that bore a close resemblance to all of the boat people.

'I haven't see the video, but I am told that it is very conclusive. There is almost no doubt that these boat people killed one of the greatest statesmen the world has seen,' he said. 'I can clearly remember the assassination and the huge impact it had on the free world. I am angered and disgusted that these murderers would seek refuge in our country.'

The Immigration Minister, Philip Ruddock, called on his critics to consider these latest claims carefully. 'This new evidence is very, very serious. If it's true, and I haven't seen the video, then we must renew our vigour in keeping these law-breakers out of our beautiful country. We can't afford to let these people infect us with their hatred and evil,' he said.

✳✳✳

A doctor had the reputation of helping couples increase the joy in their sex life, but always promised not to take a case if he felt he could not help them.

The Browns came to see the doctor, and he gave them thorough physical examinations, psychological examinations and various tests and then concluded, 'Yes, I am happy to say that I believe I can help you. On your way home from my office stop at the grocery store and buy some grapes and some doughnuts. Go home, take off your clothes and you, sir, roll the grapes across the floor until you make a bullseye in your wife's love canal. Then, on hands and knees, you must crawl to her like a leopard and retrieve the grape using only your tongue.

'Next, madam, you must take the doughnuts and from across the room, toss them at your husband until you make a ringer around his love pole. Then, like a lioness, you must crawl to him and consume the doughnut.'

The couple went home and their sex life became more and more wonderful. They told their friends, Mr and Mrs Green, that they should see the good doctor.

The doctor greeted the Greens and said he would not take the case unless he felt he could help them. So he conducted the physical examinations and the same battery of tests. Then he told the Greens the bad news. 'I cannot help you, so I will not take your money. I believe your sex life is as good as it will ever be. I cannot help.'

The Greens pleaded with him, saying, 'You helped our friends the Browns. Now, please, please help us!'

'Well, all right,' the doctor said. 'On your way home from the office, stop at the grocery store and buy some apples and a box of Cheerios . . .'

***

A guy walks into a bar with his pet monkey. He orders a drink and while he's drinking the monkey jumps all around the place. The monkey grabs some olives off the bar and eats them, then jumps onto the pool table, grabs one of the billiard balls, sticks it in his mouth and, to everyone's amazement, somehow swallows it whole.

The bartender screams at the guy, 'Did you see what your monkey just did?'

The guy says, 'No, what?'

'He just ate the cue ball off my pool table – whole!'

'Yeah, that doesn't surprise me,' replies the guy. 'He eats everything in sight, the little bastard. Sorry, I'll pay for the cue ball and stuff.'

He finishes his drink, pays his bill, pays for the stuff the monkey ate, then leaves.

Two weeks later he's in the bar again, and has his monkey with him. He orders a drink and the monkey

THE WORLD JOKE BOOK

starts running around the bar again. While the man is finishing his drink, the monkey finds a maraschino cherry on the bar. He grabs it, sticks it up his bum, pulls it out, and eats it.

The bartender is disgusted. 'Did you see what your monkey did now?' he asks.

'No, what?' replies the guy.

'Well, he stuck a maraschino cherry up his bum, pulled it out and ate it!' says the bartender.

'Yeah, that doesn't surprise me,' replies the guy. 'He still eats everything in sight, but ever since he swallowed that cue ball, he measures everything first.'

***

Several cannibals were recently hired by a big corporation. 'You are all part of our team now,' said the HR rep during the welcoming briefing. 'You get all the usual benefits and you can go to the cafeteria for something to eat, but please don't eat any of the other employees.'

The cannibals promised.

Four weeks later, their boss remarked, 'You're all working very hard and I'm satisfied with you. However, one of our secretaries has disappeared. Do any of you know what happened to her?'

The cannibals all shook their heads.

After the boss had left, the leader of the cannibals said to the others, 'Which one of you idiots ate the secretary?'

A hand was raised hesitantly. The leader of the cannibals continued, 'You fool! For four weeks we've been eating managers and no one noticed anything. Then you had to go and eat a secretary!'

***

A 'modern' Islamic couple, preparing for a religious wedding, meets with their mullah for counselling. The mullah asks if they have any last questions before they leave.

The man asks, 'We realise it is tradition in Islam for men to dance with men, and women to dance with women. But, at our wedding reception, we'd like your permission to dance together.'

'Absolutely not,' says the mullah. 'It is immoral. Men and women always dance separately.'

'So after the ceremony I can't even dance with my own wife?'

'No,' answered the mullah. 'It is forbidden in Islam.'

'Well, okay,' says the man, 'What about sex? Can we finally have sex?'

'Of course,' replies the mullah. '*Alla ho Akber*! Sex is okay within marriage to have children!'

'What about different positions?' asks the man.

'No problem,' said the mullah.

'Woman on top?' the man asks.

'Sure, go for it,' says the mullah.

'Doggy style?'

'Sure!'

'On the kitchen table?'

Yes, yes! *Alla ho Akber*!'

'Can we do it with all my four wives together on rubber sheets with a bottle of hot oil, a couple of vibrators, leather harnesses, a bucket of honey and a porno video?'

'You may indeed.'

'Can we do it standing up?'

'No,' says the mullah.

'Why not?' asks the man.

'Because that could lead to dancing.'

***

The owner of a well-established, very well-respected, third-generation family-owned garment business met with his board of directors. Due to the recession, business had been very bad. Sales were down and costs were up.

The owner and his wife had poured every penny they had back into the business in the hope of keeping it afloat, but still things looked very precarious.

The board of directors offered no solutions, so as a last resort the owner decided to seek advice from his rabbi. He poured out the story, with tears running down his face, about the three generations of family sacrifice that had gone into building this once-thriving business. He ended by asking plaintively, 'So rabbi, what should I do?'

The rabbi, a very old and wise man, said nothing for a long time and then quietly intoned, 'So here's vat I vant you to do. Get a beach chair and a Bible. Put dem in your car. Drive down to the water's edge. Sit in dis beach chair vit the Bible open on your lap and let the vind from the sea riffle the pages of the open Bible . . .'

'Yes, rabbi, yes?' encouraged the business owner, completely at a loss for any better ideas.

'. . . and ven the pages stop turning in the vind I vant you should look down at dat page and read the first thing you see. And dat vill be vat you must do,' pronounced the rabbi with great certainty.

A year passes, and the business owner returns to pay a visit to the rabbi. The man is wearing a brand new $2000 hand-made Italian suit and his wife looks stunning in her new mink coat. They have driven to see the rabbi in their new BMW 740i sedan. The business owner discreetly pulls the rabbi aside and slips an envelope to him, stuffed with money.

'Rabbi,' he whispers, 'this is a little something for you and your wife, and there's also a cheque for $25 000 towards your congregation.'

The rabbi, although very old, remembered the man. 'So, you did vat I said?'

'Absolutely!'

'You vent to the beach?'

'Yes, I did.'

'And you sat in the beach chair vit the Bible open on your lap?'

'Yes, rabbi, absolutely!'

'And you let the vind riffle through the pages until they stopped?'

'Absolutely!'

'And vat vere the first words that you read on that page?'

'Chapter Eleven.'

***

Federal Aviation Agency,
Washington DC

Dear sirs,

Since men of the Muslim religion are not allowed to look at naked women, we should replace all of our female flight attendants with strippers. Muslims would be afraid to get on the planes for fear of seeing a naked woman and, of course, every businessman in this country would start flying again in the hope of seeing a naked woman.

We would have no more hijackings, and the airline industry would have record sales.

Now why didn't Bush think of this? Why do I still have to do everything myself?

Sincerely,

Bill Clinton

★★★

A married couple are driving along a highway doing 60 km/h, the wife behind the wheel. Her husband suddenly looks over at her and says, 'Honey, I know we've been married for twenty years, but I want a divorce.'

The wife says nothing but slowly increases the speed to 70km/h.

He then says, 'I don't want you to try to talk me out of it, because I've been having an affair with your best friend and she's a better lover than you are.'

Again the wife stays quiet but speeds up as her anger increases.

'I want the house,' he insists, pressing his luck.

The wife speeds up to 80km/h.

He then says, 'I want the car as well,' but she just drives faster and faster. By now she's up to 90km/h.

'All right,' he says, 'I want the bank accounts and all the credit cards too.'

The wife slowly starts to veer towards a bridge overpass piling.

This makes him a bit nervous, so he says, 'Isn't there anything you want?'

The wife says, 'No, I've got everything I need.'

'Oh really!' he says. 'So what have you got?'

Just before they slam into the water at 100km/h, the wife smiles and says, 'The airbag.'

***

RANDOM THOUGHTS:

Food has replaced sex in my life. Now, even I can't get into my own pants.

Marriage changes passion . . . Suddenly you're in bed with a relative.

I saw a woman wearing a T-shirt with 'Guess' on it. So I said, 'Implants?'

Sign in a Chinese pet store, 'Buy one dog, get one flea'.

I got a sweater for Christmas. I really wanted a screamer or a moaner.

If flying is so safe, why do they call the airport the terminal?

I don't approve of political jokes; I've seen too many of them get elected.

Why is it that most nudists are people you don't want to see naked?

***

A sales rep, an administration clerk and their manager are walking to lunch when they find an antique oil lamp. They rub it and a genie comes out in a puff of smoke.

The genie says, 'I usually grant three wishes, so I'll give each of you just one.'

'Me first! Me first!' says the administration clerk. 'I want to be in the Bahamas, driving a speedboat, without a care in the world.' *Poof*! She's gone.

'Me next! Me next!' says the astonished sales rep. 'I want to be in Hawaii, relaxing on the beach with my personal masseuse, an endless supply of pina coladas and the love of my life.' *Poof!* He's gone.

'Okay, you're next,' the genie says to the manager.

The manager says, 'I want those two back in the office after lunch.'

Moral of the story: Always let the boss have the first say.

***

The Australian Government has announced that it is changing its emblem to a condom.

Why? Because a condom more clearly reflects the government's political stance. That is, a condom stands up to inflation, halts recreational production, destroys the next generation, protects a bunch of prints and gives you a sense of security while you're actually getting screwed.

***

Two Indians and a hillbilly were walking in the woods when all of a sudden one of the Indians ran up a hill to the mouth of a small cave. 'Wooooo! Wooooo! Wooooo!' he called into the cave and then he listened very closely until he heard a reply: 'Wooooo! Wooooo! Wooooo!'

He tore off his clothes and ran into the cave.

The hillbilly was puzzled and asked the other Indian what that was all about. Was the other Indian crazy?

'No,' said the Indian. 'It's our custom during the mating season. When Indian men see a cave, they holler, "Wooooo! Wooooo! Wooooo!" into the opening. If they get an answer back, it means there's a girl in there waiting to mate.'

Just then they saw another cave. The second Indian ran up to the opening of the cave, stopped and hollered, 'Wooooo! Wooooo! Wooooo!'

Immediately, there was an answer, 'Wooooo! Wooooo! Wooooo!' from deep inside the cave. He tore off his clothes and ran into the cave.

The hillbilly wandered around alone for a while and then he came upon a great big cave. As he looked in amazement at the size of the opening, he was thinking, 'Oh boy! Look at the size of this cave! It is bigger than those the Indians found. There must be some really big, fine women in this cave!' He stood in front of the opening and hollered with all his might. 'Wooooo! Wooooo! Wooooo!' He grinned and closed his eyes in anticipation, and then he heard the answering call, 'WOOOOOOO! WOOOOOOOO! WOOOOO-OO!' With a gleam in his eyes and a smile on his face, he raced into the cave tearing off his clothes as he ran.

The following day the newspaper headline read, NAKED HILLBILLY RUN OVER BY FREIGHT TRAIN.

***

Two Louisiana alligators are sitting on the edge of a swamp. The smaller one turns to the bigger one and says, 'I don't understand how you can be so much bigger than me. We're the same age, we were the same size as kids. I just don't get it.'

'Well,' says the bigger alligator, 'what have you been eating?'

'Lawyers, same as you,' replies the smaller alligator.

'Hmmm. Well, where do you catch 'em?'

'Down at that law firm on the edge of the swamp.'

'Same here. Hmmm. How do you catch 'em?'

'Well, crawl under a BMW and wait for someone to unlock the door. Then I jump out, bite 'em, shake the crap out of 'em and then eat 'em!'

Ah!' says the bigger alligator. 'I think I see your problem. See, by the time you get done shaking the crap out of a lawyer, there's nothing left but his lips and a briefcase.'

***

'Good morning, ma'am, I've come to ask for donations

for the Salvation Army,' said the man in the bright-red Santa suit to the woman who opened the door wearing nothing but panties and a see-through negligee.

'How do I know that?' the young woman replied. 'How do I know you're really with the Salvation Army? How do I know you aren't some sex fiend who has come to take advantage of a poor defenceless female who's all alone in her house – and will be until 5.30 p.m. this evening?'

***

Two missionaries in Africa were apprehended by a tribe of very hostile cannibals who put them in a large pot of water, built a huge fire under it, and left them there. A few minutes later, one of the missionaries started to laugh uncontrollably.

The other missionary couldn't believe it. He said, 'What's wrong with you? We're being boiled alive! They're gonna eat us! What could possibly be funny at a time like this?'

The other missionary said, 'I just peed in the soup!'

***

There were two ministers who met each Sunday morning riding to their particular church. They both enjoyed riding the bikes and talking. Then one Sunday one of the ministers was walking.

'My, what happened to your bike?' asked the other.

'Can you believe that someone in my congregation stole it?'

'No!' Then an idea struck him. 'You want to know how to get your bike back?'

'Yeah.'

'Give a fire-and-brimstone sermon on the Ten Commandments today and when you get to the part about thou shall not steal, just look at the congregation and see who looks guilty.'

Well, the next Sunday the minister came riding up on his bike.

'Hey, I see my suggestion worked!' said the other minister.

'Well, sort of. I was going along real good on the Ten Commandments and when I got to the part about adultery, I remembered where I left the bike.'

★★★

Three Kiwis and three Aussies are travelling by train to a conference. At the station, the three Aussies each buy tickets and watch as the three Kiwis buy only a single ticket.

'How are three people going to travel on only one ticket?' asks an Aussie.

'Watch and you'll see,' answers a Kiwi.

They all board the train. The Aussies take their respective seats, but all three Kiwis cram into a bathroom and close the door behind them.

Shortly after the train has departed, the conductor comes around collecting tickets. He knocks on the bathroom door and says, 'Ticket, please.' The door opens just a crack and a single arm emerges with a ticket in hand. The conductor takes it and moves on.

The Aussies see this and agree it's quite a clever idea. So after the conference, the Aussies decide to copy the Kiwis on the return trip and save some money. When they get to the station, they buy a single ticket for the return trip. To their astonishment, the Kiwis don't buy a ticket at all.

'How are you going to travel without a ticket?' asks one perplexed Aussie.

'Watch and you'll see,' answers a Kiwi.

When they board the train the three Aussies cram into a bathroom and the three Kiwis cram into another one nearby. The train departs. Shortly afterwards, one of the Kiwis leaves his bathroom and walks over to the bathroom where the Aussies are hiding. He knocks on the door and says, 'Ticket, please.'

***

Officers at a military installation were being lectured about a new computer. The training officer said the computer was able to withstand nuclear and chemical attacks.

Suddenly, he saw that one of the officers had a cup of coffee and yelled, 'There will be no eating or drinking in this room! You'll have to get rid of that coffee.'

The officer said meekly, 'Sure, but why?'

'Because a coffee spill could ruin the keyboard.'

***

Bob the builder was going through a house he had just built with the woman who owned it. She was telling him what colour to paint each room. They went into the first room and she said, 'I want this room to be painted a light blue.'

The builder went to the front door and yelled, '*Green side up!*'

When he went back into the house, she told him the next room was to be bright red.

The builder went to the front door and yelled, '*Green side up!*'

When he went back into the house, she told him that the next room was to be tan.

The builder went to the front door and yelled, 'Green side up!'

When he came back, the lady was pretty curious, so she asked him, 'I keep telling you colours, but you go out the front and yell green side up. What is that for?'

The builder said, 'Oh, don't worry about that. I've got a couple of Aussies laying the turf out front.'

***

Trev, a New Zealander, landed at Heathrow to watch the All Blacks and was not feeling well, so he decided to see a doctor. 'Hey, doc, I don't feel so good, ey,' said Trev.

The doctor gave him a thorough examination and informed Trev that he had prostate problems and that the only cure was testicular removal.

'No way, doc,' replied Trev. 'I'm gitting a second opinion, ey!'

The second pommy doctor gave Trev the same diagnosis and also advised him that testicular removal was the only cure. Not surprisingly, Trev refused the treatment.

Trev was devastated but, with only hours to go before the All Blacks' opening game, he found an expat Kiwi doctor and decided to get one last opinion from someone he could trust. The Kiwi doctor examined and him and said, 'Trev, you huv prostate suckness, ey.'

'What's the cure thin, doc, ey?' asked Trev, hoping for a different answer.

'Wull, Trev,' said the Kiwi doctor, 'wi're gonna huv to cut off your balls.'

'Phew, thunk God for thut!' said Trev. 'Those pommy bastards wanted to take my test tickets off me!'

***

One of the city's top cardiac specialists died. At his funeral, the coffin was placed in front of a huge mock-up of a heart made up of red flowers.

When the pastor finished with his sermon, and after everyone said their goodbyes, the large heart opened. The coffin rolled inside and the heart closed again.

At that moment, one of the mourners burst into a fit of laughter. Irritated by his insensitivity, the guy next to him asked, 'Why are you laughing?'

'I was just thinking about my own funeral,' the man replied. 'I'm a gynaecologist.'

***

A woman stopped by unannounced at her recently married son's house. She rang the doorbell and walked in. She was shocked to see her daughter-in-law lying on the couch, totally naked. Soft music was playing and the aroma of perfume filled the room.

'What are you doing?' she asked.

'I'm waiting for my husband to come home from work,' the daughter-in-law said. 'I'm wearing my love dress.'

'Love dress? But you're naked!' said the mother-in-law.

'My husband loves me to wear this dress,' she explained. 'It excites him no end. Every time he sees me in this dress, he instantly becomes romantic and ravages me for hours on end. He can't get enough of me.'

The mother-in-law left. When she got home, she undressed, showered, put on her best perfume, dimmed the lights, put on a romantic CD and lay on the couch waiting for her husband to arrive.

Finally her husband came home. He walked in and saw her lying there provocatively. 'What are you doing?' he asked.

'This is my love dress,' she whispered, sensually.

'Needs ironing,' he said.

***

Four Catholic ladies are having coffee together, discussing how important their children are.

The first one tells her friends, 'My son is a priest. When he walks into a room, everyone calls him "Father".'

The second woman says, 'Well, my son is a bishop. Whenever he walks into a room, people say "Your Grace".'

The third woman says smugly, 'Well, not to put you down, but my son is a cardinal. Whenever he walks into a room, people say "Your Eminence".'

The fourth Catholic woman sips her coffee in silence. The first three women give her a subtle 'Well . . . ?'

She replies, 'My son is a gorgeous, 6ft 2-inch, hard bodied, well-hung male stripper. Whenever he walks into a room, women say "Oh my God!"'

★★★

Bill Clinton, Al Gore and George W. Bush were set to face a firing squad in a small Central American country. Clinton was the first one placed against the wall and just before the order was given he yelled out, 'Earthquake!' The firing squad fell into a panic and Clinton jumped over the wall and escaped in the confusion.

Gore was the second one placed against the wall. The

squad was reassembled and Gore pondered what he had just witnessed. Just before the order was given, he yelled out, 'Tornado!' Again the squad fell apart and Gore slipped over the wall.

The last person, Bush, was placed against the wall. He was thinking. 'I see the pattern here, just scream out something about a disaster and hop over the wall.'

He confidently refused the blindfold as the firing squad was assembled. As the rifles were raised in his direction, he grinned from ear to ear and yelled, 'Fire!'

***

A Sunday school teacher was discussing the Ten Commandments with her five- and six-year-olds. After explaining the commandment to honour thy father and thy mother, she asked, 'Is there a commandment that teaches us how to treat our brothers and sisters?'

Without missing a beat, one little boy answered, 'Thou shall not kill'.

***

A teacher was giving a lesson on the circulation of blood. Trying to make the matter clearer, she said,

'Now, class, if I stood on my head, the blood, as you know, would run into it and I would turn red in the face.'

'Yes,' the class said.

'Then why is it that while I'm standing upright in the ordinary position, the blood doesn't run into my feet?'

A little fellow shouted, 'Cause your feet aren't empty.'

★★★

WEIRD HISTORY

Next time you're washing your hands and the water temperature isn't just how you like it, think about how things used to be. Here are some facts about the 1500s.

Most people got married in June because they took their yearly bath in May and still smelled pretty good by June. However, they were starting to smell, so brides carried a bouquet of flowers to hide their body odour.

Baths consisted of a big tub filled with hot water. The man of the house had the privilege of the nice clear water, then all the other sons and men, then the women and finally the children – last of all the babies.

By then the water was so dirty you could actually lose someone in it. Hence the saying, 'Don't throw the baby out with the bath water'.

Houses had thatched roofs – thick straw – piled high, with no wood underneath. It was the only place for animals to get warm, so all the dogs, cats and other small animals (mice, bugs) lived in the roof. When it rained it became slippery and sometimes the animals would slip and fall off the roof. Hence the saying, 'It's raining cats and dogs'.

There was nothing to stop things from falling into the house. This posed a real problem in the bedroom where bugs and other droppings could easily mess up the beds. Hence, a bed with big posts and a sheet hung over the top afforded some protection. That's how canopy beds came into existence.

The floor was dirt. Only the wealthy had something other than dirt, hence the saying 'dirt poor'.

The wealthy had slate floors that would get slippery in the winter when wet, so they spread thresh (straw) on the floor to help keep their footing. As the winter wore on, they kept adding more thresh until when you opened the door it would all start slipping outside. A piece of wood was placed in the entranceway, hence a 'threshold'.

In those old days, they cooked in the kitchen with a big kettle that always hung over the fire. Every day they lit the fire and added things to the pot. They ate mostly vegetables and did not get much meat. They would eat the stew for dinner, leaving leftovers in the pot to get cold overnight and then start over the next day. Sometimes the stew had food in it that had been there for quite a while. Hence the rhyme, 'Peas porridge hot, peas porridge cold, peas porridge in the pot nine days old'.

Sometimes they could obtain pork, which made them feel quite special. When visitors came, they would hang up their bacon to show off. It was a sign of wealth that a man 'could bring home the bacon'. They would cut off a little to share with guests and would all sit around and 'chew the fat'.

Those with money had plates made of pewter. Food with a high acid content caused some of the lead to leach into the food, causing lead poisoning and death. This happened most often with tomatoes, so for the next 400 years or so, tomatoes were considered poisonous.

Most people did not have pewter plates, but had trenchers, a piece of wood with the middle scooped out like a bowl. Often trenchers were made from stale bread that was so old and hard that they could be used for quite some time. Trenchers were never washed and a lot of times worms and mould got into the wood and old bread. After eating off wormy, mouldy trenchers, one would get 'trench mouth'.

Bread was divided according to status. Workers got the burnt bottom of the loaf, the family got the middle, and guests got the top, or 'upper crust'.

Lead cups were used to drink ale or whisky. The combination would sometimes knock them out for a couple of days. Someone walking along the road would take them for dead and prepare them for burial. They were laid out on the kitchen table for a couple of days and the family would gather around and eat and drink and wait to see if they would wake up. Hence the custom of holding a 'wake'.

England is old and small and the local folks started running out of places to bury people. So they would dig up coffins and would take the bones to a 'bone-house' and reuse the grave. When reopening these coffins, one out of twenty-five coffins were found to have scratch marks on the inside and they realised they had been burying people alive. So they thought they would tie a string on the wrist of the corpse, lead it through the coffin and up through the ground and tie it to a bell. Someone would have to sit out in the graveyard all night (the 'graveyard shift') to listen for the bell; thus, someone could be 'saved by the bell' or was considered a 'dead ringer'.

***

While visiting England, George W. Bush is invited to tea with the Queen. He asks her what her leadership philosophy is. She says that it is to surround herself with intelligent people. He asks how she knows if they're intelligent.

'I do so by asking them the right questions,' says the Queen. 'Allow me to demonstrate.'

She telephones Tony Blair and says, 'Mr Prime Minister, please answer this question. "Your mother has a child and your father has a child, and this child is not your brother or sister. Who is it?"'

Tony Blair responds, 'It's me, ma'am.'

'Correct. Thank you and goodbye sir,' says the Queen. She hangs up and says, 'Did you get that, Mr Bush?'

'Yes, ma'am. Thanks a lot. I'll definitely be using that!'

Upon returning to Washington, he decides he'd better put the Defence Secretary to the test. He summons Donald Rumsfeld to the White House and says, 'Don, I wonder if you'd mind answering a question for me?'

'Why, of course, sir. What's on your mind?'

'Uhh, your mother has a child, and your father has a child, and this child is not your brother or your sister. Who is it?'

Rumsfeld hems and haws and finally asks, 'Can I think about it and get back to you?'

Bush agrees and Rumsfeld leaves. Rumsfeld immediately calls a meeting with other senior officials, and they puzzle over the question for several hours, but nobody can come up with an answer. Finally, in desperation, Rumsfeld calls Colin Powell and explains his problem.

'Now look here, your mother has a child, and your father has a child, and this child is not your brother or your sister. Who is it?'

Powell answers immediately, 'It's me, of course, you idiot.'

Much relieved, Rumsfeld rushes back to the White House and exclaims, 'I know the answer, sir! I know who it is? It's Colin Powell!'

And Bush replies in disgust, 'Wrong, senator. It's Tony Blair.'

***

A man was constipated, so he decided to go to the doctor.

The doctor examined him and explained, 'I'm going to give your some suppositories. I'll insert one now, and then I'll give you another one for later this evening.'

Later that evening, the man asked his wife to insert the suppository. She agreed reluctantly, then put one hand on his shoulder and inserted the suppository.

Suddenly, her husband shrieked, 'Aaahhhhh!'

'What's wrong? Did I hurt you?' she asked.

'No – I just realised that the doctor had both his hands on my shoulders!'

***

DID BUSH REALLY SAY THAT?

'Drug therapies are replacing a lot of medicine as we used to know it.'

'It's one thing about insurance, that's a Washington term.'

'I think we ought to raise the age at which juveniles can have a gun.'

'If affirmative action means what I just described, what I'm for, then I'm for it.'

'Our priorities is our faith.'

'Families is where our nation finds hope, where wings take dream.'

'I am mindful not only of preserving executive powers for myself, but for predecessors as well.'

'You know I could run for governor, but I'm basically a media creation. I've never done anything. I've worked for my dad. I worked in the oil business. But that's not the kind of profile you have to have to get elected to public office.'

'When I was coming up, it was a dangerous world, and you knew exactly who they were. It was us versus them, and it was very clear who them was. Today, we are not sure who the they are, but we know they're there.'

'Redefining the role of the United States from enablers to keep the peace to enablers to keep the peace from peacekeepers is going to be an assignment.'

★★★

A Japanese doctor says, 'Medicine in my country is so advanced that we can take a kidney out of one man, put it in another, and have him looking for work in six weeks.'

A German doctor says, 'That is nothing. We can take a lung out of one person, put it in another, and have him looking for work in four weeks.'

A British doctor says, 'In my country, medicine is so advanced that we can take half a heart out of one person, put it in another, and have them both looking for work in two weeks.'

The American doctor, not to be outdone, says, 'You guys are way behind. We just took a man with no brain out of Texas, put him in the White House, and now half the country is looking for work.'

***

THE LAW:

Judge: Well, sir, I have reviewed this case and I've decided to give your wife $775 a week.
Husband: That's fair, your honour. I'll try to send her a few bucks myself.

***

Q: The youngest son, the twenty-year-old, how old is he?

***

Q: Were you present when your picture was taken?

***

Q: She had three children, right?
A: Yes.
Q: How many were boys?
A: None.
Q: Were there any girls?

***

Q: You say the stairs went down to the basement?
A: Yes.
Q: And these stairs, did they go up also?

***

Q: How was your first marriage terminated?
A: By death.
Q: And by whose death was it terminated?

***

Q: Can you describe the individual?
A: He was about medium height and had a beard.
Q: Was this a male or a female?

***

Q: Doctor, how many autopsies have you performed on dead people?
A: All my autopsies are performed on dead people.

***

Q: All your responses must be oral, okay?
A: Okay.
Q: What school did you go to?
A: Oral.

***

Q: Do you recall the time that you examined the body?
A: The autopsy started around 8.30 p.m.
Q: And Mr Dennington was dead at the time?
A: No, he was sitting on the table wondering why I was dong an autopsy on him.

***

Q: Are you qualified to give a urine sample?

***

Q: Doctor, before you performed the autopsy, did you check for pulse?

A: No.

Q: Did you check for blood pressure?

A: No.

Q: Did you check for breathing?

A: No.

Q: So, then it is possible that the patient was alive when you began the autopsy?

A: No.

Q: How can you be so sure, doctor?

A: Because his brain was sitting on my desk in a jar.

Q: But could the patient have still been alive nevertheless?

A: Yes, it is possible that he could have been alive and practising law somewhere.

***

A bloke arrives at the Pearly Gates, waiting to be admitted. St Peter is leafing through the Big Book to see if the bloke is worthy of entering. After several minutes, St Peter closes the book, furrows his brow, and says, 'I don't see that you ever did anything really great in your life. But I don't see anything bad, either. So, if you can tell me of one *really* good deed you did in your life, I'll let you in.'

The bloke thinks for a moment and says, 'Okay. Well there was this one time when I was driving down the highway and I saw a gang assaulting this poor girl. I slowed down and, sure enough, there they were, about fifty of them, torturing this woman. Infuriated, I got out of my car, grabbed a tyre lever out of my boot and walked straight up to the leader of the gang. He was a huge guy with a studded leather jacket and a chain running from his nose to his ear. As I walked up to the leader, the gang members formed a circle around me. So I ripped the leader's chain out of his face and smashed him over the head with the tyre lever. Then I turned around and yelled to the rest of them, 'Leave this poor, innocent girl alone! You're all a bunch of sick, deranged animals! Go home before I really teach you all a lesson in pain!'

St Peter, duly impressed, says, 'Wow! When did this happen?'

'Just a couple of minutes ago.'

★★★

A man and his young son are in the drugstore when the son sees the shelf of condoms and asks his father what they are. His father replies, 'Well son, those are condoms and they're for protection when you're having sex.'

The son then picks up one of the packs and asks why it has three in it. His father replies, 'Those are for high-school days. One for Friday, one for Saturday and one for Sunday.'

The son then picks up one with six condoms and asks, 'Why six?'

His father replies, 'Well son, those are for college men. Two for Friday, two for Saturday and two for Sunday.'

Then the son notices the twelve-pack of condoms and asks the same question.

His father replies, 'Son, those are for married men. One for January, one for February, one for March . . .'

***

A mafia godfather finds out that one of his underlings has screwed him for $10 million. The underling happens to be deaf, so the godfather brings along his consigliore, who knows sign language.

The godfather asks the underling, 'Where is the 10 million bucks you embezzled from me?'

The attorney, using sign language, asks the underling where the $10 million is hidden.

The underling signs back, 'I don't know what you're talking about.'

The attorney tells the godfather, 'He says he doesn't know what you're talking about.'

That's when the godfather pulls out a 9mm pistol, puts it to the underling's temple, cocks it and says, 'Ask him again!'

The attorney signs to the underline, 'He'll kill you for sure if you don't tell him!'

The underling signs back, 'Okay! You win! The money is in a brown briefcase buried behind the shed in my cousin Enzo's backyard in Queens!'

The godfather asks the attorney, 'Well, what'd he say?'

The attorney replies, 'He says you don't have the balls to pull the trigger.'

***

There are two kinds of pedestrians – the quick and the dead.

***

If quitters never win, and winners never quit, then who is the fool who said, 'Quit while you're ahead'?

***

One day God calls down to Noah and says, 'Noah, my old china, I want you to make me a new ark.'

Noah replies, 'No probs, God, my old Supreme Being. Anything you want. After all, you're the Guv.'

But God interrupts. 'Ah, but there's a catch this time, Noah. I want not just a couple of decks – I want twenty decks, one on top of the other.'

'Twenty decks!' screams Noah. 'Well okay, Big Man. Whatever you say. Should I fill it up with all the animals just like last time?'

'Yep, that's right. Well, sort of. However this time I want you to fill it up with fish,' God answers.

'Fish?' queries Noah.

'Yep fish. Well, to be more specific, Noah, I want carp, wall-to-wall, floor-to-ceiling carp!'

Noah looks to the skies. 'Okay God, let me get this right. You want a new ark?'

'Check.'

'With twenty decks, one on top of the other?'

'Check.'

'And you want it full of carp?'

'Check.'

'Why?' asks the perplexed Noah, who was slowly but surely getting to the end of his tether.

'Dunno,' says God. 'I just fancied a multi-storey carp ark.'

***

Get the last word in: apologise!

***

To be sung to the tune of 'If you're happy and you know it, clap your hands':

If we cannot find Osama, bomb Iraq.
If the markets hurt your Mama, bomb Iraq.
If the terrorists are Saudi
And the bank takes back your Audi
And the TV shows are bawdy,
Bomb Iraq.

If the corporate scandals growin', bomb Iraq.
And your ties to them are showin', bomb Iraq.
If the smoking gun ain't smokin'
We don't care, and we're not jokin'
That Saddam will soon be croakin',
Bomb Iraq.

Even if we have no allies, bomb Iraq.
From the sand dunes to the valleys, bomb Iraq.
So to hell with the inspections;
Let's look tough for the elections,
Close your mind and take directions,
Bomb Iraq.

While the globe is slowly warming, bomb Iraq.
Yay! The clouds of war are storming, bomb Iraq.
If the ozone hole is growing,
Some things we prefer not knowing,
(Though our ignorance is showing),
Bomb Iraq.

So here's one for dear old daddy, bomb Iraq.
From his favourite little laddy, bomb Iraq.
Saying no would look like treason.
It's the Hussein hunting season.
Even if we have no reason,
Bomb Iraq.

***

Have you noticed since everyone has a camcorder these days no one talks about seeing UFOs like they used to?

***

A Russian couple was walking down the street in Moscow one night, when the man felt a drop hit his nose. 'I think it's raining,' he said to his wife.

'No, that felt more like snow to me,' she replied.

'No, I'm sure it was just rain,' he said.

Well, as these things go, they were about to have a major argument about whether it was raining or snowing. Just then, they saw a minor Communist Party official walking towards them. 'Let's not fight about it,' the man said. 'Let's ask Comrade Rudolph whether it's officially raining or snowing.'

As the official approached, the man said, 'Tell me, Comrade Rudolph, is it officially raining or snowing?'

'It's raining, of course!' he replied, and walked on.

But the woman insisted, 'I know that felt like snow!'

The man quietly replied, 'Rudolph the Red knows rain, dear.'

★★★

Mrs Parks, the grade-six science teacher, asked her class the following question: 'Which human body part increases to ten times its normal size when stimulated?'

Nobody answered until a very angry little Mary stood up, saying, 'You should not be asking grade sixers a question like that! I'm going to tell my parents, and they'll tell the principal, and he'll fire you!' She sat down again with a sneer on her face.

Mrs Park ignored her and asked the question again.

'Which body part increases to ten times its normal size when stimulated?'

Little Mary's mouth fell open. 'Boy, is she going to get in big trouble!' she whispered to the kids around her.

Mrs Parks continued to ignore her. 'Anybody?'

Finally, Billy stood up, looked around nervously, and said, 'The body part that increases by ten times its size when it's stimulated is the pupil of the eye.'

'Very good, Billy,' Mrs Parks said.

Then, turning to Little Mary, she added, 'I only have three things to say to you, young lady. One, you have a very dirty mind; two, you didn't read your homework; and three, one day you are going to be very, very disappointed.'

★★★

The strong young man at the construction site was bragging that he could outdo anyone in a feat of strength. He made a special case of making fun of one of the older workmen. After several minutes, the older worker had had enough.

'Why don't you put your money where your mouth is?' he said. 'I will bet a week's wages that I can haul something in a wheelbarrow over to that building that you won't be able to wheel back.'

'You're on, old man,' the young guy replied.

The old man reached out and grabbed the wheelbarrow by the handles. Then he turned to the young man and said, 'All right, get in!'

***

AT THE OVAL OFFICE

George: Condi! Nice to see you. What's happening?
Condi: Sir, I have the report here about the new leader of China.
George: Great. Lay it on me.
Condi: Hu is the new leader of China.
George: That's what I want to know.
Condi: That's what I'm telling you.
George: That's what I'm asking you. Who is the new leader of China?
Condi: Yes.
George: I mean the fellow's name.
Condi: Hu.
George: The guy in China.
Condi: Hu.
George: The new leader of China.
Condi: Hu.
George: The Chinaman!
Condi: Hu is leading China.

George: Now whaddya asking me for?

Condi: I'm telling you Hu is leading China.

George: Well, I'm asking you. Who is leading China?

Condi: That's the man's name.

George: That's whose name?

Condi: Yes.

George: Will you or will you not tell me the name of the new leader of China?

Condi: Yes, sir.

George: Yasser? Yasser Arafat is in China? I thought he was in the Middle East.

Condi: That's correct.

George: Then who is in China?

Condi: Yes, sir.

George: Yasser is in China?

Condi: No, sir.

George: Then who is?

Condi: Yes, sir.

George: Yasser?

Condi: No, sir.

George: Look, Condi. I need to know the name of the new leader of China. Get me the secretary of the UN on the phone.

Condi: Kofi?

George: No thanks.

Condi: You want Kofi?

George: No.

Condi: You don't want Kofi?

George: No, but now that you mention it, I could use a glass of milk. And then get me the UN.

Condi: Yes, sir.

George: Not Yasser! The guy at the UN.

Condi: Kofi?

George: Milk! Will you please make the call?

Condi: And call who?

George: Who is the guy at the UN?

Condi: Hu is the guy in China.

George: Will you stay out of China!?

Condi: Yes, sir.

George: And stay out of the Middle East. Just get me the guy at the UN.

Condi: Kofi?

George: All right. With cream and two sugars. Now get on the phone.

Condi picks up the phone: Rice here.

George: Rice? Good idea. And a couple of egg rolls, too. Maybe we should send some to the guy in China. And the Middle East. Can you get Chinese food in the Middle East?

★★★

A boiled egg in the morning is hard to beat.

What's the definition of a will? It's a dead giveaway.

She avoided funerals because she was not a mourning person.

Those who jump off a Paris bridge are in Seine.

When a clock is hungry, it goes back four seconds.

When the electricity went off during a storm at a school the students were delighted.

The one who invented the doorknocker got a No-bell Prize.

If you don't pay your exorcist you get repossessed.

***

A man suspected his wife was seeing another man. So he hired the famous Chinese detective, Chen Lee, to watch and report any activities while he was gone.

A few days later, he received this report:

Most honourable sir, you leave house I watch house. He come to house. I watch. He and she leave house. I follow. He and she go in hotel. I climb tree. I look in window. He kiss she. She kiss he. He strip she.

She strip he. He play with she. She play with he. I play with me. I fall off tree. I not see. No fee.

Chen Lee.

***

A blonde heard that milk baths would make her beautiful. She left a note for her milkman to leave 65L of milk.

When the milkman read the note, he felt that there just be a mistake. He thought she probably meant 6.5L, so he knocked on the door to clarify the point.

The blonde came to the door, and the milkman said, 'I found your note to leave 65L of milk. Did you mean 6.5L?'

The blonde said, 'I want 65L. I'm going to fill my bathtub up with milk and take a milk bath.'

The milkman asked, 'Pasteurised?'

The blonde said, 'No, just up to my tits.'

***

A man who absolutely hated his wife's cat decided to get rid of it one day by driving it twenty blocks from his home and leaving it in the park. As he was getting home, the cat was walking up the driveway.

The next day, he decided to drive the cat forty

blocks away. Driving back up his driveway, there was the cat! He kept taking the cat further and further and the darn cat would always beat him home.

At last, he decided to drive a few kilometres away, turn right, then left, past the bridge, then right again and another right until he reached what he thought was a safe distance from his home and left the cat there. Hours later, the man called home to his wife. 'Jen, is the cat there?'

'Yes,' the wife answers, 'why do you ask?'

Frustrated, the man says, 'Put that son of a bitch on the phone. I'm lost and need directions!'

***

A parent decreed one Christmas that she was no longer going to remind her children of their thank-you note duties. As a result, their grandmother never received acknowledgements of the generous cheques she had given.

The next year things were different, however.

'The children came over in person to thank me,' the grandmother told a friend triumphantly.

'How wonderful!' the friend exclaimed. 'What do you think caused the change in behaviour?'

'Oh, that's easy,' the grandmother replied. 'This year I didn't sign the cheques.'

***

LESSONS

Parable No. 1

A little bird was flying south for the winter. It was so cold, the bird froze and fell to the ground in a large field. While it was lying there, a cow came by and dropped some dung on it. As the frozen bird lay in the pile of cow dung, it began to realise how warm it was. The dung was actually thawing him out!

He lay there all warm and happy, and soon began to sing for joy. A passing cat heard the bird singing and came to investigate. Following the sound, the cat discovered the bird under the pile of cow dung, and promptly dug him out and ate it!

Management lessons:
1. Not everyone who drops shit on you is your enemy.
2. Not everyone who gets you out of the shit is your friend.
3. When you're in deep shit, keep your mouth shut.

Parable No. 2

A crow was sitting in a tree, doing nothing all day. A small rabbit saw the crow, and asked him, 'Can I also sit like you and do nothing all day long?'

The crow answered, 'Sure, why not.'

So the rabbit sat on the ground below the crow and rested.

All of a sudden, a fox appeared, jumped on the rabbit and ate it.

Management lesson: To be sitting and doing nothing, you must be sitting very, very high up.

Parable No. 3

A turkey was chatting with a bull. 'I would love to be able to get to the top of that tree,' sighed the turkey, 'but I haven't got the energy.'

'Well, why don't you nibble on some of my droppings?' replied the bull. 'They're packed with nutrients.'

The turkey pecked at a lump of dung and found that it actually gave him enough strength to reach the first branch of the tree.

The next day, after eating some more dung, he reached the second branch. Finally, after a fourth night, there he was proudly perched at the top of the tree.

Soon he was spotted by a farmer who shot the turkey out of the tree.

Management lesson: Bullshit might get you to the top, but it won't keep you there.

Parable No. 4
The little boy rode on the donkey and the old man walked. As they went along, they passed some people who remarked, 'It was a shame the old man was walking and the boy was riding.'

The man and boy thought maybe the critics were right, so they changed positions.

Later, they passed some people who remarked, 'What a shame he makes that little boy walk.' They decided they both would walk.

Soon they passed some more people who thought they were stupid to walk when they had a decent donkey to ride. So they both rode the donkey.

Now they passed some people that shamed them by saying, 'How awful to push such a load on a poor donkey.'

The boy and man said they were probably right, so they decided to carry the donkey.

As they crossed a bridge, they lost their grip on the animal and he fell into the river and drowned.

Management lesson: If you try to please everyone, you will eventually lose your ass.

✱✱✱

DOG LETTERS TO GOD

Dear God: How come people love to smell flowers, but seldom smell one another? Where are their priorities?

Dear God: When we get to heaven, can we sit on your couch? Or is it the same old story?

Dear God: Excuse me, but why are there cars named after the jaguar, the cougar, the mustang, the cold, the stingray and the rabbit, but not one named after a dog? How often do you see a cougar riding around? We dogs love a nice ride. I know every breed cannot have its own model, but it would be easy to rename the Chrysler Eagle the Chrysler Beagle!

Dear God: If a dog barks his head off in the forest and no human hears him, is he still a bad dog?

Dear God: Is it true that in heaven dining-room tables have on-ramps?

Dear God: If we come back as humans, is that good or bad?

Dear God: More meatballs, less spaghetti please.

Dear God: When we get to the Pearly Gates, do we have to shake hands to get in?

Dear God: We dogs can understand human verbal instructions, hand signals, whistles, horns, clickers, beepers, scent IDs, electromagnetic energy fields and frisbee flight paths. What do humans understand?

Dear God: Are there dogs on other planets or are we alone? I have been howling at the moon and stars for a long time, but all I ever hear back is the beagle across the street.

Dear God: Are there mailmen in heaven? If there are, will I have to apologise?

Dear God: Can you undo what that doctor did?

A CAT LETTER TO GOD

Dear God: Do you exist? I'm just curious. I don't care.

***

DR SEUSS ON AGEING

I cannot see.
I cannot pee.
I cannot chew.
I cannot screw.
Oh my God, what can I do?
My memory shrinks.
My hearing stinks.
No sense of smell.
I look like hell.
My mood is bad – can you tell?
My body's drooping.
Having trouble pooping.
The golden years have come at last.
The golden years can kiss my arse.

***

A mechanic was removing a cylinder head from the motor of a Harley, when he spotted a world-famous heart surgeon in his shop.

The heart surgeon was waiting for the service manager to come and take a look at his bike. The mechanic shouted across the garage, 'Hey, doc, can I ask you a question?'

The famous surgeon, a bit surprised, walked over

to the mechanic working on the motorcycle. The mechanic straightened up, wiped his hands on a rag and asked, 'So, doc, look at this engine. I also can open hearts, take valves out, fix 'em, put in new parts, and when I finish this will work just like a new one. So how come I get a pittance and you get the really big money, when you and I are doing basically the same work?'

The surgeon paused, smiled, leaned over and whispered to the mechanic, 'Try doing it with the engine running!'

***

Things you can get away with saying only at Christmas:

I prefer breasts to legs.

Tying the legs together keeps the inside moist.

Smother the butter all over the breasts.

If I don't undo my trousers, I'll burst!

I've never seen a better spread!

Are you ready for seconds yet?

It's a little dry; do you still want to eat it?

Don't play with your meat.

Stuff it up between the legs as far as it will go.

Do you think you'll be able to handle all these people at once?

I didn't expect everyone to come at the same time!

You still have a little bit on your chin.

How long will it take after you put it in?

You'll know it's ready when it pops up.

Just pull the end and wait for the bang.

That's the biggest bird I've ever had!

I'm so full, I've been gobbling nuts all morning.

Wow, I didn't think I could handle all that and still want more!

***

A lady golfer, who visits a driving range to tone up before a game, is about to tee off, when she notices the man next to her.

'Pardon me, sir,' she said, 'you are aiming in the wrong direction – back towards the golf shop.'

'Oy! Tanks for dat. Vitout you, I vouldn't know. I'm blindt.'

He then turns around and then starts hitting out into the range. After a few minutes, he asks the lady how he is doing.

'Not bad,' she answers. 'Most of your shots are straight and fairly long. Only a few of them are slicing.'

'Tanks again, missus,' he replies. 'Vitout you telling, I vouldn't know dese tings.' A few shots later, he enquires again. 'Do you mind I should ask a poisonal qvuestion?'

'Not at all,' she replies.

'I don't do vell wit the ladies. Am I ugly or vat?'

'You're quite presentable,' she replies, 'I don't think that should be a problem.'

Smiling now, he exults, 'Vat a relief. I vas always afraid to ask. Again, I got to tank you.'

He was about to hit another ball when the lady interrupts him. 'Do you mind if I give you a bit of advice?' she asks.

'Vit gladness. All de help you got I vill take,' he answers.

'Lose the Jewish accent,' she replies, 'you're Chinese.'

***

Q: If you could live forever, would you and why?
A: I would not live forever, because we should not live forever, because if we were supposed to live forever, then we would live forever, but we cannot live forever, which is why I would not live forever.

Miss Alabama, 1994 Miss USA contest

'Whenever I watch TV and see those poor starving kids all over the world, I can't help but cry. I mean, I'd love to be skinny like that, but not with all those flies and death and stuff.'

Mariah Carey

'Smoking kills. If you're killed, you've lost a very important part of your life.'

Brooke Shields, during an interview
to become spokesperson for an
anti-smoking campaign

'I've never had major knee surgery on any other part of my body.'

Winston Bennett,
University of Kentucky basketball forward

'Outside of the killings, Washington has one of the lowest crime rates in the country.'
Mayor Marion Barry, Washington DC

'I'm not going to have some reporters pawing through our papers. We are the president.'
Hillary Clinton, commenting on
the release of subpoenaed documents

'That lowdown scoundrel deserves to be kicked to death by a jackass, and I'm just the one to do it.'
A congressional candidate in Texas

'I don't feel we did wrong in taking this great country away from them. There were great numbers of people who needed new land, and the Indians were selfishly trying to keep it for themselves.'

John Wayne

'Half this game is 90 per cent mental.'
Philadelphia Phillies manager Danny Ozark

'I love California. I practically grew up in Phoenix.'

Dan Quayle

'It's no exaggeration to say that the undecideds could go one way or another.'

George W. Bush, US President

'We've got to pause and ask ourselves: How much clean air do we need?'

Lee Iacocca

'I was provided with additional input that was radically different from the truth. I assisted in furthering that version.'

Colonel Oliver North, from his Iran-Contra testimony

'The word "genius" isn't applicable to football. A genius is a guy like Norman Einstein.'

Joe Theisman, NFL football quarterback and sports analyst

'We don't necessarily discriminate. We simply exclude certain types of people.'

Colonel Gerald Wellman, ROTC Instructor

'If we don't succeed, we run the risk of failure.'

Bill Clinton, US President

'We are ready for an unforeseen event that may or may not occur.'

Al Gore, Vice President

'Traditionally, most of Australia's imports come from overseas.'

Keppel Enderbery

'Your food stamps will be stopped effective March 1992 because we received notice that you passed away. May God bless you. You may reapply if there is a change in your circumstances.'

Department of Social Services,
Greenville, South Carolina

'If somebody has a bad heart, they can plug this jack in at night as they go to bed and it will monitor their heart throughout the night. And the next morning, when they wake up dead, there'll be a record.'

Mark S. Fowler, FCC chairman

✳✳✳

Everyone seems to wonder why Muslim terrorists are so quick to commit suicide. Let's see now.

No beer. No booze. No bars. No television. No baseball. No football. No basketball. No hockey. No golf. No BBQs. No hotdogs. No burgers. No lobster, shellfish or even frozen fish sticks.

Rags for clothes, towels for hats. Constant wailing from the guy next door because he is sick and there are no doctors. Twenty-four-hour wailing from a guy in the tower.

No chocolate-chip cookies. No Christmas, you can't shave, your wife can't shave.

You can't shower to wash off the smell of donkey cooked over burning camel dung. The women have to wear baggy dresses and veils at all times.

Your bride is picked by someone else. She smells just like your donkey, but your donkey has a better disposition.

Then they tell you when you die it all gets better. No mystery here!

***

A travelling salesman checked into a futuristic motel. Realising he needed a trim before the next day's meeting, he called down to the desk clerk to ask if there was a barber on the premises. 'I'm afraid not, sir,' the clerk told him apologetically, 'but down the hall is a vending machine that should serve your purposes.'

Sceptical but intrigued, the salesman located the appropriate machine, inserted 50 cents, and stuck his head into the opening, at which time the machine started to buzz and whirl. Fifteen seconds later the salesman pulled out his head and surveyed his reflection, which showed the best haircut of his life.

Two feet away was another machine with a sign that read, 'Manicures – 25 cents'. Why not, thought the salesman. He paid the money, inserted his hands into the slot, then pulled them out to see they were perfectly manicured.

The next machine had a huge sign that read, 'This Machine Provides What Men Need Most When Away from Their Wives – 50 cents'.

The salesman looked both ways, put 50 cents in the machine, unzipped his fly and, with some anticipation, stuck his penis into the opening.

When the machine started buzzing, the guy let out a shriek of agony. Fifteen seconds later, it shut off and, with trembling hands, the salesman was able to withdraw his penis – with a button sewn on the end.

★★★

Some people grow old gracefully, while others fight and scratch the whole way.

Andy's wife, refusing to give into the looks of growing old, goes out and buys a new line of expensive cosmetics guaranteed to make her look years younger.

After a lengthy sitting before the mirror applying the 'miracle' products, she asks her husband, 'Darling, honestly, if you didn't know me, what age would you say I am?'

Looking her over carefully, Andy replies, 'Judging from your skin, twenty; your hair, eighteen; and your figure, twenty-five.'

'Oh, you flatterer!' she gushed. Just as she was about to tell Andy his reward, he stopped her by saying, 'Whoa! Hold on there, sweetie! I haven't added them up yet.'

***

A missionary who had spent years showing a tribe of natives how to farm and build things to be self-sufficient gets word that he is to return home.

He realises that the one thing he never taught the natives was how to speak English, so he takes the chief and starts walking in the forest. He points to a tree and says to the chief, 'This is a tree.'

The chief looks at the tree and grunts, 'Tree'.

The missionary is pleased with the response.

They walk a little farther and the padre points to a rock and says, 'This is a rock.'

Hearing this, the chief looks and grunts, 'Rock'.

The padre is really getting enthusiastic about the results when he hears a rustling in the bushes. As he peeks over the top, he sees a couple in the midst of heavy romantic activity. The padre is really flustered and quickly says, 'Riding a bike.'

The chief looks at the couple briefly, pulls out his blowgun and kills them both.

The padre goes ballistic and yells at the chief that he has spent years teaching the tribe how to be civilised and kind to each other, so how could he just kill these people in cold blood that way?

The chief replied, 'My bike.'

✳✳✳

A man and his young wife were in the divorce court, but the custody of their children posed a problem.

The mother leapt to her feet and protested to the judge that since she brought the children into the world, she should retain custody of them.

The man also wanted custody of his children, so the judge asked for his justification.

After a long silence, the man slowly rose from his chair and replied, 'Your Honour, when I put a dollar in a vending machine and a can of Coke comes out, does the Coke belong to me or the machine?'

***

Tristian and Christian were two little prawns living in a little cave in the great reef. They had to be careful because the reef sharks chased and tried to eat them constantly.

One day Tristian said to Christian, 'I would love to be a reef shark for a change.' The Magic Cod happened to be swimming past at this exact moment and said to Tristian, 'I can turn you into a shark if you really want.'

'Great,' said Tristian, so out he went and the Cod changed him into a shark.

Tristian, now a shark, had a great time terrorising all the prawns, but after a time became bored and began to miss Christian. 'I must find Cod and see if he can change me back to a prawn.'

This he did. He came back to the little cave and knocked on the door.

'Who is it?'

'It's Tristian.'

'Go away, you are a bad shark.'

'No, no I'm not. I found Cod. I'm a prawn again, Christian.'

***

A blonde goes to a restaurant and notices there's a 'peel and win' sticker on her coffee cup. So she peels it off and starts screaming, 'I've won a motor home! I've won a motor home!'

The waitress says, 'That's impossible. The biggest prize is a free lunch.'

But the blonde keeps screaming, 'I've won a motor home! I've won a motor home!'

Finally the manager comes up and says, 'Madam, I'm sorry, but you're mistaken. You couldn't possibly have won a motor home because we didn't even have that as a prize!'

The blonde says, 'No, it's not a mistake. I've won a motor home!' And she hands the ticket to the manager, and he reads "Win a bagel".'

***

DEFINITIONS

Conference: The confusion of one person multiplied by the number present.

Etc: A sign to make others believe that you know more than you actually do.

Committee: Individuals who can do nothing individually and sit to decide that nothing can be done together.

Experience: The name men give to their mistakes.

Philosopher: A fool who torments himself during life, to be spoken of when dead.

Opportunist: A person who starts taking a bath if he accidentally falls into a river.

Miser: A person who lives poor so that he can die rich.

Boss: Someone who is early when you are late, and late when you are early.

Cigarette: A pinch of tobacco rolled in paper with fire at one end and a fool at the other.

Lecture: An art of transferring information from the notes of the lecturer to the notes of the students without passing through the minds of either.

Tears: The hydraulic force by which masculine will-power is defeated by feminine waterpower.

Dictionary: A place where success comes before work.

Conference room: A place where everybody talks, nobody listens and everyone disagrees later on.

Smile: A curve that can set a lot of things straight.

Office: A place where you can relax after your strenuous home life.

Yawn: The only time some married men get to open their mouth.

***

SOME IMPORTANT RULES OF LIFE

Murphy's First Law for Fives: If you ask your husband to pick up five items at the store and then you add one more as an afterthought, he will forget two of the first five.

Kauffmann's Paradox of the Corporation: The less important you are to the corporation, the more your tardiness or absence is noticed.

The Salary Axiom: The pay rise is just large enough to increase your taxes and just small enough to have no effect on your take-home pay.

Miller's Law of Insurance: Insurance covers everything except what happens.

First Law of Living: As soon as you start doing what you always wanted to be doing, you'll want to be doing something else.

Weiner's Law of Libraries: There are no answers, only cross-references.

Isaac's Strange Rule of Staleness: Any food that starts out hard will soften when stale. Any food that starts out soft will harden when stale.

The Grocery Bag Law: The candy bar you planned to eat on the way home from the market is hidden at the bottom of the grocery bag.

Lampner's Law of Employment: When leaving work late, you will go unnoticed. When you leave work early, you will meet the boss in the parking lot.

***

A long time ago, the Pope decided that all the Jews had to leave Rome. Naturally there was a big uproar from the Jewish community. So the Pope made a deal. He would have a religious debate with a member of the Jewish community. If the Jew won, the Jews could stay. If the Pope won, the Jews would have to leave.

The Jews realised that they had no choice. So they picked an elderly man named Moshe to represent them. Rabbi Moshe did not speak Latin. In fact, he knew very little, but he was a man of great faith and well respected in the Jewish community. The debate should be held in silence. The Pope agreed. What could be easier than a silent debate?

The day of the great debate came. Moshe and the Pope sat opposite each other for a full minute before the Pope raised his hand and showed three fingers. Moshe looked back at him and raised one finger.

The Pope waved his fingers in a circle around his head. Moshe pointed to the ground where he sat.

The Pope pulled out a wafer and a glass of wine. Moshe pulled out an apple.

The Pope stood up and said, 'I give up. This man is too good. The Jews can stay.'

An hour later, the cardinals gathered all around the Pope, asking him what happened. The Pope said, 'First I held up three fingers to represent the Holy Trinity. He responded by holding up one finger to remind me that there was still one God common to both our religions. Then I waved my finger around me to show him that God was all around us. He responded by pointing to the ground and showing that God was also right here with us. I pulled out the wine and the wafer to show that God absolved us from our sins. He pulled out an apple to remind me of original sin. He had an answer for everything. What could I do?'

Meanwhile, the Jewish community had crowded around Moshe. 'What happened?' they asked.

'Well,' said Moshe, 'first he says to me, "You Jews have three days to get out of here." So I said to him, "Up yours." Then he tells me the whole city would be cleared of Jews. So I said to him, "Listen here, Pope, the Jews stay right here."'

'And then?' asked a woman.

'Who knows?' said Moshe. 'He took out his lunch, so I took out mine.'

***

Miss Bea, the church organist, was in her eighties and had never been married. She was much admired for her sweetness and kindness to all.

The pastor came to call on her one afternoon early in the spring, and she welcomed him into her Victorian parlour. She invited him to have a seat while she prepared a little tea. As he sat facing her old pump organ, the young minister noticed a cut-glass bowl sitting on top of it, filled with water. In the water floated, of all things, a condom.

Imagine his shock and surprise. Imagine his curiosity! When she returned with tea and cookies, they began to chat. The pastor tried to stifle his curiosity about the bowl of water and its strange floater, but soon it got the better of him, and, pointing to the bowl, he asked, 'Miss Bea, will you please tell me about this?'

'Oh yes,' she replied, 'isn't it wonderful! I was walking downtown last fall, and I found this little package on the ground. The directions said to put it on my organ, keep it wet, and it would prevent all sorts of infectious diseases. And you know, I haven't had a cold all winter.'

✳✳✳

The husband dies, and thirty days later, the wife makes contact via a medium.

'What's it like over there?' asks the wife.

The husband explains, 'I wake at 5 a.m., have sex until 8 a.m., then eat my breakfast. Then I return to having sex until lunchtime, each my lunch, then return to having sex until dinner, eat my dinner and then have sex until 3 a.m., when I sleep for two hours. Then off I go again.'

'Wow!' said the wife, 'heaven sounds wonderful.'

'Heaven?' replied the husband, 'I'm a rabbit in Dubbo.'

✳✳✳

ABC Sydney Radio held a competition to finish the sentence 'It's so dry in Sydney . . .' Following are some of the entries.

It's so dry in Sydney that HIH Insurance has come out of liquidation.

It's so dry in Sydney that Gough is no longer alone as he strolls across the harbour.

It's so dry in Sydney that if the English cricket team weren't touring we'd never see ducks.

It's so dry that the Red Cross has launched a wet-blanket appeal.

It's so dry in Sydney that we're actually drinking the new Vanilla Coke.

It's so dry in Sydney that you're only permitted to eat watermelon between 8 p.m. and 8 a.m.

It's so dry in Sydney that the government has introduced a water-pistol buy-back scheme.

It's so dry in Sydney that thieves are siphoning off radiators instead of petrol tanks.

It's so dry in Sydney I'm encouraging the kids to wee in the pool.

It's so dry in Sydney that the Bulldogs have tendered to build an Oasis in every local government area.

It's so dry in Sydney that Jesus turned the wine into water.

It's so dry in Sydney that we are having to hand-feed the rocking horse.

It's so dry in Sydney that Philip Ruddock says that when the boat people threw their children overboard it was so they could walk to Australia.

It's so dry in Sydney that everyone is now an expert – because you can't find anyone who is wet behind the ears.

It's so dry in Sydney that all the bottom-of-the-harbour tax schemes are resurfacing.

It's so dry in Sydney that I saw two trees fighting over a dog.

It's so dry in Sydney that all the Baptists have become Anglicans.

It's so dry in Sydney that when my daughter fainted it took three buckets of sand to bring her around.

It's so dry in Sydney that all the dogs are marking their territory with chalk.

***

Pierre, a brave French fighter pilot, takes his girlfriend, Marie, out for a pleasant little picnic by the River Seine. It's a beautiful day, and love is in the air. Marie leans over to Pierre and says, 'Pierre, kiss me!'

Our hero grabs a bottle of merlot and splashes it on Marie's lips.

'What are you doing, Pierre?' says the startled Marie.

'I am Pierre, the fighter pilot! When I have red meat, I have red wine!'

She smiles and they start kissing. When things begin to heat up a little, Marie says, 'Pierre, kiss me lower.'

Our hero tears her blouse open, grabs a bottle of chardonnay and starts pouring it all over her breasts.

'Pierre! What are you doing?' asks the bewildered Marie.

'I am Pierre, the fighter pilot! When I have white meat, I have white wine!'

They resume their passionate interlude and things really steam up. Marie leans close to his ear and whispers, 'Pierre, kiss me lower!'

Our hero rips off her underwear, grabs a bottle of Cognac and pours it in her lap. He then strikes a match and sets it on fire. Marie shrieks and dives into the river. Standing waist deep, Marie throws her arms up and screams furiously, 'Pierre, what in hell do you think you're doing?'

Our hero stands up defiantly, and says, 'I am Pierre, the fighter pilot! If I go down, I go down in flames!'

***

Abraham is an old Jewish guy who is a yarn merchant. He lives next door to the biggest anti-Semite in town.

One day the anti-Semite calls up Abraham and says, 'Hey, Jew! I need a piece of orange yarn. The length must be from the tip of your nose to the tip of your penis. And I want it delivered tomorrow.'

Abe says, 'Okay.'

The next morning the anti-Semite is roused from sleep at 7 a.m. by the sound of running engines. He runs outside to see a row of trucks lined up one after the other, dumping truckload after truckload of orange yarn in his front yard. Soon, his yard is a 5ft-deep sea of orange yarn. Abe then presents a bill for $18 000 to the anti-Semite.

The guy starts yelling and screaming at Abe. 'What is this, Jew? This is not what I asked for! I told you I needed a piece of yarn from the end of your nose to the tip of your penis. Look at this place! What do you have to say for yourself?'

Straight-faced, Abe replies, 'I'm very careful when I deal with people like you, that's why I got a few witnesses here with me. I may be off by a few miles, so

I gave you a two per cent discount . . . but the tip of my penis was left in Poland after my circumcision!'

***

A gynaecologist had become fed up with malpractice insurance and was on the verge of burning out. Hoping to try another career where skilful hands would be beneficial, he decided to change careers and become a mechanic.

He found out from the local technical college what was involved, signed up for evening classes, attended diligently, and learned all he could.

When the time for the practical exam approached, the gynaecologist prepared carefully for weeks and completed the exam with tremendous skill.

When the results came back, he was surprised to find that he had obtained a score of 150 per cent. Fearing an error, he called the instructor, saying, 'I don't want to appear ungrateful for such an outstanding result, but I wondered if there had been an error that needed adjusting.'

The instructor said, 'During the exam, you took the engine apart perfectly, which was worth 50 per cent of the total mark. You put the engine back together again perfectly, which is also worth 50 per cent of the mark.' The instructor then went on to say, 'I gave you an extra 50 per cent because you did it all through the muffler.'

✶✶✶

The United Airlines' passenger cabin was being served by an obviously gay flight attendant who seemed to put everyone into a good mood as he served them food and drinks.

As the plane prepared to descend, he came swishing down the aisle and announced to the passengers, 'Captain Marvey has asked me to announce that he'll be landing the big scary plane shortly, lovely people. So if you could just put up your trays, that would be super.'

On his trip back up the aisle, he noticed that a well-dressed, rather exotic-looking woman hadn't moved a muscle. 'Perhaps you didn't hear me over those big brute engines. I asked you to raise your trazy-poo so the main man can pitty-pat us on the ground.'

She calmly turned her head and said, 'In my country, I am called a princess. I take orders from no one.' To which the flight attendant replied, without missing a beat, 'Well, sweet-cheeks, in my country I'm called a queen, so I outrank you. Put the tray up, bitch.'

✶✶✶

An Amish couple had just been married and had gone to a hotel for their honeymoon. The Amish man went to the front desk and asked for a room. He said this occasion was very special to them and they needed a good room.

The clerk asked if they wanted the bridal.

The Amish fellow thought about it a while and then replied, 'No, I guess not. I'll just hold onto her ears until she gets used to it.'

***

'Twas the month after Christmas, and all through the
   house
Nothing would fit me, not even a blouse.
The cookies I'd nibble, the chocolates I'd taste,
The holiday parties have gone to my waist.
When I got to the scales there arose such a number!
So I walked to the store (less a walk, more a lumber)
And remembered the marvellous meals I'd prepared;
The gravies and sauces and beef nicely rared.
The wine and the rum balls, the bread and the Brie,
And I never once said, 'No thanks, none for me'.
As I dressed myself in my husband's old shirt,
And prepared once again to do battle with dirt
I said to myself, as only I can,
'You can't spend all winter disguised as a man!'

431

So away with the last of the sour-cream dip,
Get rid of the fruit cake, every cracker and chip.
Every last bit of that wonderful food
I must strictly avoid (well it's for my own good).
It must all be dumped and totally banished
'Til all the additional ounces have vanished.
I won't have a cookie – not even a lick
And all I will chew is a celery stick.
I won't have a biscuit or fruit bread or pie.
I'll munch on a carrot and hungrily cry,
'I'm starving, I'm lonesome, and life is a bore.'
But isn't that what January's for?
Unable to giggle, no longer a riot.
So, happy new year, and to all a good diet!

***

There were two beggars sitting side by side on a street in Mexico City. One had a cross in front of him, the other one the Star of David.

Many people went by, looked at both beggars, but only put money into the hat of the one sitting behind the cross.

A priest came by, stopped and watched many, many people give money to the beggar behind the cross, but none to the beggar behind the Star of David.

Finally he went over to the beggar behind the Star

of David and said, 'Don't you understand? This is a Christian country. People aren't going to give you money if you sit there with a Star of David in front of you, especially when you're sitting beside a beggar who has a cross. In fact, they would probably give to him just out of spite.'

The Star of David beggar listened to the priest and, turning to the cross beggar, said, 'Moishe, look who's trying to teach us marketing.'

***

Two old ladies were outside their nursing home having a smoke, when it started to rain. One of the ladies pulled out a condom, cut off the end and put it over her cigarette, and continued smoking.

Miriam: 'What's that?'

Agnes: 'A condom. This way my cigarette doesn't get wet.'

Miriam: 'Where did you get it?'

Agnes: 'You can get them at the chemist.'

The next day, Miriam hobbles into the local chemist and announces to the pharmacist that she wants a box of condoms. The guy, obviously embarrassed, looks at her kind of strangely (she is, after all, more than eighty years of age), but very delicately asks, 'What brand do you prefer?'

'Doesn't matter, sonny, as long as it fits a Camel.'

The pharmacist fainted.

***

A successful rancher died and left everything to his devoted wife. She was a very good-looking woman, and determined to keep the ranch, but knew very little about ranching. So she decided to place an ad in the newspaper for a ranch hand.

Two men applied for the job. One was gay and the other a drunk.

She thought long and hard about it, and when no one else applied, she decided to hire the gay guy, figuring it would be safer to have him around the house than the drunk.

He proved to be a hard worker who put in long hours every day and knew a lot about ranching. For weeks, the two of them worked, and the ranch was doing very well. Then, one day, the rancher's widow said to the hired hand, 'You have done a really good job and the ranch looks great. You should go into town and kick up your heels.' The hired hand readily agreed and went into town one Saturday night.

However, one o'clock came and he didn't return. Two o'clock and no hired hand. He returned at around two thirty and found the rancher's widow sitting by the fireplace. She quietly called him over to her.

'Unbutton my blouse and take it off,' she said. Trembling, he did as she directed.

'Now take off my boots.' He did so, slowly.

'Now take off my socks.' He did.

'Now take off my skirt.' He did.

'Now take off my bra.' Again, with trembling hands, he did as he was told.

'Now,' she said, 'take off my panties.' He slowly pulled them down and off.

Then she looked at him and said, 'Don't you ever wear my clothes to town again!'

***

An Irishman, an Englishman and a Scotsman go into a pub and each order a pint of Guinness. Just as the bartender hands them over, three flies buzz down and one lands in each of the pints.

The Englishman looks disgusted, pushes his pint away and demands another pint.

The Scotsman picks out the fly, shrugs, and takes a long swallow.

The Irishman reaches into the glass, pinches the fly between his fingers and shakes him while yelling, 'Spit it out, ya bastard! Spit it out!'

***

The Washington Post publishes a yearly contest in which readers are asked to supply alternative meanings for various words. These were the 2001 winners.

1. Coffee (n.), a person who is coughed upon.
2. Flabbergasted (adj.), appalled over how much weight you have gained.
3. Abdicate (v.), to give up all hope of ever having a flat stomach.
4. Esplanade (v.), to attempt an explanation while drunk.
5. Willy-nilly (adj.), impotent.
6. Negligent (adj.), describes a condition in which you absentmindedly answer the door in your nightgown.
7. Lymph (v.), to walk with a lisp.
8. Gargoyle (n.), an olive-flavoured mouthwash.
9. Flatulence (n.), the emergency vehicle that picks you up after you are run over by a steamroller.
10. Balderdash (n.), a rapidly receding hairline.
11. Testicle (n.), a humorous question on an exam.
12. Rectitude (n.), the formal, dignified demeanour assumed by a proctologist immediately after he examines you.
13. Oyster (n.), a person who sprinkles his conver-

sation with Yiddish expressions.

14. Circumvent (n.), the opening in the front of boxer shorts.

15. Frisbeetarianism (n.), the belief that, when you die, your soul goes up on the roof and gets stuck there.

16. Pokemon (n.), a Jamaican proctologist.

***

Top 11 proposed names for the attack on Iraq:

11. Operation Enduring Scapegoat.

10. Operation Obliterate Iraq's Oil Infrastructure so that Dick Cheney's Halliburton can Rebuild it at a Huge Profit like after the Last War with Iraq.

9. Operation Belated Father's Day Gift.

8. Operation Because I Said So.

7. Operation We Couldn't Find bin Laden.

6. Operation Personal Vendetta.

5. Operation George Oilwell.

4. Operation Speaker Delay.

3. Operation Enron Amnesia.

2. Operation Desert Shrub.

1. Operation Just (Be) Cause.

***

Three old pilots are walking on the ramp.
First one says, 'Windy, isn't it?'
Second one says, 'No, it's Thursday!'
Third one says, 'So am I. Let's go get a beer.'

***

A man was telling his neighbour, 'I just bought a new hearing aid. It cost me $400, but it's state of the art. It's perfect.'

'Really,' answered the neighbour. 'What kind is it?'

'Twelve-thirty.'

***

Morris, an 82-year-old man, went to the doctor to get a physical. A few days later the doctor saw Morris walking down the street with a gorgeous young lady on his arm.

A couple of days later the doctor spoke to Morris and said, 'You're really doing great, aren't you?'

Morris replied, 'Just doing what you said, Doc. "Get a hot mamma and be cheerful."'

The doctor said, 'I didn't say that. I said, "You've got a heart murmur. Be careful."'

***

An elderly gent was invited to his old friends' home for dinner one evening. He was impressed by the way his mate preceded every request to his wife with endearing terms – honey, my love, darling, sweetheart, pumpkin etc.

The couple had been married almost 60 years and clearly they were still very much in love.

While the wife was in the kitchen, the man leaned over and said to his host, 'I think it's wonderful that after all these years you still call your wife those loving pet names.'

The old man hung his head, 'I have to tell you the truth,' he said, 'I forgot her name about ten years ago.'

✱✱✱

When Charles de Gaulle finally retired from public life, the British ambassador and his wife threw a gala dinner party in his honour. The ambassador's wife engaged in light conversation with Madame de Gaulle and asked, 'Your husband has been such a prominent public figure, such a presence on the French and international scene for many years. How will quiet retirement seem in comparison? What are you most looking for in these retirement years?'

'A penis,' replied Madame de Gaulle.

The room instantly fell quiet as the guests over-heard, not quite believing that they had heard it. Then le grand Charles gently leaned over to his wife and soothingly said to her, 'Ma Cherie, I believe le Engliss pronounce zat word 'appiness.'

★★★

LITTLE BILLY

On getting older:
Little Billy was sitting on a park bench munching on one candy bar after another. After the sixth one, a man on the bench across from his said, 'Son, you know eating all that candy isn't good for you. It will give you acne, rot your teeth and make you fat.'

Little Billy replied, 'My grandfather lived to be 107 years old.'

'Oh?' replied the man. 'Did you grandfather eat six candy bars at a time?'

'No,' replied Little Billy, 'he minded his own fucking business!'

On philosophy:
A teacher asks her class, 'If there are five birds sitting on a fence and you shoot one of them, how many will be left?' She calls on Little Billy.

He replies, 'None. They will all fly away with the first gunshot.'

The teacher replies, 'The correct answer is four, but I like your thinking.'

Little Billy says, 'I have a question for you. There are three women sitting on a bench having an ice-cream. One is delicately licking the sides of the triple scoop of ice-cream. The second is gobbling down the top and sucking the cone. The third is biting off the top of the ice-cream. Which one is married?'

The teacher, blushing a great deal, replies, 'Well, I suppose the one that's gobbled down the top and sucked the cone.'

To which Little Billy replied, 'The correct answer is the one with the wedding ring on, but I like your thinking.'

On English:

Little Billy goes to school and the teacher says, 'Today we are going to learn multi-syllable words, class. Does anybody have an example of a multi-syllable word?'

Little Billy says, 'Mas-tur-bate.'

Miss Rogers smiles and says, 'Wow, Little Billy, that's a mouthful.'

Little Billy says, 'No, Miss Rogers, you're thinking of a blow job.'

***

A man is waiting for his wife to give birth. The doctor comes in and informs the dad that his son was born without torso, arms or legs. The son is just a head!

But the dad loves his son and raises him as well as he can, with love and compassion. After twenty-one years, the son is now old enough for his first drink.

Dad takes him to the bar, tearfully tells the son he is proud of him and orders up the biggest, strongest drink for his boy. With all the bar patrons looking on curiously and the bartender shaking his head in disbelief, the boy takes his first sip of alcohol.

Swooop! A torso pops out!

The bar is dead silent, then bursts into a whoop of joy. The father, shocked, begs his son to drink again. The patrons chant, 'Take another drink!'

The bartender still shakes his head in dismay. *Swooop!* Two arms pop out. The bar goes wild. The father, crying and wailing, begs his son to drink again. The patrons chant, 'Take another drink!' The bartender ignores the whole affair.

By now the boy is getting tipsy, and with his new hands he reaches down, grabs his drink and guzzles the last of it. *Swooop!* Two legs pop out. The bar is in chaos. The father falls to his knees and tearfully thanks God.

The boy stands up on his new legs and tumbles to the left . . . then to the right . . . right through the front door, into the street, where a truck runs over him and kills him instantly. The bar falls silent. The father moans in grief.

The bartender sighs and says, 'He should have quit while he was a head.'

***

Two men, strangers, were seated next to each other on the plane when the first bloke turned to the second and said, 'Let's talk. I've heard that flights go quicker if you strike up a conversation with your fellow passenger.'

The second bloke, who had just opened his book, closed it slowly, took off his glasses and said to the stranger. 'What would you like to discuss?'

'Oh, I don't know,' said the first bloke. 'How about nuclear power?'

'Okay,' said the second man. 'That could be an interesting topic. But let me ask you a question first. A horse, a cow and a deer all eat grass. The same stuff. Yet a deer excretes little pellets, while a cow turns out a flat patty and a horse produces clumps of dried grass. Why do you suppose that is?'

'Jeez,' said the first bloke, 'I have no idea.'

'Well then,' said the second man, 'how is it that you feel qualified to discuss nuclear power when you don't know shit?'

***

I went to the store the other day, and I was in there for only about five minutes. When I came out there was a motorcycle cop writing a parking ticket. I went up to him and said, 'Come on, buddy, how about giving a guy a break?'

He ignored me and continued writing the ticket.

So I called him a pencil-necked Nazi. He glared at me and started writing another ticket for worn tyres!

So I called him a piece of horse shit.

He fished the second ticket and put it on the windscreen with the first. Then he started writing a third ticket! This went on for about twenty minutes – the more I abused him, the more tickets he wrote.

I didn't care. My car was parked around the corner. I try to have a little fun each day. It's important.

***

A guy sticks his head into a barber shop and asks, 'How long before I can get a haircut?' The barber looks around the shop and says, 'About two hours.'

The guy leaves.

A few days later the same guy sticks his head in the door and asks, 'How long before I can get a haircut?' The barber looks around at the shop full of customers and says, 'About three hours.' The guy leaves.

A week later the same guy sticks his head in the shop and asks, 'How long before I can get a haircut?' The barber looks around the shop and says, 'About an hour and a half.' The guy leaves.

The barber looks over at a friend in the shop and says, 'Hey, Bill, follow that guy and see where he goes. He keeps asking how long he has to wait for a haircut, but then doesn't come back.'

A little while later, Bill comes back into the shop, laughing hysterically.

The barber asks, 'Bill, where did he go when he left here?'

Bill looks up, tears in his eyes and says, 'Your house!'

***

A man was sick and tired of going to work every day while his wife stayed home. He wanted her to see what he went through, so he prayed: 'Dear Lord, I go to work every day and put in eight hours while my wife merely stays at home. I want her to know what

I go through, so please allow her body to switch with mine for a day. Amen.'

God, in his infinite wisdom, granted the man's wish. The next morning, sure enough, the man awoke as a woman. He arose, cooked breakfast for his mate, awakened the kids, set out their school clothes, fed them breakfast, packed their lunches, drove them to school, came home and picked up the dry cleaning, took it to the cleaners and stopped at the bank to make a deposit, went grocery shopping, then drove home to put away the groceries, paid the bills and balanced the cheque book. He cleaned the cat's litter box and bathed the dog.

Then it was already 1 p.m. and he hurried to make the beds, do the laundry, vacuum, dust and sweep and mop the kitchen floor. He ran to the school to pick up the kids and got into an argument with them on the way home, set out cookies and milk and got the kids organised to do their homework, set up the ironing board and watched TV while he did the ironing.

At 4.30 p.m. he began peeling potatoes and washing vegetables for salad, breaded the pork chops and snapped fresh beans for supper. After supper he cleaned the kitchen, loaded the dishwasher, folded laundry, bathed the kids and put them to bed. At 9 p.m. he was exhausted and, though his daily chores weren't finished, he went to bed where he was expected to make love, which he managed to get through without complaint.

The next morning he awoke and immediately knelt by the bed and said, 'Lord, I don't know what I was thinking. I was so wrong to envy my wife's being able to stay home all day. Please, oh please, let us trade back.'

The Lord, in his infinite wisdom replied, 'My son, I feel you have learned your lesson and I will be happy to change things back to the way they were. You'll just have to wait nine months though. You got pregnant last night.'

***

BIBLICAL HOWLERS

This purportedly comes from a Catholic primary school in the USA. Kids were asked questions about the Old and New testaments. They have not been retouched or corrected.

1. In the first book of the Bible, Guinessis, God got tired of creating the world, so he took the Sabbath off.

2. Adam and Eve were created from an apple tree. Noah's wife was called Joan of Ark. Noah built an ark, which the animals came on to in pears.

3. Lot's wife was a pillar of salt by day, but a ball of fire by night.

4. The Jews were a proud people and throughout history they had trouble with unsympathetic Genitals.

5. Samson was a strongman who let himself be led astray by a Jezebel like Delilah.

6. Moses led the Hebrews to the Red Sea, where they made unleavened bread which is bread without any ingredients.

7. The Egyptians were all drowned in the desert. Afterwards, Moses went up on Mount Cyanide to get to the ten amendments.

8. The seventh amendment is 'Thou shalt not admit adultery'.

9. Moses died before he ever reached Canada. Then Joshua led the Hebrews in the battle of Geritol.

10. The greatest miracle of the Bible is when Joshua told his son to stand still and he obeyed him.

11. David was a Hebrew king skilled at playing the liar. He fought with the Finkelsteins, a race of people who lived in Biblical times.

12. When Mary heard that she was the mother of Jesus, she sang the Magna Carta.

13. When the three wise guys from the East side arrived, they found Jesus in the manager.

14. Jesus was born because Mary had an immaculate contraption.
15. Jesus enunciated the Golden Rule, which says to do one to others before they do one to you. He also explained, 'a man doth not live by sweat alone'.
16. It was a miracle when Jesus rose from the dead and managed to get the tombstone off the entrance.
17. The people who followed the Lord were called the 12 decibels.
18. The epistles were the wives of the apostles.
19. One of the opossums was St Matthew who was also a taximan.
20. St Paul cavorted to Christianity. He preached holy acrimony, which is another name for marriage.
21. Christians have only one spouse. This is called monotony.

***

On the way to their wedding a young couple is involved in a fatal car accident. The couple find themselves sitting outside the Pearly Gates waiting for St Peter to process them into heaven. While waiting, they begin to wonder: could they possibly get married in heaven?

When St Peter shows up, they ask him.

St Peter says, 'I don't know. This is the first time anyone has asked. Let me go find out.' And he leaves.

The couple sit and wait for an answer – for a couple of months. While they wait, they discuss that *if* they were allowed to get married in heaven, should they get married, what with the eternal aspect of it all.

'What if it doesn't work?' they wonder. 'Are we stuck together *forever?*'

After yet another month, St Peter finally returns, looking somewhat bedraggled. 'Yes,' he informs the couple, 'you can get married in heaven.'

'Great!' said the couple. 'But we were just wondering, what if things don't work out? Could we also get a divorce in heaven?'

St Peter, red-faced with anger, slams his clipboard onto the ground.

'What's wrong?' asked the frightened couple.

'*Oh, come on!*' St Peter shouts. 'It took me three months to find a priest up here. Do you have *any* idea how long it'll take me to find a lawyer?'

***

KIDS IN CHURCH

Three-year old Reese: 'Our Father, Who does art in heaven, Harold be His name. Amen.'

A little boy was overheard praying: 'Lord, if you can't make me a better boy, don't worry about it. I'm having a real good time like I am.'

A Sunday school class was studying the Ten Commandments. They were ready to discuss the last one. The teacher asked if anyone could tell her what it was. Susie raised her hand, stood tall, and quoted, 'Thou shalt not take the covers off the neighbour's wife.'

After the christening of his baby brother in church, Jason sobbed all the way home in the back seat of the car. His father asked him three times what was wrong. Finally, the boy replied, 'That preacher said he wanted us brought up in a Christian home, and I wanted to stay with you guys.'

I had been teaching my three-year-old daughter, Caitlin, the Lord's Prayer for several evenings at bedtime. She would repeat after me the lines from the prayer. Finally, she decided to go solo. I listened with pride as she carefully enunciated each word, right up to the end of the prayer. 'Lead us not into temptation,' she prayed, 'but deliver us some email. Amen.'

One particular four-year-old prayed, 'And forgive us

our trash baskets as we forgive those who put trash in our baskets.'

A Sunday school teacher asked her children as they were on the way to church service, 'And why is it necessary to be quiet in church?'

One bright little girl replied, 'Because people are sleeping.'

Six-year-old Angie and her four-year-old brother, Joel, were sitting together in church. Joel giggled and talked out loud. Finally, his big sister had had enough. 'You're not supposed to talk out loud in church.'

'Why? Who's going to stop me?' Joel asked.

Angie pointed to the back of the church and said, 'See those two men standing by the door? They're hushers.'

A wife invited some people to dinner. At the table, she turned to their six-year-old daughter and said, 'Would you like to say the blessing?'

'I wouldn't know what to say,' the girl replied.

'Just say what you hear mummy say,' the wife answered.

The daughter bowed her head and said, 'Lord, why on earth did I invite all these people to dinner?'

***

Once there were twins, Joe and John. Joe was the owner of a dilapidated old boat. It so happened that John's wife died the same day that Joe's boat sank.

A few days later, a kindly old woman saw Joe and mistook him for John. She said, 'I'm sorry to hear about your loss. You must just feel terrible.'

Joe, thinking that she was talking about his boat, said, 'No, in fact I'm sort of glad to be rid of her. She was a rotten old thing right from the beginning. Her bottom was all shrivelled up and she smelled like old dead fish. She was always losing her water, she had a bad crack in the back and a pretty big hole in the front too. Every time I used her, her hole got bigger and she leaked like crazy. I guess what finally finished her off was when I rented her to four guys looking for a good time. I warned them that she wasn't very good, but they wanted to use her anyway. The fools tried to get in her all at once and she split right up the middle.'

The old lady fainted.

***

One day, while a woodcutter was cutting a branch of a tree above a river, his axe fell into the river. When he cried out, the Lord appeared and asked, 'Why are you crying?' The woodcutter replied that his axe had fallen into the water. The Lord went down into the water and reappeared with a golden axe.

'Is this your axe?' the Lord asked.

The woodcutter replied, 'No.'

The Lord again went down and came up with a silver axe. 'Is this your axe?' the Lord asked.

Again, the woodcutter replied, 'No.'

The Lord went down again and came up with an iron axe. 'Is this your axe?' the Lord asked.

The woodcutter replied, 'Yes.'

The Lord was pleased with the man's honesty and gave him all three axes to keep. The woodcutter went home happily.

One day, while he was walking with his wife along the riverbank, the woodcutter's wife fell into the river. When he cried out, the Lord again appeared and asked him, 'Why are you crying?'

'Oh Lord, my wife has fallen into the water!' The Lord went down into the water and came up with Jennifer Lopez. 'Is this your wife?' the Lord asked.

'Yes!' cried the woodcutter.

The Lord was furious. 'You cheat! That is an untruth!'

The woodcutter replied, 'Oh, forgive me, my Lord. It is a misunderstanding. You see, if I said "no" to Jennifer Lopez, you will come up with Catherine Zeta-Jones. Then if I also say "no" to her, you will thirdly come up with my wife, and I will say "yes" and then all three will be given to me. But Lord, I am a poor man and I will not be able to take care of all three wives. So that's why I said yes this time.'

The moral of the story: Whenever a man lies, it is for an honourable and useful reason.

***

FOR THE MEN

How many men does it take to open a beer?
None. It should be opened by the time she brings it.

Why is a laundromat a really bad place to pick up a woman?
Because a woman who can't even afford a washing machine will probably never be able to support you.

Why do women have smaller feet than men?
It's one of those 'evolutionary things' that allows them to stand closer to the kitchen sink.

How do you know when a woman is about to say something smart?
When she starts her sentence with 'A man once told me . . .'

How do you fix a woman's watch?
You don't. There is a clock on the oven.

Why do men fart more than women?
Because women can't shut up long enough to build up the required pressure.

If your dog is barking at the back door and your wife is yelling at the front door, who do you let in first?
The dog, of course. He'll shut up once you let him in.

What's worse than a male chauvinist pig?
A woman who won't do what she's told.

I married Miss Right.
I just didn't know her first name was Always.

I haven't spoke to my wife for eighteen months: I don't like to interrupt her.

What do you call a woman who has lost 95 per cent of her intelligence?
Divorced.

Marriage is a three-ring circus: engagement ring, wedding ring, suffe-ring.

Scientists have discovered a food that diminishes a woman's sex drive by 90 per cent.
It's called a wedding cake.

Our last fight was my fault: My wife asked me, 'What's on the TV?'
I said, 'Dust!'

In the beginning, God created the earth and rested. Then God created man and rested. Then God created woman.
    Since then, neither God nor man has rested.

Why do men die before their wives?
They want to.

Young son: Is it true, Dad? I heard that in some parts of Africa a man doesn't know his wife until he marries her?
Dad: That happens in every country, son.

A man inserted an advertisement in the classifieds: 'Wife Wanted'.
The next day he received a hundred letters. They all said the same thing: 'You can have mine!'

The most effective way to remember your wife's birthday is to forget it once.

Women will never be equal to men until they can walk down the street with a bald head and a beer gut and still think they are beautiful.

***

A man decides to buy a new rifle and scope. He goes to a rifle shop and asked the owner to show him some. The owner takes out a rifle and scope and says to the man, 'This rifle and scope is so good you can see my house all the way up on that hill.'

The man takes a look through the scope and starts laughing.

'What's so funny?' asks the owner.

'I see a naked man and a naked woman running around in the house,' the man replies.

The owner grabs the rifle and scope and looks at his house. He then hands two bullets to the man and says, 'Here are two bullets. I'll give you this rifle and scope for nothing if you take these two bullets, shoot my wife's head off and shoot the guy's penis off.'

The man takes another look through the scope and says, 'You know what? I think I can do that with one shot!'

***

A mild-mannered man was tired of being bossed around by his wife, so he went to a psychiatrist. The psychiatrist said he needed to build his self-esteem, and so gave him a book on assertiveness, which he read on the way home. He had finished the book by the time he reached his house.

The man stormed into the house and walked up to his wife. Pointing a finger in her face, he said, 'From now on, I want you to know that I am the man of this house and my word is law. I want you to prepare me a gourmet meal tonight, and when I'm finished eating my meal I expect a sumptuous dessert afterwards. Then, after dinner, you're going to draw me my bath so I can relax. And when I'm finished with my bath, guess who's going to dress me and comb my hair?'

'The funeral director,' said the wife.

***

A few years ago, the Sierra Club and the US Forest Service were presenting an alternative to Wyoming ranchers for controlling the coyote population. It seems that after years of the ranchers using the tried-and-true methods of shooting and/or trapping the predator, the 'tree-huggers' had a more humane solution.

What they proposed was for the animals to be captured alive, the males castrated and let loose again and the population would be controlled.

All the ranchers thought about this amazing idea for a couple of minutes. Finally, an old boy in the back stood up, tipped his hat back and said, 'Son, I don't think you understand the problem. Those coyotes aren't fucking our sheep – they're eating them!'

∗∗∗

Wife: Oh, come on!
Husband: Leave me alone!
Wife: It won't take long.
Husband: I won't be able to sleep afterwards.
Wife: I can't sleep without it.
Husband: Why do you think of things like this in the middle of the night?
Wife: Because I'm hot.
Husband: You get hot at the strangest times.
Wife: If you loved me, I wouldn't have to beg you.
Husband: If you loved me, you'd be more considerate.
Wife: You don't love me anymore!
Husband: Yes I do, but let's forget it for tonight.
Wife: (Sob-sob)
Husband: Alright, I'll do it.
Wife: What's the matter? Need a flashlight?

Husband: I can't find it.
Wife: Oh, for heaven's sake, feel for it!
Husband: There! Are you satisfied?
Wife: Oh yes, honey!
Husband: Is it up far enough?
Wife: Oh, that's fine.
Husband: Now go to sleep and from now on when you want the window open, do it yourself.

***

A blonde and a brunette are taking a walk. The brunette says, 'Look! A dead bird.'

The blonde looks up at the sky and says, 'Where?'

***

Hillary Clinton died and went to heaven. As she stood in front of St Peter at the Pearly Gates, she saw a huge wall of clocks behind him.

She asked, 'What are all those clocks?'

St Peter answered, 'Those are Lie Clocks. Everyone on earth has a Lie Clock. Every time you lie, the hands on your clock will move.'

'Oh,' said Hillary. 'Whose clock is that?'

'That's Mother Teresa's. The hands have never moved, indicating that she has never told a lie.'

'Whose clock is that?'

'That's Abraham Lincoln's clock. The hands have only moved twice, telling us that Abe only told two lies in his entire life.'

Hillary asked, 'Where's Bill's clock?'

'Bill's clock is in my office. I'm using it as a ceiling fan.'

***

THE PERKS OF BEING OVER 40

Kidnappers are not very interested in you.

In a hostage situation you are likely to be released first.

No one expects you to run a marathon.

People call at 9 p.m. and ask, 'Did I wake you?'

People no longer view you as a hypochondriac.

There is nothing left to learn the hard way.

Things you buy now won't wear out.

You can eat dinner at 4 p.m.

You can live without sex but not without glasses.

You keep hearing about other people's operations.

You get into heated arguments about pension plans.

You have a party and the neighbours don't even realise it.

You no longer think of speed limits as a challenge.

You quit trying to hold your stomach in, no matter who walks into the room.

You sing along with elevator music.

Your eyes won't get much worse.

Your investment in health insurance is finally beginning to pay off.

Your joints are more accurate meteorologists than the weather bureau.

Your secrets are safe with your friends because they can't remember them either.

Your supply of brain cells is finally down to manageable size.

***

GAMES FOR WHEN WE ARE OLDER

Sag. You're it!
Pin the toupee on the bald guy.
Twenty questions shouted into your good ear.
Kick the bucket.
Red rover, red rover, the nurse says bend over.
Doc, doc, goose.
Simon says something incoherent.
Hide and go pee.
Spin the bottle of Mylanta.
Musical recliners.

***

SIGNS OF MENOPAUSE

You sell your home-heating system at a yard sale.

Your husband jokes that instead of buying a wood stove, he is using you to heat the family room this winter.

Rather than just saying you are not amused, you shoot him.

You have to write post-it notes with your kids' names on them.

The Phenobarbital dose that wiped out the Heaven's Gate cult gives you four hours of decent rest.

You change your underwear after every sneeze.

***

OLD IS WHEN:

Your sweetie says, 'Let's go upstairs and make love', and you answer, 'Pick one, I can't do both!'

Your friends compliment you on your new alligator shoes, and you're barefoot.

A sexy babe catches your fancy and your pacemaker opens the garage door.

Going braless pulls all the wrinkles out of your face.

You don't care where your spouse goes, just as long as you don't have to go along.

You are cautioned to slow down by the doctor instead of by the police.

'Getting a little action' means you don't need to take any fibre today.

'Getting lucky' means you find your car in the carpark.

An 'all-nighter' means not getting up to pee.

***

Giorgio is in the country for about six months. He walks to work every day and passes a shoe store. Each day he stops and looks in the window to admire a certain pair of Bocelli leather shoes. After about two months, he saves the $300 the shoes cost, and buys them. Every Friday night the Italian community gets together at a dance in the church basement, so Giorgio seizes the opportunity to wear his new Bocelli shoes to the dance.

He asks Sophia to dance with him and, as they dance, he asks her, 'Sophia, do you weara reda panties tonighta?'

Sophia, surprised, says, 'Yes, Giorgio, I do wear red panties tonight, but how do you know?'

'I see the reflection in my new $300 Bocelli leather shoosa. How do you lika them?'

Next, he asks Rosa to dance and, after a few minutes, says to her, 'Rosa, do you weara white panties tonighta?'

'Yes, Giorgio, I do, but how do you know that?' Rosa asks.

'I see the reflection in my new $300 Bocelli leather shoosa. How do you lika them?'

Now the evening is almost over, and Giorgio asks Carmella for the last dance. Midway through the dance, Giorgio's face turns red. He gasps, 'Carmella, stilla my hearta please. Tell me you weara no panties tonighta.'

'Yes, yes, Giorgio,' Carmella answers. 'I wear no panties tonight.'

Giorgio is greatly relieved. 'Thanka God,' he says, 'I thoughta I had a cracka in my new $300 Bocelli leather shoosa.'

***

An Irish girl went to London to work as a secretary and began sending money home to her parents. After a few years they asked her to come home for a visit, as her elderly father was getting frail and very hard of hearing.

She pulled up at the family home in a Rolls Royce and stepped out wearing diamonds and a full-length fur coat. As she walked into the house, her father said, 'Hmmm, they seem to be paying secretaries awfully well in London these days.'

The girl took his hands and said, 'Dad, I've been meaning to tell you something for years, but I didn't want to put it in a letter. Obviously, I can't hide it from you any longer. I've become a prostitute.'

Her father gasped, put his hand on his chest and keeled over. The doctor was called but the old man had clearly lost the will to live. He was put to bed and the priest was called.

As the priest administered the Last Rites with the mother and daughter weeping and wailing nearby, the old man muttered weakly, 'I'm a goner – killed by my own daughter! Killed by the shame of what she's become!'

'Please forgive me,' his daughter sobbed, 'I only wanted to have nice things! I wanted to send you money and the only way I could do it was by becoming a prostitute.'

Brushing the priest aside, the old man sat bolt

upright in bed, smiling, 'Did you say *Prostitute*? I thought you said *Protestant!*'

***

DIARY OF A VIAGRA WIFE

Day 1: Just celebrated our twenty-fifth wedding anniversary with not much to celebrate. When it came time to re-enact our wedding night, he locked himself in the bathroom and cried.

Day 2: Today, he says he has a big secret to tell me. He's impotent, he says, and he wants me to be the first to know. Why doesn't he tell me something I don't know! I mean, he actually thinks I haven't noticed.

Day 3: This marriage is in trouble. A woman has needs. Yesterday, I saw a picture of Nelson's Column and burst into tears.

Day 4: A miracle has happened! There's a new drug on the market that will fix his 'problem'. It's called Viagra. I told him that if he takes Viagra, things will be just like they were on our wedding night. I think this will work. I replaced his Prozac with the Viagra, hoping to lift something other than his mood.

Day 5: What absolute bliss!

Day 6: Isn't life wonderful, but it's difficult to write while he's doing that.

Day 7: This Viagra thing has gone to his head. No pun intended! Yesterday, at Burger King, the manager asked me if I'd like a Whopper. He thought they were talking about him. But, have to admit it's very nice – don't think I've ever been so happy.

Day 8: I think he took too many over the weekend. Yesterday, instead of mowing the lawn, he was using his new friend as a weed whacker. I'm also getting a bit sore down there.

Day 9: No time to write. He might catch me.

Day 10: Okay, I admit it. I'm hiding. I mean, a girl can only take so much. And to make matters worse, he's washing the Viagra down with neat whisky! What am I going to do? I feel tacky all over.

Day 11: I'm basically being screwed to death. It's like living with a Black and Decker drill. I woke up this morning hot-glued to the bed. Even my armpits hurt. He's a complete pig. I wish he were gay. I've stopped wearing make-up, cleaning my teeth or even washing, but he still keeps coming after me! Even yawning has become dangerous.

Day 13: Every time I shut my eyes, there's a sneak attack! It's like going to bed with a scud missile. I can hardly walk and if he tries that 'Oops, sorry' thing again, I'll kill the bastard.

Day 14: I've done everything to turn him off. Nothing is working. I've even started dressing like a nun, but this just seems to make him more horny. Help me!

Day 15: I think I'll have to kill him. I'm starting to stick to everything I sit on. The cat and dog won't go near him and our friends don't come over any more. Last night I told him to go and fuck himself, and he did.

Day 16: The bastard has started to complain about headaches. I hope the bloody thing explodes! I did suggest he might try stopping the Viagra and going back to Prozac.

Day 17: I switched the pills but it doesn't seem to have made any difference. Christ! Here he comes again.

Day 18: He's back on Prozac. The lazy sod just sits there in front of the TV all day with that remote control in his hand and expects me to do everything for him. What absolute bliss!

***

A family of England supporters head out one Saturday to do Christmas shopping. While in the sports store, the son picks up an Ireland shirt and says to his sister, 'I've decided I'm going to be an Ireland supporter and would like this shirt for Christmas.'

The sister is outraged at this, promptly whacks him on the head and says, 'Go talk to your mother.'

Off he goes, with the Ireland shirt in hand, and finds his mother. 'Mum?'

'Yes, son?'

'I've decided I'm going to be an Ireland supporter and would like this shirt for Christmas.'

The mother is outraged, whacks him on the head and says, 'Go talk to your father!'

Off he goes, with the Ireland shirt in hand, and finds his father.

'Dad?'

'Yes, son?'

'I've decided I'm going to be an Ireland supporter and would like this shirt for Christmas.'

The father is outraged, whacks his son on the head and says, 'No son of mine is ever going to be seen in *that!*'

About half an hour later, they are all back in the car heading home. The father turns to his son and says, 'Son, I hope you have learned something today.'

The son replies, 'Yes, Father, I have.'

'Good, son, what is it?'

The son says, 'I've only been an Ireland supporter for an hour and already I hate you English bastards!'

***

Down south, Bubba called his attorney and asked, 'Is it true they're suing the cigarette companies for causing people to get cancer?'

'Yes, Bubba, sure is true,' responded the lawyer.

'And now someone is suing the fast-food restaurants for making them fat and clogging their arteries with all them burgers and fries, is that true, Mr Lawyer?'

'Sure is, Bubba. But why are you asking?'

'Cause what I want to know is, I was wondering, can I sue Budweiser for all the ugly women I've slept with?'

***

473

There was a boy who worked in the produce section of the market. A man came in and asked to buy half a head of lettuce. The boy told him they only sold whole heads of lettuce, but the man replied that he did not need a whole head, only half a head.

The boy said he would go and ask his manager about the matter.

The boy walked into the back room and said, 'There's some arsehole out there who wants to buy only half a head of lettuce.'

As he finished saying this, he turned around to find the man standing right behind him, so he added, 'And this gentleman wants to buy the other half!' The manager approved the deal and the man went on his way.

Later, the manager called on the boy and said, 'You almost got yourself in a lot of trouble earlier, but I must say I was impressed with the way you got yourself out of it. You think on your feet and we like that around here. Where are you from, son?'

The boy replied, 'Minnesota, sir.'

'Oh really! Why did you leave Minnesota?' asked the manager.

The boy replied, 'They're all just whores and hockey players up there.'

'Really,' replied the manager. 'My wife's from Minnesota!'

The boy replied, 'No kidding! Which team did she play for?'

***

A resolution was recently proposed in the UN to form a new union between the Turks and the Kurds. This would create a new nation along the Iraq border to be called Turds.

France vetoed the measure, pointing out their historical right to this name.

***

Do you realise that the only time in our lives when we like to get old is when we're kids? If you're less than ten years old, you're so excited about ageing that you think in fractions: 'How old are you?' 'I'm four and a half!'

You're never thirty-six and a half. You're four and a half going on five! That's the key.

You get to your teens, now they can't hold you back. You jump to the next number, or even a few ahead: 'How old are you?' 'I'm going to be sixteen!' You could be thirteen, but, hey, you're going to be sixteen.

And then the greatest day of your life is when you

become twenty-one. Even the words sound like a ceremony: You *become* twenty-one! Yes!

But then you turn thirty. Oooh, what happened there? Makes you sound like bad milk. He *turned*; we had to throw him out. There's no fun now, you're just a sour dumpling. What's wrong? What's changed? You *become* twenty-one, you *turn* thirty, then you're *pushing* forty.

Whoa! Put on the brakes, it's all slipping away. Before you know it, you *reach* fifty and your dreams are gone.

But wait! You *make* it to sixty. You didn't think you would.

So you *become* twenty-one, *turn* thirty, *push* forty, *reach* fifty and *make it* to sixty.

You've built up so much speed that you *hit* seventy! After that it's a day-by-day thing; you *hit* Wednesday.

You get into your eighties and every day is a complete cycle: you *hit* lunch; you *turn* 4.30; you *reach* bedtime.

And it doesn't end there. Into the nineties, you start going backwards. 'I was *just* ninety-two.'

Then a strange thing happens. If you make it over one hundred, you become a little kid again. 'I'm a hundred and a half!'

May you all make it to a healthy hundred and a half!

***

A truck driver is driving along the freeway. A sign comes up that reads LOW BRIDGE AHEAD. Before he knows it, the bridge is right ahead of him and he gets stuck under it. Cars are banked up for miles.

Finally, a police car comes up. The cop gets out of his car and walks around to the truck driver, puts his hands on his hips and says, 'Get stuck, heh?'

The truck driver says, 'No, I was delivering this bridge and ran out of petrol!'

***

'If I sold my house and my car, had a big garage sale and gave all my money to the church, would that get me into heaven?' I asked the children in my Sunday school class.

'No!' the children all answered.

'If I cleaned the church every day, mowed the lawns and kept everything neat and tidy, would that get me into heaven?'

Again, the answer was, 'No!'

'Well then, if I was kind to animals and gave candy to all the children, and loved my wife. Would that get me into heaven?' I asked them.

Again, they all answered, 'No!'

'Well,' I continued, 'then how can I get into heaven?'

A five-year-old boy shouted out, 'You've got to be dead!'

***

A biker walks into a yuppie bar and shouts, 'All lawyers are arseholes!' He looks around, obviously hoping for a challenge.

Finally a guy comes up to him, taps him on the shoulder and says, 'Take that back!'

The biker says, 'Why? Are you a lawyer?'

'No, I'm an arsehole!'

***

A man boarded the bus, with both of his front pants pockets filled with golf balls, and sat down next to a blonde. The blonde kept looking quizzically at him and his bulging pockets.

Finally, after many glances from her, he said, 'It's golf balls.'

The blonde continued to look at him thoughtfully and asked, 'Does it hurt as much as tennis elbow?'

***

An eight-year-old boy is walking down the road one day when a car pulls over next to him. 'If you get in the car,' the driver says, 'I'll give you $10 and a piece of candy.'

The boy refuses and keeps on walking.

A few moments later, not to take no for an answer, the man driving the car pulls over again. 'How about $20 and two pieces of candy?'

The boy tells the man to leave him alone and keeps on walking.

Still further down the road the man pulls over to the side of the road. 'Okay,' he says, 'this is my final offer. I'll give you $50 and all the candy you can eat.'

The little boy stops, goes to the car and leans in. 'Look,' he shouts to the driver, 'you bought the damned Volvo, Dad. You'll just have to live with it!'

***

Attorney-General Ashcroft is visiting an elementary school. After the typical civics presentation in the class, he announces, 'All right, boys and girls, you can ask me questions now.'

Little Bobby raises his hand and says, 'I have three questions:

1. How did Bush win the election with fewer votes than Gore?

2. Why are you using the USA Patriot Act to limit Americans' civil liberties?

3. Why hasn't the US caught Osama bin Laden yet?'

Just then the bell sounds and all the kids run out to the playground.

Fifteen minutes later, the kids come back to class and again Ashcroft says, 'I'm sorry we were interrupted by the bell. Now, you can all ask me questions.'

Little Charlene raises her hand and says, 'I have five questions:

1. How did Bush win the election with fewer votes than Gore?

2. Why are you using the USA Patriot Act to limit Americans' civil liberties?

3. Why hasn't the US caught Osama bin Laden yet?

4. Why did the bell go off twenty minutes early?

5. Where's Little Bobby?

✳✳✳

A woman was shopping at her local supermarket where she selected a litre of milk, two eggs, a small bottle of orange juice, a few lettuce leaves, one tomato and a packet of tea bags.

As she was unloading her items on the conveyor belt to check out, a drunk standing behind her watched as she placed the items in front of the cashier.

'You must be single,' said the drunk.

The woman, a bit startled but nonetheless intrigued by the drunk's intuition, looked at her six items on the belt. Seeing nothing particularly unusual about her selections, she said, 'Well, you know what, you're absolutely correct. But how on earth did you know that?'

The drunk replied, ''Cause you're ugly!'

***

A boss was complaining in a staff meeting that he wasn't getting any respect. Later that morning he went to a local sign shop and bought a small sign that read I'M THE BOSS. He then taped it to his office door.

Later that day, when he returned from lunch, he found that someone had taped a note to the sign that read, 'Your wife called. She wants her sign back.'

***

The World Health Organisation has just issued an urgent warning about BARS (Beer & Alcohol Requirement Syndrome):

A newly identified problem has spread rapidly throughout the world. The disease, identified as BARS, affects people of many different ages. Believed to have started in Ireland in 1500 BC, the disease seems to affect people who congregate in pubs and taverns or who just congregate. It is not known how the disease is transmitted but approximately three billion people worldwide are affected, with thousands of new cases appearing every day. Early symptoms of the disease include an uncontrollable urge at 5 p.m. to consume a beer or alcoholic beverage. This urge is most keenly felt on Fridays. More advanced symptoms of the disease include talking loudly, singing off-key, aggression, heightened sexual attraction/confidence, uncalled-for laughter, uncontrollable dancing and unprovoked arguing.

In the final stages of the disease, victims are often cross-eyed and speak incoherently. Vomiting, loss of memory, loss of balance, loss of clothing and loss of virginity can also occur. Sometimes death ensues, usually accompanied by the victim shouting, 'Hey, Fred, bet you can't do this!' Or 'Wanna see how fast it goes?'

If you develop any of these symptoms, it is important that you quarantine yourself in a pub with fellow victims until last call or all the symptoms have passed. Sadly, it is reported that the disease can reappear at very short notice or, at the latest, on the following Friday.

Side effects for survivors include bruising, broken limbs, lost property, killer headaches and divorce.

On the upside, there is not, and probably never will be, a permanent cure.

***

NURSERY RHYMES

Mary had a little skirt
With splits right up the sides
And every time that Mary walked
The boys could see her thighs!
Mary had another skirt
It was split right up the front
But she didn't wear that one very often!

Mary had a little lamb
Her father shot it dead.
Now it goes to school with her
Between two chunks of bread.

Little Miss Muffet
Sat on a tuffet
Her clothes all tattered and torn.
It wasn't the spider
That crept up beside her,

But Little Boy Blue and his horn!

Simple Simon met a pieman, going to the fair.
Said Simple Simon to the pieman,
'What have you got there?'
Said the pieman to Simon,
'Pies, you dickhead.'

Humpty Dumpty sat on a wall.
Humpty Dumpty had a great fall.
All the king's horses and all the king's men
Said, 'Fuck him, he's only an egg!'

Mary had a little lamb
It ran into a pylon.
10 000 volts went up its arse
And turned its wool to nylon!

Jack and Jill
Went up the hill
To have a little fun.
Jill, that dill,
Forgot her pill
And now they have a son.

★★★

A frog goes into a bank and approaches the teller. He can see from her nameplate that her name is Patricia Whack, so he says, 'Miss Whack, I'd like to get a $30000 loan to take a holiday.'

Pattie looks at the frog in disbelief and asks his name. The frog says his name is Kermit Jagger, his dad is Mick Jagger, and that it's okay, he knows the bank manager.

Pattie explains that he will need to secure the loan with some collateral. The frog says, 'Sure, I have this,' and produces a tiny porcelain elephant, about a centimetre tall, bright pink and perfectly formed.

Very confused, Pattie explains that she'll have to consult with the bank manager and disappears into a back office.

She finds the manager and says, 'There's a frog called Kermit Jagger out there who claims to know you and wants to borrow $30000, and he wants to use this as collateral.' She holds up the tiny pink elephant. 'I mean, what in the world is this?'

The bank manager looks at her and says, 'It's a knick-knack, Pattie Whack, give the frog a loan. His old man's a rolling stone.'

✱✱✱

MARKETING

The buzzword in today's business world is *marketing*. However, most people often ask for a simple explanation of marketing. Here it is:

You're a woman and you see a handsome guy at a party. You go up to him and say, 'I'm fantastic in bed.'
     That's direct marketing.

You're at a party with a bunch of friends and see a handsome guy. One of your friends goes up to him and, pointing at you, says, 'She's fantastic in bed.'
     That's advertising.

You see a handsome guy at a party. You go up to him and get his telephone number. The next day you call and say, 'Hi, I'm fantastic in bed.'
     That's telemarketing.

You're at a party and see a handsome guy. You get up and straighten your dress. You walk up to him and pour him a drink. You say, 'May I,' and reach up to straighten his tie, brushing your breast lightly against his arm and then say, 'By the way, I'm fantastic in bed.'
     That's public relations.

You're at a party and see a handsome guy. He walks up to you and says, 'I hear you're fantastic in bed.'

That's brand recognition.

You're at a party and see a handsome guy. You talk him into going home with your friend.

That's a sales rep.

Your friend can't satisfy him, so he calls you.

That's tech support.

You're on your way to a party when you realise that there could be handsome men in all these houses you're passing. So you climb onto the roof of one situated towards the centre and shout at the top of your lungs, 'I'm fantastic in bed!'

That's junk mail.

***

Recently I was diagnosed with AAADD: Age Activated Attention Deficit Disorder.

This is how it manifests itself. I decide to wash my car. As I start towards the garage, I spot the mail on the hall table. I should go through the mail before I wash the car.

I lay the car keys on the table, put the junk mail in

the rubbish bin under the table, and notice that the bin is full. So, I put the bills back on the table and take out the rubbish first. Since I'm going to be near the mailbox when I take out the rubbish anyway, I might as well pay the bills first. I see my chequebook on the table, but there is only one cheque left. My extra cheques are in my desk in the study, so I go to my desk, where I find the bottle of juice that I had been drinking. I'm going to look for my cheques, but first I need to push the juice aside so that I don't accidentally knock it over. But the juice is getting warm, and should be put in the refrigerator to keep it cold.

Heading towards the kitchen with the juice, a vase of flowers on the counter catches my eye. They need to be watered. I set the juice down on the counter and find my reading glasses, for which I've been searching all morning. I had better put them back on my desk, but first I'm going to water the flowers. I set the glasses back down on the counter, fill a container with water and suddenly spot the TV remote. Someone left it on the kitchen table. Tonight when we sit down to watch TV, we will be looking for the remote, but nobody will remember that it's on the kitchen table. I should put it back in the sitting room where it belongs, but first I'll water the flowers. I splash some water on the flowers, but most of it spills on the floor. So, I put the remote back down on the table, and get some towels to wipe up the spill. Then I head down the hall trying to remember what I was planning to do.

At the end of the day:

1. the car isn't washed;
2. the bills aren't paid;
3. there is a warm bottle of juice sitting on the counter;
4. the flowers aren't watered;
5. there is still only one cheque in my chequebook;
6. I can't find the remote;
7. I can't find my glasses;
8. And I don't remember what I did with the car keys.

I'm trying to figure out why nothing got done today. It's quite baffling because I know I was busy all day long, and I'm really tired. I know this is a serious problem, and I'll get some help for it.

★★★

The Hokey Pokey (by William Shakespeare)

O proud left foot, that ventures quick within
Then soon upon a backward journey lithe.
Anon, once more the gesture, then begin:
Command sinistral pedestal to writhe.
Commence thou then the fervid Hokey-Poke.

A mad gyration, hips in wanton swirl.
To spin! A wilde release from heaven's yoke.
Blessed dervish! Surely canst go, girl.
The hoke, the poke – banish now thy doubt
Verily, I say, 'tis what it's all about.

***

HOME HINTS

If you are choking on an ice cube, don't panic. Simply pour a cup of boiling water down your throat and presto! The blockage will be almost instantly removed.

Clumsy? Avoid cutting yourself while chopping vegetables by getting someone else to hold them while you chop away.

Avoid arguments with the missus about the toilet seat by simply peeing in the sink.

High blood pressure sufferers: simply cut yourself and bleed for a while, thus reducing the pressure on your veins.

A mousetrap, placed on top of your alarm clock, will prevent you from rolling over and going back to sleep.

If you have a bad cough, take a large laxative. Then you will be afraid to cough.

Have a bad toothache? Hit your thumb with a hammer, then you will forget about the tooth.

You only need two tools: WD-40 and duct tape. If it doesn't move and it should, use WD-40. If it moves and shouldn't, use the duct tape.

★★★

A man decides he wants to have a pig roast, so he goes out to a pig farm to buy one. He agrees on a per-pound price with the farmer and then begins to select a pig. 'How about that one?'

'Okay,' replies the farmer. The farmer then picks up the pig, puts its tail in his mouth, lets it hang from his mouth and then declares, 'This one weighs 34kg.'

'That's amazing,' the man says. 'Are you sure you can tell a pig's weight by using that method?'

'Yep,' says the farmer, 'we've used this method in our family for generations.' To prove his accuracy, the farmer puts the pig on a scale and it weighs exactly 34kg.

'My son can do it, too,' boasts the farmer. Sure enough, the farmer's son comes over, puts another pig's tail in his mouth, lets it hang and then says, 'This one weighs 38kg.' The farmer then confirms his son's accuracy with the scale.

'My wife can do it, too,' says the farmer. 'Son, go get your mother.'

The boy runs off to the house and returns a few minutes later. 'Mum can't come out right now,' says the son. 'She's busy weighing the milkman.'

***

An elephant asks a camel, 'Why are your breasts on your back?'

'Well,' says the camel, 'I think it's a strange question from someone whose dick is on his face.'

***

Scientists at NASA built a gun specifically to launch dead chickens at the windshields of airliners, military jets and the space shuttle, all travelling at maximum velocity. The idea is to simulate the frequent incidents of collisions with airborne fowl to test the strength of the windshields.

British Engineers heard about the gun and were eager to test it on the windshields of their new high-speed trains. Arrangements were made, and a gun was sent to the British engineers. When the gun was fired, the engineers stood shocked as the chicken hurled out of the barrel, crashed into the shatterproof shield, smashed it to smithereens, blasted through the control console, snapped the engineer's back rest in two and embedded itself in the back wall of the cabin like an arrow shot from a bow.

The horrified Brits sent NASA the disastrous results of the experiment, along with the designs of the windshield and begged the US scientists for suggestions.

NASA responded with a one-line memo: 'Defrost the chicken.'

***

The children were lined up on the cafeteria of a Catholic primary school for lunch. At the end of the table was a large pile of apples. The nun made a note and stuck it on the apple tray: 'Take only *one*. God is watching.'

Moving further along the lunch line, at the other end of the table, was a large pile of chocolate-chip cookies. A child had written a note: 'Take all you want. God is watching the apples.'

***

The little guy is sitting at the bar just staring into his drink. He's been sitting there for a half an hour when a big troublemaking truck driver steps next to him, grabs his drink and gulps it down in one swig.

The poor little guy starts crying.

'Come on, man. I was just giving you a hard time,' says the truck driver. 'I'll buy you another drink. I just can't stand to see a man crying.'

'This is the worst day of my life,' says the little guy between sobs. 'I can't do anything right. I overslept and was late for an important meeting, so my boss fired me. When I went to the parking lot, I found my car was stolen and I have no insurance. I grabbed a cab home but, after the cab left, I discovered I'd left my wallet in it. At home I found my wife in bed with the gardener. So I came to this bar and was thinking about putting an end to my life, and you show up and drink the darn poison.'

***

The woman entered the room and, with a knowing smile tearing her full lips, she sank into the comfort of the plush chair in the corner. The handsome stranger turned, having sensed her approach. Locking his steely grey eyes on hers, he moved slowly towards her, his experienced gaze measuring her, hypnotising her with

494

his soft murmurs of assurance. He sank to his knees before her and without a word, smoothly released her from her constraining attire.

With a sigh of surrender, she allowed his foreign hands to unleash her bare flesh. He expertly guided his hands through this tender, often hidden territory, his movements deliberate, confident in his ability to satisfy her every need. Her senses swam. She was overcome with an aching desire that had gone unfulfilled for so long.

And, just as it seemed that ecstasy was within her grasp, he paused, and for one heart-stopping moment, she thought, 'It's too big! It will never fit!' Then, with a sudden rush, it slid into place as if it had been made only for her. As pleasure and contentment washed over her, she met his steady gaze, tears of gratitude shining in her eyes. And he knew it wouldn't be long before she returned. Oh, yes, this woman would want more. She would want to do it again and again and again.

Don't you just love shopping for shoes!

✷✷✷

Evidence has been found that William Tell and his family were avid bowlers. The league records were unfortunately destroyed in a fire. Thus we'll never know for whom the Tells bowled.

***

A sceptical anthropologist was cataloguing South American folk remedies with the assistance of a tribal brujo who indicated that the leaves of a particular fern were a sure cure for any case of constipation. When the anthropologist expressed his doubts, the brujo looked him in the eye and said, 'Let me tell you, with fronds like this, who needs enemas?'

***

A thief broke into the local police station and stole all the lavatory equipment. A spokesperson was quoted as saying, 'We have absolutely nothing to go on.'

***

An Indian chief was feeling very sick, so he summoned the medicine man. After a brief examination, the medicine man took out a long, thin strip of elk hide and gave it to the chief. Instructing him to bite off, chew and swallow one inch of the leather every day. After a month, the medicine man returned to see how the chief was feeling. The chief shrugged and said, 'The thong is ended, but the malady lingers on.'

***

A famous Viking explorer returned home from a voyage and found his name missing from the town register. His wife insisted on complaining to the local civic official who apologised profusely saying, 'I must have taken Leif off my census.'

***

Ten things men understand about women:
  1.
  2.
  3.
  4.
  5.
  6.
  7.
  8.
  9.
  10.

***

There were three Indian squaws. One slept on a deer skin, one slept on an elk skin and the third slept on a hippopotamus skin. All three became pregnant and the first two each had a baby boy. The one who slept on the hippopotamus skin had twin boys. This goes to prove that the squaw of the hippopotamus is equal to the sons of the squaws of the other two hides.

***

One day when the teacher walked to the blackboard, she noticed someone had written the word 'penis' in tiny letters. She turned around and scanned the class, looking for the guilty face. Finding none, she quickly erased it, and began her class.

The next day, she went into the room and saw, in larger letters, the word 'penis' again written on the blackboard. Once again, she looked around in vain for the culprit, but found none. So she proceeded with the day's lesson.

Every morning, for about a week, she went into the classroom to find the same word written on the board. Each day's word was written larger than the previous day.

Finally, one day as she walked in, expecting to be greeted by the same word on the board, she found instead the words, 'The more you rub it, the bigger it gets!'

***

Once upon a time there was a female brain cell that, by mistake, happened to end up in a man's head. She looked around nervously, but it was all empty and quiet. 'Hello?' she cried, but no answer. 'Is there anyone here?' she cried a little louder. But still no answer.

Now the female brain cell started to feel alone and scared, so she yelled as loud as she could, 'Hello! Is there anyone here?'

Then she heard a voice from far, far away. 'Hello, we're all down here.'

✳✳✳

I was happy. My girlfriend and I had been dating for over a year, and so we decided to get married. My parents helped us in every way, my friends encouraged me, and my girlfriend? She was a dream!

There was only one thing bothering me and that was my mother-in-law-to-be. She was a career woman, smart, but most of all beautiful and sexy, and she sometimes flirted with me, which made me feel uncomfortable.

One day she called me and asked me to come over to check the wedding invitations. So I went. She was alone, and when I arrived she whispered to me that soon I was to be married, and she had feelings and desires for me that she couldn't overcome. So before I got married and committed my life to her daughter, she wanted to make love to me just once.

What could I say? I was in total shock and couldn't say a word. So she said, 'I'll go to the bedroom, and if you are up to it, just come and get me.' I just watched her delicious behind as she went up the stairs.

I stood there for a moment, and then turned around and instead went to the front door. I opened it and stepped out of the house. Her husband was standing outside and, with tears in his eyes, hugged me and said, 'We are very happy and pleased, you have passed our little test. We couldn't have asked for a better man for our daughter. Welcome to the family.'

Moral of the story: always keep your condoms in your car.

∗∗∗

Which sexual position produces the ugliest children? Ask your mum.

∗∗∗

Why do men find it difficult to make eye contact? Breasts don't have eyes.

***

Why do men want to marry virgins?
They can't stand criticism.

***

A foreign gentleman walks into a pharmacy. 'I'd like a box of condoms please,' he says.
   The pharmacist replies, 'That'll be $6 plus tax.'
   'Tacks?' the guy says. 'In my country these things stay on by themselves!'

***

A man was admitted to the hospital suffering from premature ejaculation.
Diagnosis: The doctors said it was touch and go.

***

Why do so many women fake orgasm?
Because so many men fake foreplay.

***

When is the only time a man thinks about a candlelight dinner?
When the power goes off.

***

According to a recent study, sex on television can't hurt you unless you fall off.

***

After a few years of married life, an engineer finds he is unable to perform. He goes to his doctor, and the doctor tries a few things but nothing works. Finally the doctor says to him, 'This is all in your mind,' and refers him to a psychiatrist.

After a few visits to the shrink, he confesses, 'I am at a loss as to how you could possibly be cured.' Finally the psychiatrist refers him to a witch doctor.

The witch doctor says, 'I can cure this.' He throws powder on a flame and there is a flash with billowing blue smoke. The witch doctor says, 'This is a powerful healing, but you can only use it once a year! All you have to do is say "one-two-three" and it will rise as long as you wish.'

The guy then asks the witch doctor, 'What happens when it's over?'

The witch doctor says, 'All you or your partner has to say is "one-two-three-four" and it will go down. But be warned, it will not work again for a year!'

The guy goes home and that night he is ready to surprise his wife with the good news. He is lying in bed with her and says, 'one-two-three,' and suddenly he gets a huge erection.

His wife turns over and says, 'What did you say "one-two-three" for?'

***

A woman goes to the doctor complaining of bad knee pains. After the diagnostic tests showed nothing, the doctor questions her. 'There must be something you're doing that you haven't told me. Can you think of anything that might be doing this to your knees?'

'Well,' she said a little sheepishly, 'my husband and I have sex doggy-style on the floor every night.'

'That's got to be it,' said the doctor. 'There are plenty of other positions and ways to have sex, you know.'

'Not if you're going to watch TV, there aren't,' she replied.

***

My wife and I had words, but I never got to use mine.

***

Husband: Want a quickie?
Wife: As opposed to what?

Q: How can you tell if your wife is dead?
A: The sex is the same but the dishes pile up.

Q: How can you tell if your husband is dead?
A: The sex is the same but you get the remote.

Q: Why do men name their penises?
A: Because they want to be on a first-name basis with the person who makes all their decisions.

***

If you love something, set it free. If it comes back, it was and will always be yours.

If it never returns, it was never yours to begin with.

If it just sits in your living room, messes up your stuff, eats your food, uses your telephone, takes your money and never behaves as if you actually set it free in the first place, you either married it or gave birth to it!

***

A college student picked up his date at her parents' home. He'd scraped together every cent he had to take her to a fancy restaurant.

To his dismay, she ordered the most expensive things on the menu: appetisers, lobster, champagne, the works. Finally, he asked her, 'Does your mother feed you like this at home?'

'No,' she said, 'but my mother's not looking to get laid, either!'

***

Cinderella wants to go to the ball, but her wicked stepmother won't let her.

As Cinderella sits crying in the garden, her fairy godmother appears and promises to provide Cinderella with everything she needs to go to the ball, but only on two conditions. 'First, you must wear a diaphragm.'

Cinderella agrees. 'What's the second condition?'

'You must be home by 2 a.m. Any later and your diaphragm will turn into a pumpkin.'

Cinderella agrees. The appointed hour comes and

THE WORLD JOKE BOOK

goes, and Cinderella doesn't show up. Finally, at 5 a.m. Cinderella shows up, looking lovestruck and very satisfied.

'Where have you been?' demands the fairy god-mother. 'Your diaphragm was supposed to turn into a pumpkin three hours ago!'

'I met a prince, fairy godmother. He took care of everything.'

'I know of no prince with that kind of power. Tell me his name!'

'I can't remember exactly . . . Peter, Peter, some-thing or other . . .'

***

Pinocchio had a human girlfriend who would some-times complain about splinters when they were having sex. Pinocchio therefore went to visit Geppetto to see if he could help.

Geppetto suggested he try a little sandpaper wherever indicated and Pinocchio skipped away enlightened.

A couple of weeks later, Geppetto saw Pinocchio bouncing happily through town and asked him, 'How's the girlfriend?'

Pinocchio replied, 'Who needs a girlfriend?'

***

Little Red Riding Hood was walking through the woods when suddenly the Big Bad Wolf jumped out from behind a tree and, holding a sword to her throat, said, 'Red, I'm going to screw your brains out!'

To that, Little Red Riding Hood calmly reached into her picnic basket and pulled out a 44 magnum and pointed it at him, and said, 'No you're not. You're gong to eat me, just like it says in the book!'

***

Mickey Mouse and Minnie Mouse were in the divorce court and the judge said, 'Mickey, you say here that your wife is crazy.'

Mickey replied, 'I didn't say she was crazy, I said she's fucking Goofy!'

***

One day a farmer's donkey fell into a well. The animal cried piteously for hours as the farmer tried to figure out what to do. Finally he decided the animal was old, and the well needed to be covered up anyway; it just wasn't worth it to retrieve the donkey.

He invited all his neighbours to come over and help him. They all grabbed a shovel and began to shovel dirt into the well.

At first, the donkey realised what was happening and cried horribly. Then, to everyone's amazement, he quietened down. A few shovel loads later, the farmer finally looked down the well and was astonished at what he saw.

With every shovel of dirt that hit his back, the donkey was doing something amazing. He would shake it off and take a step up. As the farmer's neighbours continued to shovel dirt on top of the animal, he would shake it off and take a step up. Pretty soon, everyone was amazed as the donkey stepped up over the edge of the well and trotted off!

Life is going to shovel dirt on you, all kinds of dirt. The trick to getting out of the well is to shake it off and take a step up. Each of our troubles is a stepping-stone. We can get out of the deepest wells just by not stopping, never giving up. Shake it off and take a step up!

Remember the five simple rules to be happy:

1. Free your heart from hatred.
2. Free your mind from worries.
3. Live simply.
4. Give more.
5. Expect less.

Enough of that crap. The donkey later came back and kicked the shit out of the farmer and tried to bury him.

Moral of the story: When you try to cover your ass, it always comes back to get you!

***

This is a story about a popular young rabbi, who on Sabbath eve, announces to the congregation that he will not renew his contract and is moving on to a larger congregation that will pay him more. There is a hush. No one wants him to leave. Epstein, who owns several car dealerships, stands up and announces, 'If the rabbi stays, I'll provide him with a new sedan every year, and his lovely wife with a mini van to transport their children!' The congregation sighs and applauds.

Goldstein, the entrepreneur and investor, stands and says, 'If the rabbi stays, I'll double his salary and establish a foundation to guarantee the college education of his children!' More sighs and applause.

Old Mrs Goldfarb, aged ninety-six, stands and announces, 'If the rabbi stays, I offer *sex*!' There is a hush. The rabbi, blushing, asks, 'Mrs Goldfarb, whatever possessed you to say that?' Mrs Goldfarb answers, 'I just asked Mr Goldfarb what we could contribute to make the rabbi stay, and he said, "Fuck the rabbi!"'

***

What with all the sadness and trauma going on in the world at the moment, it is worth reflecting on the recent death of a very important person that almost went unnoticed.

Larry La Prise, the man who wrote the song 'The Hokey Pokey', died peacefully at ninety-three. The most traumatic part for his family was getting him into the coffin.

They put his left leg in – and that's when the trouble started!

***

A woman's husband dies. He has only $20 000 to his name. After everything is done at the funeral home and cemetery, she tells her closest friend that there is no money left.

The friend says, 'How can that be? You told me he still had $20 000 left a few days before he died. How can you be broke?'

The widow says, 'Well, the funeral cost me $6000. And, of course, I had to make the obligatory donation to the temple, so that was another $2000. The rest went for the memorial stone.'

The friend says, 'Twelve thousand dollars for the memorial stone? My God, how big was it?'

Extending her left hand, the widow says, 'Three carats.'

***

While waiting for my first appointment in the reception room of a new dentist, I noticed his certificate, which bore his full name. Suddenly I remembered that a tall, handsome boy with the same name had been in my high-school class some years ago.

Upon seeing him, however, I quickly discarded any such thought. This balding, grey-haired man with the deeply lined face was too old to have been my classmate.

After he had examined my teeth, I asked him if he had attended the local high school. 'Yes,' he replied.

'When did you graduate?' I asked.

He answered, 'In 1957.'

'Why, you were in my class!' I exclaimed.

He looked at me closely and then asked, 'What did you teach?'

***

After their baby was born, the panicked father went to see the obstetrician.

'Doctor,' the man said, 'I don't mind telling you, but I'm a little upset because my daughter has red hair. She can't possibly be mine.'

'Nonsense,' the doctor said. 'Even though you and

your wife both have black hair, one of your ancestors may have contributed red hair to the gene pool.'

'It isn't possible,' the man insisted. 'This can't be, our families on both sides have had jet-black hair for generations.'

'Well,' said the doctor, 'let me ask you this. How often do you have sex?'

The man seemed a bit ashamed. 'I've been working very hard for the past year. We only made love once or twice every few months.'

'Well, there you have it,' the doctor said confidently. 'It's rust!'

✱✱✱

Long ago, when men cursed and beat the ground with sticks, it was called witchcraft. Today it's called golf.

✱✱✱

A businessman entered a tavern, sat down at the bar and ordered a double martini on the rocks. After he finished the drink, he peeked inside his shirt pocket, then he ordered another double martini. After he finished that one, he again peeked inside his shirt pocket and ordered another double martini.

Finally, the bartender said, 'Look, buddy, I'll bring

you martinis all night long. But you've got to tell me why you look inside your shirt pocket before you order a refill.'

The customer replied, 'I'm peeking at a photo of my wife. When she starts to look good, then I know it's time to go home.'

***

Relatives gathered in the waiting room of a hospital as their family member lay gravely ill. Finally, the doctor came in looking tired and sombre. 'I'm afraid I'm the bearer of bad news,' he said as he surveyed the worried faces. 'The only hope left for your loved one at this time is a brain transplant. It's an experimental procedure, very risky but it is the only hope. Insurance will cover the procedure, but you will have to pay for the brain yourselves.'

The family members sat silent as they absorbed the news. After a great length of time, someone asked, 'Well, how much does a brain cost?'

The doctor quickly responded, 'Five thousand dollars for a male brain, and two hundred dollars for a female brain.'

The moment turned awkward. Men in the room tried not to smile, avoiding eye contact with the women, but some actually smirked. A man, unable to control his curiosity, blurted out the question everyone wanted to ask: 'Why is the male brain so much more?'

The doctor smiled at the childish innocence and explained to the entire group, 'It's just standard pricing procedure. We have to mark down the price of the female brains, because they've actually been used.'

***

A bloke goes into a chemist shop and asks for some cyanide.

'I can't sell you cyanide,' said the chemist.

'Please, you must sell me some cyanide,' pleads the man.

'Sorry, I can't. Why would you want it anyway?' asks the chemist.

'I want to kill my wife,' says the man.

'Well I definitely can't sell it to you.'

The man reaches into his pocket, slowly takes out his wallet and produces a picture of his wife and slides it across to the chemist.

'Oh, I didn't realise you had a prescription,' says the chemist.

***

Washington DC (Reuters) – Fire Damages Presidential Library:

Tragically, a fire has destroyed the personal library of President George W. Bush. Both of his books have been lost. The President is reportedly devastated – apparently, he had not finished colouring the second one.

***

How can you tell when a man is well hung?
When you can just barely slip your finger in between his neck and the noose.

Why do little boys whine?
Because they're practising to be men.

How many men does it take to screw in a light bulb?
Three. One to screw in the bulb and two to listen to him brag about the screwing part.

What do you call a handcuffed man?
Trustworthy.

How does a man keep his youth?
By giving her money, furs and diamonds.

What does it mean when a man is in your bed gasping for breath and calling your name?
You didn't hold the pillow down long enough.

Why does it take 100 000 000 sperm to fertilise one egg?
Because not one will stop and ask directions.

Why do female black widow spiders kill their males after mating?
To stop the snoring before it starts.

What is the difference between men and women?
A woman wants one man to satisfy her every need. A man wants every women to satisfy his one need.

How do you keep your husband from reading your emails?
Rename the mail folder to 'Instruction Manual'.

***

There was a case in one hospital's intensive care unit where patients always died in the same bed, on Sunday morning, at around 11 a.m., regardless of their medical condition. This puzzled the doctors and some even thought that it had something to do with the supernatural. No one could solve the mystery as to why the deaths occurred around 11 a.m. on Sundays.

So a worldwide team of experts was assembled to investigate the cause of the incidents.

The next Sunday morning, a few minutes before 11 a.m., all the doctors and nurses nervously waited outside the ward to see for themselves what the terrible phenomenon was all about. Some were holding wooden crosses, prayer books and other holy objects to ward off the evil spirits.

Just when the clock struck 11, Pookie Johnson, the part-time Sunday sweeper, entered the ward and unplugged the life-support system so that he could use the vacuum cleaner!

***

A drunken man walks into a biker bar, sits down at the bar and orders a drink. Looking around, he sees three men sitting at a corner table. He gets up, staggers to the table, leans over, looks the biggest, meanest one in the face and says, 'I went by your grandma's house today and I saw her in the hallway buck naked. Man, she is a fine-looking woman!'

The biker looks at him and doesn't say a word. His buddies are confused, because he is one bad biker and would fight at the drop of a hat.

The drunk leans on the table again and says, 'I got it on with your grandma and she is good, the best I ever had!'

The biker's buddies are starting to get really mad, but the biker still says nothing.

The drunk leans on the table one more time and says, 'I'll tell you something else boy, your grandma liked it!'

At this point the biker stands up, takes the drunk by the shoulders and says, 'Grandpa, you're drunk. Go home!'

***

Bill Clinton is getting $12 million for his memoirs. His wife, Hillary, got $8 million for hers.

That's $20 million for memories from two people who for eight years repeatedly testified, under oath, that they couldn't remember anything.

***

A little girl walks into her parents' bathroom and notices for the first time her father's nakedness. Immediately, she is curious: he has equipment that she doesn't have.

She asks, 'What are those round things hanging there, daddy?'

Proudly, he replies, 'Those, sweetheart, are God's Apples of Life. Without them we wouldn't be here.'

Puzzled, she seeks Mummy out and tells her what Daddy has said. To which Mummy asks, 'Did he say anything about the dead branch they're hanging from?'

***

A man and a woman were having drinks, getting to know one another, and started bantering back and forth about male/female issues. They talked about who was better in certain sports, who were the better entertainers etc. The flirting continued for more than an hour when the topic of sex came up. So they got into an argument about who enjoyed sex more.

The man said, 'Men obviously enjoy sex more than woman. Why do you think we're so obsessed with getting laid?' He then went on for several hours arguing his point, even going so far as to ask other men in the bar for their opinions.

The woman listened quietly until the man was finished making his point. Confident in the strength of his argument, the man awaited her response.

'That doesn't prove anything,' the woman countered. 'Think about this. When your ear itches and you put your little finger in it and wiggle it around, then pull it out, which feels better – your ear or your finger?'

***

Six retired Floridians are playing poker in the condo clubhouse when Meyerwitz loses $500 on a single hand, clutches his chest and drops dead at the table.

Showing respect for their fallen comrade, the other five stand up and continue playing.

Finkelstein looks around and asks, 'So who's gonna tell his wife?'

They draw straws. Goldberg picks the short one.

They tell him to be discreet, be gentle, don't make a bad situation any worse.

'Discreet? I'm the most discreet mensch you'll ever meet. Discretion is my middle name. Leave it to me.'

Goldberg goes over to the Meyerwitz apartment and knocks on the door. The wife answers and asks what he wants.

Goldberg declares, 'Your husband just lost $500 and is afraid to come home.'

The wife says, 'Tell him to drop dead!'

'I'll go tell him,' says Goldberg.

***

The Japanese have replaced those impersonal and unhelpful Microsoft error messages with their own Japanese haiku poetry, each with only seventeen syllables: five in the first line, seven in the second, five in the third. So sublimely inscrutable!

Your file is so big.
It might be very useful.
But now it is gone.

The website you seek
Cannot be located, but
Countless more exist.

Chaos reigns within.
Reflect, repeat and reboot.
Order shall return.

Aborted effort.
Close all that you have worked on.
You ask far too much.

Windows NT crashed.
I am the Blue Screen of Death.
No one hears your screams.

Yesterday it worked.
Today it is not working.
Windows is like that.

Stay the patient course.
Of little worth is your ire.
The network is down.

A crash reduces
Your expensive computer
To a simple stone.

Three things are certain:
Death, taxes and lost data.
Guess which has occurred.

You step in the stream,
But the water has moved on.
This page is not here.

Out of memory.
We wish to hold the whole sky,
But we never will.

Having been erased,
The document you're seeking
Must now be retyped.

***

Two sisters, one blonde and one brunette, inherit the family ranch. Unfortunately, after just a few years, they are in financial trouble. In order to keep the bank from repossessing the ranch, they need to purchase a bull so that they can breed their own stock. Before leaving for another ranch to check on the possibility of buying a bull, the brunette tells her sister, 'When I get there, if I decide to buy the bull, I'll contact you to drive out after me and haul it home.'

The brunette arrives at the man's ranch, inspects the bull, and decides she wants to buy it. The man tells her that he will sell it for $599. After paying him, she drives to the nearest town to send her sister a telegram to tell her the news. She walks into the telegraph office and says, 'I want to send a telegram to my sister telling her that I've bought a bull for our ranch. I need her to hitch the trailer to our truck and drive out here so we can haul it home.'

The telegraph operator explains that he'll be glad to help her, then adds, 'It's just 99 cents a word.' Well, after paying for the bull, the brunette only has $1 left. She realises that she'll only be able to send her sister one word.

After thinking for a few minutes, she nods and says, 'I want you to send her the word "Comfortable".'

523

The operator shakes his head. 'How is she ever going to know that you want her to hitch the trailer to your truck and drive out here to haul that bull back to your ranch if you send her the word "comfortable"?'

The brunette explains, 'My sister's blonde. The word's big. She'll read it slow "come-for-da-bull".'

***

A prisoner escapes from his Californian prison where he's been kept for fifteen years. As he runs away, he finds a house and breaks into it. He finds a young couple in bed. He gets the guy out of bed, ties him up on a chair and ties the woman to the bed. He gets on top of her, kisses her on the neck, then gets up and goes to the bathroom.

While he's there, the husband tells his wife, 'Listen, this guy's a prisoner. Look at his clothes! He probably spent a lot of time in prison and hasn't seen a woman in years. I saw the way he kissed you on the neck, so if he wants sex, don't resist, don't complain, just do what he tells you and satisfy him. This guy must be dangerous. If he gets angry he might kill us both. Be strong, honey. I love you.'

To which the wife replies, 'He was not kissing my neck. He was whispering in my ear. He told me that he found you very sexy and asked if we kept any

Vaseline in the bathroom. Be strong, honey. I love you too . . .'

***

After a long night of making love, the guy rolled over and noticed a framed picture of another man on the bedside table. Naturally, he began to worry. 'Is this your husband?' he inquired nervously.

'No, silly,' she replied, snuggling up to him.

'Your boyfriend then?' he asked.

'No, not at all,' she said, nibbling away at his ear.

'Well, who is he then?' demanded the bewildered guy.

Calmly, she replied, 'That's me before the surgery.'

***

CAROLS FOR PSYCHIATRIC PATIENTS

Schizophrenia – Do You Hear What I Hear?

Multiple Personality Disorder – We Three Queens Disoriented are

Dementia – I Think I'll Be Home For Christmas

Narcissistic – Hark the Herald Angels Sing About Me!

Manic – Deck the Halls and Walls and House and Lawn and Streets and Stores and Office and Town and Cars and Buses and Trucks and Trees and Fire Hydrants and . . .

Paranoid – Santa Claus is Coming to Get Me

Borderline Personality Disorder – Thoughts of Roasting on an Open Fire

Personality Disorder – You Better Watch Out, I'm Gonna Cry, I'm Gonna Pout, Maybe I'll Tell You Why

Obsessive Compulsive Disorder – Jingle Bells, Jingle Bells, Jingle Bells, Jingle Bells, Jingle Bells . . .

***

A Chinese couple named Wong have a new baby. The nurse brings them a lovely, healthy, bouncing, definitely Caucasian baby boy.

'Congratulations!' says the nurse to the new parents.

'What will you name the baby?'

The puzzled father looks at his new baby boy and says, 'Well, two Wongs don't make a white, so I think we'll name him Sum Ting Wong.'

***

'I believe that sex is one of the most beautiful, natural, wholesome things that money can buy.'

Tom Clancy

'You know "that look" women get when they want sex? Me neither.' Steve Martin

'Having sex is like playing bridge. If you don't have a good partner, you'd better have a good hand.'

Woody Allen

'Bisexuality immediately doubles your chances for a date on Saturday night.' Rodney Dangerfield

'There are number of mechanical devices that increase sexual arousal, particularly in women. Chief among these is the Mercedes Benz 500SL.' Lynn Lavner

'Leaving sex to the feminists is like letting your dog vacation at the taxidermist.' Matt Barry

527

'Sex at age ninety is like trying to shoot pool with a rope.'
Camille Paglia

'Sex is one of the nine reasons for reincarnation. The other eight are unimportant.'
George Burns

'Women might be able to fake orgasms. But men can fake whole relationships.'
Sharon Stone

'My girlfriend always laughs during sex – no matter what she's reading.'
Steve Jobs (founder, Apple Computers)

'I saw a woman wearing a sweatshirt with "Guess" on it. So I said, "Thyroid problem?"'
Arnold Schwarzenegger

'Hockey is a sport for white men. Basketball is a sport for black men. Golf is a sport for white men dressed like black pimps.'
Tiger Woods

'My mother never saw the irony in calling me a son-of-a-bitch.'
Jack Nicholson

'Women complain about premenstrual syndrome, but I think of it as the only time of the month that I can be myself.'
Roseanne

'Clinton lied. A man might forget where he parks or where he lives, but he never forgets oral sex, no matter how bad it is.'

Barbara Bush (former US first lady)

'Women need a reason to have sex. Men just need a place.'
Billy Crystal

'According to a new survey, women say they feel more comfortable undressing in front of men than they do undressing in front of other women. They say that women are too judgmental where, of course, men are just grateful.'
Robert De Niro

'There's a new medical crisis. Doctors are reporting that many men are having allergic reactions to latex condoms. They say they cause severe swelling. So what's the problem?'
Dustin Hoffman

'There's very little advice in men's magazines, because men think, "I know what I'm doing. Just show me somebody naked."'
Jerry Seinfeld

'See, the problem is that God gives men a brain and a penis and only enough blood to run one at a time.'
Robin Williams

***

Back in the time when the samurai were important, there was a powerful emperor who needed a new chief samurai, so he sent out a declaration throughout the land that he was searching for the best one. A year passed and only three people showed up for the trials: a Japanese samurai, a Chinese samurai and a Jewish samurai.

The emperor asked the Japanese samurai to come in and demonstrate why he should be the chief samurai. The Japanese samurai opened a matchbox, and out flew a bumblebee. *Whoosh* went his razor-sharp sword, and the bumblebee dropped dead on the ground in two pieces.

The emperor exclaimed, 'This is impressive!'

The emperor then issued the same challenge to the Chinese samurai: for him to come in and demonstrate why he should be chosen. The Chinese samurai also opened a matchbox, and out buzzed a fly. *Whoosh, whoosh* went his great flashing sword, and the fly dropped dead on the ground – in four small pieces.

The emperor exclaimed in awe, 'That is really *very* impressive!'

Now the emperor turned to the Jewish samurai and asked him also to step forward and demonstrate why he should be the head samurai. The Jewish samurai also opened a matchbox, and out flew a small gnat. His lightning-quick sword went *Whoosh, whoosh, whoosh, whoosh*, but the tiny gnat was still alive and flying around.

The emperor, obviously very disappointed in this display, said, 'I see you are not up to the task. The gnat is not dead!'

The Jewish samurai just smiled and said, 'Circumcision is not meant to kill.'

***

I went to the doctor the other day and got a full brain scan. He said, 'Your brain has two parts, one left and one right. The left part has nothing right in it, and the right part has nothing left in it.'

***

Have you ever noticed that they put advertisements in with your bills now? Like bills aren't distasteful enough, they have to stuff junk mail in there with them. I get back at them. I put garbage in with my cheque when I send it in – coffee grinds, banana peels . . . I write, 'Could you throw this away for me? Thank you.'

***

Men and women are different in the morning. The men wake up aroused in the morning. We can't help it. We just wake up and we want you. And the women are thinking, 'How can he want me the way I look in the morning?' It's because we can't see you. We have no blood anywhere near our optic nerve.

***

Can you believe how many award shows they have now? They have awards for commercials. The Clio Awards. A whole show full of commercials. I taped it and then fast-forwarded through the whole thing.

***

You know those shows where people call in and vote on different issues? Did you ever notice there's always like 18 per cent 'I don't know'.

It costs 90 cents to call up and vote. They're voting 'I don't know'.

'Honey, I feel very strongly about this. Give me the phone. [Into the phone] "*I don't know!*" [Hangs up, looking proud.] Sometimes you have to stand up for what you believe you're not sure about.'

This guy probably calls sex girls for $2.95. [Into the phone] "I'm not in the mood."'

***

Did you ever hear one of those corny, positive messages on someone's answering machine? 'Hi, it's a great day and I'm out enjoying it right now. I hope you are too. The thought for the day is "Share the love". *Beep*.'

'Uh, yeah . . . This is the VD clinic calling. Speaking of being positive, your test is back. Stop sharing the love.'

***

Once upon a time there were three little pigs, the straw pig, the stick pig and the brick pig.

One day this nasty old wolf came up to the straw pig's house and said, I'm gonna huff and puff and blow your house down.' And he did!

So, the straw pig went running over to the stick pig's house and said, 'Please let me in, the wolf blew down my house.' So the stick pig let the straw pig in.

Just then the wolf showed up and said, 'I'm gonna huff and puff and blow your house down.' And he did!

So the straw pig and the stick pig went running over to the brick pig's house and said, 'Let us in, let us in. The big bad wolf just blew our houses down.'

So the brick pig let them in just as the wolf showed up.

The wolf said, 'I'm gonna huff and puff and blow your house down.' The straw pig and the stick pig were so scared! But the brick pig picked up the phone and made a call.

A few minutes passed and a big, black stretch limo pulled up. Out stepped two massive pigs in pinstriped suits and fedora hats. These pigs went over to the wolf, grabbed him by the neck and beat the living shit out of him. Then one of them pulled out a gun, stick it in the wolf's mouth and fired, killing the wolf. They then got back into their limo and drove off.

The straw pig and the stick pig were amazed. 'Who the hell were those guys?'

'They were my cousins from Brooklyn. The guinea pigs.'

***

Johnny thought he saw his feet sticking out of the end of the bed. So he got up to have a look.

***

Two Iranians meet in California. One starts to greet the other in Farsi, the language of their native country.

The other Iranian waved him away contemptuously and said, 'We're in America now. Speak Spanish!'

***

A linguistics professor was lecturing to his class one day. 'In English,' he said, 'a double negative forms a positive. In some languages though, such as Russian, a double negative is still a negative.'

'However,' he pointed out, 'there is no language wherein a double positive can form a negative.'

A voice from the back of the room piped up, 'Yeah. Right.'

***

ASKING FOR A DAY OFF

So you want a day off. Let's take a look at what you're asking for.

There are 365 days per year available for work.

There are fifty-two weeks per year in which you already have two days off per week, leaving 261 days available for work.

Since you spend sixteen hours each day away from work, you have used up 170 days, leaving only ninety-one days available.

You spend thirty minutes each day on coffee breaks, which counts for twenty-three days each year, leaving only sixty-eight days available.

With a one-hour lunch break each day, you use up another forty-six days, leaving only twenty-two days available for work.

You normally spend two days per year on sick leave. This leaves you only twenty days per year available for work.

We are off five holidays per year, so your available working time is down to fifteen days.

We generally give you fourteen days' holiday per year, which leaves only one day available for work. And I'll be damned if you're going to take that day off!

★★★

The old Cherokee chief sat in his reservation hut, smoking the ceremonial pipe, eyeing the two US government officials sent to interview him.

'Chief Two Eagles,' one official began, 'you have observed the white man for many generations. You have seen his wars and his products. You have seen all his progress, and all his problems.' The chief nodded. The official continues, 'Considering recent events, in your opinion, where has the white man gone wrong?'

The chief stared at the government officials for over a minute, and then calmly replied, 'When white man found the land, Indians were running it. No taxes. No debt. Plenty buffalo. Plenty beaver. Women did most of the work. Medicine man free. Indian men hunted and fished all the time.' The chief smiled, and added quietly, 'White man dumb enough to think he could improve system like that.'

***

Husband and wife are waiting at the bus stop. With them are their eight children. A blind man joins them after a few minutes. When the bus arrives, they find it overloaded and only the wife and her eight children are able to fit in the bus. So the husband and the blind man decide to walk.

After a while the husband gets irritated by the ticking of the stick of the blind man and says to him, 'Why don't you put a piece of rubber on the end of your stick? That ticking sound is driving me crazy!'

The blind man replies, 'If you'd have put a rubber on the end of *your* stick, we'd be sitting on the bus right now!'

***

A Jewish family is considering putting their grandfather in a nursing home. All the Jewish facilities are completely full so they have to put him in a Catholic home. After a few weeks in the Catholic facility, they come to visit grandpa.

'How do you like it here?' asks the grandson.

'It's wonderful. Everyone here is so courteous and respectful,' says grandpa.

'We're so happy for you. We were worried that this was the wrong place for you.'

'Let me tell you about how wonderfully they treat the residents here,' grandpa says with a big smile. 'There's a musician here – he's eighty-five years old. He hasn't played the violin in twenty years, and everyone still calls him "Maestro"! And there's a physician here – ninety years old. He hasn't been practising medicine for twenty-five years and everyone still calls him "Doctor"! And me, I haven't had sex for thirty years and they still call me "the fucking Jew".'

***

JEWISH HAIKU

After the warm rain
The sweet smell of camellias.
Did you wipe your feet?

Her lips near my ear,
Aunt Said whispers the name
Of her friend's disease.

Today I am a man.
Tomorrow I will return
To the seventh grade.

Testing the warm milk
On her wrists, she sighs softly.
But her son is forty.

The sparkling blue sea
Reminds me to wait an hour
After my sandwich.

Lacking fins or tail
The gefilte fish swims
With great difficulty.

Like a bonsai tree,
Your terrible posture
At my dinner table.

Beyond Valium,
The peace of knowing one's child
Is an internist.

Jews on safari –
Map, compass, elephant gun,
Hard sucking candies.

The same kimono
The top geishas are wearing
I got it at Loehmann's.

The shivah visit:
So sorry about your loss.
Now back to my problems.

Sorry I'm not home
To take your call. At the tone
Please state your bad news.

Is one Nobel Prize
So much to ask from a child
After all I've done?

Passover
Left the door open
For the Prophet Elijah.
Now our cat is gone.

Quietly murmured
At Saturday services,

Yanks 5, Red Sox 3.

Hard to tell under the lights.
White yarmulke or
Male-pattern baldness.

***

MEN VERSUS WOMEN

NAMES
If Laurie, Linda, Elizabeth and Barbara go out for lunch, they will call each other Laurie, Linda, Elizabeth and Barbara.

If Mark, Chris, Eric and Tom go out, they will affectionately refer to each other as Fat Boy, Godzilla, Peanut-Head and Scrappy.

MONEY
A man will pay $2 for a $1 item he needs.

A woman will pay $1 for a $2 item that she doesn't need but it's on sale.

EATING OUT
When the bill arrives, Mark, Chris, Eric and Tom will each throw in $20, even though it's only $32.50. None of them will have anything smaller and none

will actually admit they want change back.

When the girls get their bill, out come the pocket calculators.

BATHROOMS
A man has six items in his bathroom: a toothbrush, shaving cream, razor, a bar of soap and a towel from the Marriott.

The average number of items in the typical woman's bathroom is 337. A man would not be able to identify most of these items.

ARGUMENTS
A woman has the last word in any argument.
Anything a man says after that is the beginning of a new argument.

SUCCESS
A successful man is one who makes more money than his wife can spend.

A successful woman is one who can find such a man.

MARRIAGE
A woman marries a man expecting he will change, but he doesn't.

A man marries a woman expecting that she won't change, and she does.

DRESSING UP
A woman will dress up to go shopping, water the plants, empty the garbage, answer the phone, read a book and get the mail.

A man will dress up for weddings and funerals.

NATURAL
Men wake up as good-looking as they went to bed.

Women somehow deteriorate during the night.

OFFSPRING
Ah, children! A woman knows all about her children. She knows about dentist appointments and romances, best friends, favourite foods, secret fears and hopes and dreams.

A man is vaguely aware of some short people living in the house.

THOUGHT FOR THE DAY
Any married man should forget his mistakes. There's no use in two people remembering the same thing.

★★★

A passenger tapped the taxi driver on the shoulder to ask him a question.

The taxi driver screamed, lost control of the car, nearly hit a bus, went up on the footpath, narrowly missed a pole and stopped centimetres from a shop window.

For a second everything went quiet in the cab, then the driver said, 'Look mate, don't ever do that again. You scared the daylights out of me!'

The passenger apologised and said, 'I didn't realise that a little tap would scare you so much.'

The driver replied, 'Sorry, it's not really your fault. Today is my first day as a cab driver – I've been driving a funeral car for the past twenty-five years.'

***

Helen Clark, the Prime Minister of New Zealand, is rudely awoken at 4 a.m. by the telephone.

'Hillen, it's the hilth munster here. Sorry to bother you et thus hour but there es un emergency! I've just received word thet the Durex factory en Auckland has burned to the ground. It is istimated thet the entire New Zulland supply of condoms will be gone by the ind of the week.'

'Shuuuuut – the economy wull niver be able to cope with all those unwanted babies – we'll be ruined! We're going to hef to shup some en from abroad – Britain?'

'No chence! The Poms wull have a field day on thus one!'

'What about Australia?'

'Maybe – but we don't want them to know thet we are stuck. You call John Howard – tell hum we need one moollion condoms; tun enches long and four enches thuck! Thet way they'll know how bug the Kiwis really are!'

Helen calls John, who agrees to help the Kiwis out in their hour of need.

Three days later a van arrives in Auckland – full of boxes. A delighted Helen rushes out to open the boxes. She finds condoms: 10 inches long, 4 inches thick, all coloured green and gold. She then notices in small writing on each and every one: MADE IN AUSTRALIA. SIZE: MEDIUM.

***

A man suspected of having SARS is lying in bed with a mask over his mouth. A young auxiliary nurse appears to sponge his face and hands. 'Nurse,' he mumbles from behind the mask, 'are my testicles black?'

Embarrassed, the young nurse replies, 'I don't know Mr Lee, I'm only here to wash your face and hands.'

He struggles again to ask, 'Nurse, are my testicles black?'

Again the nurse replies, 'I can't tell. I'm only here to wash your face and hands.'

The head nurse was passing and saw the man getting a little distraught so she marched over to inquire what was wrong.

'Nurse,' he mumbled, 'are my testicles black?'

Being a nurse of longstanding, the head nurse was undaunted. She whipped back the bedclothes, pulled down his pyjamas pants, moved his penis out of the way, had a good look, pulled up the pyjamas, replaced the bedclothes and announced, 'Nothing wrong with your testicles!'

At this, the man pulled off his mask and asked again, 'I said, "Are my test results back?"'

***

OFFICE CHRISTMAS PARTY

From: Ms Pat Smith, Human Resources Director
To: All Staff
Date: December 2
Re: Christmas Party

I'm happy to inform you that the office Christmas Party will take place on December 22, starting at noon in the banquet room at Luigi's Open Pit Barbecue. No host bar, but plenty of eggnog! We'll have a small band playing traditional carols – feel free to sing along. And don't be surprised if our general manager shows up dressed as Santa Claus!

From: Pat Smith, Human Resources Director
Date: December 4
Re: Christmas Party

In no way was yesterday's memo intended to exclude our Jewish employees. We recognise that Hanukkah is an important holiday, which often coincides with Christmas, though unfortunately not this year. However, from now on we're calling it our 'Holiday Party'. The same policy applies to employees who are celebrating Kwanzaa at this time.

Happy now?

From: Pat Smith, Human Resources Director
Date: December 5
Re: Holiday Party

Regarding the note I received from a member of Alcoholics Anonymous requesting a non-drinking table, you didn't sign your name. I'm happy to accommodate this request, but if I put a sign on a table that reads 'AA Only' you wouldn't be anonymous anymore. How am I supposed to handle this?

From: Pat Smith, Human Resources Director
Date: December 6
Re: Holiday Party

What a diverse company we are! I had no idea that November 27 was the beginning of the Muslim holy month of Ramadan, which forbids eating, drinking and intimacy during daylight hours. There goes the party! Seriously, we can appreciate how a luncheon this time of year does not accommodate our Muslim employees' beliefs. Perhaps Luigi's can hold off on serving your meal until the end of the party, or else package everything for take-home in little foil swans. Will that work? Meanwhile, I've arranged for members of Overeaters Anonymous to sit furthest from the dessert buffet and pregnant women will get the table closest to the restrooms. Did I miss anything?

From: Pat Smith, Human Resources Director
Date: December 7
Re: Holiday Party

People, people, nothing sinister was intended by having our GM dress up like Santa Claus! Even if the anagram of 'Santa' does happen to be 'Satan', there is no evil connotation to our own 'little man in a red suit'. It's a tradition, folks, like sugar shock at Halloween or family feuds over the Thanksgiving turkey or broken hearts on Valentine's Day. Could we lighten up?

From: Pat Smith, Human Resources Director
Date: December 11
Re: Holiday Party

Vegetarians!? I've had it with you people! We're going to keep this party at Luigi's Open Pit Barbecue whether you like it or not, so you can sit quietly at the table furthest from the 'grill of death', as you so quaintly put it, and you'll get your #$%^&* salad, including hydroponic tomatoes . . . But you know, they have feelings too! Tomatoes scream when you slice them. I've heard them scream, I'm hearing them scream right now!

From: Karen Jones, Acting Human Resources
Director
Date: December 12
Re: Pat Smith and Holiday Party

I'm sure I speak for all of us in wishing Pat Smith a speedy recovery from her stress-related illness and I'll continue to forward your cards to her at the sanatorium. In the meantime, management has decided to cancel our Holiday Party and give everyone the afternoon of the 22nd off with full pay.

Happy holidays!

***

THINGS KIDS SAY

Q: How do you decide whom to marry?

A: You got to find someone who likes the same stuff. Like, if you like sports, she should like it that you like sports, and she should keep the chips and dip coming.

Alan, age ten.

A: No person really decides before they grow up who they're going to marry. God decides it before, and you get to find out later who you're stuck with.

Kirsten, age ten.

Q: What is the right age to get married?

A: Twenty-three is the best age because you know the person *forever* by then.

Camille, age ten.

A: No age is good to get married at. You got to be a fool to get married.
Freddie, age six.

Q: How can a stranger tell if two people are married?
A: You might have to guess, based on whether they seem to be yelling at the same kids.
Derrick, age eight.

Q: What do you think your mum and dad have in common?
A: Both don't want any more kids.
Lori, age eight.

Q: What do most people do on a date?
A: Dates are for having fun, and people should use them to get to know each other. Even boys have something to say if you listen long enough.
Lynette, age eight.

A: On the first date, they just tell each other lies, and that usually gets them interested enough to go for a second date.
Martin, age ten.

Q: What would you do on a first date that was turning sour?

A: I'd run home and play dead. The next day I would call all the newspapers and make sure they wrote about me in all the dead columns.
Craig, age nine.

Q: When is it okay to kiss someone?

A: When they're rich.
Pam, age seven.

A: The law says you have to be eighteen, so I wouldn't want to mess with that.
Curt, age seven.

A: The rule goes like this: if you kiss someone, then you should marry them and have kids with them. It's the right thing to do.
Howard, age eight.

Q: Is it better to be single or married?

A: I don't know which is better, but I'll tell you one thing. I'm never going to have sex with my wife. I don't want to be all grossed out.
Theodore, age eight.

A: It's better for girls to be single but not for boys.

Boys need someone to clean up after them.
Anita, age nine.

Q: How would the world be different if people didn't get married?
A: There sure would be a lot of kids to explain, wouldn't there?
Kelvin, age eight.

Q: How would you make a marriage work?
A: Tell your wife that she looks pretty, even if she looks like a truck.
Ricky, age ten.

***

NUDITY

I was driving with my three young children one warm summer evening when a woman in the convertible ahead of us stood up and waved. She was stark naked! As I was reeling from the shock, I heard my five-year-old shout from the back seat, 'Mum! That lady isn't wearing a seat belt!'

MORE NUDITY

A little boy got lost in the YMCA and found himself in the women's locker room. When he was spotted the women burst into shrieks, grabbing towels and running for cover. The little boy watched in amazement and then asked, 'What's the matter, haven't you ever seen a little boy before?'

***

The only cow in a small town in Poland stopped giving milk. The people did some research and found that they could buy a cow from Moscow for 2000 roubles, or one from Minsk for 1000 roubles.

Being frugal, they bought the cow from Minsk. The cow was wonderful. It produced lots of milk all the time, and the people were amazed and very happy.

They decided to acquire a bull to mate with the cow and produce more cows like it. Then they would never have to worry about the milk supply again.

They bought a bull and put it in the pasture with their beloved cow. However, whenever the bull came close to the cow, the cow would move away. No matter what approach the bull tried, the cow would move away from the bull and he could not succeed in his quest.

The people were very upset and decided to ask the rabbi, who was very wise, what to do. They told the rabbi what was happening. 'Whenever the bull approaches our cow, she moves away. If he approaches from the back, she moves forward. When he approaches her from the front, she backs off. An approach from the side and she just walks away to the other side.

The rabbi thought about this for a minute and asked, 'Did you buy this cow from Minsk?'

The people were dumfounded. They had never mentioned where they had gotten the cow. 'You are truly wise, rabbi. How did you know we got the cow from Minsk?'

The rabbi answered sadly, 'My wife is from Minsk.'

***

Two guys are moving about in a supermarket when their carts collide. One says to the other, 'Excuse me, but I'm looking for my wife.'

'What a coincidence, so am I. And I'm getting a little desperate.'

'Well, maybe I can help you. What does your wife look like?'

'She's tall, with dark hair, long legs, firm tits and a tight arse. What's your wife look like?'

'Never mind, let's look for yours!'

***

WOMEN'S QUOTE OF THE DAY
Men are like wine. They all start out like grapes, and it's our job to stomp on them and keep them in the dark until they mature into something with which you'd like to have dinner.

MEN'S COUNTER-QUOTE OF THE DAY
Women are like wine. They all start out fresh, fruity and intoxicating to the mind and then turn full-bodied with age until they go all sour and vinegary and give you a headache!

***

Dear Mr President,

With regard to your State Visit to the United Kingdom (which, I repeat, is neither a Queendom nor a great republic), some final notes to cover various aspects of your schedule:

Meeting the Royal Family
1. Elizabeth II is not the daughter of Elizabeth I.
2. She is Queen because her father was King and his father was King and so on, more or less back to some guy called Alfred the Great. It may sound a crazy way to choose a head of state, but remember Florida. She has also held down the job since

Harry S. Truman's time. Think about it.

3. The Brits do not share the American view that the Second World War began in 1941.

4. Do not try to be smart and ask if the number of Italian restaurants you see is a legacy of the Roman occupation.

5. The National Health Service is not a Commie plot. The CIA suggests that the BBC may be, but evidence is sketchy.

6. Do not ask to meet Sherlock Holmes, Robin Hood, Big Ben or Harry Potter.

7. Introduce the name David Beckham (profile attached) in conversation whenever possible. Please note that his wife is not a soccer mum.

8. During your visit, England's cricket team will be playing overseas. Show polite interest, but do not ask anyone to explain the game; greater American minds than yours have failed to understand it.

9. The UK is close to Europe, and its nearest neighbour is France, which some Brits actually like. The phrase 'cheese-eating surrender monkeys' is not widely used.

10. Among other things, the Brits invented the locomotive, the jet engine, TV, penicillin, the computer, radar, golf, the hovercraft, the sewing machine, disc brakes and (at least they claim) Viagra. The only American inventions most of

them know are the hamburger and the hot dog. Be humble.

11. We have been warned of demonstrations during your visit. Do not express surprise at the lack of tear gas, water cannon and armed troops to control them. In view of your known admiration for Sir Winston Churchill, you may think that certain gestures you will see indicate the people's home for victory in Iraq. They don't – and do not respond in kind.

***

An old couple were in a car wreck and died. When they got to heaven, St Peter was showing them around. He showed them all the mansions, the streets of gold, then took them to the Feast!

He started showing them all the wonderful foods – pork, beef, all kinds of vegies, lots of sweets. The old man asked St Peter, 'Where's the low-fat food?'

St Peter said, 'No need for low fat here.'

Then the old man asked, 'Where are the bran muffins and low-carb foods?'

St Peter said, 'No need for that either. This is heaven, you can eat whatever you want.'

The old man thinks for just a minute then turns around and decks his wife. She looks up at him in shock and said, 'Why did you do that?'

He replied, 'If it wasn't for you and those darn bran muffins, I could have been here twenty years ago!'

✱✱✱

One dark night outside a small town, a fire started inside the local chemical plant and in a blink it exploded into flames. The alarm went out to fire departments from miles around. When the volunteer fire fighters appeared on the scene, the chemical-company president rushed to the fire chief and said, 'All of our secret formulas are in the vault in the centre of the plant. They must be saved. I will give $50 000 to the fire department that brings them out intact.'

But the roaring flames held the fire fighters off. Soon more fire departments had to be called in as the situation became desperate.

As the fireman arrived, the president shouted out that the offer was now $100 000 to the fire department who could bring out the company's secret files.

From the distance, a lone siren was heard as another fire truck came into sight. It was the nearby Jewish rural-township volunteer fire company, composed entirely of men over the age of sixty-five. To everyone's amazement, the little rundown fire engine operated by this Jewish fire department passed all the newer sleek engines parked outside the plant . . . and drove straight into the middle of the inferno.

Outside the other firemen watched as the Jewish old-timers jumped off and began to fight the fire with a performance and effort never seen before. Within a short time, the Jewish old-timers had extinguished the fire and saved the secret formulas.

The grateful chemical-company president joyfully announced that for such a superhuman feat he upped the reward to $200 000, and walked over to personally thank each of the brave, though elderly, Jewish fire fighters.

The local TV news reporters rushed in after capturing the event on film, asking, 'What are you going to do with all that money?'

'Well,' said Ami Hertzfeld, the seventy-year-old fire chief, 'the first thing we are going to do is fix the brakes on this fucking truck!'

***

A blond guy gets home early from work and hears strange noises coming from the bedroom. He rushes upstairs to find his wife naked on the bed, sweating and panting. 'What's up?' he asks.

'I'm having a heart attack,' cries the woman.

He rushes downstairs to grab the phone, but just as

he's dialling, his four-year-old son comes up and says, 'Daddy! Daddy! Uncle Ted's hiding in your closet and he's got no clothes on!'

The guy slams down the phone and storms upstairs to the bedroom, past his screaming wife and rips over the wardrobe door. Sure enough, there's his brother, totally naked, cowering on the closet floor.

'You rotten bastard,' says the husband, 'my wife's having a heart attack and you're running around naked scaring the kids!'

***

TRADITIONAL CAPITALISM
You have two cows. You sell one and buy a bull. Your herd multiples and the economy grows. You sell them and retire on the income.

ENRON VENTURE CAPITALISM
You have two cows. You sell three of them to your publicly listed company, using letters of credit opened by your brother-in-law at the bank, then execute a debt/equity swap with an associated general offer so that you get all four cows back with a tax exemption for five cows. The milk rights of the six cows are transferred via an intermediary to a Cayman Island company secretly owned by the majority shareholder

who sells the rights to all seven cows back to your listed company. The annual report says the company owns eight cows, with an option on one more. Sell one cow to buy a new president of the United States, leaving you with nine cows. No balance sheet provided with the release. The public buys your bull.

AN AMERICAN CORPORATION

You have two cows. You sell one, and force the other to produce the milk of four cows. You are surprised when the cow drops dead.

A FRENCH CORPORATION

You have two cows. You go on strike because you want three cows.

A JAPANESE CORPORATION

You have two cows. You redesign them so they are one-tenth the size of an ordinary cow and produce twenty times the milk. You then create clever cow cartoon images called Cowkemon and market them worldwide.

A GERMAN CORPORATION

You have two cows. You re-engineer them so they live more than one hundred years, eat once a month, and milk themselves.

A BRITISH CORPORATION
You have two cows. Both are mad.

A RUSSIAN CORPORATION
You have two cows. You count them and learn you have five cows. You count them again and learn you have forty-two cows. You count them again and learn you have twelve cows. You stop counting cows and open another bottle of vodka.

A SWISS CORPORATION
You have 5000 cows, none of which belong to you. You charge others for storing them.

A CHINESE CORPORATION
You have two cows. You have 300 people milking them. You claim full employment, high bovine productivity, and arrest the newsman who reported the numbers.

AN ISRAELI CORPORATION
So, there are these two Jewish cows, right? The cows open a milk factory, write an ice-cream story, and then sell the movie rights. They send their calves to Harvard to become doctors. So, who needs people?

A SAUDIAN CORPORATION

You have two cows. Everybody wants your milk. You found an organisation of milk producers to raise prices. With the money, you finance terrorists to kill other breeders.

A NEW ZEALAND CORPORATION

You have two cows. That one on the left is kinda cute . . .

AN IRAQI CORPORATION

You have two cows. You execute one of them and tell the other to produce twice as much milk or it will go the same way. America notices this and sends in troops to kill you. You hide. The troops kill the remaining cow and claim that it was collateral damage and it was your fault anyway for hiding behind the cow. They steal your oil – sorry – milk for safekeeping and put an American general in charge of your corporation to ensure the safety of your remaining cows . . . Oh.

***

A little boy opened the big family Bible. He was fascinated as he fingered through the pages. Suddenly, something fell out of the Bible. He picked up the object and looked at it. What he saw was an old leaf that had been pressed between the pages. 'Mum, look what I found,' the boy called out.

'What have you got there, dear?'

With astonishment in the young boy's voice, he answered, 'I think it's Adam's underwear!'

***

RULES FOR GAY MARRIAGES

1. On the day of a gay wedding, it's bad luck for the two grooms to see each other at the gym.
2. Superstition suggests that for good luck the couple should have: something bold, something flirty, something trashy, something dirty.
3. It's customary at gay and lesbian nuptials for the parents to have an open bar during the entire ceremony.
4. Gay wedding tradition dictates that both grooms refrain from eating any of the wedding cake because it's all carbs and sugar.
5. It's considered bad luck for either of the grooms to have dated the priest.
6. During the first dance, it's considered unlucky to use glow sticks, flags, whistles or hand-held lasers.
7. For good luck at the union of a drag queen, the

    bouquet is always thrown in the face of a hated rival.

8. The reception hall must have a disco ball and at least one go-go dancer.

9. The wedding singer is not allowed to play/sing 'Let's Hear It For the Boy', 'It's Raining Men' or 'I Will Survive'.

10. The father of the bottom pays for everything!

***

You know the world has changed when you realise:
    The best rapper is a white guy.
    The best golfer is a black guy.
    And Germany doesn't want to go to war!

***

UNDERSTANDING ENGINEERS – 1

A pastor, a doctor and an engineer were waiting one morning for a particularly slow group of golfers. The engineer fumed, 'What's with these guys? We must have been waiting for fifteen minutes!'

The doctor chimed in, 'I don't know, but I've never seen such ineptitude!'

The pastor said, 'Hey, here comes the greens keeper. Let's have a word with him. Hi, George, what's with that group ahead of us? They're rather slow, aren't they?'

The greens keeper replied, 'Oh, yes, that's a group of blind fire-fighters. They lost their sight saving our clubhouse from a fire last year, so we always let them play for free any time.'

The group was silent for a moment. The pastor said, 'That's so sad. I think I'll say a special prayer for them tonight.'

The doctor said, 'Good idea. And I'm going to contact my ophthalmologist buddy and see if there's anything he can do for them.'

The engineer said, 'Why can't these guys play at night?'

UNDERSTANDING ENGINEERS – 2
What is the difference between mechanical engineers and civil engineers?

Mechanical engineers build weapons and civil engineers build targets.

UNDERSTANDING ENGINEERS – 3
The graduate with a science degree asks, 'Why does it work?'

The graduate with an engineering degree asks, 'How does it work?'

The graduate with an accounting degree asks, 'How much will it cost?'

The graduate with an arts degree asks, 'Do you want fries with that?'

UNDERSTANDING ENGINEERS – 4
Three engineering students were gathered together discussing the possible designers of the human body. One said, 'It was a mechanical engineer. Just look at all the joints.'

Another said, 'No, it was an electrical engineer. The nervous system has many thousands of electrical connections.'

The last one said, 'Actually it was a civil engineer. Who else would run a toxic waste pipeline through a recreational area?'

UNDERSTANDING ENGINEERS – 5
Normal people believe that if it ain't broke, don't fix it. Engineers believe that if it ain't broke, it doesn't have enough features yet.

UNDERSTANDING ENGINEERS – 6
An engineer was crossing a road one day when a frog called out to him and said, 'If you kiss me, I'll turn into a beautiful princess.' He bent over, picked up the frog and put it in his pocket. The frog spoke up again and said, 'If you kiss me and turn me back into a beautiful princess, I will stay with you for one week.'

The engineer took the frog out of his pocket, smiled at it and returned it to his pocket.

The frog then cried out, 'If you kiss me and turn me back into a princess, I'll stay with you and do *anything* you want.' Again the engineer took the frog out, smiled at it, and put it back into his pocket.

Finally the frog asked, 'What is the matter? I've told you I'm a beautiful princess, and that I'll stay with you for a week and do anything you want. Why won't you kiss me?'

The engineer said, 'Look, I'm an engineer. I don't have time for a girlfriend, but a talking frog, now that's cool!'

***

Two dwarves go into a bar, where they pick up two prostitutes and take them to their separate hotel rooms.

The first dwarf, however, is unable to get an erection. His depression is made worse by the fact that, from the next room, he hears his little friend shouting out cries of 'Here I come again . . . *one, two, three . . . uuh!*' all night long.

In the morning, the second dwarf asks the first, 'How did it go?'

The first mutters, 'It was so embarrassing. I simply couldn't get a hard on.'

The second dwarf shook his head, 'You think that's embarrassing? I couldn't even get on the fucking bed!'

***

ANSWERS TO EXAM QUESTIONS

What was Hitler's Christian name?
Heil.

What is a turbine?
Something an Arab wears on his head.

What is Britain's highest award for valour in war?
Nelson's Column.

Who was it that didn't like the return of the prodigal son?
The fattened calf.

What's a Hindu?
It lays eggs.

Use the word 'judicious' in a sentence to show you understand its meaning.
Hands that judicious can be as soft as your face.

Name the four seasons.
Salt, mustard, pepper, vinegar.

What changes happen to your body as you age?
When you get old, so do your bowels and you get intercontinental.

What guarantees may a mortgage company insist on?
They'll insist you're well endowed if you're buying a house.

How important are elections to a democratic society?
Sex can only happen when a male gets an election.

What is the first thing you would do to someone who has been involved in a car accident and is immobile?
Rape them in a blanket and give them a sweet cup of tea.

What is artificial respiration commonly known as?
The Kiss of Death.

What is a common treatment for a badly bleeding nose?
Circumcision.

Red, pink, orange and flamingo are the colours of the rectum.

I've said goodbye to my boyhood, now I'm looking forward to my adultery.

Monotony means being married to the same person for all your life.

I always know that it's time to get up when I hear my mother sharpening the toast.

Christians go on pilgrimages to Lord's.

A sexually transmitted disease is gonorrhoea, the penis becomes inflammable.

A major disease associated with smoking is premature death.

The equator is a menagerie lion running around the earth through Africa.

Artificial insemination is when the farmer does it to the cow instead of the bull.

Cows produce large amounts of methane, so the problem could be solved by fitting them with catalytic converters.

The process of flirtation makes water safe to drink because it removes large pollutants like grit, sand, dead sheep and canoeists.

A common disease of cereal crops is wheatgerm.

An important difference between the male and female reproductive systems is that a tube joins the testis to the exterior – called the vast difference.

Water is composed of two gins, Oxygin and Hydrogin. Oxygin is pure gin. Hydrogin is gin and water.

When you breathe, you inspire. When you do not breathe, you expire.

H_2O is hot water, and CO_2 is cold water.

To collect fumes of sulphur, hold down a deacon over a flame in a test tube.

When you smell an odourless gas, it is probably carbon monoxide.

Nitrogen is not found in Ireland because it is not found in a free state.

Three kinds of blood vessels are arteries, vanes and caterpillars.

Blood flows down one leg and up the other.

Respiration is composed of two acts: first inspiration and then expectoration.

The moon is a planet just like the earth, only it is even deader.

Dew is formed on leaves when the sun shines down on them and makes them perspire.

A super-saturated solution is one that holds more than it can hold.

Mushrooms always grow in damp places and so they look like umbrellas.

Momentum: what you give a person when they are going away.

Planet: a body of earth surrounded by sky.

Rhubarb: a kind of celery gone bloodshot.

Before giving a blood transfusion, find out if the blood is affirmative or negative.

To remove dust from the eye, pull the eye down over the nose.

For a nosebleed: put the nose much lower than the body until the heart stops.

For drowning: climb on top of the person and move up and down to make Artificial Perspiration.

For fainting: rub the person's chest or, if a lady, rub her arm above the hand instead. Or put the head between the knees of the nearest medical doctor.

For dog bite: put the dog away for several days. If he has not recovered, then kill it.

To prevent contraception, wear a condominium.

For head cold: use an agonizer to spray the nose until it drops in your throat.

To keep milk from turning sour: keep it in the cow.

The pistol of a flower is its only protection against insects.

The alimentary canal is located in the northern part of Indiana.

A permanent set of teeth consists of eight canines, eight cuspids, two molars and eight cuspidors.

The tides are a fight between the Earth and moon. All water tends towards the moon, because there is no water in the moon and nature abhors a vacuum. I get where the sun joins in this fight.

A fossil is an extinct animal. The older it is, the more extinct it is.

***

He said: I don't know why you wear a bra, you've got nothing to put in it.
She said: You wear pants, don't you?

He said: Shall we try swapping positions tonight?
She said: That's a good idea – you stand by the ironing board while I sit on the sofa.

He said: What have you been doing with all the grocery money I gave you?
She said: Turn sideways and look in the mirror!

On a wall in a ladies room: My husband follows me everywhere.
Written just below it: I do not.

***

Q: How many honest, intelligent, caring men in the world does it take to do the dishes?
A: Both of them.

Q: What's the difference between men and government bonds?
A: The bonds mature.

Q: Why are blonde jokes so short?
A: So men can remember them.

Q: How many men does it take to change a roll of toilet paper?
A: We don't know, it has never happened.

Q: Why is it difficult to find men who are sensitive, caring and good-looking?

A: They already have boyfriends.

Q: What do you call a woman who knows where her husband is every night?
A: A widow.

Q: Why are married women heavier than single women?
A: Single women come home, see what's in the fridge and go to bed. Married women come home, see what's in bed and go to the fridge.

Man says to God: 'God, why did you make woman so beautiful?'

God says to man: 'So you would love her.'

'But God,' the man says, 'why did you make her so dumb?'

God says: 'So she would love you.'

***

I bought a time machine next week.

It's going to break down last year.

So I took it to the workshop and the mechanic said, 'They don't make them like they soon will.'

***

Three men had a very late night drinking Guinness. They left in the early morning hours and went home their separate ways.

The next day, they all met for an early pint, and compared notes about who was drunker the night before. The first guy claimed that he was the drunkest, saying, 'I drove straight home and walked into the house. As soon as I got through the door, I blew chunks.'

The second guy said, 'You think that was drunk? Hell, I got into my car and wrapped my car around the first tree I saw. I don't even have insurance!'

The third guy proclaimed, 'Damn, I was the drunkest by far. When I got home, I got into a big fight with the wife, knocked a candle over and burned the whole house down!'

The room was silent for a moment. Then the first guy spoke out again, 'Listen guys. I don't think you understand. Chunks is my dog.'

***

An old farmer in Georgia had owned a large farm for several years. He had a large pond in the back that was fixed up nice with picnic tables, horseshoe courts, a basketball court etc. When it was built, the pond was shaped like a swimming pool. As he hadn't been there for a while, one evening the old farmer decided to go down to the pond and look it over.

As he neared the pond, he heard shouting and laughing. When he came closer, he saw it was a bunch of young women skinny-dipping in his pond. He made the women aware of his presence and they all went into the deep end of the pond. One of the women shouted to him, 'We're not coming out until you leave!'

The old man replied, 'I didn't come down here to watch you ladies swim or make you get out of the pond naked. I'm here to feed the alligator!'

***

This morning, from a secret cave somewhere in Pakistan, Taliban Minister for Migration Mohammed Omar warned the United States that if military action against Iraq continues, Taliban authorities will cut off America's supply of convenience-store managers.

***

One day, three men were hiking and unexpectedly came upon a large raging, violent river. They needed to get to the other side, but had no idea how to do so.

The first man prayed to God, saying, 'Please God, give me the strength to cross this river.' *Poof!* God

THE WORLD J0kE BOOK

gave him big arms and strong legs and he was able to swim across the river in about two hours, after almost drowning a couple of times.

Seeing this, the second man prayed to God, saying, 'Please God, give me the strength and the tools to cross this river.' *Poof!* God gave him a rowboat and he was able to row across the river in about an hour, after almost capsizing the boat a couple of times.

The third man had seen how this worked out for the other two, so he also prayed to God, saying, 'Please God, give me the strength and the tools – and the intelligence – to cross this river.' And *poof!* God turned him into a woman. She looked at the map, hiked upstream a couple of hundred yards, then walked across the bridge.

***

THE CHICKEN AND THE HORSE

On the farm lived a chicken and a horse that loved to play together. One day, the two were playing when the horse fell into a bog and began to sink. Scared for his life, the horse whinnied to the chicken to go get the farmer for help. Off the chicken ran, back to the farm.

Arriving at the farm, he searched and searched for the farmer, but to no avail, for he had gone to town with the only tractor. Running around, the chicken spied the farmer's new BMW Z3. Finding the keys inside, the chicken sped off with a length of rope, hoping he still had time to save his friend's life.

Back at the bog, the horse was surprised, but happy, to see the chicken arrive in the shiny BMW, and he managed to get hold of the loop of rope the chicken tossed to him. After tying the other end to the rear of the bumper of the farmer's car, the chicken then drove slowly forward and, with the aid of the powerful car, rescued the horse. Happy and proud, the chicken drove the BMW back to the farmhouse, and the farmer was none the wiser when he returned. The friendship between the two animals was cemented: best buddies, best pals.

A few weeks later the chicken fell into a mud pit and soon he, too, began to sink and cried out to the horse to save his life. The horse thought a moment, walked over and straddled the large puddle. Looking underneath, he told the chicken to grab his 'thing' and he would then lift him out of the pit. The chicken got a good grip, and the horse pulled him up and out, saving his life.

The moral of the story: when you're hung like a horse you don't need a BMW to pick up chicks!

***

A blonde is hired at the Tickle Me Elmo factory. The personnel manager explains her duties and tells her to report to work promptly at 8 a.m.

The next day at 8.45 a.m., there's a knock on the personnel manager's door. The assembly line foreman comes in and starts ranting about the new employee. He says she's incredibly slow and the whole line is backing up. The foreman takes the personnel manager down to the factory floor to show him the problem.

Sur enough, Elmos are backed up all over the place. At the end of the line is the new employee. She has a roll of material used for the Elmos and a big bag of marbles. They both watch as she cuts a little piece of fabric, wraps it around two marbles, and starts sewing the little package between Elmo's legs.

The personnel manager starts laughing hysterically. After several minutes, he pulls himself together, walks over to the blonde, and says, 'I'm sorry. I guess you misunderstood me yesterday. Your job is to give Elmo two test tickles.'

***

An old Jewish gentleman was on the operating table awaiting surgery and he insisted that his son, a renowned surgeon, perform the operation.

As he was about to get anaesthesia, he asked to

speak to his son.

'Yes, Dad, what is it?'

'Don't be nervous, son. Do your best and just remember, if it doesn't go well, if something happens to me, your mother is going to come and live with you and your wife.'

***

A man and a woman who have never met before find themselves assigned to the same sleeping room on a transcontinental train. Although initially embarrassed and uneasy over sharing a room, the two are tired and fall asleep quickly, he in the upper bunk and she in the lower.

At 2 a.m., he leans over and gently wakes the woman, saying, 'Ma'am, I'm sorry to bother you, but would you be willing to reach into the closet to get me a second blanket? I'm awfully cold.'

'I have a better idea,' she replies. 'Just for tonight, let's pretend that we're married.'

'Wow! That's a great idea!' he exclaims.

'Good,' she replies. 'Get your own damned blanket.'

***

Dad and Dave go into a pub in Cessnock with their dog Roger. Dad orders a pint. Dave orders a pint. And Roger orders a shandy.

'Christ,' says the barman, 'you've got one of them talking dogs.'

'Yep,' says Dave, 'Roger's a very, very clever dog. There's nothing much that Roger can't do.'

'Bugger it!' says the barman. 'I meant to lay a bet at the TAB and now it's getting a bit late. I won't have time to get down there.'

'No probs,' says Dave, 'just give your bet to Roger and we'll send him down to the TAB.'

So the barman tucks a $20 bill into Roger's collar and off Roger goes, barking happily.

An hour later he hasn't returned and the barman says, 'Well, it's my bloody fault for being stupid. But it's pretty bloody obvious that your dog has conned me.'

So they go out looking for Roger. And after calling 'Roger! Roger!' up and down the street, they find him in a back lane, rooting a poodle. Going hammer and tongs!

'Roger!' calls Dave, 'come here you rotten bloody mongrel!' And Roger comes out sheepishly, wagging his tail. Dave says, 'How could you do it to us, Roger? You really let us down. You've embarrassed us here with the barman.'

'Yes,' says Dad, 'you've never behaved like this before.'

And Roger looks up, sheepishly, and says, 'Well, I've never had the money before.'

***

The ground war in Afghanistan heated up yesterday when the Allies revealed plans to airdrop a platoon of crack French existentialist philosophers into the country to destroy the morale of Taliban zealots by proving the non-existence of God. Elements from the feared Jean-Paul Sartre Brigade, or 'Black Berets', will be parachuted into the combat zones to spread doubt, despondency and existential anomie among the enemy.

Hardened by numerous intellectual battles fought during their long occupation of Paris's Left Bank, their first action will be to establish a number of pavement cafes at strategic points near the front lines. There they will drink coffee and talk animatedly about the absurd nature of life and man's lonely isolation in the universe. They will be accompanied by a number of heartbreakingly beautiful girlfriends who will further spread dismay by sticking their tongues in the philosophers' ears every five minutes and looking remote and unattainable to everyone else.

Their leader, Colonel Mark-Ange Belmondo, spoke yesterday of his confidence in the success of their mission. Sorbonne graduate Belmondo, a very intense and unshaven young man in a black pullover, gesticulated wildly, and said, 'The Taliban are caught in a logical fallacy of the most ridiculous kind. There is no God and I can prove it. Take your tongue out of my ear, Juliet; I am talking.'

Marc-Ange plans to deliver an impassioned thesis on man's nauseating freedom of action with special reference to the work of Foucault and the films of Alfred Hitchcock. However, humanitarian agencies have been quick to condemn the operation as inhumane, pointing out that the effects of passive smoking from the Frenchmen's endless Gitanes could wreak a terrible toll on civilians in the area.

Speculation was mounting last night that Britain may also contribute to the effort by dropping Professor Stephen Hawking into Afghanistan to propagate his non-deistic theory of the creation of the universe.

***

She's not a babe or a chick – she's a 'breasted American'.

She's not a screamer or a moaner – she's 'vocally appreciative'.

She's not easy – she's 'horizontally accessible'.

She's not dumb – she is a 'detour off the information superhighway'.

She has not been around – she is a 'previously enjoyed companion'.

She's not an airhead – she is 'reality impaired'.

She does not get drunk or tipsy – she gets 'chemically inconvenienced'.

She does not have breast implants – she is 'surgically enhanced'.

She does not nag you – she becomes 'verbally repetitive'.

She is not a slut – she is 'sexually extroverted'.

***

A bald man with a wooden leg gets invited to a Halloween party. He doesn't know what costume to wear to hide his head and his leg so he writes to a costume company to explain his problem.

A few days later he received a parcel with the following note: 'Dear Sir, please find enclosed a pirate's outfit. The spotted handkerchief will cover your bald head and, with your wooden leg, you will be just right as a pirate. Yours very truly, Acme Costume Co.'

The man thinks this is terrible because they have just emphasised his wooden leg and so he writes a letter of complaint.

A week goes by and he receives another parcel and a note that says: 'Dear Sir, please find enclosed a monk's habit. The long robe will cover your wooden leg and, with your bald head, you will really look the party. Very truly yours, Acme Costume Co.'

Now the man is really upset since they have gone from emphasising his wooden leg to emphasising his bald head, so again he writes the company another nasty letter of complaint.

The next day he gets a small parcel and a note that reads: 'Dear Sir, please find enclosed a bottle of treacle. Pour the treacle over your bald head, stick your wooden leg up your arse and go as a toffee apple.'

***

When Jane initially met Tarzan of the jungle, she was attracted to him, and during her questions about his life, she asked him how he had sex.

'Tarzan not know sex,' he replied.

Jane explained to him what sex was.

Tarzan said, 'Oh. Tarzan use hole in trunk of tree.'

Horrified, she said, 'Tarzan, you have it all wrong, but I will show you how to do it properly.' She took off her clothes and lay down on the ground.

Here,' she said, 'you must put it in here.'

Tarzan removed his loincloth, showing Jane his considerable manhood. He stepped closer, and then gave her a mighty kick right in the crotch!

Jane rolled around in agony, for what seemed like an eternity. Eventually she managed to gasp for air and screamed, 'What did you do that for?'

He replied, 'Tarzan check for bees first.'

***

VIRUSES

The Clinton virus: Gives you a 7-inch hard drive with *no* memory.

The Lewinsky virus: Sucks all the memory out of your computer, then emails everyone about what it did.

The Ronald Reagan virus: Saves your data, but forgets where it is stored.

The Oprah Winfrey virus: Your 300mb hard drive shrinks to 100mb, then slowly expands to restabilise around 200mb.

The Jack Kevorkian virus. Deletes all old files.

The Prozac virus: Totally screws up your RAM, but your processor doesn't care.

The Arnold Schwarzenegger virus: Terminates some files, leaves, but will be back.

The Lorena Bobbitt virus: Reformats your hard drive into a 3.5-inch floppy, then discards it through Windows.

***

A nun was sitting at the airport waiting for her flight to Chicago. She looked over in the corner and saw one of those weight machines that tells your fortune and thought to herself, 'I'll give it a try and see what it tells me.'

She went over to the machine, stepped up on the scales and put her dollar in. Out came a card that read, 'You are a nun. You weigh 58kg and you are going to Chicago.'

The nun sat back down. She told herself that the machine probably gives the same card to everyone. The more she thought about it, the more curious she got, so she decided to try it again.

She went back to the machine and again put her dollar in and out came a card that read, 'You are a nun. You weigh 58kg. You are going to Chicago and you are going to play a fiddle.'

The nun said to herself, 'I know that's wrong. I have never played a musical instrument a day in my life.'

She sat back down. From out of nowhere a cowboy came over and sat down, putting his fiddle case on the seat between them. Without thinking, she opened the cowboy's case, took out the fiddle, and started playing beautiful music.

Surprised at what she had done, she looked over at the machine thinking, 'This is incredible. I've got to try this again.'

Back to the machine she went, put in another dollar and another card came out. It read, 'You are a nun. You weigh 58kg. You are going to Chicago and you are going to break wind.'

Now she knew the machine was wrong as she thought to herself, 'I've never broken wind in public a single time in my life.' But getting down off the machine she slipped, and as she was straining to keep herself from falling to the floor, she broke wind.

Absolutely stunned, she sat back down and looked at the machine. She said to herself, 'This is truly remarkable! I have got to try this again.'

She went back to the machine, put in another dollar and another card came out. It read, 'You are a nun. You weigh 58kg. You have fiddled and farted around and missed your flight to Chicago.'

***

One afternoon a wealthy lawyer was riding in the back of his limousine when he saw two men eating grass by the roadside. He ordered his driver to stop and got out to investigate.

'Why are you eating grass?' he asked one man.

'We don't have any money for food,' the poor man replied.

'Oh well, you can come with me to my house,' instructed the lawyer.

'But sir, I have a wife and two children with me!'

'Bring them along!' replied the lawyer. He turned to the other man and said, 'You come with us, too.'

'But sir, I have a wife and six children!' the second man answered.

'Bring them as well!' answered the lawyer as he headed for his limo.

They all climbed into the car, which was no easy

task, even for a car as large as a limousine. Once underway, one of the poor fellows said, 'Sir, you are too kind. Thank you for taking all of us with you.'

The lawyer replied, 'Glad to do it. You'll love my place, the grass is almost a foot tall.'

***

A man and his wife were having an argument about who should brew the coffee each morning.

The wife said, 'You should do it, because you get up first, and then we don't have to wait as long to have our coffee.'

The husband said, 'You are in charge of cooking around here and you should do it because that is your job, and I can just wait for my coffee.'

The wife replies, 'No, you should do it, and besides, it's in the Bible that the man should do the coffee.'

The husband replies, 'I can't believe that. Show me.'

So she fetched the Bible and opened the New Testament and showed him at the top of several pages, that it indeed says *Hebrews*.

***

He does not have a beer gut – he's developed a 'grain alcohol storage facility'.

He is not a bad dancer – he is 'overly caucasian'.

He does not get lost all the time – he 'investigates alternative destinations'.

He is not balding – he has 'follicle regressed'.

He is not a cradle snatcher – he prefers 'generationally different relationships'.

He does not get falling down drunk – he becomes 'accidentally horizontal'.

He does not act like a total ass – he develops a case of 'rectal-cranial inversion'.

He is not a male chauvinist pig – he is 'swine empathetic'.

He is not afraid of commitment – he is 'monogamously challenged'.

✱✱✱

A mother enters her daughter's bedroom and sees a letter on the bed. With the worst premonition, she reads it, with trembling hands.

'Mum, it is with great regret and sorrow that I'm telling you that I eloped with my new boyfriend. I found real passion and he is so nice, with all his piercings and tattoos and his big motorcycle.

But it's not only that, Mum. I'm pregnant and Ahmed said that we will be very happy in his caravan in the woods. He wants to have many more children with me and that's one of my dreams. I've learned that marijuana doesn't hurt anyone and we'll be growing it for us and his friends who are providing us with all the cocaine and ecstasy we want.

In the meantime, we'll pray for science to find the AIDS cure, for Ahmed to get better, he deserves it. Don't worry, Mum. I'm fifteen years old now and I know how to take care of myself.

Some day I'll visit for you to get to know your grandchildren.

Your daughter, Judith X.

PS: Mum, it's not true. I'm at the neighbour's house. I just wanted to show you that there are worse things in life than the school's report card that's in my desk drawer. I love you.'

***

Two church members were going door to door. They knocked on the door of a woman who clearly was not happy to see them. She told them in no uncertain terms she did not want to hear their message and then slammed the door in their faces.

To her surprise, the door did not close. In fact, it bounced back open. She tried again, really put her back into the job, and slammed the door again.

Same result. The door bounced back.

Convinced one of these rude church members was sticking a foot in the door, she reared back to give the door a slam that would teach them a lesson.

Just then, one of the church members said, 'Ma'am, before you do that again, you might want to move your cat.'

✷✷✷

A science teacher asked her students, 'Children, if you could own one mineral what would it be?'

One boy said, 'I would choose gold. It's worth lots of money and I could buy a Corvette.'

Another boy said, 'I would want platinum because it's worth more than gold and I could buy a Porsche.'

The teacher said, 'Johnny, what would you want?'

Johnny said, 'I would want silicone.'

'Why would you want silicone?' asked the teacher.

'Well, my mum got some,' he replied. 'And there's always a Porsche or Corvette sitting in our driveway.'

***

A marine was deployed to Afghanistan. While he was there he received a letter from his girlfriend. In the letter she explained that she had slept with two guys while he had been gone and she wanted to break up with him. *And* she wanted pictures of herself back.

So, the marine did what any squared-away marine would do. He went around to his buddies and collected all the unwanted photos of women he could find. He then mailed about twenty-five pictures of women (with clothes and without) to his girlfriend with the following note: 'I don't remember which one you are. Please remove your picture and send the rest back.'

***

Entries to a competition asking for a rhyme with the most romantic first line, but least romantic second line:

Love may be beautiful, love may be bliss.
But I only slept with you because I was pissed.

I thought that I could love no other
Until, that is, I met your brother.

Roses are red, violets are blue, sugar is sweet and so are you.
But the roses are wilting, the violets are dead, the sugar bowl's empty, and so is your head.

Of loving beauty you float with grace
If only you could hide your face.

Kind, intelligent, loving and hot
This describes everything you are not.

I want to feel your sweet embrace
But don't take that paper bag off your face.

I love your smile, your face and your eyes –
Damn, I'm good at telling lies!

My darling, my lover, my beautiful wife,
Marrying you screwed up the rest of my life.

I see your face when I am dreaming
That's why I always wake up screaming.

My love, you take my breath away
What have you stepped in to smell that way?

My feelings for you no words can tell
Except for maybe 'go to hell'.

What inspired this amorous rhyme?
Two parts vodka, one part lime.

***

TOP 36 OXYMORONS

36. Happily married.
35. State worker.
34. Legally drunk.
33. Exact estimate.
32. Act naturally.
31. Found missing.
30. Resident alien.
29. Genuine imitation.
28. Airline food.
27. Good grief.
26. Government organisation.
25. Sanitary landfill.
24. Alone together.
23. Small crowd.
22. Business ethics.
21. Soft rock.
20. Amtrak schedule.

19. Military intelligence.

18. Sweet sorrow.

17. Progressive liberal.

16. 'Now, then . . .'

15. Passive aggression.

14. Clearly misunderstood.

13. Peace force.

12. Extinct life.

11. Plastic glasses.

10. Terribly pleased.

9. Computer security.

8. Political science.

7. Tight slacks.

6. Definite maybe.

5. Pretty ugly.

4. Rap music.

3. Working vacation.

2. Religious tolerance.

1. Microsoft Works.

***

POLITICALLY CORRECT RED RIDING HOOD

There once was a young person named Little Red Riding Hood who lived on the edge of a large forest full of endangered owls and rare plants that would probably provide a cure for cancer if only someone took the time to study them.

Red Riding Hood lived with a nurture giver who she sometimes referred to as 'mother', although she didn't mean to imply by this term that she would have thought less of the person if a close biological link did not in fact exist.

Nor did she intend to denigrate the equal value of non-traditional households, although she was sorry if this was the impression conveyed.

One day her mother asked her to take a basket of organically grown fruit and mineral water to her grandmother's house.

'But mother, won't this be stealing work from the unionised people who have struggled for years to earn the right to carry all packages between various people in the woods?'

Red Riding Hood's mother assured her that she had called the union secretary and had a special compassionate-mission exemption form.

'But mother, aren't you oppressing me by ordering me to do this?'

Red Riding Hood's mother pointed out that it was impossible for women to oppress each other, since all women were equally oppressed until all women were free.

'But mother, then shouldn't you have my brother

carry the basket, since he's an oppressor, and should learn what it's like to be oppressed?'

And Red Riding Hood's mother explained that her brother was attending a special rally for animal rights, and besides, this wasn't stereotypical women's work, but an empowering deed that would help engender a feeling of community.

'But won't I be oppressing Grandma by implying that she's sick and hence unable to independently further her own selfhood?'

But Red Riding Hood's mother explained that her grandmother wasn't actually sick or incapacitated or mentally handicapped in any way, although that was not to imply that any of these conditions were inferior to what some people call 'healthy'.

Thus Red Riding Hood felt that she could get behind the idea of delivering the basket to her grandmother, and so she set off.

Many people believed that the forest was a forbidding and dangerous place, but Red Riding Hood knew that this was an irrational fear based on cultural paradigms instilled by a patriarchal society that regarded the natural world as an exploitable resource, and hence believed that natural predators were, in fact, intolerable competitors.

Other people avoided the woods for fear of thieves and deviants, but Red Riding Hood felt that in a truly classless society all marginalised peoples would be able to 'come out' of the woods and be accepted as valid lifestyle role models.

On her way to Grandma's house, Red Riding Hood passed a woodchopper, and wandered off the path in order to examine some flowers.

She was startled to find herself standing before a wolf, who asked her what was in the basket.

Red Riding Hood's teacher had warned her never to talk to strangers, but she was confident in taking control of her own budding sexuality and chose to dialogue with the wolf. She replied, 'I am taking my grandmother some healthful snacks in a gesture of solidarity.'

The wolf said, 'You know, my dear, it isn't safe for a little girl to walk through these woods alone.'

Red Riding Hood said, 'I find your sexist remark offensive in the extreme, but I will ignore it because of your traditional status as an outcast from society, the stress of which has caused you to develop an alternative and yet entirely valid world view. Now, if you'll excuse me, I would prefer to be on my way.'

Red Riding Hood returned to the main path, and proceeded towards her grandmother's house.

But because his status outside society had freed him from slavish adherence to linear, western-style thought, the wolf knew of a quicker route to Grandma's house.

He burst into the house and ate Grandma, a course of action affirmative of his nature as a predator.

Then, unhampered by rigid, traditionalist gender-role notions, he put on Grandma's nightclothes, crawled under the bedclothes and awaited developments.

Red Riding Hood entered the cottage and said, 'Grandma, I have brought you some cruelty-free snacks to salute you in your role of wise and nurturing matriarch.'

The wolf said softly, 'Come closer, child, so that I might see you.'

Red Riding Hood said, 'Goodness! Grandma, what big eyes you have!'

'You forgot that I am optically challenged.'

'And Grandma, what an enormous nose you have!'

'Naturally. I could have had it fixed to help my acting career, but I didn't give in to such societal pressures, my child.'

'And Grandma, what very big, sharp teeth you have!'

The wolf could not take any more of these discriminatory slurs, and in a reaction appropriate for his accustomed milieu, he leapt out of bed, grabbed Little Red Riding Hood and opened his jaws so wide that she could see her poor grandmother cowering in his belly.

'Are you forgetting something?' Red Riding Hood bravely shouted. 'You must request my permission before proceeding to a new level of intimacy!'

The wolf was so startled by this statement that he loosened his grasp on her. At the same time, the wood-chopper burst into the cottage, brandishing an axe.

'Hands off!' cried the woodchopper.

'And what do you think you're doing?' cried Little Red Riding Hood. 'If I let you help me now, I would be expressing a lack of confidence in my own abilities, which would lead to poor self-esteem and lower TER scores.'

'Last chance, sister! Get your hands off that endangered species! This is a Fisheries and Wildlife operation!' screamed the woodchopper, and when Little Red Riding Hood nonetheless made a sudden motion, he sliced off her head.

'Thank goodness you got to me in time,' said the wolf. 'The brat and her grandmother lured me in here. I thought I was a goner.'

'No, I think I'm the real victim here,' said the woodchopper. 'I've been dealing with my anger ever since I saw her picking those protected flowers earlier. And now I'm going to have such a trauma. Do you have any aspirin?'

The wolf and the woodchopper interacted together in a really, really positive way. They empowered each other in an alternative, non-traditional relationship and lived forever after in an ongoing happiness-type situation.

***

President George W. Bush got a coded message from Saddam.

It read: 370HSSV-0773H

Bush was stumped and sent for the CIA. The CIA was stumped too, so it went to the NSA. The NSA couldn't solve it either, so they asked Bill Clinton.

He suggested turning it upside down.

***

TODAY'S HISTORY LESSON

Before the Battle of Agincourt in 1415, the French, anticipating victory over the English, proposed to cut off the middle finger of all captured English soldiers. Without the middle finger it would be impossible to draw the renowned English longbow and therefore be incapable of fighting in the future.

This famous weapon was made of the native English yew tree, and the act of drawing the longbow was known as 'plucking the yew' (or 'pluck yew').

Much to the bewilderment of the French, the English won a major upset and began mocking the French by waving their middle fingers at the defeated French, saying, 'See, we can still pluck yew! *Pluck yew!*'

Over the years folk etymologies have grown up around this symbolic gesture. Since 'pluck yew' is rather difficult to say (like 'pleasant mother pheasant plucker', which is who you had to go to for the feathers used on the arrows of the longbow), the difficult consonant cluster at the beginning has gradually changed to a labiodental fricative 'F', and thus the words often used in conjunction with the one-finger-salute are mistakenly thought to have something to do with an intimate encounter.

It is also because of the pheasant feathers on the arrows that the symbolic gesture is known as 'giving the bird'.

And yew all thought yew knew everything.

***

A woman went into a store to buy her husband a pet for his birthday. After looking around, she found that all the pets were very expensive. She told the clerk she wanted to buy a pet but didn't want to spend a fortune.

'Well,' said the clerk, 'I have a very large bullfrog.

They say it's been trained to give blow jobs.'

'Blow jobs!' the woman exclaimed.

'It hasn't been proven, but we've sold thirty of them this month,' he said.

The woman thought it would be a great gag gift, and what if it's true – no more blow jobs for her!

She bought the frog. When she explained froggy's ability to her husband, he was extremely sceptical and laughed it off. The woman went to bed happy, thinking she may never need to perform this less-than-riveting act again.

In the middle of the night she was awakened by the noise of pots and pans flying everywhere, making hellacious banging and crashing sounds.

She ran downstairs to the kitchen, only to find her husband and the frog reading cookbooks.

'What are you two doing at this time?' she asked.

The husband replied, 'If I can teach this frog to cook, you're gone!'

***

Upon arriving home, a husband was met at the door by his sobbing wife. Tearfully, she explained, 'It's the pharmacist – he insulted me terribly this morning on the phone.'

Without hesitation, the husband got in his car

and drove into town to confront the pharmacist and demand an apology. Before he could say more than a word or two, the pharmacist told him, 'Now listen to my side of the story. This morning the alarm failed to go off, so I was late getting up. I went without breakfast and hurried out to my car, only to realise that I locked the house with both house and car keys inside. I had to break a window to get my keys. Then, driving a little too fast, I got a speeding ticket. When I was about three blocks from the shop I got a flat tyre. When I finally got here, there was a bunch of people waiting for me to open up. I got the store opened and started serving the people and all the time the damn phone kept ringing.'

He continued, 'Then I had to break a roll of coins against the cash register drawer to make change and they spilled all over the floor. I got down on my hands and knees to pick up the coins. The phone was still ringing. When I came up, I cracked my head on the open cash drawer, which made me stagger back against a showcase with a great number of perfume bottles on it. All of them hit the floor and broke. Meanwhile the phone was still ringing non-stop – and I finally got to answer it. It was your wife. She wanted to know how to use a rectal thermometer – and believe me, Mister, as God is my witness, all I did was tell her.'

***

A man approached a very beautiful woman in a large supermarket and said, 'I've lost my wife here in the supermarket. Can you talk to me for a couple of minutes?'

The woman looked puzzled, 'Why talk to me?' she asked.

'Because every time I talk to a woman with tits like yours, my wife appears out of nowhere.'

***

A mother of a seventeen-year-old girl was concerned that her daughter was having sex. Worried the girl might become pregnant and adversely impact the family's status, she consulted the family doctor.

The doctor told her that teenagers today were very wilful and any attempt to stop the girl would probably result in rebellion. He then told her to arrange for her daughter to be put on birth control and until then, talk to her and give her a box of condoms.

Later that evening, as her daughter was preparing for a date, the woman told her about the situation and handed her a box of condoms.

The girl burst out laughing and reached over to hug her mother saying, 'Oh Mum! You don't have to worry about that! I'm dating Susan!'

***

A Canadian was drinking in a New York bar when he got a call on his mobile phone. He hung up, grinning from ear to ear, and ordered a round of drinks for everybody in the bar because, he announced, his wife had just produced a typical Canadian baby boy weighing 25 pounds.

Nobody could believe that any new baby could weigh in at 25 pounds, but the Canuck just shrugged. 'That's about average up north, folks. Like I said, my boy's a typical Canadian baby boy.'

Congratulations showered him from all around the bar, and many exclamations of 'Wow' were heard from the patrons. One woman actually fainted due to sympathy pains.

Two weeks later, the Canadian returned to the bar. The bartender said, 'Say, you're the father of that typical Canadian baby that weighed 25 pounds at birth, aren't you? Everybody's been making bets about how big he'd be in two weeks. We were gonna call you. So how much does he weigh now?'

The proud father answered, 'Seventeen pounds.'

The bartender was puzzled and concerned. 'What happened? He already weighed 25 pounds the day he was born.'

The Canadian father took a slow swig from his

beer, wiped his lips on his shirtsleeve, leaned into the bartender and proudly said, 'Had him circumcised.'

***

Sid and Al were sitting in a Chinese restaurant.

'Sid,' asked Al, 'Are there any Jews in China?'

'I don't know,' Sid replied. 'Why don't we ask the waiter?'

When the water came by, Al asked him, 'Are there any Chinese Jews?'

'I don't know, sir, let me ask,' the waiter replied, and he went into the kitchen. He returned in a few minutes and said, 'No, sir. No Chinese Jews.'

'Are you sure?' Al asked.

'I will check again, sir,' the waiter replied and went back to the kitchen.

While he was still gone, Sid said, 'I cannot believe there are no Jews in China. Our people are scattered everywhere.'

When the waiter returned he said, 'Sir, no Chinese Jews.'

'Are you really sure?' Al asked again. 'I cannot believe there are no Chinese Jews.'

'Sir, I ask everyone,' the waiter replied exasperated. 'We have Orange Jews, Prune Jews, Tomato Jews and Grape Jews. But no Chinese Jews!'

***

George W. Bush had a heart attack and died. He went to hell where the devil was waiting for him. 'I don't know what to do here,' said the devil. 'You are on my list but I have no room for you. You definitely have to stay here, so I'll tell you what I'm going to do. I've got three folks here who weren't quite as bad as you. I'll let one of them go, but you have to take their place. I'll even let *you* decide who leaves.'

Bush thought that sounded pretty good, so he agreed.

The devil opened the first room: in it was Richard Nixon and a large pool of water. He kept diving in and surfacing empty-handed over and over and over. Such was his fate in hell.

'No!' Bush said. 'I don't think so. I'm not a good swimmer and don't think I could do that all day long.'

The devil led him to the next room: in it was Tony Blair with a sledgehammer and a room full of rocks. All he did was swing that hammer, time after time after time.

'No, I've got this problem with my shoulder. I would be in constant agony if all I could do was break rocks all day!' commented Bush.

The devil opened the third door. In it, Bush saw Bill

Clinton lying on the floor with his arms staked over his head and his legs staked in spread-eagle pose. Bent over him was Monica Lewinsky, doing what she did best.

Bush looked at this in disbelief for a while and finally said, 'Yeah, I can handle this.'

The devil smiled and said, 'Okay, Monica, you're free to go!'

***

A man goes into a library and asks for a book on suicide.

The librarian says, 'Fuck off. You won't bring it back!'

***

An Irishman arrived at JFK Airport and wandered around the terminal with tears streaming down his cheeks. An airline employee asked him if he was already homesick.

'No,' replied the Irishman, 'I've lost all my luggage!'

'How'd that happen?'

'The cork fell out!' said the Irishman.

***

A company was looking to hire someone for an important position, so they interviewed dozens of applicants and narrowed their search down to three people. In an attempt to pick one of them, they decided to give them all the same question to answer within twenty-four hours and the one with the best answer would get the job.

The question was: A man and a woman are in bed, nude. The woman is lying on her side with her back facing the man, and the man is lying on his side facing the woman's back. What's the man's name?'

After the twenty-four hours was up, the three were brought in to give their answers.

The first one said, 'My answer is, there *is* no answer.'

The second one said, 'My answer is that there is no way to determine the answer with the information we were given.'

The third one said, 'I'm not exactly sure, but I have it narrowed down to two names. It's either Willie Turner or Willie Nailer.'

He got the job.

***

HOW AUSTRALIA WAS CREATED

In the beginning God created day and night. He created day for footy, going to the beach and barbies. He created night for going prawning, sleeping and barbies. God saw that it was good. Evening came and morning came and it was the second day.

On the second day God created water – for surfing, swimming and barbies on the beach. God saw that it was good. Evening came and morning came and it was the third day.

On the third day God created the earth to bring forth plants to provide malt and yeast for beer and wood for barbies. God saw that it was good. Evening came and morning came and it was the fourth day.

On the fourth day God created animals and crustaceans for chops, sausages, steaks and prawns for barbies. God saw that it was good. Evening came and morning came and it was the fifth day.

On the fifth day God created a bloke – to go to the footy, enjoy the beach, drink the beer and eat the meat and prawns at barbies. God saw that it was good. Evening came and morning came and it was the sixth day.

On the sixth day God saw that this bloke was

lonely and needed someone to go to the footy, surf, drink beer, eat and stand around the barbie with. So God created mates and God saw that they were good blokes. God saw that it was good. Evening came and morning came and it was the seventh day.

On the seventh day God looked around at the twinkling barbie fires, heard the hiss of opening beer cans and the raucous laughter of all the blokes, smelled the aroma of grilled chops and sizzling prawns and God saw that it was good – well, almost good. God saw that the blokes were tired and needed a rest.

So God created sheilas – to clean the house, bear children, wash, cook and clean the barbie. God saw that it was not just good, it was better than that – it was bloody good!

It was Australia!

***

The Pope is visiting Washington DC and President George W. Bush takes him out for an afternoon on the Potomac, sailing on the presidential yacht, the *Sequoia*. They're admiring the sights when, all of a sudden, the Pope's hat blows off his head and out into the water. Secret-service guys start to launch a boat, but President Bush waves them off, saying, 'Wait, wait. I'll take care of this. Don't worry.'

Bush then steps off the yacht onto the surface of the water and walks out to the Holy Father's little hat, bends over and picks it up, then walks back to the yacht and climbs aboard. He hands the hat to the Pope amid stunned silence.

The next morning, the Washington Post carries a story, with front-page photos, of the event. The banner headline is BUSH CAN'T SWIM.

***

TEN HANDY HOUSEHOLD TIPS

1. If you can't find a screwdriver, use a knife. If you break off the tip, it is an improved screwdriver.
2. Try to work alone. An audience is rarely any help.
3. Above all, if what you've done is stupid, but it works, then it isn't stupid.
4. Work in the kitchen whenever you can; there are many fine tools there. It's warm and dry, and you are close to the refrigerator.
5. If it's electronic, get a new one – or consult a twelve-year-old.
6. Stay simpleminded. Get a new battery, replace the bulb or fuse, see if the tank is empty, try turning the switch 'on', or just paint over it.

7. Always take credit for miracles. If you dropped the alarm clock while taking it apart and it suddenly starts working, you have healed it.
8. Regardless of what people say, kicking, pounding and throwing sometimes *does* help.
9. If something looks level, it is level.
10. If at first you don't succeed, redefine success.

***

RULES THAT MEN WISH WOMEN KNEW

1. If you think you're fat, you probably are. Don't ask.
2. Learn to work the toilet seat. If it's up, put it down.
3. Don't cut your hair. Ever.
4. Sometimes, we're not thinking about you. Live with it.
5. Get rid of your cat.
6. Sunday = sports.
7. Anything you wear is fine. Really.
8. Women wearing wonder bras and low-cut blouses lose their right to complain about having their boobs stared at.
9. You can have too many shoes.
10. Crying is blackmail.
11. Ask for what you want. Subtle hints don't work.
12. Mark anniversaries on a calendar.

13. Yes, pissing standing up is more difficult than peeing from point-blank range. We're bound to miss sometimes.

14. Yes and no are perfectly acceptable answers.

15. A headache for seventeen months is a problem. See a doctor.

16. Don't fake it. We'd rather be ineffective than deceived.

17. Anything we said six or eight months ago is inadmissible in an argument.

18. If something can be interpreted two ways, and one of the ways makes you sad and angry, we meant the other one.

19. Let us ogle. If we don't look at other women, how can we know how pretty you are?

20. Don't rub the lamp if you don't want the genie to come out.

21. You can either ask us to do something *or* tell us how you want it done – not both.

22. Christopher Columbus didn't need directions, and neither do we.

23. You have enough dresses.

24. Nothing says 'I love you' like sex.

✶✶✶

Who was the first person to see an egg come from a chicken's arse and think, 'I bet that would be good to eat?'

If love is blind, how can we believe in love at first sight?

Why do toasters always have a setting that burns the toast to a horrible crisp, which no decent human being would eat?

What do you call male ballerinas?

Why do they call it 'getting your dog fixed' if afterwards it doesn't work anymore?

Where in the nursery rhyme does it say Humpty Dumpty is an egg?

Why does Donald Duck wear a towel when he comes out of the shower, when he doesn't usually wear any pants?

Did Adam and Eve have navels?

Do one-legged ducks swim in circles?

Whose cruel idea was it for the word 'lisp' to have an 's' in it?

Why do fat chance and slim chance mean the same thing?

And who opened that first oyster and said, 'My. Now doesn't this look yummy?'

***

An Irish priest is driving down to New York and gets stopped for speeding in Connecticut. The state trooper smells alcohol on the priest's breath and then sees an empty wine bottle on the floor of the car. He says, 'Sir, have you been drinking?'

'Just water,' says the priest.

The trooper says, 'Then why do I smell wine?'

The priest looks at the bottle and says, 'Good Lord! He's done it again!'

***

As I've matured:

I've learned that you cannot make someone love you. All you can do is stalk them and hope they panic and give in.

I've learned that one good turn gets most of the blankets.

I've learned that no matter how much I care, some people are just jackasses.

I've learned that depression is merely anger without enthusiasm.

I've learned that it is not what you wear; it is how you take it off.

I've learned that artificial intelligence is no match for natural stupidity.

I've learned that 99 per cent of the time when something isn't working in your house, one of your kids did it.

I've learned that there is a fine line between genius and insanity.

I've learned that the people who you care about most in life are taken from you too soon and all the less important ones just never go away. And the real pains in the butts are permanent.

Keep grinning – it makes people wonder what you're up to.

***

DEEP SOUTHERN QUOTES

1. Well, butter my butt and call me a biscuit.
2. It's been hotter'n a goat's butt in a pepper patch.
3. He fell out of the ugly tree and hit every branch on the way down.
4. Have a cup of coffee; it's already been saucered and blowed.
5. She's so stuck up, she'd drown in a rainstorm.
6. It's so dry, the trees are bribing the dogs.
7. My cow died last night so I don't need your bull.
8. Don't pee down my pack and tell me it's raining.
9. He's as country as cornflakes.
10. This is gooder'n grits.
11. Busier than a cat covering crap on concrete.
12. If things get any better, I may have to hire somebody to help me enjoy it.

***

NOTICE TO NORTHERNERS MOVING SOUTH

The following is a pre-approved posting whose purpose is to offer insight and advice to northerners moving south:

1. Save all manner of bacon grease. You will be instructed on how to use it shortly.
2. Stay home the two days of the year it snows. Just because you can drive on snow and ice does not mean southerners can.
3. If you run your car into a ditch, don't panic. Four men in the cab of a four-wheel pick-up with a twelve-pack of beer and a tow chain will be along shortly. Don't try to help them. Just stay out of their way. This is what they live for.
4. You can ask southerners for directions, but unless you already know the positions of key hills, trees and rocks, you're better off trying to find it yourself.
5. Remember: 'Y'all' is singular. 'All y'all' is plural. 'All y'all's' is plural possessive.
6. Get used to hearing, 'You ain't from around here, are you?'
7. Don't be worried that you don't understand anyone. They don't understand you, either.
8. The first southern expression to creep into a transplanted northerner's vocabulary is the adjective 'big ole', as in 'big ole truck' or big ole boy'.

***

Metaphors found in Year 12 HSC English essays in NSW:

Her face was a perfect oval, like a circle that had its two sides gently compressed by a Thigh Master.

He spoke with the wisdom that can only come from experience, like a guy who went blind because he looked at a solar eclipse without one of those boxes with a pinhole in it and now goes around the country speaking at high schools about the dangers of looking at a solar eclipse without one of those boxes with a pinhole in it.

She grew upon him like she was a colony of E. coli and he was room-temperature prime English beef.

She had a deep, throaty, genuine laugh, like that sound a dog makes just before it throws up.

Her vocabulary was as bad as, like, whatever.

He was as tall as a six-foot-three-inch tree.

The revelation that his marriage of thirty years had disintegrated because of his wife's infidelity came as a rude shock, like a surcharge at a formerly surcharge-free ATM.

The little boat gently drifted across the pond exactly the way a bowling ball wouldn't.

From the attic came an unearthly howl. The whole scene had an eerie, surreal quality, like when you're on vacation in another city and *Sex in the City* comes on at 7 p.m. instead of 7.30.

Her hair glistened in the rain like a nose hair after a sneeze.

The hailstones leaped from the pavement, just like maggots when you fry them in hot oil.

John and Mary had never met. They were like two hummingbirds that had also never met.

Even in his last years, Grandad had a mind like a steel trap, only one that had been left out so long, it had rusted shut.

The plan was simple, like my brother-in-law Phil. But unlike Phil, this plan just might work.

The young fighter had a hungry look, the kind you get from not eating for a while.

'Oh, Jason, take me!' she panted, her breasts heaving like a uni student on $1-a-beer night.

He was as lame as a duck. Not the metaphorical lame duck, either, but a real duck that was actually lame. Maybe from stepping on a landmine or something.

The ballerina rose gracefully en pointe and extended one slender leg behind her, like a dog at a fire hydrant.

He was deeply in love. When she spoke, he thought he heard bells, as if she were a garbage truck backing up.

She was as easy as the TV guide crossword.

She walked into my office like a centipede with 98 missing legs.

It hurt the way your tongue hurts after you accidentally staple it to the wall.

***

Two Irishmen were sitting in a pub having beer and watching the brothel across the street. They saw a

Baptist minister walk into the brothel. One of them said, 'Aye, 'tis a shame to see a man of the cloth goin' bad.' They then saw a rabbi enter the brothel, and the other Irishman said, 'Aye, 'tis a shame to see that the Jews are fallin' victim to temptation.' Then they saw a Catholic priest enter the brothel. One of the Irishmen said, 'What a terrible pity – one of the girls must be quite ill.'

***

Now that Uday and Qusay are gone, some lesser-known siblings have been discovered:

The brothers:
Guday: the half-Australian brother
Sooflay: the restaurateur
Huray: the sports fanatic
Sashay: the gay brother
Kuntay and Kintay: the twins from the African mother
Sayhay: the baseball player
Ojay: the stalker/murderer
Gulay: the singer/entertainer
Ebay: the Internet czar
Biliray: the country-music star
Ecksray: the radiologist

Puray: the blender-factory owner
Regay: the half-Jamaican brother
Tupay: the one with bad hair

The sisters:
Lattay: the coffee-shop owner
Bufay: the 140 kg sister
Dushay: the clean sister
Phayray: the zoo worker in the gorilla house
Sapheway: the grocery-store owner
Olay: the half-Mexican sister
Gudlay: the prostitute

***

Murphy was staggering home with a pint of booze in his back pocket when he slipped and fell heavily. Struggling to his feet, he felt something wet running down his leg. 'Please Lord,' he implored, 'let it be blood!'

***

Newspaper headlines for year 2035

Ozone created by electric cars now killing millions in the seventh-largest country in the world, California.

White minorities still trying to have English recognised as California's third language.

Spotted-owl plague threatens north-western United States crops and livestock.

Baby conceived naturally. Scientists stumped.

Last remaining fundamentalist Muslim dies in the American Territory of the Middle East (formerly known as Iran, Afghanistan, Syria and Lebanon).

Iraq still closed off; physicists estimate it will take at least ten more years before radioactivity decreases to safe levels.

Castro finally dies at age 112. Cuban cigars can now be imported legally, but President Chelsea Clinton has banned all smoking.

George Z. Bush says he will run for Presidency in 2036.

Postal service raises price of first-class stamp to $17.89. Reduces mail delivery to Wednesday only.

Thirty-five-year study. Diet and exercise is the key to weight loss.

Massachusetts executes last remaining conservative.

Supreme Court rules punishment of criminals violates their civil rights.

Average height of NBA players now nine feet, seven inches.

Microsoft announces it has perfected its newest version of Windows, so it crashes before installation is completed.

Celebrating Christmas now officially a felony as it offends too many people.

***

MORAL/ETHICAL DILEMMA

You are driving along in your car on a wild, stormy night, when you pass by a bus stop, and you see three people waiting for the bus:
1. An old lady who looks as if she is about to die.
2. An old friend who once saved your life.
3. The perfect partner you have been dreaming about.
Which one would you choose to offer a ride to,

knowing that there could only be one passenger in your car? Think before you continue reading . . .

You could pick up the old lady, because she is going to die, and thus you should save her first. Or, you could take the old friend because he once saved your life and this would be the perfect chance to repay him. However, you may never be able to find your perfect mate again.

One possible answer: give the car keys to the old friend and let him take the lady to the hospital. You stay behind and wait for the bus with the partner of your dreams.

However, the correct answer is to run the old lady over and put her out of her misery; have sex with the perfect partner against the bus-stop sign, and then drive off with the old friend for some beers!

***

THE 'LIVE SHEEP' EXPORT CRISIS

1. The sheep will be accused of throwing their lambs overboard. They'll say that they had photos and a video as absolute proof it happened. We'll be told that these are not the type of sheep to be allowed back into Australia. You can see a statement, such as, 'They will never set hoof on our shores.'

2. They'll be accused of being queue-jumping sheep. What about all the other sheep in the sheep camps waiting to be allowed back in?
3. The sheep will be attacked for not having passports and proper documentation or having thrown it overboard.
4. We'll be told that it is cruel to allow the sheep out of detention on the ship so they can do what normal lambs do. The Minister will say the detention of the lambs is for their own good so they won't be disappointed about being locked up again.
5. It's possible we'll be told that although a plane flew directly over the boat containing the sheep, they saw nothing.
6. If all of the above fails, the sheep will be accused of being potential terrorists with links to Osama Baa Laden.

✱✱✱

BOB HOPE

On turning seventy: 'You still chase women, but only downhill.'

On turning eighty: 'That's the time of your life when even your birthday suit needs pressing.'

On turning ninety: 'You know you're getting old when the candles cost more than the cake.'

On turning one hundred: 'I don't feel old. In fact I don't feel anything until noon. Then it's time for my nap.'

On giving up his early career, boxing: 'I ruined my hands in the ring. The referee kept stepping on them.'

On sailors: 'They spend the first six days of each week sowing their wild oats, then they go to church on Sunday and pray for crop failure.'

On never winning an Oscar: 'Welcome to the Academy Awards or, as it's called at my home, Passover.'

On golf: 'Golf is my profession. Show business is just to pay the green fees.'

On presidents: 'I have performed for twelve presidents and entertained only six.'

On why he chose showbiz for his career: 'When I was born, the doctor said to my mother, "Congratulations, you have an eight-pound ham."'

On receiving the Congressional Gold Medal: 'I feel very humble, but I think I have the strength of character to fight it.'

On his family's early poverty: 'Four of us slept in the one bed. When it got cold, mother threw on another brother.'

On his six brothers: 'That's how I learned to dance. Waiting for the bathroom.'

On his early failures: 'I would not have had anything to eat if it wasn't for the stuff the audience threw at me.'

On going to heaven: 'I've done benefits for *all* religions. I'd hate to blow the hereafter on a technicality.'

***

A flight attendant was stationed at the departure gate to check tickets. As a man approached, she extended her hand for the ticket, and he opened his trench coat and flashed her. Without missing a beat she said, 'Sir, I need to see your ticket, not your stub.'

***

A lady was picking through the frozen turkeys at the grocery store, but couldn't find one big enough for her family. She asked a stock boy, 'Do these turkeys get any bigger?'

The stock boy replied, 'No, ma'am, they're dead.'

***

The cop got out of his car and the kid who was stopped for speeding rolled down his window. 'I've been waiting for you all day,' the cop said.

The kid replied, 'Yeah, well I got here as fast as I could.'

***

A couple is dressed and ready to go out for the evening. They turn on a nightlight, turn the answering machine on, cover their cockatiel and put the cat in the backyard.

The taxi arrives and the couple open the front door to leave their house.

The cat they had put into the yard scoots back into the house. They don't want the cat shut in the house because she always tries to eat the bird.

The wife goes out to the taxi while the husband

goes inside to get the cat. The cat runs upstairs, the man in hot pursuit.

The wife doesn't want the driver to know the house will be empty so she explains to the taxi driver that her husband will be out soon. 'He's just gone upstairs to say goodbye to my mother.'

A few minutes later, the husband gets into the car. 'Sorry I took so long,' he says. 'Stupid bitch was hiding under the bed. Had to poke her with a coat hanger to get her to come out. Then I had to wrap her in a blanket to keep her from scratching me. But it worked. I hauled her fat arse downstairs and threw her into the backyard.'

***

At an outdoor press conference, Al Gore was addressing harsh criticism of being 'lifeless as a statue'.

'That's absurd,' Gore stoically stated. 'When elected, the people of America will see just how passionate and alive I truly am.'

Embarrassed for her husband, Tipper leaned in to whisper, 'Honey, you have a pigeon on your head.'

***

WHY GOD CREATED CHILDREN

After creating heaven and earth, God created Adam and Eve, and the first thing He said was '*Don't*.'

'Don't what?' Adam asked.

'Don't eat the forbidden fruit,' God said.

'Forbidden fruit? We have forbidden fruit? Hey, Eve, we have forbidden fruit!'

'No way!'

'Yes way!'

'Do *not* eat the fruit!' said God.

'Why?'

'Because I am your Father and I said so,' God replied, wondering why He hadn't stopped creation after making the elephants.

A few minutes later, God saw His children having an apple break and He was annoyed. 'Didn't I tell you not to eat the fruit?' God asked.

'Uh huh,' Adam replied.

'Then why did you?' said the Father.

'I don't know,' said Eve.

'She started it!' Adam said.

'Did not.'

'Did too!'

'*Did not!*'

Having had it with the two of them, God's punishment was that Adam and Eve should have children of their own.

Thus the pattern was set and it has never changed.

***

In ancient Greece, Socrates held knowledge in high esteem. One day an acquaintance met the great philosopher and said, 'Socrates, do you know what I just heard about your friend?'

'Hold on a minute,' Socrates replied. 'Before telling me anything, I'd like you to pass a little test. It's called the Triple Filter Test.'

'Triple filter?'

'That's right,' Socrates continued. 'Before you talk to me about my friend, it might be a good idea to take a moment and filter what you're going to say. The first filter is Truth. Have you made absolutely sure that what you are about to tell me is true?'

'No,' the man said, 'actually just heard about it and . . .'

'All right,' said Socrates. 'So you don't really know if it's true or not. Now let's try the second filter, the filter of Goodness. Is what you are about to tell me about my friend something good?'

'No, on the contrary . . .'

'So,' Socrates continues, 'you want to tell me something bad about him, but you're not certain it's true. You may still pass the test though, because there's one filter left: the filter of Usefulness. Is what you want to tell me about my friend going to be useful to me?'

'No, not really.'

'Well,' concluded Socrates, 'if what you want to tell me is neither true nor good nor even useful, why tell it to me at all?'

This is why Socrates was a great philosopher and held in such high esteem. It also explains why he never found out his best friend was banging his wife.

***

The secret of a good sermon is to have a good beginning and a good ending and have the two as close together as possible.   George Burns

Santa Claus has the right idea – visit people only once a year.   Victor Borge

My wife is a sex object – every time I ask for sex, she objects.   Les Dawson

I was married by a judge. I should have asked for a jury.   Groucho Marx

Whatever women do they must do twice as well as men to be thought half as good. Luckily, this is not difficult. Charlotte Whitton

My wife has a slight impediment in her speech – every now and then she stops to breathe.
Jimmy Durante

The male is a domestic animal that, if treated with firmness and kindness, can be trained to do most things. Jilly Cooper

I never hated a man enough to give his diamonds back. Zsa Zsa Gabor

Only Irish coffee provides in a single glass all four essential food groups: alcohol, caffeine, sugar and fat. Alex Levine

Don't go around saying the world owes you a living. The world owes you nothing. It was here first.
Mark Twain

My luck is so bad that if I bought a cemetery, people would stop dying. Ed Furgol

What's the use of happiness? It can't buy you money.
Henny Youngman

Youth would be an ideal state if it came a little later in life.
Herbert Henry Asquith

The secret of staying young is to live honestly, eat slowly and lie about your age.
Lucille Ball

A woman drove me to drink – and I hadn't even the courtesy to thank her.
W.C. Fields

I once had a rose named after me and I was very flattered. But I was not pleased to read the description in the catalogue: 'No good in a bed, but fine up against a wall'.
Eleanor Roosevelt

***

These questions about Australia were posted on an Australian Tourism website and obviously the answers came from an Aussie.

Q: I have never seen it rain on Australian TV shows, so how do the plants grow? (UK)
A: We import all plants fully grown and then just sit around watching them die.

Q: Will I be able to see kangaroos in the street? (USA)

A: Depends on how much you've been drinking.

Q: I want to walk from Perth to Sydney – can I follow the railroad tracks? (Sweden)

A: Sure, it's only three thousand miles. Take lots of water.

Q: Is it safe to run around in the bushes in Australia? (Sweden)

A: So it's true what they say about Swedes.

Q: It is imperative that I find the names and addresses of places to contact for a stuffed porpoise. (Italy)

A: Let's not touch this one.

Q: Are there any ATMs in Australia? Can you send me a list of them in Brisbane, Cairns, Townsville and Hervey Bay? (UK)

A: What did your last slave die from?

Q: Can you give me some information about hippo racing in Australia? (USA)

A: A-fri-ca is the big triangle-shaped continent south of Europe. Aus-tra-lia is that big island in the middle of the Pacific, which does not . . . oh forget it. Sure, the hippo racing is every Tuesday night at Kings Cross. Come naked.

Q: Which direction is north in Australia? (USA)
A: Face south and then turn 90 degrees. Contact us when you get here and we'll send the rest of the directions.

Q: Can I bring cutlery into Australia? (UK)
A: Why? Just use your fingers like we do.

Q: Can you send me the Vienna Boys' Choir schedule? (USA)
A: Aus-tri-a is that quaint little country bordering Ger-man-y, which is . . . oh forget it. Sure, the Vienna Boys' Choir plays every Tuesday night in Kings Cross, straight after the hippo races. Come naked.

Q: Do you have perfume in Australia? (France)
A: No, *we* don't stink.

Q: I have developed a new product that is the fountain of youth. Can you tell me where I can sell it in Australia? (USA)
A: Anywhere significant numbers of Americans gather.

Q: Can I wear high heels in Australia? (UK)
A: You are a British politician, right?

Q: Can you tell me the regions in Tasmania where the female population is smaller than the male populations? (Italy)
A: Yes, gay nightclubs.

Q: Do you celebrate Christmas in Australia? (France)
A: Only at Christmas.

Q: Are there killer bees in Australia? (Germany)
A: Not yet, but for you, we'll import them.

Q: Are there supermarkets in Sydney, and is milk available all year round? (Germany)
A: No, we are a peaceful civilisation of vegan hunter-gatherers. Milk is illegal.

Q: Please send a list of all doctors in Australia who can dispense rattlesnake serum. (USA)
A: Rattlesnakes live in A-meri-ca, which is where *you* come from. All Australian snakes are perfectly harmless, can be safely handled and make good pets.

Q: I have a question about a famous animal in Australia, but I forget its name. It's a kind of bear and lives in trees. (USA)

A: It's called a Drop Bear. They are so called because they drop out of gum trees and eat the brains of anyone walking underneath them. You can scare them off by spraying yourself with human urine before you go out walking.

Q: I was in Australia in 1969 on R&R and I want to contact the girl I dated while I was staying in Kings Cross. Can you help? (USA)

A: Yes, and you will still have to pay her by the hour.

Q: Will I be able to speak English most places I go? (USA)

A: Yes, but you'll have to learn it first.

✳✳✳

PHILOSOPHIES FROM BATHROOMS

Friends don't let friends take home ugly men. (Women's rest room, Starboard, Dewey Beach)

Remember, it's not 'How high you are', it's 'Hi, how are you?' (Rest stop off Route 81, West Virginia)

648

No matter how good she looks, some other guy is sick and tired of putting up with her crap. (Men's room, Linda's Bar and Grill, Chapel Hill, North Carolina)

Make love, not war. Hell, do both. Get married! (Women's rest room, The Filling Station, Bozeman, Montana)

A woman's rule of thumb: if it has tyres or testicles, you're going to have trouble with it. (Women's rest room, Dick's Last Resort, Dallas, Texas)

No wonder you always go home alone. (Sign over mirror in men's rest room, Ed Debevic's, Beverly Hills)

Beauty is only a light switch away. (Perkins Library, Duke University, Durham, North Carolina)

Fighting for peace is like screwing for virginity. (The Irish Times, Washington DC)

It's hard to make a comeback when you haven't been anywhere. (Written in the dust on the back of a bus, Flagstaff, Arizona)

If voting could really change things, it would be illegal. (Revolution Books, New York, New York)

Don't trust anything that bleeds for five days and doesn't die. (Men's rest room, Murphy's, Champaign)

Please don't throw your cigarette butts in the urinal. It makes them soggy and hard to light. (The Janitor)

What are you looking up on the wall for? The joke is in your hands. (Men's rest room, Lynagh's, Lexington)

***

Think about this:
1. The number of physicians in the US is 700 000.
2. The number of accidental deaths caused by physicians per year is 120 000.
3. The number of accidental deaths per physician is 0.171 (US Department of Health & Human Services).

Then think about this:
1. The number of gun owners in the US is 80 000 000.
2. The number of accidental gun deaths per year (all age groups) is 1500.

3. The number of accidental deaths per gun owner is 0.0000188.

Statistically, doctors are approximately 9000 times more dangerous than gun owners.

Fact: Not everyone has a gun, but almost everyone has at least one doctor.

Please alert your friends to this alarming threat. We must ban doctors before this gets out of hand. As a public health measure, I have withheld the statistics of lawyers for fear that the shock could cause people to seek medical attention.

***

There were two brothers. One was very good and one was very bad. He did all the things that men should not do in life and didn't care who he hurt.

The bad brother died. He was still missed by his brother since he loved him despite everything.

Years later, the good brother died and went to heaven. Everything was beautiful there and he was very happy.

One day, he asked God where his brother was, as he hadn't seen him. God said that he was sorry but his brother lived a terrible life and went to hell instead.

The good brother then asked God if there was any way for him to see his brother. So God gave him the power of vision to see into hell and there was his brother sitting on a bench with a keg of beer under one arm and a gorgeous blonde on the other.

Confused, the good brother said to God, 'I am so happy that you let me into heaven with you. It is so beautiful here and I love it. But I don't understand, if my brother was bad enough to go to hell, why does he have the keg of beer and a gorgeous blonde? It hardly seems like a punishment.'

God said unto him, 'Things are not always as they seem, my son. The keg has a hole in it; the blonde does not.'

***

Gay Bob goes into the doctor's office and has some tests run. The doctor comes back and says, 'Bob, I'm not going to beat around the bush. You have HIV.'

Bob is devastated. 'Doc, what can I do?'

Doc says, 'Eat one sausage, one head of cabbage, twenty unpeeled carrots drenched in hot sauce, ten chilli peppers, forty walnuts and forty peanuts, one huge box of All Bran cereal and top it off with 5L of prune juice.'

Bob asks, 'Will that cure me, Doc?'

'No, but it should leave you with a better understanding of what your arse is for!'

***

Catholicism: If shit happens, I deserve it.
Protestantism: Shit won't happen if I work harder.
Judaism: Why does this shit always happen to me?
Buddhism: When shit happens, is it really shit?
Islam: If shit happens, take a hostage.
Hinduism: This shit happened before.
Hare Krishna: Shit happens Rama lama ding-dong.
Rastafarianism: Let's smoke this shit.
Atheist: No shit.

***

WHAT TO SAY TO A COP

1. I can't reach my licence unless you hold my beer.
2. Sorry, officer, I didn't realise my radar detector wasn't plugged in.
3. Aren't you the guy from the Village People?
4. Hey, you must've been doin' about 140 to keep up with me!
5. I thought you had to be in good physical condition to be a cop.
6. You're not gonna check the truck, are you?
7. I pay your salary!
8. Gee, officer, that's terrific. The last officer only gave

me a warning, too!

9. I was trying to keep up with the traffic. Yes, I know there are no other cars around. That's how far ahead of me they are.

10. 'Son, your eyes look red, have you been drinking?' Reply: 'Gee officer, your eyes look glazed, have you been eating doughnuts?'

***

What would have happened if three wise Jewish women had gone to Bethlehem instead of three wise men?

They would have:

Asked directions.

Arrived on time.

Helped deliver the baby.

Hired someone to clean the stable.

Made a casserole.

And brought practical gifts.

And what would they have said to each other after they left?

'Did you see the sandals Mary was wearing with that shmatta?

'That baby doesn't look anything like Joseph!'

'Virgin? I knew her in school!'

'Can you believe they let all of those disgusting animals in there?'

'I heard that Joseph doesn't have a job.'

'And that donkey they are riding has seen better days.'

'We'll just see how long it will take to get your casserole dish back.'

***

Why God gave the Jews Ten Commandments

God first went to the Egyptians and asked if they would like a commandment. 'What's a commandment?' they asked.

'Well, it's like, *Thou shall not commit adultery*,' replied God.

The Egyptians thought about it then said, 'No thanks.'

So then God went to the Assyrians and asked them if they would like a commandment. They also asked, 'What's a commandment?'

'Well,' said God, 'it's like, *thou shall not steal*.'

The Assyrians immediately replied, 'No way. That would ruin our economy.'

So finally God went to the Jews and asked them if they wanted a commandment.

They asked, 'How much?'

God said, 'They're free.'

The Jews said, 'Great! We'll take *ten!*'

***

Three little boys were concerned because they couldn't get anyone to play with them. They decided it was because they had not been baptised and didn't go to Sunday school.

So they went to the nearest church. Only the janitor was there. One said, 'We need to be baptised because no one will come out and play with us. Will you baptise us?'

'Sure,' said the janitor.

He took them into the bathroom and dunked their heads in the toilet bowl, one at a time. Then he said, 'Now go out and play.'

When they got outside, dripping wet, one of them asked, 'What religion do you think we are?'

The oldest one said, 'We're not Katlick, because they pour the water on you. We're not Bablist because they dunk all of you in it. We're not Methdiss because they just sprinkle you.'

The littlest one said, 'Didn't you smell that water?'

'Yes. What do you think that means?'

'I think that means we're Pisscopalians.'

***

INNER STRENGTH:

If you can start the day without caffeine;

If you can be cheerful, ignoring aches and pains;

If you can resist complaining and boring people with your troubles;

If you can eat the same food every day and be grateful for it;

If you can overlook when people take things out on you;

If you can take criticism and blame without resentment;

If you can face the world without lies and deceit;

If you can conquer tension without medical help;

If you can relax without liquor;

If you can sleep soundly every night . . .

YOU ARE PROBABLY THE FAMILY DOG.

***

On a visit to Boston I noticed a parking meter with a paper bag over it that said, 'Broken'. A sceptical traffic officer removed the bag, inserted a coin in the meter and turned the dial. It worked perfectly.

As the officer began to write a parking ticket, the car's owner rushed out of a nearby building. 'What are you doing?' he yelled after a quick glance at the meter. 'There's plenty of time left!'

***

I just organised some plastic surgery for my wife. I cut up all her credit cards.

***

While suturing a laceration on the hand of a 74-year-old Texan rancher, a doctor and the old man started talking about George W. Bush being in the White House.

The old Texan observed, 'Well, ya know, Bush is a "post turtle".'

Not knowing what the old man meant, the doctor asked him what a post turtle was.

The old man answered, 'When you're driving down a country road and you come across a fence post with a turtle balanced on top, that's a post turtle.'

The old man saw a puzzled look on the doctor's face, so he continued to explain, 'Think about it this way. He didn't get up there by himself, he doesn't belong up there, and he can't get anything done while he's up there. You just want to help the poor stupid bastard get down.'

***

Dear Tech Support,

Last year I upgraded from Boyfriend 5.0 to Husband 1.0 and noticed a distinct slowdown in the overall performance, particularly in the flower and jewellery applications, which operated flawlessly under Boyfriend 5.0.

In addition, Husband 1.0 uninstalled many other valuable programs, such as Romance 9.5 and Personal Attention 6.5, and then installed undesirable programs such as NFL 5.0, NHL 4.3, MLB 3.0 and NBA 3.6.

Conversation 8.0 no longer runs, and Housecleaning 2.6 simply crashes the system. I've tried running Nagging 5.3 to fix these problems, to no avail. What can I do?

Signed, Desperate.

Dear Desperate,

First, keep in mind that Boyfriend 5.0 is an Entertainment Package, while Husband 1.0 is an Operating System. Try to enter the command: 'c:/ ITHOUGHTYOULOVEDME' to download Tears 6., which should automatically install Guilt 3.0. If that application works as designed, Husband 1.0 should then automatically run the applications Jewellery 2.0 and Flowers 3.5.

Remember, though, that overuse of the above application can cause Husband 1.0 to default to Grumpy Silence 2.5, Happy Hour 7.0, or Beer 6.1. Beer 6.1 is a very bad program that will create Snoring Loudly 10.8. Whatever you do, *do not* install Mother-in-Law 1.0 or reinstall another Boyfriend program. These are not supported applications and will crash Husband 1.0. In summary, Husband 1.0 is a great program, but it does have limited memory and cannot learn new applications quickly.

You might consider buying additional software to improve memory and performance. I personally recommend Hot Food 3.0 and Lingerie 7.7.

Good luck, Tech Support.

***

Walking through San Francisco's Chinatown, a tourist from the Midwest was fascinated with all the Chinese restaurants, shops, signs and banners. He turned a corner and saw a building with the sign MOISHE PLOTNIK'S CHINESE LAUNDRY.

'Moishe Plotnik?' he wondered, 'How does that fit in Chinatown?'

So he walked into the shop and saw a fairly standard looking Chinese laundry. He could see that the proprietors were clearly aware of the uniqueness of the name, as there were baseball hats, T-shirts and coffee mugs emblazoned with MOISHE PLOTNIK'S CHINESE LAUNDRY. There was also a fair selection of Chinatown souvenirs, indicating that the name alone had brought many tourists into the shop.

The tourist selected a coffee cup as a conversation piece to take back to his office. Behind the counter was a smiling old Chinese gentleman who thanked him for his purchase. The tourist asked, 'Can you tell me how this place got a name like Moishe Plotnik's Chinese Laundry?'

The old man answered, 'Ahh . . . everybody asks me that. It's the name of the owner.'

Looking around, the tourist asked, 'Is he here now?'

'He is right here,' replied the old man. 'He is me.'

'Really? You're Chinese. How did you ever get a name like Moishe Plotnik?'

'It's simple,' said the old man. 'Many, many years ago when I came to this country, I was standing in line at the documentation centre. The man in front of me was a Jewish gentleman from Poland. The lady at the counter looked at him and said, "What is your name?" He said, "Moishe Plotnik". Then she looked at me and said, "What is your name?" I said "Sam Ting."'

***

KIDS AND RELIGION

A Sunday school teacher asked her class, 'What is Jesus's mother's name?'

One child answered, 'Mary.'

The teacher then asked, 'Who knows what Jesus's father's name was?'

A little kid said, 'Verge.'

Confused, the teacher asked, 'Where did you get that?'

The kid said, 'Well, you know they are always talking about Verge 'n' Mary.'

***

A mother was preparing pancakes for her sons, Kevin, five, and Ryan, three. The boys began to argue over who would get the first pancake.

Their mother saw the opportunity for a moral lesson. 'If Jesus were sitting here, he would say, "Let my brother have the first pancake, I can wait."'

Kevin turned to his younger brother and said, 'Ryan, you be Jesus!'

***

A man was walking down the street when he was accosted by a particularly dirty and shabby looking homeless man who asked him for a couple of dollars for dinner.

The man took out his wallet, extracted $10 and asked, 'If I give you this money, will you buy some beer with it instead?'

'No, I had to stop drinking years ago,' the homeless man replied.

'Will you use it to gamble instead of buying food?' the man asked.

'No, I don't gamble,' the homeless man said. 'I need everything I can get just to stay alive.'

'Will you spend it on greens fees at a golf course instead of food?' the man asked.

'Are you nuts?' replied the homeless man. 'I haven't played golf in twenty years!'

'Will you spend the money on a woman in the red-light district instead of food?' the man asked.

'What disease would I get for ten lousy bucks?' exclaimed the homeless man.

'Well,' said the man, 'I'm not going to give you the money. Instead, I'm going to take you home for a terrific dinner cooked by my wife.'

The homeless man was astounded. 'Won't your wife be furious with you for doing that? I know I'm dirty, and I probably smell pretty disgusting.'

The man replied, 'That's okay. I just want her to see what a man looks like who's given up beer, gambling, golf and sex.'

***

Employee: I'm sorry, but I can't come in today. My doctor says I suffer from Anal Glaucoma.
Boss: Anal Glaucoma? What's that?
Employee: I just can't see my arse coming to work today!

***

An Indian walks into a cafe with a shotgun in one hand and a bucket of buffalo manure in the other. He says to the waiter, 'Me want coffee.'

The waiter says, 'Sure, Chief, coming right up.' He gets the Indian a tall mug of coffee, and the Indian drinks it down in one gulp, picks up the bucket of manure, throws it in the air, blasts it with the shotgun, then just walks out.

The next morning, the Indian returns. He has his shotgun in one hand and a bucket of buffalo manure in the other. He walks up to the counter and says to the waiter, 'Me want coffee.'

The waiter says, 'Whoa, Tonto. We're still cleaning

up your mess from the last time you were here. What the heck was all that about, anyway?'

The Indian smiles and proudly says, 'Me training for upper-management position. Come in, drink coffee, shoot shit, leave mess for others to clean up, disappear for rest of day.'

***

A defence attorney was cross-examining a police officer during a felony trial.

Q: Officer, did you see my client fleeing the scene?

A: No, sir, but I subsequently observed a person matching the description of the offender running several blocks away.

Q: Officer, who provided this description?

A: The officer who responded to the scene.

Q: A fellow officer provided the description of this so-called offender. Do you trust your fellow officers?

A: Yes, sir, with my life.

Q: With your life? Let me ask you this then officer. Do you have a room where you change your clothes in preparation for your daily duties?

A: Yes, sir, we do.

Q: And do you have a locker in that room?

A: Yes, sir, I do.

Q: And do you have a lock on your locker?

A: Yes, sir.

Q: Now, why is it then, officer, if you trust your fellow officers with your life that you find it necessary to lock your locker in a room you share with those same officers?

A: Well, you see sir, we share the building with the court complex, and sometimes lawyers have been known to walk through that room.

***

An American, a Briton and an Iraqi are in a bar one night having a beer. The Yankee drinks his beer and suddenly throws his glass in the air, pulls out a gun and shoots the glass to pieces. He says, 'In the States our glasses are so cheap that we don't need to drink from the same ones twice.'

The Brit, obviously impressed by this, drinks his beer, throws his glass into the air, pulls out his gun and shoots the glass to pieces. He says, 'In the British Isles we have so much sand to make the glasses that we don't need to drink out of the same glass twice either.'

The Iraqi, cool as a cucumber, picks up his beer and drinks it, throws his glass into the air, pulls out his gun and shoots the Yank and the Brit. He says, 'In

Baghdad we have so many Americans and British that we don't need to drink with the same ones twice.'

***

In the beginning God created the heavens and the Earth.

And the Earth was without form, and void, and darkness was upon the face of the deep.

And the devil said, 'It doesn't get any better than this.'

And God said, 'Let there be light,' and there was light.

And God said, 'Let the earth bring forth grass, the herb yielding seed, and the fruit tree yielding fruit.' And God saw that it was good.

And the devil said, 'There goes the neighbourhood.'

And God said, 'Let us make Man in our image, after our likeness, and let them have dominion over the fish of the sea, and over the fowl of the air and over the cattle, and over all the Earth, and over every creeping thing that creepeth upon the Earth.' And so God created Man in his own image; male and female he created them.

And God looked upon Man and Woman and saw that they were lean and fit.

And the devil said, 'I know how I can get back at this game.'

And God populated the earth with broccoli and cauliflower and spinach, green and yellow vegetables of all kinds, so Man and Woman would live long and healthy lives.

And the devil created McDonald's. And McDonald's brought forth the 79-cent double cheeseburger. And the devil said to Man, 'You want fries with that?'

And Man said, 'Super size them.' And Man gained five pounds.

And God created the healthful yoghurt, that Woman might keep her figure that Man found so fair.

And the devil brought forth chocolate. And Woman gained five pounds.

And God said, 'Try my crispy fresh salad.'

And the devil brought forth Ben and Jerry's and Woman gained 10 pounds.

And God said, 'I have sent thee heart-healthy vegetables and olive oil with which to cook them.'

And the devil brought forth chicken-fried steak so big it needed its own platter. And Man gained 10 pounds and his bad cholesterol went through the roof.

And God brought forth running shoes and Man resolved to lose those extra pounds.

And the devil brought forth cable TV with remote

control so Man would not have to toil to change channels. And Man gained another 20 pounds.

And God said, 'You're running up the score, devil.'

And God brought forth the potato, a vegetable naturally low in fat and brimming with nutrition.

And the devil peeled off the healthful skin and sliced the starchy centre into chips and deep-fried them. And the devil created sour-cream dip.

And Man clutched his remote control and ate the potato chips swaddled in cholesterol. And the devil saw and said, 'It is good.' And Man went into cardiac arrest.

And God sighed and created quadruple bypass surgery.

And the devil cancelled Man's health insurance. Then God showed Woman how to peel the skin off chicken and cook the nourishing wholegrain brown rice.

And the devil created light beer so Man could poison his body with alcohol while feeling righteous because he had to drink twice as much of the now-insipid brew to get the same buzz. And Man gained another 10 pounds.

And God created the life-giving tofu.

And Woman ventured forth into the land of Godiva chocolate and upon returning asked Man, 'Do I look fat?'

And the devil said, 'Always tell the truth.'

And Man did.

And Woman went out from the presence of Man and dwelt in the land of the divorce lawyer, east of the marriage counsellor.

And Woman put aside the seeds of the earth and took unto herself comfort food.

And God brought forth Weight Watchers. It didn't help.

And God created exercise machines with easy payments.

And Man brought forth his Visa at 21 per cent. And the exercise machine went to dwell in the closet of Nod, east of the polyester leisure suit.

And in the fullness of time, Woman received the exercise machine from Man in the property settlement.

***

A husband and wife were having a fancy French dinner party for some important guests. The wife was very excited about this and wanted everything to be perfect. At the very last minute, she realised that she didn't have any snails for the dinner party, so she asked her husband to run down to the beach with the bucket to gather some snails.

Very grudgingly he agreed. He took the bucket, walked out the door, down the steps and out to the beach. As he was collecting the snails, he noticed a beautiful woman strolling alongside the water just a little further down the beach. He kept thinking to himself, 'Wouldn't it be great if she would even just come down and talk to me?' He went back to gathering the snails. All of a sudden he looked up and the beautiful woman was standing right over him.

They started talking and she invited him back to her place. They ended up spending the night together. At seven o'clock the next morning he woke up and exclaimed, 'Oh no! My wife's dinner party!'

He gathered all his clothes, put them on real fast, grabbed his bucket, and ran out the door. He ran down the beach all the way to his apartment. He ran up the stairs of his apartment. He was in such a hurry that when he got to the top of the stairs, he dropped the bucket of snails. There were snails all down the stairs. The door opened just then, with a very angry wife standing in the doorway wondering where he'd been all this time. He looked at the snails all down the stairs, then looked at his wife, then back at the snails and said, 'Come on guys, we're almost there!'

***

A man moved into a nudist colony. He received a letter from his grandmother asking him to send her a current photo of himself in his new location. Too embarrassed to let her know that he lived in a nudist colony, he cut a photo in half, but accidentally sent the bottom half of the photo.

He was really worried when he realised that he'd sent the wrong half, but then remembered how bad his grandmother's eyesight was, and hoped she wouldn't notice.

A few weeks later, he received a letter from his grandmother. It said, 'Thank you for the picture. Change your hairstyle – it makes your nose look too short. Love, Grandma.'

✱✱✱

Moishe Rabinowitz in the late 1930s fled his native land of Germany. He sold all his assets and converted them to gold and then had five sets of solid gold false teeth made.

When he arrived in New York the customs official was perplexed as to why anybody would have five sets of gold teeth. So Moishe explained. 'We Orthodox Jews have two separate sets of dishes for meat products and dairy products, but I am so kosher and religious I also have separate sets of teeth.'

The customs official shook his head and said, 'Well that accounts for two sets of teeth. What about the other three?'

Moishe then said, 'Well, us very religious Orthodox Jews use separate dishes for Passover, but I am so religious I have separate teeth, one for meat and one for dairy food.'

The Customers official slapped his head and then said, 'You must be a very religious man with separate teeth for food and dairy products and likewise for Passover. That accounts for four sets of teeth. What about the fifth set?'

'Well, to tell you the truth, once in a while I like a ham sandwich.'

***

Proudly showing off his newly leased downtown apartment to a couple of friends late one night, the drunk yuppie led the way to his bedroom where there was a big brass gong. 'What's that big brass gong for?' one of the friends asked.

'Issss nod a gong. Isss a talking clock,' the drunk replied.

'A talking clock?'

'Yep.'

'How does it work?' the second friend asked,

squinting at it.

'Watch,' the yuppie said. He picked up a hammer, gave it a ear-shattering pound and stepped back.

The three stood looking at one another for a moment in silence.

Suddenly, someone on the other side of the wall screamed, 'For fuck's sake, you wanker, it's ten past three in the fucking morning!'

***

'What's the usual tip?' a man growled when Jason, a college student, delivered his pizza.

'Well,' Jason replied, 'this is my first delivery, but the other guys said that if I got a quarter out of you, I'd be doing great.'

'Is that so?' grunted the man. 'In that case, here's twenty dollars.'

'Thanks,' Jason said, 'I'll put it in my college fund.'

'By the way, what are you studying?' enquired the man.

Jason replied, 'Applied psychology.'

***

A man walks out into the street and manages to get a taxi just going by. He gets into the taxi, and the cabbie says, 'Perfect timing. You're just like Dave.'

'Who?'

'Dave Bronson. There's a guy who did everything right. Like my coming along when you needed a cab. It would have happened like that to Dave every single time.'

'There are always a few clouds over everybody.'

'Not Dave. He was a terrific athlete. He could have gone on the pro tour in tennis. He could golf with the pros. He sang like an opera baritone and danced like a Broadway star.'

'He was something, huh?'

'He had a memory like a trap. Could remember everybody's birthday. He knew all about wine, which fork to eat with. He could fix anything. Not like me. I change a fuse and the whole neighbourhood blacks out.'

'No wonder you remember him.'

'Well, I never actually met Dave.'

'Then how do you know so much about him?'

'I married his widow!'

***

A blonde girl enters a store that sells curtains. She tells the salesman, 'I would like to buy a pink curtain in the size of my computer screen.'

The surprised salesman replies, 'But, madam,

computers do not have curtains!'

And the blonde says, 'Hello! I've got Windows!'

***

Inland Revenue sends their auditor to a synagogue. The auditor is doing all the checks and then turns to the rabbi and says, 'I noticed that you buy a lot of candles.'

'Yes,' answers the rabbi.

'Well rabbi, what do you do with the candle drippings?' he asks.

'A good question,' notes the rabbi. 'We actually save them up and when we have enough, we send them back to the candle maker and every now and then they send us a free box of candles.'

'Oh,' replies the auditor, somewhat disappointed that his unusual question actually had a practical answer. So he thought he'd go on, in his obnoxious way.

'Rabbi, what about all those matzo purchases? What do you do with the crumbs from the matzo?'

'Ah yes,' replies the rabbi, calmly. 'We actually collect up all the crumbs from the matzo and when we have enough, we send them in a box back to the manufacturer and every now and then, they send a free box of matzo balls.'

'Oh,' replies the auditor, thinking hard how to fluster the rabbi.

'Well, rabbi' he continues, 'what do you do with all the foreskins from the circumcisions?'

'Yes, here too, we do not waste,' answers the rabbi. 'What we do is save up all the foreskins and when we have enough we actually send them to the Inland Revenue.'

'Inland Revenue?' questions the auditor in disbelief.

'Ah yes,' replies the rabbi, 'Inland Revenue – and about once a year they send us a little prick like you.'

***

A man walks into a restaurant with a full-grown ostrich behind him and, as he sits, the waitress comes over and asks for their order. The man says, 'I'll have a hamburger, fries and a Coke,' and turns to the ostrich. 'What's your order?'

'I'll have the same,' says the ostrich.

A short time later the waitress returns with the order. 'That will be $6.40 please.' And the man reaches into his pocket and pulls out the exact amount.

The next day, the man and the ostrich come again and the man says, 'I'll have a hamburger, fries and a Coke.'

And the ostrich says, 'I'll have the same.'

Once again the man reaches into his pocket and pays the exact amount.

This becomes a routine until late one evening the two enter again.

'The usual?' asks the waitress.

'No, this is Friday night, so I will have a steak, baked potato and salad,' says the man.

'Same for me,' says the ostrich.

A short time later the waitress comes with the order and says, 'That will be $12.62.' Once again the man pulls the exact amount out of his pocket and places it on the table.

'How do you manage to always come up with the exact money out of your pocket every time?'

'Well,' says the man, 'several years ago I was cleaning the attic and found an old lamp. When I rubbed it a genie appeared and offered me two wishes. My first wish was that if I ever had to pay for anything, I'd just put my hand in my pocket and the right amount of money would always be there.'

'That's brilliant!' says the waitress. 'Most people would wish for a million dollars or something, but you'll always be as rich as you want for as long as you live!'

'That's right! Whether it's a gallon of milk or a Rolls Royce, the exact money is always there,' says the man.

The waitress asks, 'One other thing sir, what's with the ostrich?' The man sighs and answers, 'My second wish was for a tall chick with long legs who agrees with everything I say!'

***

A lady, about eight months pregnant, got on a bus. She noticed the man opposite her smiling at her. She immediately moved to another seat. This time the smile turned into a grin, so she moved again. The man seemed more amused. When on the fourth move the man burst out laughing, she complained to the driver and he had the man arrested.

The case came up in court. The judge asked the man what he had to say for himself. He replied, 'Well, Your Honour, it was like this. When the lady got on the bus, I couldn't help but notice her condition. She sat under a sign that said "The Double Mint Twins are coming", and I grinned. Then she moved and sat under a sign that said "Logan's Liniment will reduce the swelling", and I had to smile. Then she placed herself under a sign that said "William's Big Stick Did the Trick", and I could hardly contain myself. But, Your Honour, when she moved the fourth time and sat under a sign that said "Goodyear Rubber could have prevented this accident", I just lost it.'

'Case dismissed!'

***

An American tourist in London found himself needing to take a leak something terrible. After a long search he just couldn't find any public toilet to relieve himself, so he went down one of the side streets to take care of business. Just as he was unzipping, a London police officer showed up.

'Look here, old chap, what are you doing?' the officer asked.

'I'm sorry,' the American replied, 'but I really gotta take a leak.'

'You can't do that here,' the officer told him. 'Look, follow me.'

The police officer led him to a beautiful garden with lots of grass, pretty flowers and manicured hedges. 'Here,' said the policeman, 'whiz away.'

The American tourist shrugged, turned, unzipped and started pissing on the flowers. 'Ahhh,' he said in relief. Then turning towards the officer, he said, 'This is very nice of you. Is this British courtesy?'

'No,' retorted the policeman, 'it's the French Embassy.'

***

Bessie, the church gossip and self-appointed arbiter of the church's morals, kept sticking her nose into other people's business. Several residents were unappreciative of her activities, but feared her enough to maintain their silence.

She made a mistake, however, when she accused George, a new member, of being an alcoholic after she saw his pick-up truck parked in front of the town's only bar one afternoon. She commented to George and others that everyone seeing it there would know what he was doing.

George, a man of few words, stared at her for a moment and just walked away. He didn't explain, defend or deny. He said nothing.

Later that evening, George quietly parked his pick-up in front of Bessie's house – and left it there all night.

✲✲✲

A first-grade teacher, Ms Neelam, was having trouble with one of her students studying at YPS Patiala. The teacher asked, 'Singh Jr, what is your problem?'

Singh Jr answered, 'I am too smart for the first grade. My sister is in the third grade and I'm smarter than she is. I think I should be in the third grade, too!'

Ms Neelam had had enough. She took Singh Jr to the principal's office. While Singh Jr waited in the outer office, the teacher explained to the principal what the situation was. The principal told Ms Neelam he would give the boy a test and if he failed to answer any of his questions he was to go back to the first grade and behave. She agreed.

Singh Jr was brought in and the conditions were explained to him and he agreed to take the test.

Principal: 'What is three times three?'

Singh Jr: 'Nine.'

Principal: 'What is six times six?'

Singh Jr: 'Thirty-six.'

And so it went with every question the principal thought a third-grader should know. The principal looked at Ms Neelam and told her, 'I think Singh Jr can go to the third grade.'

Ms Neelam said to the principal, 'I have some of my own questions. Can I ask him?'

The principal and Singh Jr both agreed.

Ms Neelam asked, 'What does a cow have four of that I have only two of?'

Singh Jr, after a moment, said, 'Legs.'

Ms Neelam: 'What is in your pants that you have, but I do not have?'

Singh Jr: 'Pockets.'

Ms Neelam: 'What does a dog do that a man sometimes steps into?'

Singh Jr: 'Pants.'

Ms Neelam: 'What starts with a C and ends with

a T, is hairy, oval, delicious and contains thin whitish liquid?'

Singh Jr: 'Coconut.'

Ms Neelam: 'What goes in hard and pink then comes out soft and sticky?'

The principal's eyes opened really wide and before he could stop the answer, Singh Jr was taking charge: 'Bubblegum.'

Ms Neelam: 'What does a man do standing up, a woman does sitting down and a dog does on three legs?'

The principal's eyes opened really wide and before he could stop the answer, Singh Jr said, 'Shake hands.'

Ms Neelam: 'Now I will ask some "Who am I" sorts of questions, okay?'

Singh Jr: 'Yep.'

Ms Neelam: 'You stick your poles inside me. You tie me down to get me up. I get wet before you do.'

Singh Jr: 'Tent.'

Ms Neelam: 'A finger goes in me. You fiddle with me when you're bored. The best man always has me first.'

The principal was looking restless, a bit tense, and took a large swig of vodka.

Singh Jr: 'Wedding ring.'

Ms Neelam: 'I come in many sizes. When I'm not well, I drip. When you blow me, you feel good.'

Singh Jr: 'Nose.'

Ms Neelam: 'I have a stiff shaft. My tip penetrates. I come with a quiver.'

Singh Jr: 'Arrow.'

Ms Neelam: 'What word starts with an F and ends in K that means a lot of heat and excitement?'

Singh Jr: 'Firetruck.'

The principal breathed a sign of relief and said to the teacher: 'Send Singh Jr to Delhi University. I got the last ten questions wrong myself!'

***

A wife and husband are having dinner one night and engage in a casual conversation.

Wife: What would you do if I died? Would you get married again?

Husband: Definitely not!

Wife: Why not? Don't you like being married?

Husband: Of course I do.

Wife: When why wouldn't you remarry?

Husband: Okay, I'd get married again.

Wife: You would? (With a hurtful look on her face.)

Husband: (Makes audible groan.)

Wife: Would you sleep with her in our bed?

Husband: Where else would we sleep?

Wife: Would you replace my pictures with hers?

Husband: That would seem like the proper thing to do.

Wife: Would you play golf with her?

Husband: I guess so.

Wife: Would she use my golf clubs?

Husband: No, she's left-handed.

Wife: (Silence.)

Husband: Shit!

***

On her radio show, Dr Laura Schlesinger said that, as an observant Orthodox Jew, homosexuality is an abomination according to Leviticus 18:22, and cannot be condoned under any circumstance.

The following response is an open letter to Dr Laura, penned by a US resident, which was posted on the Internet.

Dear Dr Laura,

Thank you for doing so much to educate people regarding God's Law. I have learned a great deal from your show, and try to share that knowledge with as many people as I can. When someone tries to defend the homosexual lifestyle, for example, I simply remind them that Leviticus 18:22 clearly states it to be an abomination. End of debate.

I do need some advice from you, however, regarding some other elements of God's Law and how to follow them.

1. When I burn a bull on the altar as a sacrifice, I know it creates a pleasing odour for the Lord – Lev. 1:9. The problem is my neighbours. They claim the odour is not pleasing to them. Should I smite them?

2. I would like to sell my daughter into slavery, as sanctioned in Exodus 21:7. In this day and age, what do you think would be a fair price for her?

3. I know that I am allowed no contact with a woman while she is in her period of menstrual uncleanliness – Lev. 15:19-24. The problem is how do I tell? I have tried asking, but most women take offence.

4. Lev. 25:44 states that I may indeed possess slaves, both male and female, provided they are purchased from neighbouring nations. A friend of mine claims that this applies to Mexicans, but not Canadians. Can you clarify? Why can't I own Canadians?

5. I have a neighbour who insists on working on the Sabbath. Exodus 35:2. The passage clearly states he should be put to death. Am I morally obligated to kill him myself?

6. A friend of mine feels that even though eating shellfish is an abomination – Lev. 11:10 – it is a lesser abomination than homosexuality. I don't agree. Can you settle this? Are there 'degrees' of abomination?

7. Lev. 21:20 states that I may not approach the altar of God if I have a defect in my sight. I have to admit that I wear reading glasses. Does my vision have to be 20/20, or is there some wiggle room here?

8. Most of my male friends get their hair trimmed, including the hair around their temples, even though this is expressly forbidden by Lev. 19:27. How should they die?

9. I know from Lev. 11:6-8 that touching the skin of a dead pig makes me unclean, but may I still play football if I wear gloves?

10. My uncle has a farm. He violates Lev. 19:19 by planting two different crops in the same field, as does his wife by wearing garments made of two different kinds of thread (cotton/polyester blend). He also tends to curse and blaspheme a lot. Is it really necessary that we go to all the trouble of getting the whole town together to stone them? (Lev. 24:10-16.) Couldn't we just burn them to death at a private family affair like we do with people who sleep with their in-laws? (Lev. 20:14)

I know you have studied these things extensively and thus enjoy considerable expertise in such matters, so I am confident you can help. Thank you again for reminding us that God's word is eternal and unchanging.

Your adoring fan,

James M. Kauffman, Ed.D.

Professor Emeritus, Dept of Curriculum, Instruction and Special Education, University of Virginia

***

Be sure to lock your doors and windows at home! A Sydney man was found dead in his home over the weekend. Detectives at the scene found the man face down in his bathtub. The tub had been filled with milk, sugar and cornflakes. A banana was sticking out of his arse.

Police suspect a cereal killer.

***

A mother complained to the doctor about her daughter's strange eating habits. 'All day long she lies in bed and eats yeast and car wax. What will happen to her, doctor?' the mother asked.

'Eventually,' said the doctor, 'she will rise and shine.'

***

The Lone Ranger and Tonto walked into a bar one day and sat down to drink a beer. After a few minutes, a tall cowboy walked in and said, 'Who owns the big white horse outside?'

The Lone Ranger stood up, hitched his gun belt, and said, 'I do. Why?'

The cowboy looked at the Lone Ranger and said, 'I just thought you would like to know that your horse is just about dead outside.'

The Lone Ranger and Tonto rushed outside and sure enough, Silver was about dead from heat exhaustion. The Lone Ranger got him some water and made him drink it. Soon Silver started to feel better. The Lone Ranger turned to Tonto and said, 'Tonto, I want you to run around Silver and see if you can create enough of a breeze to make him start to feel better.'

Tonto said, 'Sure, Kemosabe,' and took off running circles around Silver. Not able to do anything but wait, the Lone Ranger returned to the bar to finish his drink.

A few minutes later, another cowboy struts to the bar and asks, 'Who owns that big white horse outside?'

The Lone Ranger stands again and says, 'I do. What's wrong with him this time?'

The cowboy says to him, 'Nothin' much. I just wanted you to know you left your Injun running.'

✳✳✳

A farmer goes out one day and buys a brand new stud rooster for his chicken coop. The new rooster struts over to the old rooster and says, 'Okay, old timer, time for you to retire.' The old rooster replies, 'Come on, surely you can't handle all of these chickens. Look what it has done to me. Can't you just let me have the two old hens over in the corner?'

The young rooster says, 'Beat it. You're washed up and I'm taking over.'

The old rooster says, 'I tell you what, young stud. I will race you around the farmhouse. Whoever wins gets the exclusive domain over the entire chicken coop.'

The young rooster laughs, 'You know you don't stand a chance, old man. So, just to be fair, I will give you a head start.'

The old rooster takes off running. About fifteen seconds later the young rooster takes off running after him. They round the front porch to the farmhouse and the young rooster has closed the gap. He is already about 10 centimetres behind the old rooster and gaining fast.

The farmer, meanwhile, is sitting in his usual spot

on the front porch when he sees the roosters running by. He grabs his shotgun and – *boom* – he blows the younger rooster to bits. The farmer sadly shakes his head and says, 'Shucks, that's the third gay rooster I've bought this month.'

Moral of the story: Don't mess with the old timbers. Age and treachery will always overcome youth and skill.

***

IDIOTS IN SERVICE

This week, our phones went dead and I had to contact the repair people. They promised to come between 8 a.m. and 7 p.m. When I asked if they could give me a smaller time window, the pleasant gentleman asked, 'Would you like us to call you before we come?

I replied that I didn't see how he would be able to do that since our phones weren't working.

He also requested that we report future outages by email.

(Whose email works without a telephone line?)

***

IDIOTS AT WORK

I was signing the receipt for my credit card purchase

when the clerk noticed I had never signed my name on the back of the credit card. She informed me that she could not complete the transaction unless the card was signed. When I asked why, she explained that it was necessary to compare the signature I had just signed on the receipt. So I signed the credit card in front of her.

She carefully compared the signature to the one I had just signed on the receipt. As luck would have it, they matched!

***

IDIOTS IN THE NEIGHBOURHOOD
I live in a semi-rural area. We recently had a new neighbour call the local township administrative office to request the removal of the Koala Crossing sign on our road.

The reason: too many koalas were being hit by cars and she didn't want them to cross there anymore.

***

Now I lay me
Down to sleep
I pray the Lord
My shape to keep.
Please no wrinkles,

Please no bags.
And please lift my butt
Before it sags.
Please no age spots,
Please no grey.
And as for my belly,
Please take it away.
Please keep me healthy,
Please keep me young,
And thank you, Dear Lord
For all that you've done.

***

A local business was looking for office help. They put a sign in the window, stating the following: 'HELP WANTED. Must be able to type, must be good with a computer, and must be bilingual. We are an Equal Opportunity Employer.'

A short time afterwards, a dog trotted up to the window, saw the sign and went inside. He looked at the receptionist and wagged his tail, then walked over to the sign, looked at it and whined.

Getting the idea, the receptionist got the office manager. The office manager looked at the dog and was surprised, to say the least. However, the dog looked determined, so he led him into the office.

Inside, the dog jumped up on the chair and stared at the office manager.

The manager said, 'I can't hire you. The sign says you have to be able to type.' The dog jumped down, went to the typewriter and proceeded to type out a perfect letter. He took out the page and trotted over to the manager and gave it to him, then jumped back on the chair.

The manager was stunned, but then told the dog, 'The sign says you have to be good with a computer.' The dog jumped down again and went to the computer. The dog proceeded to enter and execute a perfect program that worked flawlessly the first time.

By this time the manager was totally dumbfounded. He looked at the dog and said, 'I realise that you are a very intelligent dog and have some interesting abilities. However, I still can't give you a job.'

The dog jumped down and went to a copy of the sign and put his paw on the sentences that told about being an Equal Opportunity Employer. The manager said, 'Yes, but the sign also says that you have to be bilingual.'

The dog looked at the manager calmly and said, 'Meow!'

✷✷✷

I was at the airport checking in at the gate when an airport employee asked, 'Has anyone put anything in your baggage without your knowledge?'

To which I replied, 'If it was without my knowledge, how would I know?'

She smiled knowingly and nodded. 'That's why we ask.'

***

The stoplight on the corner buzzes when it's safe to cross the street. I was crossing with a co-worker when she asked if I knew what the buzzer was for. I explained that it signals blind people when the light is red.

Appalled, she responded, 'What on earth are blind people doing driving?'

***

At a goodbye luncheon for an old and dear co-worker who was leaving the company due to 'downsizing', the manager commenced cheerfully, 'This is fun. We should do this more often.'

Not a word was spoken. Everyone just looked at each other with that cow-in-the-headlights stare.

***

The Washington Post asked readers to take any word from the dictionary, alter it by adding, subtracting or changing one letter and then supply a new definition. Here are a few winners:

1. Intaxication: Euphoria at getting a tax refund that lasts until you realise it was your money to start with.

2. Reintarnation: Coming back to life as a hillbilly.

3. Bozone (n.): The substance surrounding stupid people that stops bright ideas from penetrating. (The bozone layer, unfortunately, shows little sign of breaking down in the near future.)

4. Foreploy: Any misrepresentation about yourself for the purpose of getting laid.

5. Cashtration (n.): The act of buying a house, which renders the subject financially impotent for an indefinite period.

6. Giraffiti: Vandalism spray-painted very, very high.

7. Sarchasm: The gulf between the author of sarcastic wit and the person who doesn't get it.

8. Inoculatte: To take coffee intravenously when you are running late.

9. Hipatitis: Terminal 'cool'ness.

10. Osteopornosis: A degenerate disease.

11. Karmageddon: It's like, when everybody is sending off all these really bad vibes, right? And then, like, the Earth explodes and it's, like, a serious bummer.

12. Decafalon (n.): The gruelling event of getting through the day consuming only things that are good for you.

13. Glibido: All talk and no action.

14. Dopeler effect: The tendency of stupid ideas to seem smarter when they come at you rapidly.

15. Arachnoleptic fit (n.): The frantic dance performed just after you've accidentally walked through a spider web.

16. Beelzebug (n.): Satan in the form of a mosquito that gets into your bedroom at three in the morning and cannot be cast out.

17. Caterpallor (n.): The colour you turn after finding half a grub in the fruit you're eating.

18. Ignoranus: A person who's both stupid and an arsehole.

***

My husband, not happy with my mood swings, bought me a mood ring the other day so he would be able to monitor my moods. When I'm in a good mood it turns green.

When I'm in a bad mood it leaves a big fucking red mark on his forehead.

Maybe next time he'll buy me a diamond.

***

THINGS TO SAY WHEN YOU'RE STRESSED:

1. Okay! Okay! I take it back. Unfuck you!
2. You say I'm a bitch like it's a bad thing.
3. Well, this day was a total waste of make-up.
4. Well, aren't we a bloody ray of sunshine?
5. Don't bother me. I'm living happily ever after.
6. Do I look like a people person?
7. This isn't an office; it's hell with fluorescent lighting.
8. I started out with nothing and still have most of it left.
9. Therapy is expensive. Popping bubble wrap is cheap. You choose.
10. Why don't you try practising random acts of intelligence and senseless acts of self-control?
11. I'm not crazy. I've been in a very bad mood for thirty years.
12. Sarcasm is just one more service I offer.
13. Do they ever shut up on your planet?
14. I'm not your type. I'm not inflatable.
15. Stress is when you wake up screaming and you realise you haven't gone to sleep yet.
16. Back off! You're standing in my aura.
17. Don't worry, I forgot your name too.

18. I work forty-five hours a week to be this poor.
19. Not all men are annoying. Some are dead.
20. Wait – I'm trying to imagine you with a personality.
21. Chaos, panic, and disorder – my work here is done.
22. Ambivalent? Well, yes and no.
23. You look like shit. Is that the style now?
24. Earth is full. Go home.
25. A hard-on doesn't count for personality growth.
26. You are depriving some village of an idiot.
27. If arseholes could fly, this place would be a fucking airport!

***

A little old man shuffled ever so slooooowly into an ice-cream parlour, pulled himself ever so slooooowly, painfully, onto a stool. After catching his breath, he ordered a banana split.

The waitress asked kindly, 'Crushed nuts?'

'Nope,' he replied, 'arthritis.'

***

I never quite figured out why the sexual urges of men and women differ so much. And I never figured out the whole Venus and Mars thing. I have never figured out why men think with their head and women think with their heart. I have never figured out why the sexual desire gene gets thrown into a state of turmoil when it hears the words 'I do'.

For example: One evening last week, my wife and I were getting into bed. Well, the passion starts to heat up and she eventually says, 'I don't feel like it, I just want you to hold me.'

I said, '*What?*' What was that?'

So she says the words that every husband on the planet dreads to hear: 'You're just not in touch with my emotional needs as a woman enough for me to satisfy your physical needs as a man.' She responded to my puzzled look by saying, 'Can't you just love me for who I am and not for what I do for you in the bedroom?'

Realising that nothing was going to happen that night, I rolled over and went to sleep.

The very next day I opted to take the day off work to spend time with her. We went out to a nice lunch and then went shopping to a big department store. I walked around with her while she tried on several different very expensive outfits. She couldn't decide which one to take so I told her we'll just buy them all! She wanted new shoes to complement her new clothes, so I said let's get a pair for each outfit.

We went to the jewellery department where she picked out a pair of diamond earrings. Let me tell you, she was so excited. She must have thought I was one wave short of a shipwreck! I started to think she was testing me because she asked for a tennis bracelet when she doesn't even know how to play tennis. I think I threw her for a loop when I said, 'That's fine, honey.' She was almost nearing sexual satisfaction from all of the excitement.

Smiling with excited anticipation, she finally said, 'I think this is all, dear, let's go to the cashier.'

I could hardly contain myself when I blurted out, 'No honey, I don't feel like it.'

Her face just went completely blank as her jaw dropped with a baffled, '*What?*'

I then said, 'Really honey! I just want you to *hold* this stuff for a while. You're just not in touch with my financial needs as a man enough for me to satisfy your shopping needs as a woman.'

And just when she had this look like she was going to kill me, I added, 'Why can't you just love me for who I am and not for the things I buy you?'

Apparently, I won't be having sex again until sometime after pigs fly over a frozen hell while monkeys fly out her bum.

***

A man walking on the beach picks up a bottle and rubs it. Out pops a genie.

'Master, I can grant any two wishes you desire.'

The man thinks for a second and says, 'I want to be hard all the time and get all the arse I want.'

'As you wish.'

There is a loud poof, and the man turns into a toilet seat.

***

How many members of the Bush Administration are needed to replace a light bulb?

Seven.

1. One to deny that a lightbulb needs to be replaced.
2. One to attack and question the patriotism of anyone who has questions about the light bulb.
3. One to blame the previous administration for the need for a new light bulb.
4. One to arrange the invasion of a country rumoured to have a secret stockpile of light bulbs.
5. One to get together with Vice President Cheney and figure out how to pay Halliburton Industries one million dollars for a light bulb.
6. One to arrange a photo-op session showing Bush changing the light bulb while dressed in a flight

suit and wrapped in an American flag.

7. And one to explain to Bush the difference between screwing a light bulb and screwing the country.

★★★

A little girl walks into a pet shop and asks in the sweetest little lisp, 'Excuthe me, mithter, do you keep wittle wabbits?'

The shopkeeper gets down on his knees, so that he's on her level, and asks, 'Do you want a wittle white wabby or a soft and fuwwy black wabby or maybe one like that cute wittle brown wabby over there?

She in turn puts her hands on her knees, leans forward and says in a quiet voice, 'I don't fink my pyfon weally gives a phuck.'

★★★

It started out innocently enough.

I began to think at parties now and then – to loosen up. Inevitably, though, one thought led to another, and soon I was more than just a social thinker.

I began to think alone – 'to relax', I told myself – but I knew it wasn't true. Thinking became more and more important to me, and finally I was thinking all the time.

I began to think on the job. I knew that thinking and employment don't mix, but I couldn't stop myself. I began to avoid friends at lunchtime so I could read Thoreau and Kafka. I would return to the office dizzied and confused, asking, 'What is it exactly we are doing here?'

Things weren't going so great at home either. One evening I had turned off the TV and asked my wife about the meaning of life. She spent that night at her mother's.

I soon had a reputation as a heavy thinker. One day the boss called me in. He said, 'Jim, I like you, and it hurts me to say this, but your thinking has become a real problem. If you don't stop thinking on the job, you'll have to find another job.'

This gave me a lot to think about. I came home early after my conversation with the boss. 'Honey,' I confessed, 'I've been thinking . . .'

'I know you've been thinking,' she said, 'and I want a divorce!'

'But honey, surely it's not that serious.'

'It is serious,' she said, lower lip aquiver. 'You think as much as college professors and college professors don't make any money, so if you keep on thinking, we won't have any money!'

'That's a faulty syllogism,' I said impatiently, and she began to cry.

I'd had enough. 'I'm going to the library,' I snarled as I stomped out the door. I headed for the library, in the mood for some Nietzsche, with NPR on the radio. I roared into the parking lot and ran up to the big glass doors – they didn't open. The library was closed. To this day, I believe that a higher power was looking out for me that night.

As I sank to the ground, clawing at the unfeeling glass, whimpering for Zarathustra, a poster caught my eye. 'Friend, is heavy thinking ruining your life?' it asked. You probably recognise that line. It comes from the standard Thinker's Anonymous poster. Which is why I am what I am today: a recovering thinker. I never miss a TA meeting. At each meeting we watch a non-educational video; last week it was *Porky's*. Then we share experiences about how we avoided thinking since the last meeting. I still have my job, and things are a lot better at home.

Life just seemed easier, somehow, as soon as I stopped thinking. Soon, I will be able to vote for a Republican . . .

***

Why did the man want to live to be 102?
He heard very few people die at that age.

***

A father walks into a cafe with his young son. The boy is holding a 20-cent coin. Suddenly, the boy starts going blue in the face. The father realises the boy has swallowed the coin and starts shouting for help.

A well-dressed and attractive woman is sitting in the cafe reading her newspaper and sipping a cappuccino. Looking up, she puts her coffee cup down, neatly folds the newspaper, gets up and makes her way, unhurried, to the boy. She then drops his pants, takes hold of the boy's testicles and starts to squeeze and twist, gently at first and then more firmly.

After a few seconds the boy convulses violently and coughs up the coin, which the woman deftly catches in her free hand.

Releasing the boy's testicles, the woman hands the coin to the father and walks back to her seat without saying a word.

The father rushes over and starts thanking her. 'I've never seen anybody do anything like that before,' he says. 'Are you a doctor?'

'No,' the woman replied, 'a divorce lawyer.'

***

A professor at a Texas university was giving a lecture on the supernatural. To get a feel for his audience, he asked, 'How many people here believe in ghosts?'

About ninety students raised their hands.

'Well, that's a good start. Out of those of you who believe in ghosts, do any of you think you've seen a ghost?'

About forty students raised their hands.

'That's really good. I'm really glad you take this seriously. Has anyone here ever talked to a ghost?' About fifteen students raised their hands.

'Has anyone here ever touched a ghost?'

Three students raised their hands.

'That's fantastic. Now let me ask you a further question. Have any of you ever made love to a ghost?'

Way in the back, Bubba raised his hand.

The professor took off his glasses and said, 'Son, all the years I've been giving this lecture, no one has ever claimed to have made love to a ghost. You've got to come up here and tell us about your experience.'

The big redneck student replied with a nod and a grin, and began to make his way up to the podium. When he reached the front of the room, the professor asked, 'So, Bubba, tell us what it's like to have sex with a ghost.'

Bubba replied, 'I'm sorry . . . from way back there I thought you said "goats".'

***

Three men died on Christmas Eve and were met by St Peter at the Pearly Gates. 'In honour of this holy season,' St Peter said, 'you must each possess something that symbolises Christmas to get into heaven.'

The first man fumbled through his pockets and pulled out a lighter. He flicked it on. 'It represents a candle,' he said.

'You may pass through the Pearly Gates,' St Peter said.

The second man reached into his pocket and pulled out a set of keys. He shook them and said, 'They're bells.'

St Peter said, 'You may pass through the Pearly Gates.'

The third man started searching desperately through his pockets and finally pulled out a pair of women's panties.

St Peter looked at the man with a raised eyebrow and asked, 'And just what do those symbolise?'

The man replied, 'They're Carols.'

***

If you had bought $1000 of Nortel stock one year ago, it would now be worth $49. With Enron, you would have $16.50 of the original $1000. With Worldcom, you would have less than $5 left.

If you had bought $1000 worth of Budweiser (the beer, not the stock) one year ago, drank all the beer, then turned in the cans for the 10-cent deposit, you would have $214.

Based on the above, my investment advice is to drink heavily and recycle.

***

The congregation honours a rabbi for twenty-four years of service by sending him to Hawaii for a week, all expenses paid. When he walks into his hotel room, there's a beautiful nude girl lying on the bed. She says, 'Hi, rabbi. I'm a little something extra that the president of the board paid for!'

The rabbi is incensed! He picks up the phone, calls the board president and says, 'Greenberg, where is your respect? I am the moral leader of our community. As your rabbi, I am very, very angry with you.'

The girl gets up and starts to get dressed. The rabbi turns to her and says, 'Where are you going? I'm not angry with you.'

***

A story is told of a Jewish man who was riding on the subway reading a neo-Nazi newspaper. A friend of his, who happened to be riding in the same subway car, noticed this strange phenomenon.

Very upset, he approached the newspaper reader. 'Moshe, have you lost your mind? Why are you reading a neo-Nazi newspaper?'

Moshe replied, 'I used to read the Jewish newspaper, but what did I find? Anti-Semitism in Europe, terrorism in Israel, Jews disappearing through assimilation and intermarriage. Jews living in poverty.

'So I switched to the neo-Nazi newspaper. Now what do I find? Jews own all the banks. Jews control the media. Jews are all rich and powerful. Jews rule the world. The news is so much better!'

***

A little boy and a little girl attended the same school and became friends. Every day they would sit together to eat their lunch. They discovered that they both brought chicken sandwiches every day!

This went on all through the fourth and fifth grades, until one day he noticed that her sandwich wasn't a chicken sandwich.

He said, 'Hey, how come you're not eating chicken. Don't you like it anymore?'

She said, 'I love it, but I have to stop eating it.'

'Why?' he asked.

She pointed to her lap and said, 'Cause I'm starting to grow little feathers down there!'

'Let me see,' he said.

'Okay,' and she pulled up her skirt.

He looked and said, 'That's right. You are! Better not eat any more chicken.'

He kept eating his chicken sandwiches until one day he brought peanut butter. He said to the little girl, 'I have to stop eating chicken sandwiches. I'm starting to get feathers down there too!'

She asked if she could look, so he pulled down his pants for her.

She said, 'Oh my God, it's too late for you. You've already got the neck and the gizzards!'

★★★

As he was flying down the road yesterday, he noticed a cop with a radar gun sitting on top of a bridge. Naturally, he was pulled over. The cop walked up to the car and asked him. 'What's the hurry?'

He replied, 'I'm late for work.'

'Oh yeah,' said the cop. 'What do you do?'

'I'm a rectum stretcher,' he responded.

The cop said, 'What? A rectum stretcher? What

does a rectum stretcher do?'

He said, 'Well, I start with one finger, then I work my way up to two fingers, then three, then four, then my whole hand. Then I work until I can get both hands in there, and then slowly stretch it until it's about six foot wide.'

'What the hell do you do with a six foot arsehole?'

'You give him a radar gun and park him on top of a bridge.'

***

A garbo is going along a street picking up the wheelie bins and emptying them into his truck.

He gets to one house where the bin hasn't been left out, so he has a quick look for it. He goes round the back but still can't see it, so he knocks on the door.

There's no answer, so he knocks again.

'Alright mate, where's your bin?' asks the garbo.

'I bin on toilet,' replied the Japanese bloke, looking perplexed.

Realising the Japanese fellow has misunderstood, the garbo smiles and says, 'No mate. Where's ya dustbin?'

'I dust bin on toilet, I told you,' says the Japanese man.

'Mate,' says the garbo, 'you're misunderstanding me. Where's your wheelie bin?'

'Okay, okay,' says the Japanese man. 'I wheelie bin having wank.'

***

A young broker goes out and buys a brand new Ferrari GTO. It costs him $500 000. He takes it out for a spin and stops at a red light.

An old man on a moped, looking about a hundred years old, pulls up next to him. The old man looks over at the sleek, shiny car and says, 'What kind of car ya' got there sonny?'

The young man replies, 'A Ferrari GTO. It cost half a million dollars.'

'That's a lot of money,' says the old man. 'Why does it cost so much?'

'Because this car can do up to 500k's an hour!'

The moped driver says, 'Mind if I take a look inside?'

'No problem,' replies the owner. So the old man pokes his head in the window and looks around. Then, sitting back on his moped, the old man says, 'That's a pretty nice car all right. But I'll stick with my moped!'

Just then the light changes, so the guy decides to show the old man just what his car can do. He floors it, and within 30 seconds, the speedometer reads 160kph.

Suddenly, he notices a dot in his rear-view mirror. It seems to be getting closer! He slows down to see what it could be. And suddenly, *Whoooooooossshhh!* Something whips by him, going much faster!

'What on earth could be going faster than my Ferrari?' the young man asks himself. He floors the accelerator and takes the Ferrari up to 250kph. Then, up ahead of him, he sees that it's the old man on the moped!

Amazed that a moped could pass his Ferrari, he gives it more gas and passes the moped at 300kph. *Whoooooooossshhh!*

He's again feeling pretty good until he looks in his mirror and sees the old man gaining on him *again!* Astounded by the speed of this old guy, he floors the pedal and takes the Ferrari all the way up to 500kph. Not ten seconds later, he sees the moped bearing down on him again! The Ferrari is flat out, and there's nothing he can do!

Suddenly, the moped ploughs into the back of his Ferrari, demolishing the rear end. The young man stops and jumps out, and unbelievably the old man is still alive.

He runs up to the mangled old man and says, 'Oh my God! Is there anything I can do for you?'

The old man whispers with his dying breath, 'Can you unhook my suspenders from your side-view mirror?'

***

For those of us getting along in years, here is a little secret for building your arm and shoulder muscles. You might want to adopt this regimen. Three days a week works well.

Begin by standing straight, with a 2kg potato sack in each hand. Extend your arms straight out from your sides and hold them there as long as you can. Try to reach a full minute. Relax.

After a few weeks, move up to 5kg potato sacks, and then to 20kg potato sacks. And eventually try to get to where you can lift a 50kg potato sack in each hand and hold your arms straight out for more than a minute.

After you feel confident at this level, start putting a couple of potatoes in each of the sacks, but be careful not to overdo it.

***

It is hard to find a joke without a dirty word or two in it. Here is one with none:

Two tall trees, a birch and a beech, are growing in the woods. A small tree begins to grow between them, and the beech says to the birch, 'Is that a son of a beech or a son of a birch?'

The birch says he cannot tell. Just then a woodpecker lands on the sapling. The birch says, 'Woodpecker, you are a tree expert. Can you tell if that is a son of a beech or a son of a birch?'

The woodpecker takes a taste of the small tree. He replies, 'It is neither a son of a beech nor a son of a birch. It is, however, the best piece of ash I have ever put my pecker in.'

✳✳✳

YEAR'S BEST HEADLINES

Crack Found on Governor's Daughter

Something Went Wrong in Jet Crash, Expert Says

Police Begin Campaign to Run Down Jaywalkers

Iraqi Head Seeks Arms

Is There a Ring of Debris around Uranus?

Prostitutes Appeal to Pope

Miners Refuse to Work after Death

Juvenile Court to Try Shooting Defendant

War Dims Hope for Peace

Red Tape Holds Up New Bridges

Kids Make Nutritious Snacks

Typhoon Rips Through Cemetery: Hundreds Dead

***

At New York's Kennedy Airport today, an individual later discovered to be a public school teacher was arrested trying to board a flight while in possession of a ruler, a protractor, a setsquare, a slide rule and a calculator.

At a morning press conference, Attorney General John Ashcroft said he believes the man is a member of the notorious Al-gebra movement. He is being charged by the FBI for carrying weapons of maths instruction.

'Al-gebra is a fearsome cult,' Ashcroft said. 'They desire average solutions by means and extremes, and sometimes they go off on tangents in search of absolute value. They use secret code names like 'x' and 'y' and refer to themselves as 'unknowns', but we have determined they belong to a common denominator of the axis of medieval with coordinates in every country.

'As the Greek philanderer Isosceles used to say, "There are three sides to every triangle",' Ashcroft declared.

When asked to comment on the arrest, President Bush said, 'If God had wanted us to have better weapons of maths instruction, He would have given us more fingers and toes.

'I am gratified that our government has given us a sine that it is intent on protracting us from these math-dogs who are willing to disintegrate us with calculus disregard. Murky statisticians love to inflict plane on every sphere of influence,' the President said, adding, 'Under the circumferences, we must differentiate their root, make our point and draw the line.'

President Bush warned, 'These weapons of maths instruction have the potential to decimal everything in their math on a scalene never before seen unless we become exponents of a higher power and begin to factor in random facts of vertex.'

Attorney General Ashcroft said, 'As our great leader would say, read my ellipse. Here is one principle he is uncertainty of: "Though they continue to multiply, their days are numbered as the hypotenuse tightens around their necks."'

***

King Ozymandias of Assyria was running low on cash after years of war with the Hittites. His last great possession was the Star of the Euphrates, the most valuable diamond in the ancient world. Desperate, he went to Croesus, the pawnbroker, to ask for a loan.

'I'll give you 100 000 dinars for it,' says Croesus.

'But I paid a million dinars for it!' the king protests. 'Don't you know who I am? I am the *king!*'

Croesus shrugs his shoulders. 'When you wish to pawn a star, makes no difference who you are.'

***

One day George W. Bush and Dick Cheney walk into a diner. A waitress walks up to them and asks if she can take their order. Bush leans close to her and says, 'Honey, can I have a quickie?'

The waitress is appalled and yells at the President about women's rights and storms away.

Cheney then says to Bush, 'George, it's pronounced 'quiche'.'

***

A little boy wanted $100 very badly and prayed for weeks, but nothing happened. Then he decided to write God a letter requesting the $100. When the postal authorities received the letter addressed to God, The World, they decided to send it to John Howard.

The Prime Minister was so amused that he instructed his secretary to send the little boy a $5 note. Mr Howard thought this would appear to be a lot of money to a little boy.

The little boy was delighted with the $5 note and sat down to write a thank you note to God, which read: 'Dear God, thank you very much for sending the money. However, I noticed that for some reason you sent it through Canberra and, as usual, those arseholes deducted $95 in taxes!'

★★★

What if there were no hypothetical questions?

If a deaf person swears, does his mother wash his hands with soap?

If someone with multiple personalities threatens to kill himself, is it considered a hostage situation?

Is there another word for synonym?

What do you do when you see an endangered animal eating an endangered plant?

If a parsley farmer is sued, can they garnish his wages?

Would a fly without wings be called a walk?

Why do they lock gas station bathrooms? Are they afraid someone will clean them?

If a turtle doesn't have a shell, is he homeless or naked?

If the police arrest a mime, do they tell him he has the right to remain silent?

Why do they put Braille on the drive-through bank machines?

How do they get deer to cross the road only at those yellow road signs?

What was the best thing before sliced bread?

One nice thing about egotists: they don't talk about other people.

Do infants enjoy infancy as much as adults enjoy adultery?

If one synchronised swimmer drowns, do the rest drown, too?

If you spin an Oriental man in a circle three times, does he become disoriented?

Can an atheist get insurance against acts of God?

***

JEWISH WOMEN

The Harvard School of Medicine did a study of why Jewish women like Chinese food so much. The study revealed that this is due to the fact that 'Won ton' spelled backwards is 'not now'.

There is a big controversy on the Jewish view of when life begins. In Jewish tradition, the foetus is not considered viable until it graduates from medical school.

Q: Why don't Jewish mothers drink?
A: Alcohol interferes with their suffering.

Q: Why do Jewish mothers make great parole officers?

A: They never let anyone finish a sentence.

Q: What's a Jewish-American princess's favourite position?

A: Facing Bloomingdale's.

When the doctor called Mrs Liebenbaum to tell her that her cheque came back, she replied, 'So did my arthritis.'

A man called his mother in Florida, 'Mom, how are you?'

'Not too good,' said the mother, 'I'm very weak.'

The son said, 'Why are you so weak?'

She said, 'Because I haven't eaten in thirty-eight days.'

The son said, 'That's terrible. Why haven't you eaten in thirty-eight days?'

The mother answered, 'Because I don't want my mouth to be filled with food if you should call.'

A Jewish boy comes home from school and tells his mother he has a part in the play. She asks, 'What part is it?'

The boy says, 'I play the part of the Jewish husband.'

723

The mother scowls and says, 'Go back and tell the teacher you want a speaking part.'

Q: Where does a Jewish husband hide money from his wife?
A: Under the vacuum cleaner.

Q: How many Jewish mothers does it take to change a light bulb?
A: (Sigh) 'Don't bother, I'll sit in the dark. I don't want to be a nuisance to anybody.'

Short summary of every Jewish holiday: They tried to kill us, we won, let's eat.

Did you hear about the bum who walked up to a Jewish mother on the street and said, 'Lady, I haven't eaten in three days.'
'Force yourself,' she replied.

Q: What's the difference between a Rottweiler and a Jewish mother?
A: Eventually the Rottweiler lets go.

Jewish telegram: 'Begin worrying. Details to follow.'

Q: Why are Jewish men circumcised?

A: Because Jewish women don't like anything that isn't 20 per cent off.

***

A Japanese company and a Californian company decided to have a canoe race on the Columbia River. Both teams practised hard and long to reach their peak performance before the race.

On the big day, the Japanese won by a mile.

Afterwards, the Californian team became very discouraged and depressed. The management of the Californian company decided that the reason for the crushing defeat had to be found. A 'measurement team' made up of senior management was formed to investigate and recommend appropriate action.

Their conclusion was that the Japanese had eight people rowing and one person steering, while the Californians had one person rowing and eight people steering.

So the management of the Californian company hired a consulting company and paid them incredible amounts of money. They advised that too many people were steering the boat and not enough people were rowing.

To prevent losing to the Japanese again next year, the rowing team's management structure was totally reorganised to four steering supervisors, three area steering superintendents and one assistant superintendent steering manager.

They also implemented a new performance system that would give the one person rowing the boat greater incentive to work harder. It was called the 'Rowing Team Quality First Program', with meetings, dinners and free pens for the rower. 'We must give the rower empowerment and enrichment through this quality program.'

The next year the Japanese won by two miles. Humiliated, the management of the Californian company laid off the rower for poor performance, halted development of a new canoe, sold the paddles and cancelled all capital investments for new equipment.

Then they used the money saved by giving a High Performance Award to the steering managers and distributed the rest of the money as bonuses to the senior executives.

***

Paddy and Mick have been drinking pints of Guinness all night and it's time to go home.

They stagger from the pub.

Paddy says to Mick, 'Let's steal a bus to go home in.'

'Good idea,' says Mick. So off they go to the bus depot.

They break in and look around, but Paddy says, 'Can't find a 71.'

'That's okay,' says Mick. 'We'll take a 75 and walk from the roundabout.'

***

A middle-aged woman standing nude looks in the bedroom mirror and says to her husband. 'I look horrible. I'm fat, my boobs and my backside are getting saggier by the day. I find a new wrinkle every morning and I think I'll have to go up yet *another* dress size.'

Sitting down with her head in her hands, she continues, 'I just feel so old and ugly. Can you please at least pay me one compliment?'

The husband replies, 'Well, if it's any consolation, your eyesight's fucking perfect!'

***

Little Leroy came into the kitchen where his mother was making dinner. His birthday was coming up and he thought this was a good time to tell his mother what he wanted. 'Mum, I want a bike for my birthday. Little Leroy was a bit of a troublemaker. He had gotten into trouble at school and at home. Leroy's mother asked him if he thought he deserved to get a bike for his birthday. Little Leroy, of course, thought he did.

Leroy's mother, being a Christian woman, wanted Leroy to reflect on his behaviour over the last year. 'Go to your room, Leroy, and think about how you have behaved this year. Then write a letter to God and tell him why you deserve a bike for your birthday.'

Little Leroy stomped up the stairs to his room and sat down to write God a letter.

Letter 1: 'Dear God, I have been a very good boy this year and I would like a bike for my birthday. I want a red one. Your friend, Leroy.'

Leroy knew that wasn't true. He had not been a very good boy this year so he tore up the letter and started over.

Letter 2: 'Dear God, I have been an okay boy this year. I still would really like a bike for my birthday. Leroy.'

Leroy knew he could not send this letter to God either. So he wrote a third letter.

Letter 3: 'God, I haven't been a good boy this year. I am very sorry. I will be a good boy if you send me a bike for my birthday. Please! Thank you. Leroy.'

Leroy knew, even if it was true, this letter was not going to get him a bike.

By now, Leroy was very upset. He went downstairs

and told his mother that he wanted to go to church. Leroy's mother thought her plan had worked as Leroy looked very sad. 'Just be home in time for dinner,' Leroy's mother told him.

Leroy walked down the street to the church on the corner. Little Leroy went into the church and up to the altar. He looked around to see if anyone was there. Leroy bent down and picked up a statue of the Virgin Mary. He slipped it under his shirt and ran out of the church, down the street, into the house and up to his room and sat down with a piece of paper and a pen.

Leroy began to write his letter to God.

Letter 4: 'GOD, I'VE GOT YOUR MAMA. IF YOU WANT TO SEE HER AGAIN, SEND THE BIKE. SIGNED YOU KNOW WHO.'

***

My friend drowned in a bowl of muesli. A strong currant pulled him in.

I went to a seafood disco last week – and pulled a muscle.

Our ice-cream man was found lying on the floor of his van covered with hundreds and thousands. Police say he topped himself.

Guy goes into the doctor's. 'Doc, I've got a cricket ball stuck up my backside.'

'How's that?'

'Don't you start!'

Two elephants walk off a cliff . . . *boom, boom*!

Police arrested two kids yesterday. One was drinking battery acid, the other was eating fireworks. They charged one and let the other one off.

A man walked into the doctor's. He said, 'I've hurt my arm in several places.'

The doctor said, 'Well, don't go there any more.'

Ireland's worst air disaster occurred early this morning when a small two-seater Cessna plane crashed into a cemetery. Irish search and rescue workers have recovered 1826 bodies so far, and expect that number to climb as digging continues into the night.

***

A fellow in a golf comp turns up without a caddy, so requests one from the crows. A 95-year-old gent steps forward. 'I'll be your caddy,' says the frail old bloke.

'You won't be able to lift the bag.'

'No problem. I workout every day, fit as a fiddle.'

'But will you be able to hear when I ask for a club?'

'Not a problem, perfect hearing.'

'But what about tracking the ball from a distance?'

'20-20 vision, not a problem.'

The golfer tees off and whacks the ball almost out of sight.

'Now are you sure you can carry the bag?'

The old bloke picks up the bag.

'Did you see where the ball went?' asks the golfer.

'Yep.'

'Okay, let's go. So, where did the ball go?'

'I forgot,' says the old bloke.

***

A man falls asleep on the beach for several hours and gets horrible sunburn. He goes to the hospital and is promptly admitted after being diagnosed with second-degree burns.

The doctor prescribes continuous intravenous feeding with saline and electrolytes, a sedative and a Viagra pill every four hours.

The nurse, rather astounded, said, 'What good will Viagra do him?'

The doctor replied, 'It'll keep the sheets off his legs.'

***

THOUGHTS ON THE PRESIDENT

Well, we're all excited because President Bush has started his 35-day vacation. He's down there in Crawford, Texas, and on the first day of his vacation he went fishing. He didn't find any fish. But he believes they're there and that his intelligence is accurate.

David Letterman

Some good news for the economy. President Bush went on a month-long vacation.   Jay Leno

The United States is putting together a Constitution now for Iraq. Why don't we just give them ours? It's served us well for 200 years, and we don't appear to be using it anymore. So what the hell?   Jay Leno

The White House says that the vacation in Texas will give President Bush the chance to unwind. My question is: when does the guy wind?

David Letterman

If you add up all the time he's spent on the ranch, he's spent more time in hiding than bin Laden and Hussein put together.   Bill Maher

732

President Bush's economic team is now on their Jobs & Growth bus tour all across America. I think the only job they've created so far is for the guy driving the bus.   Jay Leno

They're saying Arnold will get 95 per cent of the vote. At least according to his brother, Jeb Schwarzenegger.
                                                    Craig Kilborn

Finally, a candidate who can explain the Bush Administration's position on civil liberties in the original German.
 Bill Maher on Schwarzenegger running for Governor

President Bush is supporting Arnold. But a lot of Republicans are not, because he is actually quite liberal. Karl Rove said if his father wasn't a Nazi, he wouldn't have any credibility with conservatives at all.   Bill Maher

Apparently, Arnold was inspired by President Bush, who proved you can be a successful politician in this country even if English is your second language.
                                                    Conan O'Brien

President Bush has been silent on Schwarzenegger. Of course, he can't pronounce Schwarzenegger.

David Letterman

Here's how bad California looks to the rest of the country. People in Florida are laughing at us.

Jay Leno

***

New York magazine sponsors a contest each year in which contestants take a well-known expression in a foreign language, change a single letter, and provide a definition for the new expression. Here are some winners:

Harlez-vous Francais. Can you drive a French motorcycle?
Ex post fucto. Lost in the mail.
Veni, vipi, vici. I came, I'm a very important person, I conquered.
Cogito eggo sum. I think, therefore I waffle.
Rigor morris. The cat is dead (after a cat-food TV advert.)
Respondez s'il vous plaid. Honk if you're Scottish.
Que sera serf. Life is feudal.
Le roi est mort. Jive le roi. The king is dead. No kidding.

Pro bozo publico. Support your local clown.

Monage a trois. I am three years old.

Felix navidad. Our cat has a boat.

Haste cuise. Fast French food.

Veni, vidi, vice. I came, I saw, I partied.

Quip pro quo. Fast retort.

Aloha oy. Love; greetings; farewell, from such a pain you would never know.

Visa la France. Don't leave your chateau without it.

Amicus puriae. Platonic friend.

L'etat, c'est moo. I'm bossy around here.

Cogito, ergo spud. I think, therefore I yam. (okay, more than one letter)

Veni, vidi, velcro. I came, I saw, I stuck around. (Another exception)

Ich bit ein berliner. He deserved it.

Zitgeist. The Clearasil doesn't quite cover it up.

E pluribus anum. Out of any group, there's always one arsehole.

***

I recently picked a new primary care physician. After two visits and exhaustive lab tests, he said I was doing 'fairly well' for my age.

A little concerned about that comment, I couldn't resist asking him, 'Do you think I'll live to be eighty?'

He asked, 'Well, do you smoke tobacco or drink beer?'

'Oh no,' I replied. 'I've never done either.'

Then he asked, 'Do you eat rib-eye steaks, greasy food and barbecued ribs?'

I said, 'No. I've heard that grease and red meat are very unhealthy.'

'Do you spend a lot of time in the sun?' he asked.

'No, I don't,' I said.

He said, 'Do you gamble, drive fast cars or fool around?'

'No,' I said, 'I've never done any of those things.'

He looked at me and said, 'Then why on earth do you want to live to be eighty?'

***

One night, an 87-year-old woman came home from bingo to find her husband in bed with another woman. She became violent and ended up pushing him off the balcony of their twentieth-floor apartment, killing him instantly.

Brought before the court on the charge of murder, she was asked if she had anything to say in her own defence.

'Your Honour,' she began coolly, 'I figured that at ninety-two, if he could fuck, he could fly.'

736

***

A few minutes before the church service started, the townspeople were sitting in their pews and talking.

Suddenly, Satan appeared at the front of the church. Everyone started screaming and running for the front entrance, trampling each other in a frantic effort to get away from evil incarnate.

Soon everyone had exited the church except for one elderly gentleman who sat calmly in his pew without moving, seemingly oblivious to the fact that God's ultimate enemy was in his presence.

So Satan walked up to the old man and said, 'Don't you know who I am?'

The man replied, 'Yep, sure do.'

'Aren't you afraid of me?' Satan asked.

'Nope, sure aren't,' said the man.

'Don't you realise I can kill you with a word?' asked Satan.

'Don't doubt it for a minute,' returned the old man, in an even tone.

'Did you know that I could cause you profound horrifying agony for all eternity?' persisted Satan.

'Yep,' was the calm reply.

'And you're still not afraid?' asked Satan.

'Nope,' said the old man.

More than a little perturbed, Satan asked, 'Well,

why aren't you afraid of me?'

The man calmly replied, 'Been married to your sister for forty-eight years.'

***

Some of the artists of the sixties are revising their hits with new lyrics to accommodate the ageing baby boomers. This is good news for those feeling a little older and missing those great old tunes.

Herman's Hermits
'Mrs Brown, You've Got a Lovely Walker'

The Bee Gees
'How Can You Mend a Broken Hip'

Bobby Darin
'Splish, Splash, I Was Havin' a Flash'

Ringo Starr
'I Get By With a Little Help From Depends'

Roberta Flack
'The First Time Ever I Forget Your Face'

Johnny Nash
'I Can't See Clearly Now'

Paul Simon
'Fifty Ways to Lose Your Liver'

The Commodores
'Once, Twice, Three Times to the Bathroom'

Marvin Gaye
'I Heard it Through the Grape Nuts'

Procol Harum
'A Whiter hade of Hair'

Leo Sayer
'You Make Me Feel Like Napping'

The Temptations
'Papa's Got a Kidney Stone'

ABBA
'Denture Queen'

★★★

Farmer Joe lived on a quiet rural highway. But, as time went by, the traffic slowly built up at an alarming rate. The traffic was so heavy and so fast that his chickens were being run over at a rate of three to six a day.

So one day Farmer Joe called the sheriff's office and said, 'You've got to do something about all of these people driving so fast and killing all of my chickens.'

'What do you want me to do?' asked the sheriff.

'I don't care, just do something about those crazy drivers.'

So the next day, he had the county workers go out and erect a sign that said: SLOW. SCHOOL CROSSING.

Three days later Farmer Joe called the sheriff and said, 'You've got to do something about these drivers. The 'school crossing' sign seems to make them go even faster.'

So again, the sheriff sent out the county workers and they put up a new sign: SLOW. CHILDREN AT PLAY.

That really sped them up. So Farmer Joe called and called and called every day for three weeks.

Finally, he asked the sheriff, 'Your signs are doing no good. Can I put up my own sign?'

The sheriff told him, 'Sure thing, put up your own sign.'

He was going to let Farmer Joe do just about anything in order to get him to stop calling every day to complain. The sheriff got no more calls from Farmer Joe.

Three weeks later, curiosity got the better of the sheriff and he decided to give Farmer Joe a call.

'How's the problem with those drivers? Did you put up your sign?'

'Oh, I sure did. And not one chicken has been killed since then. I've got to go. I'm very busy.' He hung up the phone.

The sheriff was really curious now and he thought to himself, 'I'd better go out there and take a look at that sign, it might be something that *we* could use to slow down drivers.'

So the sheriff drove out to Farmer Joe's house and his jaw dropped the moment he saw the sign. It was spray-painted on a sheet of wood: NUDIST COLONY. GO SLOW AND WATCH OUT FOR THE CHICKS!

***

How many dogs does it take to change a light bulb?

Golden Retriever: 'The sun is shining, the day is young, we've got our whole lives ahead of us and you're inside worrying about a stupid burned-out bulb.'

Border Collie: 'Just one. And then I'll replace any

wiring that's not up to code and repaint the wall where you scuffed it in the dark, before moving on to the plumbing.'

Dachshund: 'You know I can't reach that stupid lamp!'

Rottweiler: 'Make me!'

Boxer: 'Who cares? I can play with my squeaky toy in the dark.'

Lab: 'Oh, me, me! Pleeeeeeze let me change the light bulb! Can I? Can I? Huh? Huh? Can I? Pleeeeeeze, please, please, please pick me!'

German Shepherd: 'I'll change it as soon as I've led everyone from the dark room, made sure no one was hurt, checked to make sure I haven't missed any, and made one more perimeter patrol to see that no one has tried to take advantage of the dark situation.'

Jack Russell: 'I'll just pop it in while I'm bouncing off the walls and furniture.'

Old English Sheep Dog: 'Light bulb? I don't see a light bulb. I don't see a lamp. Where am I? Where are you?'

Cocker Spaniel: 'Why change it? If I pee on the carpet in the dark I won't get caught till you step in it.'

Chihuahua: 'Yo quiero Taco Bulb.'

Pointer: 'I see it, there it is, there it is . . . right there.'

Greyhound: 'It isn't moving. Who cares?'

Blue Heeler: 'First, let me put all the light bulbs in a little circle.'

Poodle: 'I'll just blow in the Border Collie's ear and he'll do it. By the time he finishes rewiring the house, my nails will be dry.'

***

The other day I heard that the Taliban are getting upset because people keep referring to them as 'towel heads'. Apparently, they do not wear towels on their heads, they wear sheets. In the future, when you refer to them, please use their correct name – 'sheet heads'.

Thank you.

***

Three guys and a woman are stuck in an elevator. While they're stuck, they strike up a conversation.

The first guy says, 'I'm a Y.U.P.P.I.E. You know, Young, Urban, Professional, Peaceful, Intelligent, Ecologist.'

The second guy says, 'I'm a D.I.N.K.Y. You know, Double, Income, No Kids, Yet.'

The third guy says, 'I'm a R.U.B. Rich, Urban, Biker.'

They turn to the woman and ask her, 'What are you?'

She replies, 'I'm a W.I.F.E. You know, Wash, Iron, Fuck, Etc.'

***

A very modest man was in the hospital for a series of tests, the last of which had left his bodily systems extremely upset. Upon making several false-alarm trips to the bathroom, he figured that the latest episode was just that, so he stayed put.

Suddenly, however, he filled his bed with diarrhoea and was embarrassed beyond his ability to remain rational.

In a complete loss of composure, he jumped out of bed, gathered up the bed sheets and threw them out the hospital window.

A drunk was walking by the hospital when the sheets landed on him. The drunk started yelling, cursing and swinging his arms violently in an attempt to free himself of the sheets. He ended up with the soiled sheets in a tangled pile at his feet.

As the drunk stood there, staring down at the sheets, a hospital security guard who had witnessed the entire incident, walked up to him and asked, 'What the heck is going on?'

The drunk, still staring down at the sheets, replied, 'I think I just beat the shit out of a ghost.'

✳✳✳

Saddam Hussein has admitted to having weapons of mass destruction. He says Shane Warne's mum gave them to him.

✳✳✳

Answers provided by sixth-graders in a history test:

Ancient Egypt was inhabited by mummies and they all wrote in hydraulics. They lived in the Sarah Dessert. The climate of the Sarah is such that all the inhabitants have to live elsewhere.

Moses led the Hebrew slaves to the Red Sea where they made unleavened bread, which is bread made without any ingredients. Moses went up on Mount Cyanide to get the ten commandments. He died before he ever reached Canada.

The Greeks were a highly sculptured people, and without them we wouldn't have history. The Greeks also had myths. A myth is a female moth.

Socrates was a famous Greek teacher who went around giving people advice. They killed him. Socrates died from an overdose of wedlock. After his death, his career suffered a dramatic decline.

In the Olympic Games, Greeks ran races, jumped, hurled biscuits and threw Java.

Julius Caesar extinguished himself on the battlefields of Gaul. The Ides of March murdered him because they thought he was going to be made king. Dying, he gasped out, 'Tee hee, Brutus.'

Joan of Arc was burnt to a steak and was canonised by Bernard Shaw.

Queen Elizabeth was the 'Virgin Queen'. As a queen

she was a success. When she exposed herself before her troops they all shouted 'hurrah'.

It was an age of great inventions and discoveries. Gutenberg invented removable type and the Bible. Another important invention was the circulation of blood. Sir Walter Raleigh is a historical figure because he invented cigarettes and started smoking.

Sir Francis Drake circumsized the world with a 100-foot clipper.

The greatest writer of the Renaissance was William Shakespeare. He was born in the year 1564, supposedly on his birthday. He never made much money and is famous only because of his plays. He wrote tragedies, comedies and hysterectomies, all in Islamic pentameter. Romeo and Juliet are an example of a heroic couple. Romeo's last wish was to be laid by Juliet.

Writing at the same time as Shakespeare was Miguel Cervantes. He wrote *Donkey Hote*. The next great author was John Milton. Milton wrote *Paradise Lost*. Then his wife died and he wrote *Paradise Regained*.

Delegates from the original 13 states formed the Contented Congress. Thomas Jefferson, a Virgin, and

Benjamin Franklin were two singers of the Declaration of Independent. Franklin discovered electricity by rubbing two cats backward and declared, 'A horse divided against itself cannot stand'. Franklin died in 1790 and is still dead.

Abraham Lincoln became America's greatest Precedent. Lincoln's mother died in infancy, and he was born in a log cabin, which he built with his own hands. Abraham Lincoln freed the slaves by signing the Emasculation Proclamation. On the night of April 14, 1865, Lincoln went to the theatre and got shot in his seat by one of the actors in a moving picture show. They believe the assinator was John Wilkes Booth, a supposingly insane actor. This ruined Booth's career.

Johann Bach wrote a great many musical compositions and had a large number of children. In between he practised on an old spinster that he kept up in his attic. Bach died from 1750 to the present. Bach was the most famous composer in the world and so was Handel. Handel was half German, half Italian and half English. He was very large.

Beethoven wrote music even though he was deaf. He was so deaf he wrote loud music. He took long walks in the forest even when everyone was calling for him.

Beethoven expired in 1827 and later died for this.

The nineteenth century was a time of a great many thoughts and inventions. People stopped reproducing by hand and started reproducing by machine. The invention of the steamboat caused a network of rivers to spring up. Cyrus McCormick invented the McCormick raper, which did the work of a hundred men. Louis Pasteur discovered a cure for rabbits. Charles Darwin was a naturalist who wrote the Organ of the Species. Madman Curie discovered the radio. Karl Marx became one of the Marx Brothers.

***

One Christmas Eve, a frenzied young man ran into a pet shop looking for an unusual Christmas gift for his wife. The shop owner suggested a parrot named Chet, which could sing well-known Christmas carols. This seemed like the perfect gift. 'How do I get him to sing?' the young man asked, excitedly.

'Simply hold a lighted match directly under his feet,' was the shop owner's reply.

The shop owner held a lighted match under the parrot's left foot. Chet began to sing, 'Jingle Bells! Jingle Bells!' The shop owner then held another match under the parrot's right foot. Then Chet's tune changed, and the air was filled with, 'Silent Night, Holy Night'.

The young man was so impressed that he bought the bird and ran home as quickly as he could with Chet under his arm. When his wife saw her gift she was overwhelmed.

'How beautiful!' she exclaimed. 'Can he talk?'

'No,' the young man replied, 'but he can sing. Let me show you.' So the young man whipped out his lighter and placed it under Chet's left foot, as the shopkeeper has shown him, and Chet crooned, 'Jingle Bells!'

The man then moved the lighter to Chet's right foot, and out came, 'Silent Night, Holy Night'.

The wife, her face filled with curiosity, asked, 'What if we hold the lighter between his legs?'

The man did not know. 'Let's try it,' he answered, eager to please his wife. So they held the lighter between Chet's legs. Chet twisted his face, cleared his throat, and the little parrot sang out loudly like it was the performance of his life, 'Chet's nuts roasting on an open fire . . .'

***

REDNECK MEDICAL TERMS

Benign: What you be after you be eight.
Artery: The study of paintings.
Bacteria: Back door to cafeteria.
Barium: What doctors do when patients die.
Caesarean section: A neighbourhood in Rome.
Cat scan: Searching for kitty.
Cauterise: Made eye contact with her.
Colic: A sheep dog.
Coma: A punctuation mark.
D&C: Where Washington is.
Dilate: To live long.
Enema: Not a friend.
Fester: Quicker than someone else.
Fibula: A small lie.
Genital: Non-Jewish person.
Hangnail: What you hang your coat on.
Impotent: Distinguished, well known.
Labour pain: Getting hurt at work.
Medical staff: A doctor's cane.
Morbid: A higher offer than I bid.
Nitrates: Cheaper than day rates.
Node: I knew it.
Outpatient: A person who has fainted.
Pap Smear: A fatherhood test.
Pelvis: Second cousin to Elvis.

Post-operative: A letter carrier.
Recovery Room: Place to do upholstery.
Rectum: Damn near killed him.
Secretion: Hiding something.
Seizure: Roman emperor.
Tablet: A small table.
Terminal illness: Getting sick at the airport.
Tumour: More than one.
Urine: Opposite of you're out.
Varicose: Nearby.

***

CODE OF ETHICAL BEHAVIOUR FOR PATIENTS

Do not expect your doctor to share your discomfort.

Involvement with the patient's suffering might cause him to lose valuable scientific objectivity.

Be cheerful at all times.

Your doctor leads a busy and trying life and requires all the gentleness and reassurance he can get.

Try to suffer from the disease for which you are being treated.

Remember that your doctor has a professional reputation to uphold.

Do not complain if the treatment fails to bring relief.

You must believe that your doctor has achieved a deep insight into the true nature of your illness, which transcends any mere permanent disability you may have experienced.

Never ask your doctor to explain what he is doing or why he is doing it.

It is presumptuous to assume that such profound matters could be explained in terms that you would understand.

Submit to novel experimental treatment readily.

Though the surgery may not benefit you directly, the resulting research paper will surely be of widespread interest.

Pay your medical bills promptly and willingly.

You should consider it a privilege to contribute, however modestly, to the wellbeing of physicians and other humanitarians.

Do not suffer from ailments that you cannot afford.

It is sheer arrogance to contract illnesses that are beyond your means.

Never reveal any of the shortcomings that have come

to light in the course of treatment.

The patient-doctor relationship is a privileged one, and you have a sacred duty to protect him from exposure.

Never die while in your doctor's presence or under his direct care.

This will only cause him needless inconvenience and embarrassment.

***

A virile young Italian gentleman was relaxing at his favourite bar in Rome when he managed to attract a spectacular young blonde. Things progressed to the point where he invited her back to his apartment, and after some small talk, they retired to his bedroom and made love.

After a pleasant interlude, he asked with a smile, 'So, you finish?'

She paused for a second, frowned and replied, 'No.'

Surprised, the young man reached for her and the lovemaking resumed. This time she thrashed about wildly and there were screams of passion. The lovemaking ended and again the young man smiled, and asked, 'You finish?'

Again, after a short pause, she returned his smile, cuddled closer to him and softly said, 'No.'

Stunned, but damned if this woman was going to outlast him, the young man reached for the woman again. Using the last of his strength, he barely managed it, but they climaxed simultaneously, screaming, bucking, clawing and ripping the bed sheets. The exhausted man fell onto his back gasping. Barely able to turn his head, he looked into her eyes, smiled proudly and asked again, 'You finish?'

Barely able to speak, she whispers in his ear, 'No! I Norwegian!'

***

A sign in the window of a funeral home in Philadelphia, PA:

WE WOULD RATHER DO BUSINESS WITH 1000 AL-QAEDA TERRORISTS THAN WITH A SINGLE AMERICAN.

***

One night George W. Bush was awakened in the White House by the ghost of George Washington. Bush asked the ghost, 'Mr Washington, sir, what is the best thing I can do to help the American people?'

'Set an honest and honourable example, George, just as I did.'

The following evening, the ghost of Thomas Jefferson appeared before Bush in the dark bedroom. 'Mr Jefferson, sir,' Bush asked, 'what is the best thing I can do to help the American people?'

'Preserve the land for future generations and stay out of foreign affairs.'

Bush wasn't sleeping well the next night and saw yet another figure moving in the shadows. It was Abraham Lincoln. 'Mr Lincoln, sir, what is the best thing I can do to help the American people?' George asked.

'Go to the theatre more!'

***

WHAT WOULD YOU DO?

You are the President of the United States.

Scientists have discovered a meteor that is headed towards the earth.

They have calculated that it will strike France in two days, at approximately 2.30 a.m. The meteor is large enough to completely wipe France from the face of the earth. France and the United Nations have requested that the United States send all available ships and aircraft to help evacuate the country. Among the ships and planes you could be sending are many that are being used to fight the war on terror overseas.

As President, you must decide. Do you:

A. Stay up late on the night of the impact to watch the coverage live?

B. Tape it and watch it in the morning?

***

PARIS (AP) – France announced today that it plans to ban fireworks at Euro Disney following last night's display that caused soldiers at a nearby army garrison to surrender.

***

A reporter goes to Israel to cover the fighting. She is looking for something emotional and positive and of human interest. Something like that guy in Sarajevo who risked his life to play the cello every day in the town square.

In Jerusalem, she hears about an old Jew who had been going to the Western Wall to pray twice a day, every day, for a long, long time. So she goes to check it out.

She goes to the Western Wall and there he is!

757

She watches him pray and after about 45 minutes, when he turns to leave, she approaches him for an interview.

'I'm Rebecca Smith, CNN News. Sir, how long have you been coming to the Western Wall and praying?'

'For about fifty years.'

'Fifty years! That's amazing! What do you pray for?'

'I pray for peace between the Jews and the Arabs. I pray for all the hatred to stop and I pray for our children to grow up in safety and friendship.'

'How do you feel after doing this for fifty years?'

'Like I'm talking to a fucking wall!'

***

Recently, Iraq delivered to the United Nations a 12 000-page report denying it had weapons of mass destruction. Knowing President Bush doesn't have the attention span to read 12 000 pages, the Iraqis also provided an executive summary written in the style of the President's favourite author, Dr Seuss. Here is a copy of the document obtained from an anonymous source deep inside Vice President Dick Cheney's secret hideout.

I am Saddam.
Saddam I am.

I am the ruler of Iraq.
The country that you would attack.

You are Bush.
Bush you are.
The fame of you has spread afar.

You do not like me, Bush, I know.
You would not like me in a show.
You would not like me in the snow.
You simply wish that I would go.

You say I used to slaughter Kurds.
You say that I use naughty words.
You say I have an evil stash
Of weapons of destruction (mass),
Of bombs and missile, germs and gas.

You say I tried to kill your pop.
Oh, how I wish that you would stop!
I promise you I have no stash
Of weapons of destruction (mass).

I do not have them near or far.
I did not hide them in my car.
I did not hide them in a bar.

I did not hide them in a hole.
I did not hide them up a pole.

I did not hide them in a grave.
I did not hide them in a cave.

I did not hide them in a dish.
I did not hide them in a knish.

I did not hide them in my coat.
I did not hide them in a goat.

I did not hide them in a trunk.
I did not hide them in my bunk.

I did not hide them anywhere.
In short, they simply are not there.

The inspectors came and looked,
And looked, and looked, and looked, and looked.

They looked high and they looked low,
Every place that they could go.

They looked in every hole and crack.
Each drawer and closet, bag and sack.

They found nothing in a trunk, or
Even in my private bunker.

They did not find a single stash
Of weapons of destruction (mass) . . .
And *still* you won't get off my ass!

I've done all that I can do.
The rest, dear Bush, is up to you.

Please don't be angry, don't be sore.
We don't need to have a war.

Let's go back to the good old days
When your dad and Reagan sang my praise.

I was your faithful ally then.
Why can't we be friends again?

I say, let's let this whole thing drop.
(My best regards to your dear pop.)

✳✳✳

NEW POTENTIAL IRAQI TOWN NAMES

1. Wherz-Myroof
2. Mykamel-Isded
3. Oshit-Disisbad
4. Waddi-El-Izgowinon
5. Pleez-Ztopdishit
6. Kizz-Yerass-Goodbi
7. Ikantstan-Dosnomore
8. Wha-Tafuk-Wazi-Tinkin
9. Myturbin-Izburnin

★★★

SIGNS THAT YOU'VE GROWN UP

1. Your house plants are alive, and you can't smoke any of them.
2. Having sex in a single bed is out of the question.
3. You keep more food than beer in the fridge.
4. Six in the morning is when you get up, not when you go to bed.
5. You hear your favourite song in an elevator.
6. You watch the weather channel.
7. Your friends marry and divorce instead of hook up and break up.
8. Jeans and sweater no longer qualify as 'dressed up'.

9. You're the one calling the police because those damn kids next door won't turn down the stereo.

10. Older relatives feel comfortable telling sex jokes around you.

11. You don't know what time Hungry Jack's closes any more.

12. Sleeping on the couch makes your back hurt.

13. Dinner and a movie is the whole date instead of the beginning of one.

14. You go to the chemist for ibuprofen and antacid, not condoms and pregnancy tests.

15. A $4 bottle of wine is no longer 'pretty good'.

16. You actually eat breakfast food at breakfast time.

17. 'I just can't drink the way I used to,' replaces, 'I'm never going to drink that much again.'

18. Ninety per cent of the time you spend in front of a computer is for real work.

19. You drink at home to save money before going to a bar.

20. You read this entire list looking desperately for a sign that doesn't actually apply to you and can't find one to save your sorry old arse.

✱✱✱

WORDS TO LIVE BY:

Always keep your words soft and sweet, just in case you have to eat them.

Always read stuff that will make you look good if you die in the middle of it.

Drive carefully. It's not only cars that can be recalled by their maker.

Eat a live toad in the morning and nothing worse will happen to you for the rest of the day.

If you can't be kind, at least have the decency to be vague.

Never buy a car you can't push.

Never put both feet in your mouth at the same time, because then you don't have a leg to stand on.

Nobody cares if you can't dance well. Just get up and dance.

The early worm gets eaten by the bird, so sleep late.

When everything's coming your way, you're in the wrong lane.

Birthdays are good for you; the more you have, the longer you live.

Ever notice that the people who are late are often much jollier than the people who have to wait for them?

If ignorance is bliss, why aren't more people happy?

You may be only one person in the world but you may also be the world to one person.

Some mistakes are too much fun to only make once.

Don't cry because it's over; smile because it happened.

A truly happy person is one who can enjoy the scenery on a detour.

Happiness comes through doors you didn't even know you left open.

✶✶✶